Behavioral Group Therapy, 1979

An Annual Review

Dennis Upper
Steven M. Ross
Editors

Research Press Company

2612 N. Mattis Avenue
Champaign, Illinois 61820

ISBN 0-87822-197-2

ISSN 0191-5681

CONTENTS

Preface

Although the uses of behavior therapy procedures and techniques for the individual client have been well documented in the psychological literature of the past 20 years, it is only relatively recently that clinicians and researchers have begun to explore the application of behavioral procedures in group therapy settings. This situation seems all the more strange in light of the fact that behavior therapy, with its strong emphasis on skill acquisition and social reinforcement, should lend itself particularly well to group implementation, as well as facilitating the evaluation of treatment effectiveness.

In a recent review of the literature on the behavioral treatment of emotional, avoidance, and social skills problems in a group therapy context (Upper & Ross, 1977), we concluded that, despite the advantages to both clinicians and clients of conducting behavioral treatment in groups, clinical developments and research in this area were still at a relatively rudimentary level. The majority of behavioral group therapy studies in the literature which we reviewed featured the direct transfer of individually oriented procedures, such as systematic desensitization, to a group of clients with homogeneous problems. Only a limited amount of attention was given to whether or not group interaction variables (such as group discussion, sharing ideas and feelings, and mutual feedback among members) could be used to improve the effectiveness of individually developed therapies conducted in a group.

Despite the relatively rudimentary level of the behavioral group therapy research at the time of our review, we felt that there were a number of indications of a burgeoning interest on the part of clinicians and researchers in undertaking the types of studies which were needed in order to improve the technology of behavioral group therapy and to allow its extension to new treatment populations and environments. These included: (1) studies in which group process variables were manipulated in a programed way and the effects on treatment outcome carefully evaluated; (2) investigations which involved testing the limits of various techniques through comparative factorial studies across different sets of clients, therapists, problematic behaviors, and treatment environments; (3) appropriate "process studies" (including outcome measures) designed to clarify how the intervention procedures actually operated in the group context; (4) parametric studies to standardize and operationalize the most efficient procedures for individuals and groups; and (5) studies aimed at developing standardized assessment procedures with adequate reliability and validity for use in behavioral group therapy.

The present volume (and the series which it initiates) reflects our continuing interest in following the growth and development of behavioral group therapy and perhaps even in contributing to that growth by providing a forum for behaviorally oriented clinicians and researchers who are doing group work. We wish to express our thanks to the authors of these articles for being so prompt and conscientious in preparing and revising their manuscripts, to Jeannette Farris for her secretarial assistance, and to Ann Wendel and Rick Stephens of Research Press for their unfailing optimism about our project and their invaluable help in its realization. We would also like to express our deepest appreciation to our families, friends, and professional colleagues for their encouragement and support of our efforts.

Finally, it should be noted that both editors contributed equally to the preparation of this volume and that the order of editorship is arbitrary.

REFERENCES

Upper, D., & Ross, S. M. Behavioral group therapy: 1. Emotional, avoidance, and social skills problems of adults. In M. Hersen, R. M. Eisler, & P. M. Miller (Eds.), *Progress in behavior modification* (Vol. 5). New York: Academic Press, 1977.

Aims and Scope

Behavioral Group Therapy: An Annual Review is a multidisciplinary serial publication which is aimed at presenting significant research reports, clinical group studies, review articles, and other material related to the application of behavioral treatment procedures in group therapy settings. The primary purposes of this *Annual Review* are: (1) to serve as an up-to-date and central source of information about the important recent clinical work and research involving behavioral group therapy, (2) to indicate areas of needed research and to stimulate scientific inquiry in these areas, and (3) to provide a forum for communication among those doing clinical work and research of this type. In order to serve a desirable and needed training function, its articles include case material, detailed descriptions of therapeutic methods, and transcriptions of group therapy sessions in order to illustrate how target behaviors are identified, how treatment methods are selected and applied, how difficulties are handled, and how therapeutic progress is evaluated. Articles which critically analyze and discuss important theoretical, social, professional, and ethical issues involved in the practice of behavioral group therapy also are included.

This *Annual Review* has two major thrusts, one theoretical and one practical. The theoretical thrust is designed to answer the question: "Will research and case material using behavioral group approaches enable us to understand group psychotherapy in general as a lawful, predictable process?" The practical thrust is directed to the question: "Can analyzing group therapy from a learning point of view direct our attention to practical improvements in the practice of group therapy, whatever the theoretical persuasion of the therapist?" Even more specifically, this series addresses the question of which behavioral procedures have proven to be particularly amenable to implementation in group therapy situations and with what types of problematic behaviors and patient populations.

Included in this series will be articles describing behavioral group treatment in the following areas: (1) emotional and avoidance behaviors, (2) habitual and addictive behaviors, (3) children's behaviors and family interactions, (4) adolescent and delinquent behaviors, (5) adult social and sexual behaviors, (6) behaviors of institutionalized patients and inmates, (7) miscellaneous target behaviors and techniques (e.g., group treatment of stuttering, chronic pain, etc.), and (8) behavioral marital therapy. Although the scope of the *Annual Review* is broad enough to include a wide range of content and settings, two general limitations are observed. First, the *Annual Review*'s focus is on the application of behavioral procedures in group therapy settings, rather than on the more general area of behavior modification with a group of patients, such as through the use of hospital token economies or structured classroom programs. Second, although significant work is being done in the area of applying behavioral techniques in vocational counseling and training groups, this *Annual Review* concentrates on group work in which more "clinical" behavioral problems such as those enumerated above are the targets for change.

Contributors

Elgan L. Baker, Jr.

Texas Research Institute of Mental Sciences, Texas Medical Center, Houston, Texas

Jeffrey R. Bedell

Florida Mental Health Institute, Tampa, Florida

Betty J. Blythe

School of Social Work, University of Washington, Seattle, Washington

Judith Coché

Institute for Behavioral Education, King of Prussia, Pennsylvania

Henry S. G. Cutter

Veterans Administration Hospital, Brockton, Massachusetts

Howard J. Doueck

School of Social Work, University of Washington, Seattle, Washington

John V. Flowers

Program in Social Ecology, University of California at Irvine, Irvine, California

Myles Genest

Department of Psychology, University of Waterloo, Waterloo, Ontario, Canada

Kay Gustafson

Veterans Administration Hospital, Omaha, Nebraska

Henry A. Jordan

Institute for Behavioral Education, King of Prussia, Pennsylvania

Arthur J. Lange

Center for Counseling, Special Services and Learning Skills, University of California at Irvine, Irvine, California

Leonard S. Levitz

Institute for Behavioral Education, King of Prussia, Pennsylvania

W. Charles Lobitz

Department of Psychiatry, University of Colorado Medical School, Denver, Colorado

Anne L. McGihon

Department of Psychology, McGill University, Montreal, Quebec, Canada

Kevin B. McGovern

Columbia Psychiatric Clinic, Portland, Oregon

Ruta M. Montvila

Department of Psychology, McGill University, Montreal, Quebec, Canada

Timothy J. O'Farrell

Veterans Administration Hospital, Brockton, Massachusetts

William E. Piper

Department of Psychology, McGill University, Montreal, Quebec, Canada

David L. Sansbury

School of Education, The American University, Washington, D.C.

Steven P. Schinke

School of Social Work, University of Washington, Seattle, Washington

Carl Schrader

Project Entry Day Center, Long Island Jewish-Hillside Medical Center, Queens Village, New York

Dennis C. Turk

Department of Psychology, Yale University, New Haven, Connecticut

Lawrence R. Weathers

Florida Mental Health Institute, Tampa, Florida

Part One

The Behavioral Group Therapy Process

Goldstein, Heller, and Sechrest (1966) have differentiated between the process of doing therapy *in* groups and that of doing therapy *through* groups. In the former case, therapy is more therapist centered and individual oriented; in general, this approach is more directive, interpretive, and focused on the behaviors of individual group members, as in the case of group systematic desensitization. Many of the "in-group" studies reported in the literature employ intervention techniques which were developed for use in individual therapy and which are employed in a group context primarily for the sake of efficiency of therapists' time. To date, only a limited amount of attention has been accorded to whether or not group interaction variables might enhance these individually developed therapies conducted in a group.

The "through-groups" approach is more group centered; the therapist tends to be less overtly active, to promote member-to-member (rather than member-to-therapist) interactions, and to be more oriented toward group-wide influences on individual patients. Viewed in this way, behavioral group therapy may be viewed as a process in which the group leader trains the group members to become behavioral engineers for one another. As training progresses and the group members learn to appropriately reinforce, prompt, model, and shape each other's behavior, the leader gradually fades to a less active role. Ideally, then, the next step in the

1

treatment process would be fading out the group itself, while programing the generalization of new behavior outside the group and teaching members to engineer their own behavior.

The three chapters in Part One focus on the role of the group in behavioral group therapy, with a special emphasis placed on the identification and manipulation of those aspects of group process which will enhance treatment outcome. In Chapter 1, John V. Flowers reviews the history of behavioral group interventions, describes a method for analyzing both behavioral and nonbehavioral groups, and presents a comprehensive model for conducting interactive behavioral group therapy (i.e., behavior therapy *through* a group). Of particular interest to therapists interested in doing behavioral group work are Flowers's specific suggestions, based upon his extensive research in this area, about facilitating group process and enhancing therapeutic outcome by manipulating: (1) the frequency, content, and valence of messages given and received by group members; (2) the type and amount of members' activity within the group; and (3) a number of variables indicating group cohesion. Another significant aspect of Flowers's article is its focus on therapist-training issues. According to Flowers, if behavioral group therapy is to be a systematic and objective set of techniques that are trainable, the assessment of the training itself must also be objective; toward this end, he presents a preliminary method of objectively assessing behavioral group therapist skill and discusses its implications for therapist training.

David L. Sansbury, in Chapter 2, begins by citing a number of advantages of conducting behavioral therapy in groups, including savings in therapist time and effort, enhanced opportunities to learn through modeling, an increased likelihood of discrimination learning and generalization, and the opportunity for a far more thorough behavioral analysis. After summarizing the research findings and clinical descriptions which suggest the value of the group context for behavior therapy, Sansbury generates nine potentially testable hypotheses regarding the specific role of the group in behavioral group therapy. He goes on to suggest techniques by which therapists can effectively manage such aspects of group process as cohesion, commonality, and the selection of protherapeutic norms in such a way as to improve the effectiveness of the behavioral treatment.

In Chapter 3, William E. Piper, Ruta M. Montvila, and Anne L. McGihon discuss the development of a process analysis system as a means of better defining relevant group process issues and, thereby, of refining therapeutic interventions. The system consists of a modified version of the Hill Interaction Matrix in which any group verbal behavior can be placed in one of the 16 cells of the matrix. Examples of various uses of the system are provided, as well as areas for future research and development of the system.

The systems discussed by Flowers and Piper et al. offer a variety of ideas for operationalizing and monitoring group interventions. Future research will need to explore normative and parametric issues: What types of process are appropriate for what stages of what types of groups? What are the limits within which process is constructive and what are the indications for when group process becomes harmful? Can process analysis methodology be used to test for generalization and maintenance outside the group? These are only a few of the many questions which can be raised at this stage in this fertile area.

REFERENCES

Goldstein, A. P., Heller, K., & Sechrest, L. B. *Psychotherapy and the psychology of behavior change*. New York: Wiley, 1966.

Chapter 1

Behavioral Analysis of Group Therapy and a Model for Behavioral Group Therapy

John V. Flowers

Abstract

This chapter briefly reviews the history of behavioral interventions in group contexts, pointing out that most such interventions are not group therapy at all, but are actually behavior therapy done in a group of clients. When behavior therapy is attempted in interactive groups, i.e., by means of group process, the need for basic research on group therapy as a unique form of intervention becomes apparent. The second section of this chapter presents a behavioral method of analyzing both behavioral and nonbehavioral groups and presents the results of this analysis to date. The third section of this chapter presents a model for conducting interactive behavioral group therapy and summarizes the outcome findings to date. The final section addresses leadership training issues and presents a preliminary method of objectively assessing behavioral group therapist skill.

Chapter 1

Behavioral Analysis of Group Therapy and a Model for Behavioral Group Therapy

John V. Flowers

Abstract

INTRODUCTION

Behavioral group therapy can have three different definitions. It can mean a specific type of behavioral therapy that has originated in individual practice and is being used in a group setting. When behavioral group therapy has this definition, the group is usually composed of individuals with a similar problem, e.g., unassertive behavior, fear of public speaking, a weight problem, etc. The intervention is usually a large scale version of an already recognized technique. This is therapy done *in* the group, as opposed to therapy done *by* the group (Upper & Ross, S., 1977). The second possible meaning of the term "behavioral group therapy" is behavioral intervention in an already existing therapy group. In this case, the problems of the individual group members may be extremely varied. Usually one behavioral intervention is employed (e.g., conditioning against silence or conditioning task persistence) and all of the other therapeutic interventions are not specifically behavioral. This therapy is done by the group, but it is not really behavioral group therapy. Rather, this is some form of traditional group therapy which is potentially made more effective by the use of behavioral principles. Finally, behavioral group therapy can mean behavior therapy accomplished by the group. In this case, the individuals' problems may be extremely varied, but the interventions are specific and systematic. In this type of group the interventions must be matched to the client problem, executed by the entire group, and based on learning principles.

The first meaning of behavioral group therapy, behavior change techniques developed in individual therapy and performed in the group, is the most common meaning. Moreover, it is historically common for a psychotherapy developed with individuals to be transformed into group therapy. For instance, Freudian individual therapy was transformed into analytic group therapy (Slavson, 1963). Similarly, Rogerian individual client-centered therapy was transformed into Rogerian group therapy (Gordon, 1955; Rogers, 1971). Despite the fact that such transformations are common, they can be troublesome. In analytic group therapy, where the correctness and timing of interpretations are emphasized, the therapist can either yield therapeutic control by allowing client-to-client interactions or can maintain therapeutic control by conducting the group with primarily therapist-to-client interactions. In this latter case, the group resembles individual therapy with onlookers.

In Rogerian or "active listening" types of group therapy, where client-to-client interaction is almost always encouraged, the therapist's problem is different. Here the therapist can either continue to employ the very "soft" mode of reflection, thereby losing impact and therapeutic control when interpretations, advisements, and self-disclosures are employed in client-to-client interactions, or the therapist can employ more powerful statements to maintain leadership control. Given the Rogerian model, Gibb (1971) maintains that the therapist should not employ advisement or interpretations to maintain group control. Instead, the therapist should use self-disclosure as a group facilitation tool. Not only does this technically violate the initial therapeutic model, but by being perceived as a client, the therapist also has the problem of losing therapeutic effectiveness.

There are fewer problems in transferring individual behavior techniques to group use. In some behavioral therapy performed with groups (not by the group), such as group desensitization, very little client-to-client interaction is needed; hence, there are fewer problems of intervention change due to group interactions. Even when there is frequent client-to-client interaction in a behavioral group therapy, such as group assertion training (Booraem & Flowers, 1978), the interaction is highly structured, thus preserving the integrity of the therapeutic technique. While there are undoubtedly differential effects when a specific behavioral intervention is performed in a group rather than individually, these effects do not change the basic therapy as much as when the intervention is not behavioral.

Since most research on behavior therapy is done at universities and since the most common phobia found at universities is test anxiety, the most common form of behavior therapy researched in groups is desensitization with test-anxious students. Cohen (1969); Crighton and Jehu (1969); Freeling and Shember (1970); Graff, Maclean, and Loving (1971); Ihli and Garlington (1969); McManus (1971); Meichenbaum (1972); Mitchell and Ingham (1970); Nawas, Fishman, and Pucel (1970); Suinn (1968); and Suinn and Hall (1970) have all conducted test anxiety desensitization groups with generally good results. Other investigators have performed group desensitization with snake phobics (Ritter, 1968), spider phobics (Rachman, 1966; Robinson & Suinn, 1968), agoraphobics (Watson, Mullett, & Pillay, 1973), and those who are afraid of public speaking or have stagefright (Kondas, 1967; Paul & Shannon, 1966).

In addition to desensitization, behavior therapists have conducted groups for weight control (Bornstein & Sipprelle, 1973; Hagen, 1974; Wollersheim, 1970), depression (Lewinsohn, Weinstein, & Alper, 1970), geriatric problems (Linsk, Howe, & Pinkston, 1975), smoking reduction (Koenig & Masters, 1965; Marrone,

Marksamer, & Salzberg, P., 1970; Whitman, 1972), alcohol problems (Miller, E., Dvorak, & Turner, 1960), hysteria (Kass, Silvers, & Abroms, 1972), and children's problems (Clement, 1968; Clement, Fazzone, & Goldstein, 1970; Hinds & Roehlke, 1970). L. Miller and O. Miller (1970) have conducted behavior groups to help welfare recipients help themselves. Ross, D., Ross, S., and Evans (1971) formed a behavioral group to help modify the behavior of one client. This group is reminiscent of the early communal groups (Kanter, 1972) in which the group was formed to help reintegrate one member into the commune. Finally, a number of investigators have done social skills training groups (Booraem & Flowers, 1972; Fensterheim, 1972; Hedquist & Weinhold, 1970; Lomont, Gilner, Spector, & Skinner, 1969; MacDonald, Lindquist, Kramer, McGrath & Rhyne, 1975; Rathus, 1972; Sarason & Ganzer, 1973; Schinke & Rose, 1976). In each of the above cases, a specific mode of behavior therapy is employed in, not performed by, the groups. While such groups are often effective and efficient, and while they are therapy done in groups, they are not group therapy.

The second, less general meaning of behavioral group therapy has been the use of specific behavioral interventions within an existing therapy group. Here the existing therapy group is viewed as an a priori intervention that can be influenced behaviorally. In most cases the groups are defined as "eclectic," which means that the therapist does whatever he or she feels will produce positive change. Aiken (1965); Oakes (1962a, 1962b); Oakes, Droge, and August (1960, 1961); Rickard and Timmons (1961); H. Salzberg (1961); Simkins and West (1965); Ullmann, Krasner, and Collins (1961); and Wagner (1966) have employed conditioning techniques to increase one or another form of verbal participation, usually with the assumption (Yalom, 1975) that participation is a major curative factor for group members. Heckel, Wiggins, and Salzberg, H. (1962) conditioned against silence in group therapy. Hastorf (1965) and Hauserman, Zweback, and Plotkin (1972) conditioned for on-task behavior in the therapy group. Liberman (1970, 1971) used reinforcement to increase cohesion and thereby increase positive client outcome. Abudabbah, Prandoni, and Jensen (1972) conditioned disclosure, while Bednar, Zelhart, Greathouse, and Weinberg (1970) used reinforcement to shape task persistence. In each of these cases, the experimenters assumed that a group discussion of individual problems could help the client. The experimenters then employed behavioral principles to strengthen those aspects of the group process that they considered essential for positive client change.

The final meaning of behavioral group therapy is seen in a group in which behavioral forms of intervention are performed in and by the group. Behavioral group therapy of this type is emerging but does not fully exist at present. It still needs further development. This type of group therapy would not be problem specific. It would help group members with a variety of problems, i.e., within broad limits would attempt to intervene with any problems with which the group member wished assistance. However, while the problems could be highly varied, the group intervention, selected to match the problem, would be systematic, repeatable, and assessable. The work of Krumboltz and Potter (1973), Lawrence and Sundel (1972), Lazarus (1968), and Rose (1967, 1969, 1972, 1977) seems to be directed toward this final definition of group therapy.

It is this final definition of behavioral group therapy that is the subject of the rest of this chapter. It is our belief that further development of behavioral group therapy done by the group requires three separate research efforts. First, group therapy must be understood as a unique noneclectic intervention that can be analyzed in terms of learning principles (Lieberman, Lakin, & Whitaker, 1968); this is the focus of the next section of this chapter. Second, a step-by-step method of conducting behavioral group therapy must be created and verified; this is the focus of the third section of this chapter. Finally, the issues of training and assessing group leaders must be investigated; this is the focus of the final section of this chapter. Throughout, the interaction of group process variables (such as cohesion), behavioral intervention steps, and leadership variables (such as sensitivity) must be inspected.

BEHAVIORAL ANALYSIS OF GROUP THERAPY

Beyond the issue of the therapeutic content of individual statements, which will be taken up in the next section, our behavioral analysis of group therapy involves the evaluation of: (1) the patterns of positive, negative, and neutral messages and the effects of these patterns on group members' behavior both in and out of the group; (2) the syntax of messages and the effects of different forms of syntax on group members' behavior both in and out of the group; (3) the patterns and types of individual activity within the group and the effects of this activity on group performance and later individual behavior; and (4) the effects of group cohesion on total group and individual functioning.

Analysis of Positive and Negative Messages in Group Therapy

The frequency and distribution patterns of positive, negative, and neutral messages can be assessed in two ways. External raters can be used to judge how a message was sent or received, i.e., as positive, negative, or neutral. An alternative method is to have the group members gather the data themselves via a process that can occur alongside the interactions of the group. We have employed both methods (Flowers, Booraem, Brown, & Harris, 1974; Flowers, Booraem, & Seacat, 1974; Flowers, Kenney, & Rotheram, in press; Flowers, Kenney, & Rotheram, Note 1), and it has become apparent that there is substantial agreement between them. The choice was made to emphasize the latter method, client collection of data, because external raters, whether rating live, from videotape, or from audiotape, are not always available.

Any procedure in which the group members collect the data must be automatic and must not interfere with normal group interaction. We have employed colored tokens which are exchanged with positive and negative messages (blue for positive and red for negative). The tokens are numbered so that exact patterns of distribution can be obtained at any point.

Pilot research demonstrated that, in groups where tokens were both given (the color of the token being based on how the giver intended the message) and taken (based on how the receiver views the valence of the message), the group process was severely disrupted. Having tokens taken, without the sender giving any token for intent, also proved to be disruptive and unreliable, although this process did prove to be a useful therapy tool in some cases (Flowers, 1975).

Having the receiver take the token demanded that he or she judge the behavior of another, with consequent disruptions as group members argued over the valence of many messages. Secondly, some clients initially took tokens at the slightest sign of positive or negative valence, while others initially took them only if the message was very powerful. Thus, it seemed that having tokens given with the intended message was the least disruptive and most reliable method of client data collection.

There are two disadvantages to this method of data collection. One is that the intent of the group member delivering the message may not correspond with how the message was received. This problem exists in any interaction. In terms of therapy, this problem is alleviated by the fact that the receiver can question the valence of any message. In terms of research, the problem between possible differences of intent and reception is actually solved by the definition of reinforcement. The final definition is neither what was intended nor what was judged by the receiver as positive, negative, or neutral; it is what effect messages have on subsequent behavior.

A second disadvantage of this data-gathering process is that it may affect group process, substantially changing what is being assessed. Our data (Flowers, Booraem, Brown, & Harris, 1974; Flowers, Note 2) indicate that this method of measurement is highly reactive in one form of group therapy. In groups where there are both a high percentage of therapist-to-client interactions and a low frequency of valenced (positive or negative) messages, the token method itself increases the frequency of both client-to-client interactions and valenced messages without any other intervention being employed. While we would argue, for reasons outlined in the section on cohesion, that such a change is beneficial to the group, it is also clear that the token procedure cannot be used to assess such forms of group therapy. If most group therapy were conducted in this manner, the utility of the token procedure would be severely limited; however, as Lieberman, Yalom, and Miles (1973) point out, such groups are the exception rather than the rule. Thus, with this one exception, the token procedure has proven to be a useful assessment device, irrespective of the form of therapy being done in the group.

Data from various studies (Flowers & Booraem, 1976; Flowers, Booraem, Brown, & Harris, 1974; Flowers, Booraem, & Seacat, 1974; Flowers et al., in press; Flowers, Note 2; Flowers, Booraem, & Hartman, Note 3) yield a set of consistent findings:

(1) Overall, group therapy is more effective in terms of client change if there is an increase in the percentage of positive and negative messages employed by the entire group. Individual clients demonstrating the most improvement are those with the highest levels of such valenced input.

(2) On specific problems, input can be more powerful, i.e., more effective in terms of client change, if it is from other clients rather than from the therapists.

(3) A high proportion (when compared to the group session mean) of negative messages delivered to a single client reduces the client's ability to hear the delivered messages; however, negative messages delivered to the therapist are heard very clearly (probably because of a different learning history).

(4) Individuals (including therapists) who deliver a high proportion of negative messages are also less receptive to group input than are other group members.

In summary, an increase in the proportion of positive and negative messages, especially if that increase is from other group members, is beneficial to the group in terms of client change. However, any imbalance in valenced messages compared to the group norm, either in terms of messages sent or received, is not beneficial. Thus, the most effective groups are those that employ a high proportion of valenced messages, but employ them "democratically," i.e., without a disproportionate number being either sent or received by any particular group member.

Behavioral Analysis of Syntax

Behavioral analysis of the syntax of messages is important because differences in syntax often define differences in therapeutic approach. Of the most common forms of speech (questions, interpretations, self-disclosures, reflections, and advisements) one would expect to find a high proportion of interpretations in analytic types of group therapy and a high proportion of reflection in Rogerian or "active listening" types of group. One would also expect to find a high proportion of advisement (often in instruction form) in behavioral groups. All groups would employ questions for information gathering; however, within the large class of questions, one would expect analytic groups to emphasize the question "why," while behavioral groups would be expected to emphasize "what" questions.

Results from an early study (Flowers, Note 2) were somewhat different from this prediction. Analytic group therapists did use more interpretation than behavioral group therapists; however, so did client-centered therapists. There were no differences in the amount of advisement used between any of the three group therapy types; however, there was a clear difference in the type of advisement used. Both analytic and client-centered therapists used more pure advice, while behavioral therapists used more instruction and alternatives.

In the analytic groups the most common advisement was in the approximate form of "You should . . . ," while in the client-centered group the most common form was "If I were you, I would. . . ." In both the analytic and the client-centered groups, time in this phase of group was primarily spent in various forms of persuasion; in the behavioral groups, time was primarily spent in either generating alternatives or in clarifying instructions. Instruction here means a clear step-by-step procedure that the client can follow to accomplish the specified task. Alternatives here means that the client is offered at least two choices of action rather than being told what he or she should or could do. The behavioral group therapists in this study were not doing behavioral therapy in the group, but were attempting to conduct group therapy employing behavioral principles. Thus, the data may not be representative of behavior therapists doing a single behavioral intervention (e.g., desensitization, assertion training, etc.) in a group of homogenous clients.

Additionally, behavioral group therapists employed more questions than either analytic or client-centered group therapists; however, the time a client spent answering behavioral group therapists' questions was significantly less than that spent answering either analytic or client-centered group therapists' questions. Client-centered group therapists did employ more reflection than other group therapists, but all group therapists used the same amount of reflection in the assessment phase of a problem.

Three points suggested by this study are important. First, interpretations, which are highly frequent in analytic and also in client-centered group therapy, were judged positively by the sender, but negatively by the receiver. Thus, in terms of the analysis above, interpretations are almost axiomatic double messages in terms of valence. Further analysis needs to be done in terms of interpretations and client change; however, it is our present prediction that this form of syntax will be difficult to use therapeutically in a group because of the mixed valence issues.

Second, "why" questions, which are more frequent in both analytic and client-centered groups, elicit very long and time-consuming responses from clients. Further analysis and assessment of the clarity of such responses is needed. It is our present contention that "why" questions would probably elicit less clear responses than other forms of interrogatives and that the length of the responses is an indicator of the troublesome nature of this form of question. Behavior therapists in group ask significantly more questions and yet the total client response time is significantly less than in the other forms of group therapy. We would contend that "what" questions get clearer and shorter answers.

The third area, advicement, is where we have followed up these initial findings most adequately to date. In a subsequent study (Flowers, Note 4), it was found that therapists could be trained to use alternatives and instruction as opposed to advice. More importantly, it was found that clients improved more on problems where either alternatives or instruction were employed than they did when advise was used.

Since this study also showed that direct advice was judged as being more reinforcing by the sender and less by the receiver, while alternatives and instructions were judged as being less reinforcing by the sender but more reinforcing by the receiver, it is clear why advice continues to be employed. In fact, advice continues to be employed in almost all forms of therapy despite the common assumption (Frank, 1964; Strupp & Wallach, 1965) that it does not work well in therapy. Our data indicate that the common belief that direct advice does not work well is true. However, other forms of advisement, such as alternatives and instructions, do work. It is hoped that precisely this type of behavioral analysis of group process will lead to the development of a behavioral group therapy model that will not be subject to the allegation that behavior therapy is too "simple" to deal with complex human problems.

It is clear that more work needs to be done both in classifying the syntax in use in various groups and in assessing what syntactical forms elicit what types of group and outcome behavior. The important issue is that different types of therapy groups differ in their use of syntax and that different types of syntax lead to different results. If group therapists are going to be trained to understand and to do what is effective, this type of analysis must be continued.

Behavioral Analysis of the Type and
Amount of Activity Within the Group

The relationship of individual activity within the group to other aspects of group process and to individual change is another necessary area of analysis. With as simple a question as whether or not participation leads to client improvement, mixed results have been found (Bassin, 1962; Sechrest & Berger, 1961). Using the token data, the present form of analysis can easily identify four individual participation variables: total amount of token use (where use refers to giving and receiving tokens), type of use (input versus output), input valence (percentage of tokens the individual was given that were positive), and output valence (percentage of tokens the individual gave that were positive).

With relation to the first variable, the total tokens given and received, our data indicate that more active clients improve more than less active clients (Flowers & Booraem, 1976; Flowers, Note 2). Moreover, a more recent study (Flowers, Hartman, & Booraem, Note 5) indicates that total token use correlates very highly with a separate count of total statements made. Thus, a count of total token use indicates total activity as well as valenced activity.

The variable of giving versus receiving tokens indicates whether the client is in the role of shaper or shapee in any session. In line with Guerney's (1969) double change hypothesis, we have found (Flowers & Kidder, Note 6) that group members who adopt both roles over sessions change more than those who adopt predominantly one or the other. The advantage of this methodology with relation to both total activity and role is that easily collected data give the group leaders an objective count of what has occurred, rather than the leaders' having to rely on their subjective impressions for such data.

Our research on input and output valence yields complicated results. One repeated finding (Flowers, Booraem, & Seacat, 1974; Flowers et al., in press; Flowers et al., Note 1; Flowers, Note 2) is that a group member who gives a high proportion of negative messages is less sensitive than other group members in the session in which those messages were given. Sensitivity here means the match between the subject's recall of events and the objective data. A second finding is that a negative message delivered without an accompanying positive message is not heard clearly. A high proportion of such messages sent to a client (when compared to other clients in the session) reduces that client's sensitivity to the entire session. The exception to this latter finding is that experienced therapists increase in sensitivity when they receive a high proportion of negative messages in any session. Since confrontive groups are very common (Lieberman et al., 1973) and since feedback that can be attended to is essential for learning, the therapist needs to be aware of exactly who is encountering and being encountered in ways that reduce the impact of group messages and group interventions. Our data do not demonstrate that negative feedback does not work. In fact, too high a percentage of overall positive feedback reduces positive outcome results (Flowers et al., Note 1). Our data indicate that when negative feedback either given or received is out of balance for that client in relation to other clients in that session, the client does not demonstrate change on problems discussed in that session. Furthermore, if this pattern continues, the client often terminates attendance before the group is over. Again, the token methodology provides the therapist with an accurate assessment of which clients may be at risk by keeping a running tally of the proportion exchanged. The individual token exchanges also help the therapist by giving an additional visual signal of which behaviors are being reinforced and punished and which messages are being delivered in solely negative ways.

Obviously, individual activity patterns also affect the entire group process. Within group therapy, the term "cohesion" has been employed to attempt to describe the ingredient or group process that leads to group effectiveness (Lott, A. & Lott, B., 1961; Schachter, Ellerston, McBride, & Gregory, 1968; Yalom, 1975; Yalom & Rand, 1966). However, with the exception of the work of Liberman (1970, 1971), the term cohesion has never been well operationalized. The suggestion that group therapists should strive for group cohesion, since cohesion is important for group functioning, is vague both in terms of what to do and what to expect.

Cohesion

One of our major research efforts has been directed at operationally defining group cohesion in terms of a set of covarying components. To date (Flowers, 1978; Flowers et al., in press; Flowers et al., Note 1; Flowers et al., Note 3), starting with a suggestion of Krumboltz and Potter (1973), we have identified the following eight variables as indicative (and productive when the variables are manipulated) of group cohesion:

(1) Increased percentage of eye contact with the speaker
(2) Increased percentage of client-client interactions
(3) Decreased number of members on whom or by whom negative messages are repeatedly focused
(4) Increased use of negative messages by the entire group
(5) Increased frequency of self-disclosure
(6) Client change in patterns of activity from session to session (activity, role, input and output flexibility)
(7) Increase in self-reported satisfaction with sessions
(8) Increased numbers of group members trusted by other group members

In addition to its importance in the process analysis of group therapy, cohesion is also important because clients improve more on problems discussed within groups or sessions with high cohesion than on problems considered within groups or sessions with lower cohesion (Flowers et al., Note 3). Simply put, increased group cohesion leads to increased group effectiveness in terms of client outcome. The operationalization of cohesion allows the therapist to manipulate this important variable. As more operational components are found to be a part of the cohesion network, more methods of influencing group process will be understood and available to the group leader. How leaders are presently being trained to generate cohesion will be specified in the final leadership section of this chapter.

Behavioral Analysis of Outcome

Since the final criterion of judgment of a group's effectiveness is client change, outcome assessment is a necessary component of any behavioral analysis of group therapy. As the literature demonstrates (e.g., Bednar & Lawlis, 1971), client outcome assessment has been a difficult issue. For therapy groups that are based on theories of personality change, the most employed assessment methods have been personality tests or generalized self-reports, which yield ambiguous results at best (Bednar & Lawlis, 1971). Such assessment is inappropriate for group therapy for two reasons. In terms of groups emphasizing behavior change of any type, there is a very weak correspondence of such tests and actual behavior change (Paul, 1966). In terms of any group that deals with varied client problems as they are disclosed, generalized testing is an inadequate assessment of such a therapy modality (Goldfried & Kent, 1972).

Behavioral groups dealing with a single problem such as smoking or weight control can assess outcome more easily since only one behavior needs to be assessed. Furthermore, many such behaviors can be objectified in terms of pounds gained or lost, number of cigarettes smoked, etc. Assessment is more difficult when the problems are disclosed and dealt with ad-lib. In terms of changes that can be externally verified, such as getting a job, dating, going to school, we have employed external verification (Flowers & Booraem, 1976) as the criterion of outcome. When such relatively easy external verification of change is not possible, therapist opinion (Langer & Abelson, 1974), other group member opinion (Skindrud, 1973), or self-reports (Lang, 1968, 1977) are too biased to be employed as outcome measures. Thus, easy to collect or not, adequate outcome analysis must be based on external evidence of client change. For this reason, we have begun to employ a new client outcome assessment method that can be used when direct therapist or experimenter verification is not possible (Flowers et al., Note 3; Flowers, Note 4; Flowers & Kidder, Note 6; Flowers, Hartman, & Mann, Note 7).

Problem cards (Goodman, 1969), which will be fully explained in the next section, are completed by each client prior to each session. On these the client writes (briefly) two problems that he or she is presently experiencing and names an external rater who could judge any change in the client's coping (positive or negative) with this problem. About 10% of the problems are of a type such that no rater can be named. After every group session, any problem that was disclosed and not previously written on a problem card is then written down with the name of an external rater. At the end of each session, both sets of cards are collected.

At various times during the course of therapy, the specified raters are given lists of problems and rate the client's positive or negative change in dealing with the problem; however, the rater is unaware of which problems have, in fact, been disclosed and discussed in the therapy group. Additionally, the client and other group members also assess each disclosed problem in the same manner. This in-group assessment is done so that the therapist can judge the group members' perception of client change in relation to the criterion provided by the external raters.

The therapist can choose to implement this procedure at any time depending on the research and/or clinical questions to be answered. For example, in groups of short duration, we tend to employ this procedure only at the termination point for outcome research purposes, while in groups of longer duration we tend to sample every 10 to 12 sessions to keep track of client progress and give the therapists necessary feedback.

In cases where the client can name two raters, both of whom he or she thinks can accurately assess positive or negative change, both raters are contacted. In our experience this happens on less than 25% of the problems. When this fortunate event does occur, we have found that external rater reliability (correlation) is between .8 and .9 for all such problems in a single group. The correlations between other group members' ratings or between those of other group members and external raters are significantly lower and range between −.4 and .7, with a mean of between .3 and .4 in any single group.

While these data support a number of the points made above, this method is not primarily designed to insure reliability but is designed to eliminate rater bias. Client improvement is judged on the raters' differences in ratings of discussed and nondiscussed problems. Thus, a client who was rated at 7 (greatly improved) on both discussed and nondiscussed problems would not be considered to have improved as a function of the group, even though the rating showed improvement. A client who was rated 5 on a nondiscussed problem and 6 on a discussed problem would be scored as improving one point by virtue of the group, and a client who scored 5 on a discussed problem and 6 on a nondiscussed problem would be scored as having deteriorated one point because of the group. This assessment method is deliberately conservative, ignoring nonspecific generalization effects. Generalization research is now being undertaken based on the prediction of which nondiscussed problems should improve most due to their similarity to discussed problems.

While rater bias has been removed, there is still the potential bias in terms of the client selection of the problem to be disclosed. Our data (Flowers et al., Note 3; Flowers et al., Note 7) have also been analyzed, holding problem difficulty and immediacy constant, with no change in results. Research is in progress in which the client discloses randomly from the problem card, which we feel will provide an even more powerful test of this methodology.

This method of assessment allows the group therapist to assess specific outcome of any type without relying on biased data or inappropriately nonspecific tests. On those problems where only self-report is possible, the therapist can estimate the bias of the client as a self-reporter by comparing his or her ratings with external ratings on all other problems.

A MODEL FOR BEHAVIORAL GROUP THERAPY

The present model, hopefully one of many that will be formulated for behavioral group therapy, is an outgrowth of the research program on behavioral analysis of group therapy outlined above. Since much of the research of this model is more recent than that cited above, many of the results reported below are not presently published or presented, and some are actually from studies not yet completed. Readers who want the exact data or design may request them from the author.

The basic model involves steps through which a client progresses in the solution of any problem. These steps are:

(1) disclosure
(2) behavioral assessment
(3) problem solving
(4) group intervention
(5) evaluation

While there are exceptions to this sequence which will be described below, it accounts for more than 90% of the group activity in the present form of behavioral group therapy. The reader should realize that all clients are not at identical points of this sequence simultaneously. Client A may be problem solving as Client B discloses. Moreover, Client A may be in an intervention phase with relation to one problem and in an assessment phase with relation to another. Finally, this sequence is not a lock-step arrangement in that, if an intervention fails with a client, it may be necessary to return to the assessment or even the disclosure phase to try again.

While other forms of group therapy could point to any or all of these steps and claim that they are also part of that therapy, the difference in behavioral group therapy lies in the systematic sequencing of steps and the behavioral methods employed in each.

Disclosure

While disclosure is obviously part of almost all group therapy, very little work has been done on how to systematically elicit frequent and germane disclosures. This may not seem to be an issue to therapists working with moderately troubled, intelligent, verbal clients; however, most mental health services are delivered to clients who are more disturbed, less verbal, and, at least superficially, less intelligent. Disclosure is more frequent in groups with a high proportion of client-to-client interaction (Flowers, Booraem, Brown, & Harris, 1974; Flowers et al., in press), which can be encouraged in a low client-to-client interaction group simply by using the token procedure outlined above (Flowers, 1978). Disclosure is also more frequent in groups with higher levels of cohesion (Flowers et al., in press). Cohesion levels can be facilitated by employing the tokens in the following manner. Negative messages (red tokens) to a group member should be either preceded or followed by a positive message from either the person delivering the negative message or from another group member. Our data (Flowers, Note 2) indicate that this form of "buffering" increases session and overall group cohesion.

Beyond encouraging client-to-client interaction and facilitating the development of group cohesion, another technique that can be used to increase disclosure rates is problem cards (Goodman, 1969). Prior to the group session, each member writes down two current problems, one judged more difficult or immediate and one judged less difficult or immediate. When asked to disclose, the client can choose to disclose either problem, to disclose something else that has come to his or her mind, or to disclose nothing at all. These cards serve multiple purposes. First, they serve as a prompt and a pregroup preparation. In comparing groups with no cards, groups with one problem on a card, and groups with two problems on a card, we find that in those without problem cards, members disclose less frequently and each disclosure takes longer to assess. In groups whose members write one problem prior to group, problems are disclosed more frequently and are easier to assess; however, more members refuse to disclose than when members bring cards with two problems written. Second, the card serves as an initial method of problem operationalization. The reason for the use of index cards rather than sheets of paper is that such cards require brevity and often clearer operationalization by the writer. Finally, use of a card with two problems gives the client a choice other than "I will" or "I will not" share with the group. Combined use of cohesion facilitation, increased client-to-client interaction, and problem cards elicits two to four times as many disclosures as comparison groups, giving the therapists and group members the initial material they need to conduct the therapy group (Flowers, Note 2).

Behavioral Assessment

After a problem has been disclosed, the next task in any therapy group is usually assessment. In behavioral group therapy, behavioral assessment (Kanfer & Saslow, 1969) is employed. Obviously different problems require different types and amounts of assessment; however, one general rule is to ask every necessary question, but never to ask "why." Since the question "why" is the most common assessment employed in most other therapy groups, this one rule leads to a major difference between behavioral and other forms of group therapy. This warning against the "why" question cannot be overemphasized. Our data indicate that when such questions are allowed (not encouraged, merely allowed) the assessment phase requires over three times as long with reduced outcome results. Moreover, it is difficult to reduce "why" questioning, either in trainees or in clients, and this becomes even more difficult the more experience the client or trainee has had in psychology.

Assessment proceeds by asking "what" is the problem. Such assessment can involve questions of frequency, duration, and/or intensity. While initial clarification is done by asking the client questions or by using reflection, the majority of the assessment does not rely on the client's memory, but involves record keeping between group sessions. Thus, the major question is not what happened yesterday, but, "Are you willing to keep track of what happens tomorrow?" Records that will be shared with the group are an integral part of behavioral group therapy assessment. Such record keeping can involve any combination of the variables such as frequency and duration, as well as the variables of "where," "when," and "with whom," as appropriate.

The assessment of "how" is a special question that is asked when there is reason to believe that the client is performing some action incorrectly, usually because of anxiety or behavioral deficit. Assessment of "how" is best done as an analogue in the group by asking the client to demonstrate in front of the group "how" he or she does something or intends to do something.

While assessment of "how" always involves the assessment of action, all other assessment can be done in one of the five areas that for training purposes we call the F.A.T.E.S. Whether the client is called upon to assess the behavior of (1) fantasy, (2) action, (3) thought, (4) emotion, or (5) sensation depends on the initial disclosure and preliminary group questions. (Sensation would be more correctly titled perception, but no easy acronym can then be used.) One clear limitation that we have found is that most clients have difficulty assessing more than two things at a time; loading the client with a shotgun assessment will usually result in no out-of-group assessment being done.

When the assessment involves intensity, as it often does in the assessment of emotion and sensation, we have found it useful to help the client construct an intensity scale from 0 to 10 as Wolpe and Lazarus (1966) do with subjective units of discomfort. While such a scale is obviously not objective data, its use can help the client discriminate differing levels of anger, stress, enthusiasm, hunger, craving, etc. While such discriminations can be useful within the group sessions, most of the assessment is done between group sessions in the client's natural environment.

A special issue in the assessment process involves emotional induction and reduction. Many therapy group leaders view emotional induction as the curative factor in group therapy, and "getting in touch with one's feelings" has become almost synonymous with many forms of group therapy. Our research indicates that emotional induction is indeed important in group therapy, but that emotional induction is an early step in the therapeutic process leading to behavior change. Emotional induction can occur in the disclosure and assessment phases of group therapy when the client re-experiences (in memory) the aversive consequences of the problem. From both self-ratings and external ratings, we have found that such emotional induction is much more likely in a more cohesive group. More important therapeutically, we have found that such induction is directly related to later outcome if, and only if, the emotionality is reduced prior to problem solving. This is not to say that behavioral changes will not occur without such induction. However, and especially on problems rated as more difficult, more change is found if the client is emotional during the assessment phase, provided that the client is then calmer during later phases of the group process.

Problem Solving

In other forms of group therapy this phase is often confused with intervention, mainly because many other therapy groups rely heavily on advice and persuasion to get the client to change. Problem solving does not guarantee change—it is a prerequisite for optimum change. The exception to this is when the client needs to be taught problem-solving skills as the primary therapeutic goal. In this case the skills, not the problem, are the group focus, and the analogue intervention described in the intervention section is employed.

When a problem is to be solved rather than problem solving being taught as a skill, the first step is the generation of a maximum number of alternative solutions. Our research indicates that more alternatives are generated in a situation in which criticism is postponed. As the research indicates (Flowers, 1978), alternatives lead to more client change than advice. Units of advice, such as "You should . . . ," "You could . . . ," "If I were you I would . . . ," are usually responded to with "Yes . . . , but . . . ." In our token groups this shows up as a blue (positive), then a red (negative) token from the client to the advice giver. When criticism is removed, the client tends not to eliminate the alternatives one after the other; instead, a list of possibilities is created. Often, this list contains alternatives that would not have been created if the possibilities had been judged as they were generated. After generating alternatives, the client is faced with a choice among options rather than a choice of each option sequentially. Our research indicates a significant drop in the frequency of "Yes . . . but . . ." messages when possible solutions are offered in this manner.

The simple choice of the best alternative does not produce behavior change. Group therapists often mistake a client's choosing an alternative for commitment and for what is necessary to get fulfillment. The choice of which alternative is best is an important step in the problem-solving process, but it does not mean that the client is going to do anything. Making the best choice also involves the inspection of the consequences of attempting the alternative, and an inspection of the client's skills and resources. Here, it is essential that the client choose from among multiple possibilities, for even if the client imagines negative consequences to all the alternatives, some will be less catastrophic than others. The group can also serve as a reality check in this inspection of the consequences, skills, and resources.

Often, the client can narrow his or her initial choices down to two possibilities and then have severe difficulty deciding between the two. A technique that we have found useful at this point involves taking out a coin and asking, "If the two are that close overall, how about flipping a coin?" About 40% of the clients choose without tossing the coin. Of the remaining 60%, almost a third reverse the coin's "decision," and many state that they realized what they wanted the coin to show as it was in the air.

The final step in this process is a public commitment by the client that he or she will not rechoose without *outside* data that he or she is willing to bring to the group. If there is more a client needs to know in order to choose, this additional information is specified, including how it can be obtained, and this is made into a homework assignment. If there is no additional outside information that can be reasonably obtained, then clients are asked to agree that they will not redecide on the basis of internal data (e.g., worry) since they have already processed such data repeatedly in the past. If subsequent external data indicate that another choice is more advantageous, the client may redecide. It is best to have such decision changes made after the client shares both the new data and his or her problem-solving steps with the group. This step is designed to head off the worry trap that prevents many clients from attempting problem solutions. The technique is employed to break the behavioral chain of test . . . abortive operation one . . . test . . . abortive operation two, etc., that so often defines chronic worry. If the tests were legitimate, this chain would not be so troublesome. However, the tests are usually reflective of highly volatile internal states rather than being assessments of external reality. This step is introduced to increase the frequency of the classic problem strategy of test . . . operate . . . test . . . exit (Miller, G., Galanter, & Pribram, 1960).

Group Intervention

There are two basic interventions leading to behavior change that can be employed in the present form of behavioral group therapy: an analogue in the group, and a self-control contract with the group. Analogues, where the client practices the behavior change in the group, are quite common in group therapy (Morris & Cinnamon, 1974; Pfieffer & Jones, 1970); however, such analogues tend to be employed without a clear understanding of their therapeutic purpose in the client's life. In behavioral group therapy, analogue instigations are employed if practicing a specific behavior in the group is a prerequisite for successful performance of that behavior in the client's life. While the variety of possible analogues is almost endless, the most common involve: (1) social skill acquisition, (2) self-reinforcement, (3) relaxation training, (4) problem-solving skill acquisition, and (5) stress inoculation.

Social skill acquisition can involve the client practicing any verbal or nonverbal interaction the client is having difficulty performing in his or her life. It can involve practice in: reinforcing others, confronting others, receiving reinforcement, receiving criticism, requesting, refusing, being more or less verbal, touching more or less, and so on. Such rehearsal involves both verbal and nonverbal coaching. For more detailed information on social skill acquisition, the reader is directed to Whiteley and Flowers (1978).

Increasing self-reinforcement and/or decreasing self-punishment are other common analogue interventions. In the present form of behavioral group therapy, this type of training is made easier by the use of self-administered tokens accompanying verbal statements to indicate self-reinforcement and self-punishment (Flowers, 1975). Our research (Cohn, Mann, Booraem, & Flowers, in press) has demonstrated that the increase of self-reinforcement alone is an effective group therapy intervention in terms of client improvement.

A third common analogue that is employed in behavioral group therapy is the use of relaxation training for anxiety reduction. Often coupled with outside relaxation training procedures, clients in the group are instructed to monitor and reduce muscle tension levels. Other group members monitor tension indicators such as rapidity of speech, breathing, body tightness, and they prompt behavior which helps the client bring the anxiety under some voluntary control. Members in many types of therapy groups often reflect on other members' tension indicators; however, the present form of behavioral group therapy has members do so systematically. Specific group members are assigned to watch for specific indicators and to have the client systematically identify and deliberately practice behaviors that reduce tension levels.

Related to the analogue of relaxation training is the analogue of stress inoculation (Meichenbaum, 1977), in which the client is supported for continued coping action under signs of obvious stress. This is a very difficult analogue, requiring considerable therapist expertise. Stress levels can be somewhat manipulated by adjusting external input (usually support and encounter), but they should be changed in small steps. Safe stress inoculation requires a prior assessment of a hierarchy of stress cues. It differs from desensitization in that continued coping under high levels of stress is encouraged; however, unlike implosion (Morris, 1975), stress flooding is not attempted.

When problem solving becomes an analogue intervention (D'Zurilla & Goldfried, 1971), the issue is not the specific problem (in fact, the initial problem dealt with in the analogue should be trivial), but rather the problem-solving process itself. The steps are the same as in the section on problem solving above, except that the group input is faded in later stages and the client is supported for good individual problem solving rather than for choosing a good solution.

Obviously, an analogue can be devised for any behavior that the client can practice in the group. However, such use of therapeutic time and energy should always have a clear purpose that is assessable in the client's life. Since the group will terminate and is not designed as a substitute for living, the purpose of any in-group practice is generalization to an appropriate external environment. Analogues should not be employed without a clear understanding of how, where, and with whom this specific behavior change will help the client in his or her life. If analogues are employed simply because they seem like the right thing to do at the moment, they can be wasteful at best and destructive at worst.

Ultimately, the final intervention for the behavior change leading to improved life functioning is self-control. Even if there is prior analogue training, the client finally is being asked to change in the real world, which is beyond the group's control. The first step toward generalization, if the intervention has been an analogue, or to actualization, if the client has chosen an alternative, is public commitment (Kanfer, 1975). This is not the same as a choice. A public commitment is a clear statement to the group that a client will try to change. In line with the research of Kanfer (1975), our research shows that a public commitment is more likely to be made if: (1) it is somewhat vague, (2) it has no set completion date, (3) it is made in a more cohesive group, (4) there has been prior emotional induction, (5) no public accountability has been established, and (6) fewer obstacles to success have been found to exist (Flowers, Note 2; Flowers et al., Note 7).

However, commitment and fulfillment are not the same thing. Fulfillment includes making a thorough attempt and collecting data indicating success or failure. If the alternative fails, such data are important for further intervention attempts. Our research indicates that fulfillment is more likely if: (1) the alternative is specific and operationally defined; (2) the time for fulfillment is specified; (3) the group is cohesive, but will punish a nonattempt (not punish an attempt which did not work); (4) both emotional induction and reduction preceded the commitment; (5) accountability is systematic and public; and (6) the client possesses the skills and resources requisite to make the attempt.

Thus, the factors that facilitate a commitment reduce the likelihood of fulfillment and vice versa. The issue is one of timing. In this form of behavioral group therapy, commitment is urged when conditions for commitment are favorable. The group's task is then to change the rules, one by one, to favor fulfillment. In terms of self-control, we see a teetertotter that must be managed to get maximum outcome. To confuse commitment and fulfillment is not merely to trust to luck for outcome, it is to trust a long shot. The advantage of a behavioral group is that the factors of both commitment and fulfillment can be identified and managed.

Evaluation

After all is said and done, the issue is outcome. Does the client change in advantageous ways? Since group therapy deals with problems on an ad-lib basis, there is no standardized test that can fully assess group therapy results. A therapeutic strength of group therapy is also a source of methodological problems. It is our belief that group therapy outcome assessment is best done on a problem-by-problem basis. When employing client records as an evaluation device, we have found that clients agree with external raters if they are called upon to make fewer inferences. We get our best reliability if we ask the client to record frequency, next best if we ask for duration, only fair reliability if we ask for intensity, and practically no reliability if we ask general questions or ask for opinions (Flowers & Kidder, Note 6). The group therapist should obviously use any evaluation that is helpful therapeutically, including self-reports, generalized tests, etc. When possible, evaluation from all sources should be shared with the client, since learning requires feedback. The obvious limit is that evaluation should not become so burdensome that it makes the process aversive.

LEADERSHIP

The first issue in terms of leadership in this form of behavioral group therapy is that there need to be two leaders. There are a number of reasons for this requirement. First, when the leader is concentrating on or involved in a particular interaction, there should be another leader directing his or her attention to the other group members. This second leader is looking for signs of stress, noninvolvement, potential participation, etc. The second reason for having two leaders is that negative messages should almost always be delivered with accompanying positive messages. If one therapist delivers a negative message that he or she cannot truthfully "buffer" and if no other group member delivers a closely accompanying positive message, it is the responsibility of the second therapist to deliver the positive message. Another reason for two leaders is that group therapy is extremely complex and one leader can neither always know what to do nor always adequately and accurately perceive what has happened. For this reason, it is essential that the two leaders compare plans prior to the group and compare their understanding of what has occurred shortly after the session. It is also important that they be able to disagree, allowing that disagreement to be resolved in the future, i.e., by what the client does in his or her life or in future group sessions. Similarly, it is important that the therapists be able to disagree (and exchange red tokens) in the group therapy session. While it is important that the clients perceive the therapists as having expertise, it is equally important that the therapists should not be perceived as infallible or as always presenting a unified front "against" the client.

For leaders to effectively conduct the form of behavioral group therapy presented here, they must know standard behavioral interventions such as desensitization, assertion training, operant methods, self-control, problem solving, etc. When a client can be helped by such standard interventions, it is the therapists' responsibility to know how to proceed, since it is unlikely that another group member will know the specifics of the necessary intervention.

Beyond being skilled behavior therapists, the behavioral group therapists must also be skilled in influencing group process. In terms of the variables already mentioned as elements of group cohesion, the group leaders need to allow and facilitate client-to-client interaction. While this can be done by silence, it is best accomplished by selective reinforcement of group member interactions. Thus, when one client attempts to help another in a manner the therapists see as appropriate, the group leaders can encourage client-to-client interaction, maintain therapeutic influence, and increase the probability of such interactions in the future (both directly and via modeling) by nondisruptive praise of the client-helper.

The behavioral group therapists also need to encourage and to serve as models for the giving of positive and negative messages (i.e., shaping). The group leaders also must "buffer" negative messages that are not likely to be clearly heard. The therapists must be skilled in operant techniques and must monitor what behaviors the various group members (including the therapists) are attempting to reinforce, punish, and extinguish. Without such awareness, the leaders cannot verify what intended positive and negative messages are actually operant in the group.

The behavioral group therapists need to be aware of the ongoing patterns of activity of each group member. Here, token counts can be extremely helpful. Not only do the therapists need to know which clients are at risk because of proportionately high negative input or output, the leaders need to be aware of which clients are changing their behavior patterns from session to session and which clients are not. Whether this type of in-group behavior is labeled flexibility, risk taking, or experimentation, the crucial point is that such in-group behavior change leads to improved outcome.

To accomplish these tasks, the behavioral group therapists have the same tools that they have always had: prompts, instructions, demonstrations, reinforcement, punishment, and extinction. As always, the therapists can attempt to influence behavior, the in-group behavior, by intervention with the antecedent, behavior, or consequence. The task is more complex, but also can be more powerfully accomplished because of the potential impact of group interaction.

In addition to these overt skills, the behavioral group therapists must be able to discriminate what has occurred in the group,
i.e., they must be sensitive. By sensitivity, we specifically mean
(Flowers, Booraem, & Seacat, 1974; Flowers et al., in press;
Flowers et al., Note 1; Flowers, Hartman, & Booraem, Note 5)
that the therapists' memory of what has occurred, whether that be
of a client's frequency of participation or the content of a client's
disclosure, must match with objective data of that same event. In
addition to research on conditions which disrupt and elicit such
disclosure, and how such sensitivity can be assessed and taught
(Flowers, Booraem, & Seacat, 1974; Flowers et al., in press;
Flowers et al., Note 1), we have recently (Flowers et al., Note 5)
investigated using sensitivity measures along with other variables
as an objective measure of the effectiveness of a behavioral group
therapist.

Two sets of eight trainees each were trained in a 10-week
behavioral group therapy course including a weekly practicum in
which the trainees rotated as group leaders. Two experienced behavioral group therapists, unaware of the following data, independently ranked the trainees in terms of each trainee's ability to
conduct behavioral group therapy. Trainees who were ranked highest also: (1) were most sensitive to individual activity patterns
every session, (2) demonstrated the most sensitivity improvement
over the 10 sessions, (3) demonstrated the greatest increase in sensitivity when in the therapist role, and (4) were the most sensitive
to their own behavior when they were in either the therapist or
client role. The highest ranked leaders were also trusted by group
members when they led the group. Finally, almost all trainees increased the number of statements they made when they were the
assigned leader (Matarazzo & Small, 1963). Highest ranked leaders
were those members who increased the least.

What this method may yield is an objective group leadership
assessment device that can be employed at any point in the training. If behavioral group therapy is to be a systematic and objective
set of techniques that is trainable, the assessment of the training
itself must also be objective. This is both a scientific responsibility
and an ethical one. Trainees become independent therapists who
attempt to intervene with clients who are in real need of the best
possible help.

In this author's experience, many group leaders indicate that
they prefer group therapy to individual therapy because group therapy is easier. From the present perspective, if a leader finds that
group therapy is easier than individual therapy, that leader is not
doing the difficult job that is required. Behavioral group therapy is

difficult, but it can be very effective. It can be taught and learned, and the therapists can not only know what they are doing, but can know that they know.

REFERENCE NOTES

1. Flowers, J. V., Kenney, B. J., & Rotheram, M. J. *The effects of differing proportions of positive and negative feedback on sensitivity, satisfaction and trust of group members.* Paper presented at the Western Psychological Association Convention, San Francisco, Cal., April 1974.
2. Flowers, J. V. *The training of group therapists and the analysis of group therapy: A behavioral approach.* Research address to the First Joint Convention of the California State Psychological Association and the California Association of School Psychologists and Psychometrists, Anaheim, Cal., March 1975.
3. Flowers, J. V., Booraem, C. D., & Hartman, K. A. *Client improvement on higher and lower intensity problems as a function of group cohesiveness.* Paper presented at the Western Psychological Association Convention, Seattle, Wash., April 1977.
4. Flowers, J. V. *The differential effects of simple advice, alternatives, and instructions in group psychotherapy.* Paper presented at the Western Psychological Association Convention, San Francisco, Cal., April 1974.
5. Flowers, J. V., Hartman, K. A., & Booraem, C. D. *Group therapist training: An objective assessment of individual's leadership ability.* Paper presented at the Western Psychological Association Convention, Seattle, Wash., April 1977.
6. Flowers, J. V., & Kidder, S. W. *The relationship between role flexibility and client outcome in group therapy.* Paper presented at the Western Psychological Association Convention, San Francisco, Cal., April 1978.
7. Flowers, J. V., Hartman, K. A., & Mann, R. J. *Supervised client led group therapy: The effects of rotating client and leaders on group therapy outcome.* Paper presented at the Western Psychological Association Convention, San Francisco, Cal., April 1978.

REFERENCES

Abudabbah, N., Prandoni, J. R., & Jensen, D. E. Application of behavior principles to group therapy techniques with juvenile delinquents. *Psychological Reports,* 1972, *31,* 375–380.

Aiken, G. E. Changes in interpersonal descriptions accompanying the operant conditioning of verbal frequency in groups. *Journal of Verbal Learning and Verbal Behavior,* 1965, *4,* 243–247.

Bassin, A. Verbal participation and improvement in group therapy. *International Journal of Group Psychotherapy,* 1962, *12,* 369–373.

Bednar, R. L., & Lawlis, G. F. Empirical research in group psychotherapy. In A. E. Bergin & S. L. Garfield (Eds.), *Handbook of psychotherapy and behavior change: An empirical analysis.* New York: Wiley, 1971.

Bednar, R. L., Zelhart, P. F., Greathouse, L., & Weinberg, S. Operant conditioning principles in the treatment of learning and behavior problems with delinquent boys. *Journal of Counseling Psychology,* 1970, *17,* 492–497.

Booraem, C. D., & Flowers, J. V. Reduction of anxiety and personal space as a function of assertion training with severely disturbed neuropsychiatric inpatients. *Psychological Reports,* 1972, *30,* 923–929.

Booraem, C. D., & Flowers, J. V. A procedural model for the training of assertive behavior. In J. M. Whiteley & J. V. Flowers (Eds.), *Approaches to assertion training.* Monterey, Cal.: Brooks/Cole, 1978.

Bornstein, P., & Sipprelle, C. Group treatment of obesity by induced anxiety. *Behaviour Research and Therapy,* 1973, *11,* 339–441.

Clement, P. Operant conditioning in group psychotherapy with children. *Journal of School Health,* 1968, *38,* 271–278.

Clement, P., Fazzone, R., & Goldstein, B. Tangible reinforcers and child group therapy. *American Academy of Child Psychiatry Journal,* 1970, *7,* 409–427.

Cohen, R. The effects of group interaction and progressive hierarchy presentation on desensitization of test anxiety. *Behaviour Research and Therapy,* 1969, *7,* 15–26.

Cohn, N. B., Mann, R. J., Booraem, C. D., & Flowers, J. V. Methods of increasing self-reinforcement in group therapy and the effects on therapy outcome. *International Journal of Group Psychotherapy,* in press.

Crighton, J., & Jehu, D. Treatment of examination anxiety by systematic desensitization or psychotherapy in groups. *Behaviour Research and Therapy,* 1969, *7,* 245–248.

D'Zurilla, T. J., & Goldfried, M. R. Problem solving and behavior modification. *Journal of Abnormal Psychology,* 1971, *78,* 107–126.

Fensterheim, H. Behavior therapy: Assertive training in groups. In C. J. Sager and H. S. Kaplan (Eds.), *Progress in group and family therapy.* New York: Brunner/Mazel, 1972.

Flowers, J. V. Role playing and simulation methods in psychotherapy. In F. H. Kanfer and A. J. Goldstein (Eds.), *Helping people change: Methods and materials.* New York: Pergamon Press, 1975.

Flowers, J. V. The effect of therapist support and encounter on the percentage of client-client interactions in group therapy. *Journal of Community Psychology,* 1978, *6,* 69–73.

Flowers, J. V., & Booraem, C. D. The use of tokens to facilitate outcome and monitor process in group psychotherapy. *International Journal of Group Psychotherapy,* 1976, *26,* 191–201.

Flowers, J. V., Booraem, C. D., Brown, T. R., & Harris, D. E. An investigation of a technique for facilitating patient-to-patient interactions in group therapy. *Journal of Community Psychology,* 1974, *2,* 39–42.

Flowers, J. V., Booraem, C. D., & Seacat, G. F. The effect of positive and negative feedback on members' sensitivity to other members in group therapy. *Psychotherapy: Theory, Research and Practice*, 1974, *11*, 346–450.

Flowers, J. V., Kenney, B. J., & Rotheram, M. J. Group therapy cohesion and group member behavior: An experimental study. *Small Group Behavior*, in press.

Frank, G. H. The effect of directive and non-directive statements by therapists on the content of patient verbalizations. *Journal of General Psychology*, 1964, *71*, 323–328.

Freeling, N., & Shember, K. The alleviation of test anxiety by systematic desensitization. *Behaviour Research and Therapy*, 1970, *8*, 293–299.

Gibb, J. R. The effects of human relations training. In A. E. Bergin & S. L. Garfield (Eds.), *Handbook of psychotherapy and behavior change: An empirical analysis*. New York: Wiley, 1971.

Goldfried, M. R., & Kent, R. Traditional versus behavioral assessment: A comparison of methodological and theoretical assumptions. *Psychological Bulletin*, 1972, *77*, 409–420.

Goodman, G. An experiment with companionship therapy: College students and troubled boys—assumptions, selection and design. In B. G. Guerney (Ed.), *Psychotherapeutic agents: New roles for nonprofessionals, parents and teachers*. New York: Holt, Rinehart, & Winston, 1969.

Gordon, T. *Group-centered leadership*. Boston: Houghton-Mifflin, 1955.

Graff, R., Maclean, G., & Loving, A. Group reactive inhibition and reciprocal inhibition therapies with anxious college students. *Journal of Counseling Psychology*, 1971, *18*, 431–436.

Guerney, B. G. (Ed.). *Psychotherapeutic agents: New roles for nonprofessionals, parents and teachers*. New York: Holt, Rinehart, & Winston, 1969.

Hagen, R. L. Group therapy versus bibliotherapy in weight reduction. *Behavior Therapy*, 1974, *5*, 222–234.

Hastorf, A. H. The "reinforcement" of individual actions in a group situation. In L. Krasner & L. P. Ullmann (Eds.), *Research in behavior modification*. New York: Holt, Rinehart, & Winston, 1965.

Hauserman, N. , Zweback, S., & Plotkin, A. Use of concrete reinforcement to facilitate verbal initiations in adolescent group therapy. *Journal of Consulting and Clinical Psychology*, 1972, *38*, 90–96.

Heckel, R. V., Wiggins, S. L., & Salzberg, H. C. Conditioning against silences in group therapy. *Journal of Clinical Psychology*, 1962, *18*, 216–217.

Hedquist, F. J., & Weinhold, B. K. Behavioral group counseling with socially anxious and unassertive college students. *Journal of Counseling Psychology*, 1970, *17*, 237–242.

Hinds, W., & Roehlke, H. A learning theory approach to group counseling with elementary school children. *Journal of Counseling Psychology*, 1970, *17*, 49–55.

Ihli, K. L., & Garlington, W. K. A comparison of group vs. individual desensitization of test anxiety. *Behaviour Research and Therapy*, 1969, *7*, 207–209.

Kanfer, F. H. Self-management methods. In F. H. Kanfer & A. P. Goldstein (Eds.), *Helping people change: Methods and materials*. New York: Pergamon Press, 1975.

Kanfer, F. H., & Saslow, G. Behavioral diagnosis. In C. M. Franks (Ed.), *Behavior therapy: Appraisal and status*. New York: McGraw-Hill, 1969.

Kanter, R. M. *Commitment and community*. Cambridge, Mass.: Harvard University Press, 1972.

Kass, D. J., Silvers, F. M., & Abroms, G. M. Behavioral group treatment of hysteria. *Archives of General Psychiatry*, 1972, *26*, 42–50.

Koenig, K. P., & Masters, J. Experimental treatment of habitual smoking. *Behaviour Research and Therapy*, 1965, *3*, 235–243.

Kondas, O. Reduction of examination anxiety and stage-fright by group desensitization and relaxation. *Behaviour Research and Therapy*, 1967, *5*, 275–281.

Krumboltz, J. D., & Potter, B. Behavioral techniques for developing trust, cohesiveness, and goal accomplishment. *Educational Technology*, 1973, *13*, 26–30.

Lang, P. J. Fear reduction and fear behavior: Problems in treating a construct. In J. M. Shlien (Ed.), *Research in psychotherapy* (Vol. 3). Washington, D.C.: American Psychological Assn., 1968.

Lang, P. J. Physiological assessment of anxiety and fear. In J. D. Cone & R. P. Hawkins (Eds.), *Behavioral assessment: New directions in clinical psychology*. New York: Brunner/Mazel, 1977.

Langer, E. J., & Abelson, R. P. A patient by another name. . .: Clinician group differences in labeling bias. *Journal of Consulting and Clinical Psychology*, 1974, *42*, 4–9.

Lawrence, H., & Sundel, M. Behavior modification in adult groups. *Social Work*, 1972, *17*, 2, 34–43.

Lazarus, A. A. Behavior therapy in groups. In G. M. Gazda (Ed.), *Basic approaches to group psychotherapy and group counseling*. Springfield, Ill.: Charles C. Thomas, 1968.

Lewinsohn, P. M., Weinstein, M. S., & Alper, T. A behavioral approach to the group treatment of depressed persons: A methodological contribution. *Journal of Clinical Psychology*, 1970, *26*, 525–532.

Liberman, R. A behavioral approach to group dynamics: 1. Reinforcement and prompting of cohesiveness in group therapy. *Behavior Therapy*, 1970, *1*, 141–175.

Liberman, R. P. Reinforcement of cohesiveness in group therapy: Behavioral and personality changes. *Archives of General Psychiatry*, 1971, *25*, 168–177.

Lieberman, M. A., Lakin, M., & Whitaker, D. S. The group as a unique context for therapy. *Psychotherapy: Theory, Research, and Practice*, 1968, *5*, 29–36.

Lieberman, M. A., Yalom, I. D., & Miles, M. B. *Encounter groups: First facts*. New York: Basic Books, 1973.

Linsk, N., Howe, M. W., & Pinkston, E. M. Behavioral group work in a home for the aged. *Social Work*, 1975, *20*, 454–463.

Lomont, J., Gilner, F., Spector, N., & Skinner, K. Group assertion training and group insight therapies. *Psychological Reports*, 1969, *25*, 463–470.

Lott, A. J., & Lott, B. E. Group cohesiveness, communication level, and conformity. *Journal of Abnormal and Social Psychology,* 1961, *62,* 408–412.

MacDonald, M. L., Lindquist, C. U., Kramer, J. A., McGrath, R. A., & Rhyne, L. L. Social skills training: The effects of behavior rehearsal in groups on dating skills. *Journal of Counseling Psychology,* 1975, *22,* 224–230.

McManus, M. Group desensitization of test anxiety. *Behaviour Research and Therapy,* 1971, *9,* 51–56.

Marrone, R. L., Merksamer, M. A., & Salzberg, P. M. A short duration group treatment of smoking behavior by stimulus saturation. *Behaviour Research and Therapy,* 1970, *8,* 347–352.

Matarazzo, J., & Small, I. An experiment in teaching group psychotherapy. *Journal of Nervous Mental Disease,* 1963, *36,* 252–263.

Meichenbaum, D. H. Cognitive modification of test anxious college students. *Journal of Consulting and Clinical Psychology,* 1972, *39,* 370–380.

Meichenbaum, D. H. *Cognitive-behavior modification: An integrative approach.* New York: Plenum, 1977.

Miller, E., Dvorak, B., & Turner, D. A method of creating aversion to alcohol by reflex conditioning in a group setting. *Quarterly Journal of Studies on Alcohol,* 1960, *21,* 424–431.

Miller, G. A., Galanter, E., & Pribram, K. H. *Plans and the structure of behavior.* New York: Holt, Rinehart, & Winston, 1960.

Miller, L., & Miller, O. Reinforcing self-help group activities of welfare recipients. *Journal of Applied Behavior Analysis,* 1970, *3,* 57–64.

Mitchell, K., & Ingham, R. The effects of general anxiety on group desensitization of test anxiety. *Behaviour Research and Therapy,* 1970, *8,* 69–78.

Morris, R. J. Fear reduction methods. In F. H. Kanfer & A. J. Goldstein (Eds.), *Helping people change: Methods and materials.* New York: Pergamon Press, 1975.

Morris, K. T., & Cinnamon, K. H. *A handbook of verbal group exercises.* Springfield, Ill.: Charles C. Thomas, 1974.

Nawas, M., Fishman, S., & Pucel, J. A standardized desensitization program applicable to group and individual treatments. *Behaviour Research and Therapy,* 1970, *8,* 49–56.

Oakes, W. F. Effectiveness of signal light reinforcers given various meanings on participation in group discussion. *Psychological Reports,* 1962, *11,* 469–470. (a)

Oakes, W. F. Reinforcement of Bales' categories in group discussion. *Psychological Reports,* 1962, *11,* 427–435. (b)

Oakes, W. F., Droge, A. E., & August, B. Reinforcement effects on participation in group discussion. *Psychological Reports,* 1960, *7,* 503–514.

Oakes, W. F., Droge, A. E., & August, B. Reinforcement effects on conclusions reached in group discussion. *Psychological Reports,* 1961, *9,* 27–34.

Paul, G. L. *Insight vs. desensitization in psychotherapy.* Stanford: Stanford University Press, 1966.

Paul, G. L., & Shannon, D. T. Treatment of anxiety through systematic desensitization in therapy groups. *Journal of Abnormal Psychology*, 1966, *71*, 124–135.

Pfieffer, J. W., & Jones, J. E. *A handbook of structured experience for human relations training* (4 vols.). Iowa City, Iowa: University Associates Press, 1970.

Rachman, S. Studies in desensitization II: Flooding. *Behaviour Research and Therapy*, 1966, *4*, 1–6.

Rathus, S. A. An experimental investigation of assertive training in a group setting. *Journal of Behavior Therapy and Experimental Psychiatry*, 1972, *3*, 81–86.

Rickard, H. C., & Timmons, E. O. Manipulating verbal behavior in groups: A comparison of three intervention techniques. *Psychological Reports*, 1961, *9*, 729–736.

Ritter, B. The group desensitization of children's snake phobias using vicarious and contact desensitization procedures. *Behaviour Research and Therapy*, 1968, *6*, 1–6.

Robinson, C., & Suinn, R. Group desensitization of a phobia in massed sessions. *Behaviour Research and Therapy*, 1968, *7*, 319–321.

Rogers, C. R. The process of the basic encounter group. In R. W. Siroka, E. K. Siroka, & G. A. Schloss (Eds.), *Sensitivity training and group encounter*. New York: Grosset & Dunlap, 1971.

Rose, S. D. A behavioral approach to group treatment of children. In E. J. Thomas (Ed.), *The socio-behavioral approach and applications to social work*. New York: Council on Social Work Education, 1967.

Rose, S. D. A behavioral approach to the group treatment of parents. *Social Work*, 1969, *14*, 21–29.

Rose, S. D. *Treating children in groups*. San Francisco: Jossey-Bass, 1972.

Rose, S. D. *Group therapy: A behavioral approach*. Englewood Cliffs, N.J.: Prentice-Hall, 1977.

Ross, D. M., Ross, S. A., & Evans, T. A. The modification of extreme social withdrawal by modeling with guided participation. *Journal of Behavior Therapy and Experimental Psychiatry*, 1971, *2*, 273–279.

Salzberg, H. C. Manipulation of verbal behavior in a group psychotherapeutic setting. *Psychological Reports*, 1961, *9*, 183–186.

Sarason, I. G., & Ganzer, V. J. Modeling and group discussion in the rehabilitation of juvenile delinquents. *Journal of Counseling Psychology*, 1973, *20*, 442–449.

Schachter, S., Ellerston, N., McBride, D., & Gregory, D. An experimental study of cohesiveness and productivity. In D. Cartright & A. Zander (Eds.), *Group dynamics*. New York: Harper & Row, 1968.

Schinke, S. P., & Rose, S. D. Interpersonal skill training in groups. *Journal of Counseling Psychology*, 1976, *23*, 442–448.

Sechrest, L. B., & Berger, B. Verbal participation and perceived benefit from group psychotherapy. *International Journal of Group Psychotherapy*, 1961, *11*, 49–59.

Simkins, L., & West, J. Modification of verbal interaction in triad groups: Preliminary report. *Psychological Reports*, 1965, *16*, 684.

Skindrud, K. Field evaluation of observer bias under overt and covert monitoring. In L. A. Hamerlynck, L. C. Handy, & E. J. Mash (Eds.), *Behavior change: Methodology, concepts and practice.* Champaign, Ill.: Research Press, 1973.

Slavson, S. S. *Textbook in analytic group psychotherapy.* New York: International Universities Press, 1963.

Strupp, H. H., & Wallack, M. S. A further study of psychiatrists' responses in quasi-therapeutic situations. *Behavioral Science,* 1965, *10,* 113–134.

Suinn, R. The desensitization of test-anxiety by group and individual treatment. *Behaviour Research and Therapy,* 1968, *6,* 385–387.

Suinn, R., & Hall, R. Marathon desensitization groups: An innovative technique. *Behaviour Research and Therapy,* 1970, *8,* 97–98.

Ullmann, L., Krasner, L., & Collins, B. Modification of behavior through verbal conditioning: Effects in group therapy. *Journal of Abnormal and Social Psychology,* 1961, *62,* 128–132.

Upper, D., & Ross, S. M. Behavioral group therapy: 1. Emotional, avoidance, and social skills problems of adults. In M. Hersen, R. M. Eisler, & P. M. Miller (Eds.), *Progress in behavior modification* (Vol. 5). New York: Academic Press, 1977.

Wagner, M. Reinforcement of verbal productivity in group therapy. *Psychological Reports,* 1966, *19,* 1217–1218.

Watson, J. P., Mullett, G. E., & Pillay, H. The effects of prolonged exposure to phobic situations upon agoraphobic patients treated in groups. *Behaviour Research and Therapy,* 1973, *11,* 531–545.

Whiteley, J. M., & Flowers, J. V. (Eds.), *Approaches to assertion training.* Monterey, Cal.: Brooks/Cole, 1978.

Whitman, T. Aversive control of smoking behavior in a group context. *Behaviour Research and Therapy,* 1972, *10,* 97–104.

Wollersheim, J. Effectiveness of group therapy based upon learning principles in the treatment of overweight women. *Journal of Abnormal Psychology,* 1970, *76,* 462–474.

Wolpe, J., & Lazarus, A. A. *Behavior therapy techniques: A guide to the treatment of neurosis.* Oxford: Pergamon Press, 1966.

Yalom, I. D. *The theory and practice of group psychotherapy* (2nd ed.). New York: Basic Books, 1975.

Yalom, I. D., & Rand, K. Compatibility and cohesiveness in therapy groups. *Archives of General Psychiatry,* 1966, *13,* 267–276.

Chapter 2

The Role of the Group in Behavioral Group Therapy

David L. Sansbury

Abstract

This chapter examines two related questions concerning behavioral group therapy: What is the additive value of the group context? How can the group process issues which emerge in behavioral groups be effectively managed? Relevant research findings and expert opinion are presented which support the chapter's thesis that the group context can enhance the therapeutic outcome of many behavioral approaches if the group process issues are effectively managed by the therapist. Nine potential assets of conducting behavior therapy in groups are identified, and the group process issues of commonality, cohesion, and protherapeutic group norms are discussed, along with suggested techniques for their effective management.

INTRODUCTION

In this volume a variety of treatment techniques are presented for the alleviation of a wide range of problematic behaviors, and all of the treatments have the common element of being conducted in a group context. This chapter explores the implications of the group setting for behavioral group therapy, with an examination of the value of the group context and of the actual and potential influences of group processes on the conduct and outcome of behavioral group therapy.

The first question to be addressed is, "What is the additive value, if any, of conducting the various behavior therapy procedures in a group therapy context?" A very critical position was taken by Lieberman (1975) regarding the extension of a behavioral orientation into the group setting. He notes that this extension assumes implicitly that the leader is in precise control of the situation and, thus, is able to carry out the various behavioral techniques. He argues that, in fact, the therapist's power and influence are much more diffused in groups than in the dyadic relationship and that the nature of the reward-punishment system in groups differs from that in dyads. The precision of the techniques is dependent upon how the social system evolves. Also, he points out that the behaviorists often assume naively ". . . that group members will do just the right thing at the right time so that they will be facilitative, and that producing these responses in the collective is open to strategies in accordance with social learning theory" (p.443). Further, he notes that there is wide agreement that the group reward functions are most closely related to the evolving group norms, which may not necessarily be in agreement with the behavioral therapist's intentions. He refers to unidentified "recent studies" which he believes indicate that group norms are not primarily a function of the leader's behavior.

Lieberman (1975) concludes his argument:

> Thus, approaching change induction in groups with a behavioral orientation presents some tricky theoretical and technical issues which tend, as yet, not to be addressed in the behavioral literature. As with most theories of change derived from examination of dyadic experience, the failure of behavioral approaches to take account of the most salient features of groups, namely that they represent a complex social system not only with unique properties for change, but also with unique problems, reduces the power of change strategies that have demonstrated success in the dyadic context. (p. 443)

In contrast to Lieberman, Lawrence and Sundel (1972) downplay the importance of group dynamics as a major consideration in the conduct of treatment groups. They argue that, in the treatment model of social group work, a client becomes a member of the group as a means of solving a problem of concern to himself and/or significant others. The goal of treatment is not that the client learns to be a good group member but that each member changes his behavior in relationships outside the group. Group functioning objectives, such as cohesiveness, democratic leadership, and self-revealing communication, are relevant only to the degree that they facilitate the achievement of treatment goals. Group functioning objectives thus are seen as means to an end, not ends in themselves (Lawrence & Sundel, 1972).

In contrast to these two positions, it is the thesis of this chapter that the group context can enhance the therapeutic outcomes of many behavioral approaches if the group process issues are effectively managed by the leader and if that effective management involves the systematic application of known social learning principles.

THE VALUE OF THE GROUP CONTEXT FOR BEHAVIOR THERAPY

In presenting a general rationale for conducting behavior therapy in groups, Lazarus (1968) touched on several potential values of the group context. He cited not only the savings in therapists' time and effort but also the enhanced likelihood of discrimination learning, a wider range of experiences and opinions, and lessened feelings of isolation. He also noted that aspects of the patient's problems which may not have been evident during the early diagnostic phase often become clearly delineated in the group. The value of the group for diagnostic purposes was also cited by Goldstein and Wolpe (1972):

> The group setting offers an opportunity for a far more thorough behavioral analysis than does individual therapy. When dealing with the patient in an individual session, the therapist is able to observe his behavior in relation to only one person—the therapist—which gives little knowledge of the patient's possible responses to other people. (p. 129)

Time Saving

The research basis of Lazarus's assumption that behavioral groups represent a savings of time and effort is rather meager but nevertheless supportive. Lazarus (1961) published the first report in which desensitization was applied in groups. He tested 35 adults with phobic disorders in a study which compared the effects of desensitization groups with interpretive groups and interpretive groups plus relaxation. His results strongly favored the desensitization groups, which also averaged the fewest number of sessions.

Paul and Shannon (1966) reported the first investigation of group desensitization involving both a central life problem and a no-treatment control group. Ten chronically anxious males received nine sessions of group desensitization and were compared with individuals who received individual desensitization, insight-oriented psychotherapy, an attention-placebo treatment, and no treatment. The posttreatment results showed that group desensitization subjects had significantly reduced anxiety, not only in the specific target areas of anxiety, but on related interpersonal anxieties as well, suggesting a significant generalization effect. In comparison with individual treatments, the group desensitization procedure was found to be as effective as individual desensitization in all areas and was superior to individual insight-oriented psychotherapy and control groups. A two-year follow-up study of the groups (Paul, 1968) showed that the earlier superiority of both individual and group desensitization over individual insight-oriented psychotherapy and attention-placebo treatments was not only maintained, but the group treatment was found to show even greater reduction in emotionality than any individual treatment.

Although the value of their study is limited by the few subjects, Ihli and Garlington (1969) also found that group desensitization was equally as effective as individual desensitization and represented a considerable saving in therapist time. Finally, Krumboltz and Thoresen (1964) studied the effects of reinforcement and model-reinforcement counseling in both individual and group settings. In general, they found both settings equally effective, although sex-by-group and treatment-by-group interactions did occur.

Another study bearing on the value of conducting a behavioral approach to treatment in a group context was performed by Hafner and Marks (1976). They compared the contributions of diazepam (Valium), group exposure, and anxiety evocation in the *in vivo* treatment of agoraphobics using a flooding procedure. No specific emphasis was placed on developing the group as a group, though. A comparison of group versus individual treatment showed both to be effective, with slight differences favoring the group approach. Also, the group method showed a trend of increasing improvement after treatment which was not shown by the individually treated group. Therapists reported the group treatments easier to conduct and the patients more willing to enter into the anxiety-arousing situations when treated in a group.

Thus, the available comparative research indicates that, with several behavioral techniques, group treatment is at least as effective as individual treatment and can represent a significant saving of therapist time.

Enhanced Learning Through Modeling

Zupnick (1971) has suggested that group therapy can be conceptualized as exposing individuals to multiple peer models, and this availability of multiple models increases the value of conducting behavior therapy in groups. Recent studies by Kazdin (1973, 1974) and Meichenbaum (1971) lend empirical support to the value of group members as models as they develop coping skills.

Investigating the characteristics of models which would be most effective in reducing avoidance behavior, Meichenbaum found that the perceived similarity between models and observer is enhanced by having the model portray, at first, the behaviors, thoughts, and feelings that are similar to those of the client. Then, client change is effected by having the models demonstrate a sequence of coping skills, as opposed to mastery skills, that can be employed by the client to overcome the deficit. In his study, the models demonstrated not only desirable behaviors, but also coping cognition, re-evaluation, ways of coping with feelings of frustration and self-doubt, and self-reinforcing statements.

Kazdin (1974) provided evidence that covert modeling can effectively reduce avoidance behavior and that the efficacy of modeling is dependent upon the similarity of the model and observer in terms of age and sex. Also, of the two experimental groups which imagined a model of similar age and sex, the group that also imagined a model who was initially hesitant, anxious, and worried but eventually coped with the task (coping model) tended to show greater change compared with the groups imagining a mastery model. The latter model appeared confident, relaxed, and unbothered while performing each task with ease.

Thus, there is research support for the assertion that one clear value of conducting behavior therapy in groups is the opportunity for learning to occur as members watch other members develop coping skills for handling their problems. The value of being in a group with several members as models is strongly supported by a recent study by Kazdin (1976). He studied the effects of having subjects imagine a single model performing assertively versus imagining four different models varied by age and sex. Also, half of the subjects in each group imagined favorable consequences following the covert model behavior while the other half imagined no consequences. The results indicated that: (1) covert modeling led to significant increases in assertive behaviors which generalized to novel role-playing situations and were maintained up to a 4-month follow-up evaluation, and (2) imagining several models engaging in assertive behavior, with favorable consequences following model performance, enhanced treatment effects. In general, the multiple model-reinforcement group was significantly more assertive than the other treatment groups. Earlier, Bandura and Menlove (1968) had studied the comparative effectiveness of single-model versus multiple-model treatments in the vicarious extinction of avoidance behavior in children. While both treatments effected significant reductions in children's avoidance behavior, only the multiple-model treatment weakened their fears sufficiently to enable them to perform potentially threatening interactions with dogs.

While modeling is a potent means of evoking behavior change, several studies substantiate the importance of providing guided participation following modeling for both increasing the acquisition of desired behaviors, and reducing avoidance behaviors. Friedman (1971) studied the differential effects of information, modeling, and role playing on the acquisition of assertive behavior. He assigned 101 subjects randomly to one of six treatment conditions: live modeling, directed role playing, improvised role playing, modeling plus directed role playing, reading an assertive script, and reading a nonassertive script. In the male subjects, modeling plus directed role playing was the most effective treatment, while the women showed greatest change following the improvised role playing.

The following two studies have focused on reducing avoidance behavior using guided participation following modeling. Bandura, Blanchard, and Ritter (1969) compared the effectiveness of participant modeling, symbolic modeling, and standard desensitization in the treatment of snake phobia. In the participant modeling condition, after demonstrating the desired behavior, the model guides the observer personally through the steps involved, directly assisting if necessary. In the study, 92% of the participant modeling subjects significantly reduced their phobia. This method was more successful than the symbolic modeling condition, and both modeling groups proved superior to the standard desensitization treatment group.

In order to study the relative efficacy of two covert modeling procedures and guided participant modeling in treating avoidance behavior, Thase and Moss (1976) assigned eight subjects randomly to one of four treatment conditions: covert modeling with a similar other as model, covert modeling with themselves as model, live modeling followed by the model guiding the subject's participation, and a delayed-treatment control group. The guided modeling group was significantly more effective in reducing general and specific self-reported fears and had significantly greater approach behavior than the other three groups.

These three studies, then, point to the importance of having the group members try out the desired new behaviors in the group setting where there is the provision for guidance and feedback on performance. The next section reviews the effects of increased member-to-member talking and increased cohesion on behavioral group therapy outcome.

Member-to-Member Interactions

The existence of the group as an audience which can dispense social reinforcement is another value of group therapy. In a series of studies, Scott (1957, 1959a, 1959b) examined the importance of social reinforcement for the modification of attitudes in role-playing situations. In the first study, college students were asked to participate in a debate before a class of their peers and to adopt a position that was not in accord with their own beliefs about the issues being debated. Then, the subjects were led to believe that they had either won or lost the debate on the basis of a class vote. The declared "winners" demonstrated a greater change in attitude toward the adopted positions than did the "losers." In the next two studies, the college students debated in front of a panel of judges and again were told they had won the debate when they were in the group who argued for a position contrary to their own. Again the declared "winners" changed their attitudes significantly in the direction of the debated position while the "losers" did not.

Two studies have been specifically designed to examine the influence of group processes on behavioral group therapy outcome. Cohen (1969) randomly assigned 25 highly test-anxious subjects to four groups. In two groups, the subjects were desensitized to test anxiety and participated in interactions with other group members on intra-experimental situations and extra-experimental experiences. In the other two desensitization groups, there was no opportunity for interaction among members of the group. These four experimental groups were compared with each other and the two control groups. The results indicate that the groups with interaction were superior in reducing test anxiety. In discussing the results, Cohen speculated that the group interaction improved desensitization by: (1) providing an additional desensitization experience by allowing people to talk about anxiety-provoking topics in a non-threatening supportive environment, and (2) serving a motivational function as students see that others who have similar problems can successfully cope with them.

A further step toward understanding how groups may enhance behavioral treatment was taken by Hand, Lamontagne, and Marks (1974), who studied the role of social cohesion as a facilitator of improvement during the group behavioral treatment of agoraphobia using an *in vivo* flooding procedure. They reasoned that a cohesive group would increase the motivation of the members to perform the required treatment exercises and to continue applying the learned techniques after the termination of treatment. Subjects were assigned to either a structured or an unstructured treatment group. The structured group was designed to enhance group cohesion through the use of half-hour discussion periods before and after each daily session and intermingled 15-minute discussions between the 45-minute treatment sessions. In the structured groups, the therapist elicited discussion of achievements and fostered intermember talking. These group members also were given the expectation that the group would facilitate treatment. In the unstructured group, members were asked not to talk with each other but to discuss problems individually with the therapist. Thus, intermember discussion was minimized.

During and immediately after each treatment session, members of both groups responded to a five-item questionnaire designed to measure group cohesion. Patients rated the help received from the group as a whole, help received from individual patients, help given to individual patients, perceived liking from the other patients, and liking of the other patients. On each item, the structured group members gave significantly higher ratings than those in the unstructured group. Also, the members of the structured group rated the group as more helpful in their treatment than the therapist and saw the group as having a calming effect on their fears. At the end of treatment, both groups showed equal and significant improvement on the target behaviors. Yet, at the follow-up periods 3 and 6 months later, the structured group was superior to the unstructured group in treatment outcome. Clinical impressions by the therapists included the observations that members experience tension reduction upon finding that others share their fears and anxieties; a member's sense of helping others in the group is a major motivation in the treatment group; and a member's knowledge that other patients are going through the same procedures boosted both feelings of confidence and competition, resulting in better treatment performance. They also noted that there was no group panic or contagion when one member became hysterical and physically distraught during treatment.

Intrigued by the findings of Hand et al. (1974), Teasdale, Walsh, Lancashire, and Mathews (1977) attempted to replicate the beneficial effects of the structured group approach. They studied the treatment outcome of using a flooding procedure with agoraphobics in structured groups. Their findings did not replicate the continued improvement of the treatment group but showed the same plateau following the termination of treatment as was found with the unstructured groups in the Hand et al. study. They did note, though, that group process measures showed that the groups in this study did not attain the degree of cohesion reported by Hand et al.

Summary

At this point, a number of potential assets of conducting behavior therapy in groups has been identified. These assets are stated below as research hypotheses with the hope of fostering further research in the field.

Hypothesis 1. With the techniques of desensitization, modeling plus reinforcement, and flooding, group approaches to treatment will save therapist time and effort with equal or increased effectiveness.

Hypothesis 2. The availability of multiple models which display the acquisition of coping skills to a range of problems will increase member motivation to change and will enhance behavior change.

Hypothesis 3. In comparison with individual behavior therapy, a more thorough behavioral analysis is possible in behavioral group therapy.

Hypothesis 4. In comparison with individual behavior therapy, there are lessened feelings of isolation and uniqueness of individual problems experienced in behavioral group therapy, which results in a lowering of initial anxiety.

Hypothesis 5. Knowledge that others are experiencing the same treatment procedures increases feelings of confidence in the treatment and increases motivation to continue treatment.

Hypothesis 6. Having others observe one's progress increases motivation to do well, leading to increased likelihood of entering into the more anxiety-provoking aspects of the treatment.

Hypothesis 7. Discussions of anxiety-provoking topics in a supportive group environment act as a mild form of desensitization.

Hypothesis 8. In a group context, discrimination learning is enhanced because of the variety of feedback sources available.

Hypothesis 9. In comparison with individual behavior therapy, new coping behaviors learned in behavioral group therapy will generalize to a wider range of situations.

GROUP PROCESS ISSUES

The above list represents a potential that may be available when behavior therapy is carried out in a group context. In any group, and particularly in therapeutic groups, certain group process issues will emerge, and they carry with them the potential for enhancing or disrupting the tasks of the group. Too often the behavioral group leader either ignores the group processes occurring in the group or views them only as a distraction and seeks to minimize their influence. There is a third way—actively managing the emergence of the major group process issues in such a way that they improve the effectiveness of the behavioral treatment. Thus, the second question to be addressed is, "How do the group process issues of commonality, cohesion, and norms relate to behavioral groups, and what are effective therapist techniques for influencing their emergence?"

Commonality

Patients typically approach treatment assuming that they are unique in their fears, anxieties, impulses, and difficulties. While therapist statements of having treated similar problems may bring a little relief, the disconfirmation of this dread of uniqueness, accomplished through the initial sharing in a behavior therapy group, is a powerful source of relief. The mutual recognition that others share the same difficulties and are similarly motivated for treatment dramatically reduces anxiety in the group. Hand et al. (1974), as well as Teasdale et al. (1977), have commented on this phenomenon occurring in their groups.

While the feeling of commonality can come about spontaneously, the therapist can facilitate its occurrence by a number of behaviors prior to and during the first session. Treatment groups formed with maximum homogeneity of patient problems is one potent approach. Alternatively, in groups which include an array of target behaviors, the therapist can strive to select members on the basis of similar educational and socioeconomic backgrounds. During the first session, the use of structured exercises designed to facilitate the members' discussion of their reasons for being there and their goals for treatment sets the stage for discovering similarities and initiates a sense of "we-ness."

The feeling of not being all alone in one's misery may reduce anxiety and promote a positive feeling toward the other group members. During this initial sharing, members may experience a belonging to the group, and collectively the group may convey an acceptance to the member that he or she has a legitimate place in the group. An acceptance of the group as an agent of help and the individual's acceptance in the group by the other members is a necessary step in the development of cohesion.

Cohesion

From the sense of being in the right place and being accepted as a legitimate member by others, there develops a sense of oneness of purpose that binds the members together. This developing sense of unity and attraction is referred to as cohesion, and without it the beneficial nonspecific aspects of the group context are not available to enhance the behavioral treatment. Nearly all writers in the field of group work mention cohesion as the core of a successful group. Bednar and Lawlis (1971) reviewed the available literature to determine whether there was a basis for inferring that group cohesion is related to desirable group therapy outcome. In general, they concluded that the data were consistent with the view that the concept of group cohesion, broadly defined, represents an aspect of group process essential to effective treatment. Cohesion appears to grow out of shared group experience, a process that results in "earned" trust, and its dynamic importance lies in the feeling of safety it can provide. A cohesive group provides the basis for meaningful self-exploration, giving and receiving interpersonal feedback, and a sense of being understood and valued.

How can the group leader directly influence the level of group cohesion? The research conducted by Liberman (1970) provides convincing evidence for the use of social learning and operant conditioning procedures to influence its development. He demonstrated that, by ". . . prompting and reinforcing intermember behavior that reflects mutual recognition, interest, concern, and acceptance, the therapist can help the group members resolve their problems with intimacy and foster group cohesiveness" (p. 145).

Krumboltz and Potter (1973) extended Liberman's concepts by both specifying the group behaviors which operationally define group cohesion and providing an extensive list of leader behaviors and group exercises which could facilitate the development of cohesion. In addition to leader behaviors designed to cue, reinforce, or extinguish member behaviors, they emphasize the use of modeling, confronting, and norm setting. For example, the leader could model statements expressing a liking for the group or statements referring to the group as a whole, could confront members' attempts to form subgroups, and could set norms by explicitly defining desired behavior—all in an attempt to increase group cohesion.

Group Norms

"The more cohesive the group, the greater the probability that members will develop uniform opinions and other behaviors with respect to matters of consequence to the group" (Lott, 1961, p. 284). One major result of increased cohesion is the greater value attached to the group and the development of group norms regarding permissable, desired, and unapproved group behaviors. Members take on greater and greater reinforcement value for each other. Accompanying the increased attraction for the group is the increased fear that deviant attitudes or behaviors will result in rejection, thus depriving the member of reinforcement. Therefore, the group will develop a capacity to control the behavior of the members through an established system of rewards and punishments, and it is critical that the norms developed further the therapeutic task of the group.

Lawrence and Sundel (1972) stress the importance of establishing protherapeutic group norms early in the life of a time-limited behavioral group and suggest that a pre-group interview and therapist modeling and prompting are effective techniques to bring about such group norms. During the intake interview they establish the following five rules as important for the success of the group: (1) members must attend every meeting, (2) members must refrain from outside socializing until the series of meetings is completed, (3) group discussions must be focused on contemporary events related to the members' problems, (4) members must refrain from hostile confrontation with each other, and (5) members must work on assigned tasks between group meetings. Because the rules are stated during the intake interview, it is easier to enforce them in the group. Within the group, the leader can use modeling, prompts, selective reinforcement, and references to the rules to help facilitate the development of appropriate norms which then become enforced by the members themselves.

The expected result of the effective management of these group process issues of commonality, cohesion, and protherapeutic norms is reduced member anxiety, increased interaction, increased motivation, and a supportive, encouraging environment for treatment. Feelings of altruism will most likely develop. Members, then, are more willing to work on the problems which brought them to the group, and the process of change is quickened. The sense of "we-ness" and group support motivates members to continue working between sessions and after the group treatment has formally ended.

CONCLUSIONS

With reference to the two positions cited early in this chapter, Lieberman (1975) presents a valid caution to behavioral group therapists when he points out that the group context brings with it a potential for undermining the effectiveness of behavioral techniques. Yet, rather than simply focusing on potential limitations, this chapter has recognized that danger and has argued for the effective management of the group process in order to *enhance* therapeutic outcome. Recent research tends to support this possibility. Although they do stress the importance of protherapeutic group norms, Lawrence and Sundel (1972) appear to downplay the importance of the group process issues. Most lacking in their approach is attention to the systematic development of other group processes which enhance the likelihood of acceptance of these desired norms by the group member. Their approach is a good start but not sufficiently broad in scope to ensure the desired results. This chapter has stressed the development of the necessary preconditions for the evolution of protherapeutic norms—commonality and cohesion.

Exploration of the role of the group in behavioral group therapy is just beginning. While this chapter has proposed a framework for understanding the development of group process issues in behavioral groups, the theory is based largely upon extrapolations from nonbehavioral groups and a few related research studies. Research specifically on behavioral groups is needed to substantiate or modify our current conceptualizations, and a good beginning would be a naturalistic study of the developmental trends in a variety of behavioral groups in a fashion analogous to Lundgren's (1977) study of T-groups. Later investigators could study the relationship between various group leader behaviors designed to enhance group process issues and the emergence of those issues, as well as their relation to the success of the group. By exploring the various related aspects of group process issues in behavioral groups, this trend of research will eventually merge with the larger field of small group research and should yield a broader theory of groups and group leadership, one which takes into account the influence of leader-imposed structure in therapy groups. Finally, through this research effort, the contributions of operant and social learning theory to the enhancement of group leader behavior will become more widely recognized and new systematic techniques will be developed.

REFERENCES

Bandura, A., Blanchard, E. B., & Ritter, B. Relative efficacy of desensitization and modeling approaches for inducing behavioral, affective and attitudinal changes. *Journal of Personality and Social Psychology*, 1969, *13*, 173–199.

Bandura, A., & Menlove, F. L. Factors determining vicarious extinction of avoidance behavior through symbolic modeling. *Journal of Personality and Social Psychology*, 1968, *8*, 99–108.

Bednar, R. L., & Lawlis, G. F. Empirical research in group psychotherapy. In A. E. Bergin & S. L. Garfield (Eds.), *Handbook of psychotherapy and behavior change: An empirical analysis*. New York: Wiley, 1971.

Cohen, R. The effects of group interaction and progressive hierarchy presentation on desensitization of test anxiety. *Behaviour Research and Therapy*, 1969, *7*, 15–26.

Friedman, P. H. The effects of modeling and role-playing on assertive behavior. In R. Rubin, H. Fensterheim, A. Lazarus, & C. Franks (Eds.), *Advances in behavior therapy*. New York: Academic Press, 1971.

Goldstein, A., & Wolpe, J. Behavior therapy in groups. In H. I. Kaplan & B. Sadock (Eds.), *New models for group therapy*. New York: Jason Aronson, Inc., 1972.

Hafner, J., & Marks, I. Exposure *in vivo* of agoraphobics: Contributions of diazepam, group exposure, and anxiety evocation. *Psychological Medicine*, 1976, *6*, 71–88.

Hand, I., Lamontagne, Y., & Marks, I. M. Group exposure (flooding) *in vivo* for agoraphobics. *British Journal of Psychiatry*, 1974, *124*, 588–602.

Ihli, K. L., & Garlington, W. K. A comparison of group vs. individual desensitization of test anxiety. *Behaviour Research and Therapy*, 1969, *7*, 207–209.

Kazdin, A. E. Covert modeling and the reduction of avoidance behavior. *Journal of Abnormal Psychology*, 1973, *81*, 87–95.

Kazdin, A. E. Effects of covert modeling and reinforcement on assertive behavior. *Journal of Abnormal Psychology*, 1974, *83*, 240–252.

Kazdin, A. E. Effects of covert modeling, multiple models, and model reinforcement on assertive behavior. *Behavior Therapy*, 1976, *7*, 211–222.

Krumboltz, J. D., & Potter, B. Behavioral techniques for developing trust, cohesiveness, and goal accomplishment. *Educational Technology*, 1973, *13*, 26–30.

Krumboltz, J. D., & Thoresen, C. E. The effect of behavioral counseling in group and individual settings on information-seeking behavior. *Journal of Counseling Psychology*, 1964, *11*, 324–333.

Lawrence, H., & Sundel, M. Behavior modification in adult groups. *Social Work*, 1972, *17*, 2, 34–43.

Lazarus, A. A. Group therapy of phobia disorders by systematic desensitization. *Journal of Abnormal and Social Psychology*, 1961, *63*, 504–510.

Lazarus, A. A. Behavior therapy in groups. In G. M. Gazda (Ed.), *Basic approaches to group psychotherapy and group counseling*. Springfield, Ill.: Charles C. Thomas, 1968.

Liberman, R. A behavioral approach to group dynamics: 1. Reinforcement and prompting of cohesiveness in group therapy. *Behavior Therapy,* 1970, *1,* 141–175.

Lieberman, M. A. Group methods. In F. H. Kanfer & A. P. Goldstein (Eds.), *Helping people change: Methods and materials.* New York: Pergamon Press, 1975.

Lott, B. E. Group cohesiveness: A learning phenomenon. *Journal of Social Psychology,* 1961, *55,* 275–286.

Lundgren, D. C. Developmental trends in the emergence of interpersonal issues in T-groups. *Small Group Behavior,* 1977, *8,* 179–200.

Meichenbaum, D. H. Examination of model characteristics in reducing avoidance behavior. *Journal of Personality and Social Psychology,* 1971, *17,* 298–307.

Paul, G. L. Two year follow-up of systematic desensitization in groups. *Journal of Abnormal Psychology,* 1968, *73,* 119–130.

Paul, G. L., & Shannon, D. T. Treatment of anxiety through systematic desensitization in therapy groups. *Journal of Abnormal Psychology,* 1966, *71,* 124–135.

Scott, W. A. Attitude change through reward of verbal behavior. *Journal of Abnormal and Social Psychology,* 1957, *55,* 72–75.

Scott, W. A. Cognitive consistency, response reinforcement, and attitude change. *Sociometry,* 1959, *22,* 219–229. (a)

Scott, W. A. Attitude change by response reinforcement: Replication and extension. *Sociometry,* 1959, *22,* 328–335. (b)

Teasdale, J. D., Walsh, P. A., Lancashire, M., & Mathews, A. M. Group exposure for agoraphobics: A replication study. *British Journal of Psychiatry,* 1977, *130,* 186–193.

Thase, M. E., & Moss, M. K. The relative efficacy of covert modeling procedures and guided participant modeling on the reduction of avoidance behavior. *Journal of Behavior Therapy and Experimental Psychiatry,* 1976, *7,* 7–12.

Zupnick, S. Effects of varying degrees of a peer model's performance on extinction of a phobic response in an individual or group setting. *Proceedings of the 79th Annual Convention of the American Psychological Association,* 1971, *6,* 433–434. (Summary)

Chapter 3

Process Analysis in Therapy Groups: A Behavior Sampling Technique with Many Potential Uses

William E. Piper
Ruta M. Montvila
Anne L. McGihon

Abstract

Process analysis is presented as a conceptual bridge between the behavioral orientation and traditional orientations to group therapy. A number of uses of process analysis for treatment, training, and research are considered. Resistance to the development and use of behavioral process analysis systems in therapy groups is related to conceptual and practical issues. Some of the authors' experiences in developing a process analysis system and some suggestions for future work involving process analysis are given.

INTRODUCTION

Process analysis of therapy session material represents a natural converging point for the behavioral orientation and traditional orientations to group treatment. Relative to the behavioral orientation, traditional orientations place more emphasis on constructs from psychodynamic theories, more emphasis on constructs that view the group as a whole, and less emphasis on constructs from learning theories (Rose, 1977; Shaffer & Galinsky, 1974). Despite these differences both behavioral and traditional orientations share a common interest in group process. The behavioral orientation emphasizes the value of directly monitoring observable behavior and communicating summary information about the behavior to interested parties. Traditional approaches emphasize that the patient's behavior in a therapy group is representative of his behavior in external interpersonal situations, particularly small groups (Yalom, 1975). This "social microcosm" assumption suggests that the therapy group provides a useful opportunity for the direct observation of maladaptive interpersonal behaviors. There would seem to be much merit in traditionally oriented group therapists capitalizing on behavioral recording categories and in behavior therapists capitalizing on the group therapy situation as a valuable source of data. The fact that substantial collaboration regarding process analysis has not occurred does not negate the potential value of such a mutual enterprise. It does, however, lead one to consider the uses of behavioral process analysis systems in therapy groups in light of a number of obstacles, some conceptual and some practical in nature.

For purely descriptive reasons, there is no substitute for a specific process analysis of a therapy session. The notion that one cannot rely on labels of techniques or the theoretical orientation, training, or experiences of therapists for an accurate representation of what occurs in a therapy session has been demonstrated in the literature (Lieberman, Yalom, & Miles, 1973; Truax, 1966). Furthermore, the weakness of relying on the therapist's or patient's memory or recording skills is increased in group therapy, where a number of individuals are emitting behavior, sometimes simultaneously. The therapist's attention in a therapy group is not only divided among a number of people, but also among different tasks, some therapeutic and some managerial in nature. For the purposes of this chapter, process analysis will refer to the monitoring of ongoing therapy session material by an external observer (neither therapist nor patient).

The present authors have found it useful to define several basic concepts that are relevant to considering the uses of process analysis. The first concept is the notion of optimal group therapy process. It includes both therapeutic and integrative processes. Therapeutic processes underlie those techniques and responses of patients that are seen to be most directly related to patient improvement. Ultimately these are empirically determined over time as a function of outcome investigations. From the behavioral point of view these processes are associated with such techniques as rewarding, modeling, flooding, desensitizing, role playing, providing feedback, and restructuring cognitions. Therapeutic processes are frequently referred to as "on-task" or work processes. They are to be distinguished from "off-task" processes which serve goals other than attainment of treatment objectives. Such goals could include making friends among members of a therapy group or simply having a good time in a therapy group. While neither of these goals represents treatment objectives, one may find that substantial time is devoted to processes which serve them.

Integrative processes refer to those techniques and responses of patients which are seen to be most directly related to keeping the group together. Ultimately these are empirically determined by investigating promptness, attendance, and drop-out rate. From the psychodynamic point of view such concepts as therapeutic relationship (Frank, 1973), sentience (Miller, E., & Rice, 1967), and cohesion (Yalom, 1975) are associated with integrative processes. They are to be distinguished from disintegrative processes which serve to dissolve or break up a group. Any activity in a group may be located along a task dimension (on-task, off-task) and along a maintenance dimension (integration, disintegration). Optimal process in a therapy group can be viewed as consisting of a high level of on-task (therapeutic) processes, as well as a greater proportion of integrative processes than disintegrative processes, so that the members remain together to work (see Figure 1).

Optimal process (on-task, integrative) in a behaviorally oriented therapy group may be exemplified by patients reinforcing one another for practicing target behaviors in the group or for reporting about such practice outside the group. In a dynamically oriented therapy group, optimal process may be exemplified by patients demonstrating shared interest in the exploration of the relationship between a patient's defensive style in the group and difficulties he experiences outside the group. In marked contrast to optimal process, yet similar in salience, is off-task, disintegrative activity. Such activity is not a therapeutic process and contributes to the dissolution of a group. Examples include the expression of

Figure 1. Task and Maintenance Dimensions*

TASK DIMENSION

	On-task	Off-task
Integrative	optimal process	
Disintegrative		

MAINTENANCE DIMENSION

*Any behavior in a group can be placed in one of the four quadrants.

animosity and hostility, even if subtle, that is never examined in the group, the monopolization of the group by a few outspoken members, the formation of subgroups that exclude other members of the group, the use of humor as a means of belittling members of the group, and the absence of concern when fellow patients miss part or all of sessions or leave the group.

More subtle, but equally important types of process include activity that is therapeutic yet disintegrative and activity that is not therapeutic yet integrative. Recognition of these processes is likely to be more difficult. On-task, disintegrative activity might involve applying behavioral exercises in monotonous or mechanical ways, communicating accurate but demoralizing interpersonal feedback, or delivering interpretations that arouse considerable anxiety but do not direct the patient(s) to ways of working with the material. A therapist in such a group might not understand why "correctly executed technique" is resulting in the death of his group. Off-task, integrative behavior might involve pleasant discussions of current events, explorations of patient commonalities, or amiable greetings by the therapist at the onset of sessions. A therapist may discover that tolerance of occasional digressions into such off-task activities is well rewarded in the form of a cohesive group that is also willing to spend time working on therapeutic tasks.

The present authors have defined two additional concepts that are also relevant to the uses of process analysis in group therapy. These are the scope of observation and the specificity of observation. A narrow scope of observation involves only a small part of a group, perhaps one or two members and their interaction. A broad scope involves an entire group and makes possible an overview of an entire group's functioning. High specificity involves detailed categorization of behavior, e.g., response-by-response ratings over a 15-minute period. Low specificity involves general categorization of behavior, e.g., the report that 15 minutes were spent "on-task" with type A therapeutic process. Different purposes may be served by these differing types of observations. Next, let us consider some of the potential uses of process analysis in group therapy.

TREATMENT USES OF PROCESS ANALYSIS

For treatment, information from a process analysis can be used to advise the therapist and patients about adjustments that need to be made in order to better achieve treatment objectives (Clement, Roberts, & Lantz, 1976; Lewinsohn, Weinstein, & Alper, 1970; Lindberg, Morrill, & Kilstrom, 1974; Linsk, Howe, & Pinkston, 1975; Zweback, 1976).

A broad-scope process analysis that uses general categorizations provides an overview concerning how much time is spent "on-task," on what type of therapeutic processes, and by whom. Similar information is available for off-task, integrative and disintegrative processes. An implicit positive effect of analyzing such information is the pressure it puts on the therapists to clearly define and recognize these processes when they occur in treatment. Subsequent adjustments might involve the entire group (Rose, 1977), e.g., spending less time socializing and more time problem solving, less time reporting on external experiences and more time practicing skill behaviors, or might involve certain individuals, e.g., spending less time talking and more time thinking, less time observing and more time providing feedback.

A narrow-scope process analysis that uses specific categorizations provides a detailed summary of some of the members' behavior (Paden, Himelstein, & Paul, 1974). Thus, the precise nature of the members' behavior can be documented, e.g., in what way and how well members responded or performed during desensitization, flooding, or role-playing procedures.

TRAINING USES OF PROCESS ANALYSIS

For ongoing therapist training (Pattinson, Rardin, & Lindberg, 1977), process data may be used to inform the therapist and supervisor about the therapist's skills in applying techniques and managing the group. Also, if there is an ongoing training aspect for patients that is associated with treatment, e. g., learning to monitor others' (Flowers & Booraem, 1976) and one's own behaviors (Frederiksen & Miller, P., 1976), process data may be used to inform the patient about his accuracy. As Rose (1977) has noted, such data also provide the therapist with an estimate of the patient's reliability in monitoring behavior outside of the session.

RESEARCH USES OF PROCESS ANALYSIS

For research, one may wish to examine the relationship between process variables and any of a number of other variables monitored prior, concurrent, or subsequent to the process analysis. Such variables may include previous training for the therapist, pretherapy training for the patient (Heitler, 1976; Wogan, Getter, Amdur, Nichols, & Okman, 1977; Yalom, Houts, Newell, & Rand, 1967), patient attendance and drop-out rate, patient and therapist satisfaction with treatment, and patient improvement (Strassberg, Roback, Anchor, & Abramowitz, 1975). In addition, in research projects involving the comparison of two or more therapy techniques, a process analysis serves the purpose of clearly differentiating the techniques (Vernallis, Holson, Shipper, & Butler, 1972).

FACTORS AFFECTING THE USE OF PROCESS ANALYSIS

Despite a variety of potential uses, resistance to utilization of process analysis systems, as well as resistance to collaboration between behaviorally oriented and dynamically oriented group therapists regarding process analysis, exists. This can be related to several conceptual and practical issues. On the conceptual side, what behaviorally oriented and dynamically oriented group therapists may share is a narrow view of the potential uses of process analysis. At the risk of oversimplification, the present authors believe that a tendency may exist for group therapists from a behavioral orientation to focus more on therapeutic processes from a narrow scope using specific observations. Such a therapist may obtain a detailed summary of a patient's assertive behavior during a dyadic, role-play sequence. The categories might include extent of eye contact, number of verbal hesitations, tone of voice and appropriateness of content. This type of analysis would provide a useful summary of a patient's ability to be appropriately assertive. In contrast, the therapist may have relatively little interest in the other member of the dyad, the remaining members of the group, or the relationship between the behavior of the focal patient and the behavior of the other patients in the group.

Rose (1977) has identified a number of process variables which he believes are conducive to individuals making behavioral change in therapy groups. His examples include: moderate therapist activity, delegation of leadership to patients, even distribution of patient participation, expression of statements with feeling content, and minimal coercive or punishing interactions. Each of these variables seems intuitively linked to integrative processes. All represent general categories which can be monitored rather easily as part of a broad-scope process analysis. Yet they may represent variables that are commonly ignored, that are left to the subjective impression of behaviorally oriented therapists, or that are assessed by self-report scales (Hand, Lamontagne, & Marks, 1974). A notable exception is the work of Liberman (1971), who used two process analysis systems to monitor cohesiveness in group therapy.

A parallel tendency may exist for group therapists from a dynamic orientation to focus more on integrative processes from a broad scope using general observations. Such a therapist may note that a male patient's attempt to bolster the low self-esteem of an attractive female patient is constantly interrupted by the other patients in the group. He may summarize the activity by noting that jealousy on the part of the other women and competition on the part of the other men represent counterforces to the integrity of a working group. In contrast, he may have relatively little interest in how individuals specifically behave during the interaction. These differences in focus signify blind spots among therapists of differing orientations. However, they also draw attention to the wide range of information that can be obtained from process analysis, information that can be used to enrich and improve one's practice of group therapy.

On the practical side, the costs associated with process analysis have probably seemed prohibitive to many group therapists, particularly those with a narrow conception of its uses. Clearly, substantial costs (in time and manpower) are part of using a process analysis system. Costs are associated with training raters, monitoring, summarizing, and communicating the final information to interested parties. Unfortunately, most investigators have had to incur additional costs associated with developing a new system or modifying an existing system to meet specific requirements. At a minimum, this involves creating a new scoring manual. If the inertia of developing relevant systems could be overcome, the remaining costs associated with merely using a system would neither seem nor be so large. As it now stands, a great deal of the developing phase of work remains to be done.

THE USE OF PROCESS ANALYSIS SYSTEMS

In a recent review of theories of group development (Hare, 1973), several developed process analysis systems for groups are described. These include systems of interaction process analysis (Bales, 1950), work and emotionality analysis (Stock & Thelen, 1958), sign process analysis (Mills, 1964), and member-to-leader analysis (Mann, 1967). While some of these systems have received considerable use, e.g., Bales's I.P.A., the predominant use of these systems has been with classroom study groups and T-groups. They have rarely been used with therapy groups.

During the last several years, the present authors' work with process analysis has involved the modification of a system that has also existed for a number of years, the Hill Interaction Matrix (HIM) (Hill, 1965). This system, which has been used predominantly with therapy groups, was chosen on the basis of its conceptual relevance to the orientation of the therapy groups with which we were working (long-term, outpatient, group-psychodynamic) and on the basis of promising reliability data. The system focuses a great deal on classifying therapeutic processes from a broad scope using general categorizations, e.g., levels of work and nonwork. Our initial attempts to use the HIM 16-cell matrix were ungratifying both from the standpoint of conceptual clarity and reliability. We found that ratings were highly overloaded in some cells and underloaded in others. This indicated that the system was not sensitively differentiating among units. We spent considerable time trying to decide between category redefinition and reliability determination. The product of our deliberations was a modification which resembled the original structurally, i.e., a two-dimensional, 16-cell matrix, but which differed substantially from the original's unit and category definitions (see Figure 2).

The two dimensions of the matrix are content and work. Content refers to the subject of a statement. It consists of topic, group, personal, and relationship categories. Topic statements are general discussion subjects. Group statements identify the group as a unit. Personal statements provide information about individual members. Relationship statements indicate how two parties within the group affect each other. Work refers to the investigation of a problem, i.e., a symptom, an unobtained goal, or an obstacle to goal attainment. This applies to members, subgroups or the group as a whole. The

Figure 2. The Modified Hill Interaction Matrix*

CONTENT DIMENSION

WORK DIMENSION	Topic	Group	Personal	Relationship
Conversational Nonwork				
Affective Nonwork				
Undocumented Work				
Documented Work				

*Any statement made in a group can be placed in one of the sixteen cells. Modified from *Hill Interaction Matrix,* W. F. Hill. Los Angeles: Youth Studies Center, University of Southern California, 1965.

work dimension consists of conversational nonwork, affective nonwork, undocumented work, and documented work categories. Conversational nonwork statements are neutral material that does not deal with a problem. Affective nonwork statements are affect-laden material that does not deal with a problem. Undocumented work statements identify a problem. Documented work statements identify a problem and offer evidence. Any statement made in the group can be placed within one of the 16 cells.

(Topic/Conversational)

Sara: Oh, really?

(Personal/Affective Nonwork)

Eric: You might try taking the wax out of your ears and listen.

(Personal/Documented Work)

Donna: I've been trying to talk, but with Richard talking all the time, there hasn't been an opportunity to get a word in.

Once satisfied with such category definitions and reliability, we proceeded to a third consideration, economy. Given that ratings were based on statement-by-statement units of a 1½ hour audio-taped session, monitoring time was considerable (approximately 5 to 6 hours). The main output was frequency and time percentages for each of the 16 cells of the system for each of the members of the group. We began comparing the output based on the entire 1½ hours with the output based on subsamples, e.g., the middle hour. Several simple computer programs were used for this purpose. We were pleasantly surprised to discover that we could rate as little as 45 minutes of the entire 90 minutes and obtain a highly representative output. This was confirmed for two different therapy groups. The most representative 45-minute segment was the period just after the first 30 minutes and just before the last 15 minutes. Thus, for our purposes we determined empirically that we could cut the monitoring time in half.

The following is an excerpt from a group therapy session with corresponding ratings:

(Group/Documented Work)

Therapist: The group seems to be establishing a pattern that may be creating some problems. Last week the men did most of the talking and Linda was upset about that. It seems that again tonight the men are monopolizing the conversation and the women are sitting it out.

(Personal/Undocumented Work)

Alice: Yeah, and Richard probably feels guilty now.

(Personal/Conversational Nonwork)

Richard: No, I don't.

(Relationship/Undocumented Work)

Alan: Well, I was just looking at Linda and wondering which one of us she was angry with now. I was wondering why she might be angry with me, what I might have done.

(Personal/Documented Work)

Eric: Usually, Linda gets into the conversation. But tonight she hasn't said a word. The same goes for Donna. They both must be pretty angry.

TRAINING STUDENTS AS RATERS

Over the last year our work has also involved the development of a training program for a set of undergraduate student raters ($n = 7$). Training consisted of relevant reading material (a new manual, papers concerning reliability), practice, reliability feedback, discussions, and more practice. In addition, some clinical issues associated with conducting group therapy from a group-psychodynamic orientation were covered. We found that, on a part-time basis (3 hours of meeting time with the raters per week, 6 hours of work time from each rater per week), a group of raters could be trained to use the system with very good inter-rater reliabilities after one academic semester.

Two types of reliability coefficients were obtained from ratings that the students conducted during a second academic semester. The first concerned the percent of unit-by-unit cell agreement between two raters for a therapy session. Percentages of perfect agreement were calculated for 10 therapy sessions from each of two therapy groups. The mean percent agreement for the 20 sessions was 71.2% with a range from 57.9% to 82.2%. The second type of coefficient concerned the correlation between two raters' distribution of cell scores for a therapy session. This is known as marginal agreement reliability (Waxler & Mishler, 1966). Pearson product-moment correlation coefficients were calculated for five sessions from each of the above two therapy groups. The mean correlation coefficient for the 10 sessions was .95, with a range from .86 to .99.

Overall, we found undergraduate students to be a good resource for conducting process analysis. We attempted to make the training program a useful learning experience in return for work as a rater. To date that enterprise appears to have been mutually rewarding. It has certainly lessened the cost factor associated with monitoring.

PROPOSED RESEARCH

Presently we are entering an exciting phase regarding the research use of our process analysis data. We will soon have process analysis data available for a number of therapy groups that have been part of a patient pretraining investigation (Piper, Debbane, Garant, & Bienvenu, in press). This investigation involved a controlled comparison between three outpatient therapy groups which used a new, cognitive-experiential approach to pretraining and two groups which did not. Pretrained groups evidenced significantly higher patient attendance and significantly fewer drop-outs than groups that were not pretrained. Soon we will be able to examine a number of relationships between the process variables and pre-training procedures, attendance, drop-out rate, and outcome.

In addition, our system is now developed to the point that we can obtain process analysis data summaries within a short time (within a week). This opens the door for the use of our data for training and treatment purposes. We anticipate using computer printout summaries of therapy sessions in weekly therapist supervision sessions. For example, a summary may indicate that large portions of a session are monopolized by a few patients who produce relatively low work scores. It may also be apparent that most therapist interventions result in only temporary interruptions of this pattern. A comparison of these interventions with more successful interventions might indicate that the latter go beyond mere description of what is occurring to include either a documented interpretation or a suggestion for an alternate activity. The process analysis may also suggest that such interventions are most effective when presented as a combination of co-therapist statements. In this way, the summaries can provide empirical information concerning the amount and sources of work during a session, the type and effect of therapists' interventions, and the nature of the working relationship between co-therapists. Clearly, not until we were able to develop a reliable, economical system for obtaining process analysis data could we entertain such uses.

It has been our experience that the development of a process analysis system need not be an all-or-nothing investment. Our work with process analysis has occurred on a part-time basis over several years. We have sought and discovered ways to keep costs manageable, e.g., by using undergraduate students and subsampling procedures to reduce monitoring time. Had we chosen a less complex matrix with more discrete categories, the costs would have been even less. We suggest that investigators who are just beginning to develop or use a process analysis system choose only a few relevant categories with clearly defined behavioral referents. Our prediction is that, in most cases, the payoff regarding the uses of the system will outweigh the costs. We are aware that brief lip service is frequently paid to the desirability of using process analysis systems in therapy investigations. We hope that this chapter might inspire development and use of process analysis systems in future work involving therapy groups.

REFERENCES

Bales, R. F. *Interaction Process Analysis: A method for the study of small groups*. Reading, Mass.: Addison-Wesley, 1950.

Clement, P. W., Roberts, P. V., & Lantz, C. E. Mothers and peers as child behavior therapists. *International Journal of Group Psychotherapy*, 1976, *26*, 335–359.

Flowers, J. V., & Booraem, C. D. The use of tokens to facilitate outcome and monitor process in group psychotherapy. *International Journal of Group Psychotherapy*, 1976, *26*, 191–201.

Frank, J. D. *Persuasion and healing*. Baltimore, Md.: The Johns Hopkins University Press, 1973.

Frederiksen, L. W., & Miller, P. M. Peer-determined and self-determined reinforcement in group therapy with alcoholics. *Behaviour Research and Therapy*, 1976, *14*, 385–388.

Hand, I., Lamontagne, Y., & Marks, I. M. Group exposure (flooding) *in vivo* for agoraphobics. *British Journal of Psychiatry*, 1974, *124*, 588–602.

Hare, P. A. Theories of group development and categories for interaction analysis. *Small Group Behavior*, 1973, *4*, 259–304.

Heitler, J. B. Preparatory techniques in initiating expressive psychotherapy with lower-class, unsophisticated patients. *Psychological Bulletin*, 1976, *83*, 339–352.

Hill, W. F. *Hill Interaction Matrix*. Los Angeles: Youth Studies Center, University of Southern California, 1965.

Lewinsohn, P. M., Weinstein, M. S., & Alper, T. A behavioral approach to the group treatment of depressed persons: A methodological contribution. *Journal of Clinical Psychology*, 1970, *26*, 525–532.

Liberman, R. P. Behavioral group therapy: A controlled clinical study. *British Journal of Psychiatry*, 1971, *119*, 534–544.

Lieberman, M. A., Yalom, I. D., & Miles, M. B. *Encounter groups: First facts*. New York: Basic Books, 1973.

Lindberg, F. H., Morrill, R. S., & Kilstrom, D. R. Group therapy with hospitalized patients: Increasing therapeutic interaction using a feedback-escape technique. *Small Group Behavior*, 1974, *5*, 486–494.

Linsk, N., Howe, M. W., & Pinkston, E. M. Behavioral group work in a home for the aged. *Social Work*, 1975, *20*, 454–463.

Mann, R. D. *Interpersonal style and group development*. New York: Wiley, 1967.

Miller, E. J., & Rice, A. K. *Systems of organization*. London: Tavistock, 1967.

Mills, T. M. *Group transformation: An analysis of a learning group*. Englewood Cliffs, N.J.: Prentice-Hall, 1964.

Paden, R. C., Himelstein, H. C., & Paul, G. L. Videotape versus verbal feedback in the modification of meal behavior of chronic mental patients. *Journal of Consulting and Clinical Psychology*, 1974, *42*, 623–624.

Pattinson, P. R., Rardin, M. W., & Lindberg, F. H. Effects of immediate feedback on the therapeutic content of group leader's statements. *Small Group Behavior*, 1977, *8*, 303–311.

Piper, W. E., Debbane, E. G., Garant, J., & Bienvenu, J. P. Pretraining for group psychotherapy: A cognitive-experiential approach. *Archives of General Psychiatry*, in press.

Rose, S. D. *Group therapy: A behavioral approach.* Englewood Cliffs, N.J.: Prentice-Hall, 1977.

Shaffer, J. B. P., & Galinsky, M. D. *Models of group therapy and sensitivity training.* Englewood Cliffs, N.J.: Prentice-Hall, 1974.

Stock, D., & Thelen, H. A. *Emotional dynamics and group culture: Experimental studies of individual and group behavior.* New York: New York University Press, 1958.

Strassberg, D. S., Roback, H. B., Anchor, K. N., & Abramowitz, S. I. Self-disclosure in group therapy with schizophrenics. *Archives of General Psychiatry,* 1975, *32,* 1259–1261.

Truax, C. B. Reinforcement and nonreinforcement in Rogerian psychotherapy. *Journal of Abnormal Psychology,* 1966, *71,* 1–9.

Vernallis, F. F., Holson, D. G., Shipper, J. C., & Butler, D. C. The treatment process in saturation group therapy. *Psychotherapy: Theory, Research and Practice,* 1972, *9,* 135–138.

Waxler, N. F., & Mishler, E. G. Scoring and reliability problems in interaction process analysis: A methodological note. *Sociometry,* 1966, *29,* 28–40.

Wogan, M., Getter, H., Amdur, M. J., Nichols, M. F., & Okman, G. Influencing interaction and outcomes in group psychotherapy. *Small Group Behavior,* 1977, *8,* 25–46.

Yalom, I. D. *The theory and practice of group psychotherapy* (2nd ed.). New York: Basic Books, 1975.

Yalom, I. D., Houts, P., Newell, G., & Rand, K. Preparation of patients for group therapy: A controlled study. *Archives of General Psychiatry,* 1967, *17,* 416–427.

Zweback, S. Use of concrete reinforcement to control content of verbal initiations in group therapy with adolescents. *Psychological Reports,* 1976, *38,* 1051–1057.

Part Two

Behavioral Group Therapy in Clinical Practice

The five chapters included in this section represent diverse applications of the group setting to various clinical problems. The problem areas include sexual dysfunction, child and adolescent problems, cognitive modification/assertiveness training, and smoking reduction.

Chapter 4 by Kevin B. McGovern serves as a general introduction to behavioral group treatment of sexual dysfunction. He reviews group interventions which have been designed to ameliorate such problems as anorgasmia, preorgasmia, secondary inorgasmia, rapid ejaculation, erectile failure, and sexual dissatisfaction. Of major interest to the practicing clinician will be his section on therapeutic strategies. Here, practical issues such as client selection, fears and expectations, use of co-therapists, etc., are discussed with clear implications for the treatment setting.

Chapter 5 by W. Charles Lobitz and Elgan L. Baker, Jr. also deals with sexual dysfunction, but more specifically with a series of interventions for single males with no regular partner who suffered from chronic erectile dysfunction. Interestingly, almost all the work with erectile dysfunctional men has been done with men who have partners. Thus, Lobitz and Baker take a coping skills approach to enable their male clients who do not have partners to deal with performance anxiety with a future partner. The fact that the group members were given an opportunity to interact with a female co-therapist seemed particularly important for these men.

The next three chapters cover a variety of problems. Chapter 6, by Steven P. Schinke, Betty J. Blythe, and Howard J. Doueck, describes a very broad treatment package for smoking reduction. Although several of the specific techniques in the package such as thought stopping, *in vivo* practice, relaxation training, etc., have been used extensively in individual therapy, it is clear that the group was explicitly shaped to reward the use of these procedures as well as progress toward smoking reduction goals. The package, employed within a group context, shows considerable promise compared to similar techniques which have typically not been used in combination with one another or in group settings. Future research will need to focus on the effective components as well as the contribution made by the group itself.

Arthur J. Lange's chapter, Chapter 7, first presents a fairly extensive description of his own cognitive-behavioral model for group behavior therapy and next provides examples of how each therapeutic step of his model is actually carried out within a more general therapy group and later how the principles and procedures can be applied within the context of an assertiveness training group.

The final chapter, Chapter 8, by Carl Schrader deals with children and adolescents. First, he critically reviews the adolescent behavioral group literature. After outlining methodological weaknesses with the group research reviewed, Schrader describes an ongoing program which is designed to overcome many of the design problems discussed. In concluding, he lists difficulties encountered in working with adolescents as well as some practical suggestions for overcoming these difficulties.

Chapter 4

An Analysis of Behavioral Group Treatment Programs Designed to Modify Sexual Dysfunction

Kevin B. McGovern

Abstract

Over the last decade, clinicians have developed effective therapeutic procedures for the assessment and treatment of sexual dysfunction. Although many therapists have adopted a co-therapy model for treating couples with sexual concerns, recent studies have demonstrated that behavioral group treatment programs may also be employed for the treatment of sexually dysfunctional couples and individuals. These behavioral group programs have been designed to modify a variety of specific sexual concerns including anorgasmia, preorgasmia, secondary inorgasmia, rapid ejaculation, erectile failure, and sexual dissatisfaction. In this chapter these behavioral group treatment programs are reviewed. In addition, a number of crucial therapeutic strategies are presented. Finally, the major limitations and advantages of these behavioral group treatment programs are discussed.*

*The author wishes to express his gratitude to both Drs. Joseph LoPiccolo and Carol Kirkpatrick for their assistance with the development of a behavioral group treatment program for sexually dysfunctional couples. His wife, Nancy, and his son, Ryan, born on January 30, 1978, are to be recognized for their love and patience. Finally, the author wishes to thank Candy Schmid for her timely assistance with this manuscript.

INTRODUCTION

Over the last 10 years, there has been a radical change in the clinical assessment and treatment of sexual dysfunction. Prior to the historic efforts of Masters and Johnson (1970), many sexual concerns were perceived to be symptoms of an underlying pathological disorder. Accordingly, many of these problems were approached through more traditional forms of psychotherapy. Fortunately, at the Reproductive Institute in St. Louis, Masters and Johnson developed an efficient method for treating sexual dysfunction. As their research efforts became publicized, other clinicians modified this therapeutic model and developed other treatment alternatives (Annon, 1974; Barbach, 1976; Kaplan, 1974; LoPiccolo, J., & Lobitz, W., 1972).

As these innovative treatment approaches evolved, outdated concepts such as "frigidity" and/or "impotence" were reexamined and replaced by more sensible definitions. For example, women with sexual concerns were no longer labeled "cold" or "frigid." Instead, women's sexual problems were redefined as anorgasmia, preorgasmia, secondary inorgasmia, low levels of sexual arousal, dyspareunia, and/or vaginismus. Anorgasmic or preorgasmic women (these terms are used interchangeably in the literature) do not experience orgasms through any type of physical stimulation including masturbation, oral stimulation, manual stimulation, and/or coital activity. In contrast, secondary inorgasmic women experience orgasms, but are dissatisfied with the frequency of their orgasmic responses or the manner in which they become orgasmic. Dyspareunia refers to a condition in which women experience pain during sexual intercourse. Vaginismus, another painful condition, occurs because of an involuntary muscle spasm which makes penetration virtually impossible.

In addition, the word "impotence" was replaced by a number of male sexual concerns, including rapid ejaculation, premature ejaculation, primary and secondary erectile failure, retarded ejaculation, and/or low levels of sexual arousal. Rapid or premature ejaculation refers to a condition in which the male ejaculates quickly during self-stimulation, foreplay, or coital activities. Men with primary erectile failure can rarely, if ever, obtain a firm erection during self-stimulation, foreplay, or coital activities. Secondary or situational erectile failure occurs when a man cannot consistently achieve an erection or frequently loses his erection during some form of sexual activity. Retarded ejaculation or ejaculatory incompetence refers to a condition in which a man can obtain an erection but cannot ejaculate. Men and women hampered by low levels of sexual arousal usually find the majority of their sexual activities routine, boring, and nonarousing.

Clinicians have demonstrated that the majority of these sexual concerns can be effectively altered through a number of well designed therapy programs. Instead of just analyzing or discussing the underlying reasons for a particular sexual concern, trained therapists utilizing behaviorally oriented procedures began to ask their clients to learn new adaptive attitudes and behaviors. In addition, reading materials and audiovisual aids were used to supplement these basic treatment procedures. As clients began to learn new behaviors and attitudes, they shared their newly learned skills with their sexual partners. By participating in a comprehensive treatment program, individuals hampered by sexual dysfunction could alleviate their nonadaptive perceptions, attitudes, and behaviors.

Many clinicians have adopted a co-therapy model for treating couples with sexual concerns (Kaplan, 1974; Lobitz, W., & LoPiccolo, J., 1972; LoPiccolo, J., & LoPiccolo, L., 1978; Masters & Johnson, 1970). This approach, utilizing a female and male co-therapist to advise a couple with sexual problems, has proven to be an effective treatment procedure. Recently, other therapists have demonstrated that group treatment programs may be as effective as the co-therapist model for the treatment of sexual dysfunction (Barbach, 1974; McGovern, Kirkpatrick, & LoPiccolo, J., 1976; Schneidman & McGuire, 1976; Zilbergeld, 1975). In addition to increasing the number of people who can obtain treatment, the group therapy approach affords clients an opportunity to learn valuable information about sexual behavior from other group members. Through group participation, group members can re-evaluate their perceptions, attitudes, and behaviors about human sexuality in a supportive setting.

In this chapter, a review of the innovative behavioral group treatment programs for clients with sexual dysfunction will be presented. Recently, group therapy programs have been designed for preorgasmic women, secondary inorgasmic women, couples concerned about a variety of sexual problems, and men with erectile failure and/or rapid ejaculation. After reviewing these programs, a number of fundamental treatment procedures will be discussed. Finally, the advantages and limitations of a behavioral group therapy approach will be reviewed.

A REVIEW OF BEHAVIORAL GROUP TREATMENT PROGRAMS FOR SEXUAL DYSFUNCTION

Since clinicians have already demonstrated that sexually dysfunctional couples could be adequately treated by a co-therapy team (Kaplan, 1974; Lobitz, W., & LoPiccolo, J., 1972; LoPiccolo, J., & Lobitz, W., 1972; Masters & Johnson, 1970), recent studies have been designed to determine whether a behavioral group treatment approach is an efficient way to provide treatment for sexually dysfunctional individuals and/or couples. Over the last 4 years a number of behavioral group treatment programs have been designed to assist clients hampered by preorgasmic and/or secondary inorgasmic dysfunction, primary and/or secondary erectile failure, rapid ejaculation, and sexual boredom. These preliminary reports demonstrated that a number of the behavioral group treatment programs were beneficial.

Behavioral Group Treatment Programs for Women

Therapists (Barbach, 1976; Heiman, LoPiccolo, L., & LoPiccolo, J., 1976; LoPiccolo, J., & Lobitz, W., 1972) have observed that preorgasmic women can become orgasmic by learning a series of self-stimulation skills. Recent studies have demonstrated that preorgasmic women can learn these important self-stimulation procedures while attending preorgasmic women's groups. Utilizing a basic nine-step self-stimulation program, Barbach (1974) reported a high level of success with the group treatment of 83 preorgasmic women. In this study, two female therapists met with six women for two 1½-hour sessions per week for 5 weeks. During these 10 therapeutic meetings, the six women had an opportunity to learn reasonable ways to reach orgasm through adequately designed homework assignments. The participants were expected to practice specific homework assignments for approximately 1 hour per day. Barbach reported that approximately 92% of the first 83 women treated were orgasmic through masturbation by the end of 10 sessions.

An extensive 8-month follow-up study of 17 of these women (Wallace & Barbach, 1974) demonstrated that 16 of them were able to reach orgasm through a nonmanual masturbatory procedure. Furthermore, 87% of the women indicated that they were orgasmic in partner-related activities. Although these women did not become "fixated on their initial mode of achieving orgasm" (Wallace & Barbach, 1974, p. 149), the participants reached orgasm more consistently through self-stimulation than through partner-related activities.

Schneidman and McGuire (1976) developed a similar group treatment program for preorgasmic women. After identifying a population of preorgasmic women, 10 women below the age of 35 and 10 women above the age of 35 from the population were randomly placed into two psychotherapy groups. All of these women had regular sexual partners. During the course of this group treatment program, clients had an opportunity to learn how to reach orgasm through self-stimulation. The treatment program consisted of four major components: (1) education and audiovisual instruction, (2) group discussion, (3) couple-oriented therapy, and (4) self-stimulation. The participants were also encouraged to have their partners participate in the homework assignments at home. A review of the 6-month follow-up data revealed that 80% of the women below the age of 35 were able to reach orgasm with vibrators, masturbation, or with a vibrator used during intercourse. In contrast, 60% of the women over 35 were orgasmic via self-stimulation or partner-related activities.

Price and A. Heinrich (Note 1) developed a group treatment program for secondary inorgasmic women. Fourteen clients were placed into two eight-member groups. Each group consisted of seven women and one female therapist. Although every woman in these groups was able to reach orgasm through self-stimulation prior to treatment, they were dissatisfied with the manner in which they reached orgasm or the frequency of their orgasms. The major goal of this group therapy program was to teach these women a new method to experience orgasm with their sexual partners. The clients attending this group were *not expected* to be orgasmic in intercourse by the end of the treatment.

The basic therapeutic format included: (1) a discussion of the previous week's homework assignment, (2) a review of the weekly topic to be discussed, and (3) the outlining of the next set of homework instructions. The therapist described the group therapy program as primarily educational. The co-therapist provided the group members with basic information regarding sexuality and used a film to display self-stimulation procedures. During a number of group meetings, the therapist discussed "bridging techniques." These procedures allowed women to explain to their partners how they might experience an orgasm through some form of sexual expression.

A posttreatment evaluation and a 2-month study demonstrated that the treatment program was effective for 10 of the 12 women. These 10 women indicated that they were able to reach orgasm through another mode of stimulation, other than self-stimulation, with their partners present. The data demonstrated that the clients were able to become orgasmic either in a new position, through a new form of stimulation, or were experiencing a different type of orgasmic intensity.

Behavioral Group Treatment Programs for Men

Zilbergeld (1975) described a group treatment program for men with premature ejaculation and/or erectile failure. During this program, the co-therapists met with their male clients for 12 2-hour sessions. The group format included: (1) relaxation training, (2) visual imagery, (3) the stop-start method, (4) assertiveness training, and (5) the resolution of sexual myths. The author concluded that, by the end of treatment, two-thirds of the men had reached their goals. The major advantages of the group approach were: (1) modeling, (2) peer support and understanding, and (3) a realization among group members that normal-looking and normal-sounding people also have sexual problems. Finally, the rationale of utilizing a heterogenous population and a male-female co-therapy team was discussed.

W. Lobitz and Baker (in press) designed a group treatment program for single men with erectile dysfunction. During the course of treatment, these clients learned: (1) relaxation training, (2) self-directed *in vivo* desensitization, (3) a variety of self-stimulation procedures, (4) the stop-start technique (Semans, 1956), and (5) the squeeze technique (Masters & Johnson, 1970). At the end of the treatment, 66% of the men showed significant improvement. Although this program had a positive effect on the majority of males treated, the authors did not feel that the procedures were adequate for men with primary erectile failure. On follow-up, only one of the three men with primary erectile failure could successfully engage in intercourse 90% of the time.

W. Lobitz and Baker (in press) and Zilbergeld (1975) observed that their clients with severe erectile failure also were uncomfortable in developing social contacts. Since they experienced high levels of anxiety and were fearful of another sexual failure, they continued to avoid heterosexual social contacts. They concluded that men with severe erectile failure also need to learn a repertoire of social skills. Fortunately, behavior therapists have developed practical methods for enhancing an individual's social skills and general comfortableness in heterosexual interactions (Gambrill, 1977; Heimberg, R., Montgomery, Madsen, & Heimberg, J., 1977; McGovern, Arkowitz, & Gilmore, 1975; McGovern & Burkhard, 1976).

Behavioral Group Treatment Programs for Couples

McGovern, Kirkpatrick, and J. LoPiccolo (1976) described a behavioral group treatment program for sexually dysfunctional couples. Four dysfunctional couples were provided with 15 3-hour sessions of group psychotherapy. The first 13 sessions were held on a weekly basis, while the last 2 sessions were spread over a 6-week period. Four of the women were preorgasmic and three of the men were hampered by rapid ejaculation. During the course of group psychotherapy, the women were taught methods for changing their orgasmic responses, while the men learned how to control their rapid ejaculation. Comparison of the pre- and posttreatment follow-up data showed that this group treatment program was successful in changing the orgasmic response cycle of the preorgasmic women and the ejaculatory response of men. This program seemed to be highly successful for three of the four couples attending.

Kaplan, Kohl, Pomeroy, Offit, and Hogan (1974) demonstrated how rapid ejaculation could be successfully treated through a group psychotherapy program. Four couples met with several therapists once a week for six 45-minute sessions. During the course of therapy, these couples learned how to use the stop-start procedure. A 4-month follow-up study revealed that all of the couples reported that they were able to adequately control their ejaculatory response during coital activities.

In another study, Golden, Price, A. Heinrich, and W. Lobitz (Note 2) contrasted the effects of group therapy with the individual treatment of couples with sexual dysfunction. The 17 couples selected for this study were heterosexual and had been living together for a period of at least 6 months. The men's sexual performance was hampered by rapid ejaculation. Some of the women could be classified as having a secondary orgasmic dysfunction (McGovern, Stewart, & LoPiccolo, J., 1975). The major goals of this program were to increase the men's latency and to enable the women to reach orgasm more comfortably. Eleven couples were assigned to group treatment and six to individual treatment.

The therapeutic procedures included: (1) the presentation of didactic material; (2) teaching reasonable sexual skills, such as the squeeze technique and the stop-start procedure; (3) discussing various communication techniques; and (4) viewing two films, *The Squeeze Technique* and *Reaching Orgasm*. The couples were also asked to engage in homework assignments that included sensate focus exercises, specific communication techniques, and a behavioral maintenance program. The results revealed that the behavioral group therapy program was comparable to individual couple therapy. The data further demonstrated that, after treatment, the couples in both treatment modalities were more satisfied with their sexual interactions. More specifically, the men were able to control their ejaculation and to prolong intercourse. The women were more satisfied with their overall ability to experience orgasm. In addition, the couples spent more time engaging in foreplay activities and described their sexual interactions as more satisfactory.

J. LoPiccolo and Miller (1975) designed a treatment program

for enhancing the sexual relationships of couples. The initial study was conducted with 12 couples who were not hampered by sexual dysfunction. Instead, these couples were interested in making their sexual relationships more spontaneous and interesting. The participants in this group therapy program met for three 3-hour sessions during a 2-day period. The couples also agreed to participate in a follow-up session 2 weeks later. The therapeutic program was coordinated by a male and female co-therapist. All of the couples attending this program were expected to complete a series of homework assignments given after the second session.

During the course of the 3-hour sessions, the couples: (1) practiced a variety of communication skills, (2) discussed their expectations and fears, (3) reviewed audiovisual materials, (4) learned sensate focus exercises (Masters & Johnson, 1970), and (5) described to their mates the types of sexual behaviors that were pleasant and aversive. The 12 couples completed several self-report inventories before the group therapy program began, after the 2-week posttherapy session, and 3 months after the program had been completed. A comparison of the pre- and posttreatment scores on the Sexual Interaction Survey (LoPiccolo, J., & Steger, 1974) revealed that the 12 couples participating in this group treatment program achieved reasonable therapeutic gains.

Behavioral Group Treatment Programs for Individuals Without Partners

Since the couple-oriented form of psychotherapy does not usually incorporate single individuals without partners, R. Heinrich and Price (Note 3) have recently developed a group treatment program for men and women without partners. In this program, the co-therapists treated 10 men and 10 women who sought treatment for premature ejaculation and a preorgasmic condition. Each group consisted of 10 clients and was coordinated by a male and female co-therapist. The sessions lasted 2 hours weekly over an 8-week period.

During the first phase of psychotherapy, the group participants were provided with basic information about their sexuality. They also had an opportunity to discuss a number of sexual myths. After this segment, the clients then viewed the films *Reaching Orgasm* and *The Squeeze Technique*. In addition to the larger 10-member groups, the clients were subdivided into smaller group meetings. At the submeetings, the therapists of the same sex reviewed the homework assignment of each individual. The last four therapy meetings were basically used to allow the individuals to learn more reasonable social skills. Since many of the participants were not involved in a steady relationship, they were given this opportunity to role play a number of social behaviors that would allow them to cultivate their own stable partners.

A 2-month follow-up study revealed that 7 of the 9 women were able to reach orgasm 50% of the time through some form of sexual stimulation. In addition, 8 of the 10 men were able to control their latency for a sufficient period of time. The authors were enthusiastic that the mixed group allowed both men and women to alleviate their myths about human sexual behavior. In addition, the authors cautioned that the men who were the least successful had a difficult time communicating their concerns and feelings to their sexual partners.

FUNDAMENTAL THERAPEUTIC STRATEGIES

In the previous section, an overview of behavioral group treatment programs designed to modify dysfunctional sexual behavior was provided. These studies demonstrated that sexually dysfunctional clients can learn adaptive sexual attitudes and behaviors while participating in a behavioral group therapy program. In the following section, a number of fundamental therapeutic strategies that can significantly influence behavioral group therapy programs will be discussed. These therapeutic strategies are derived from the group studies reviewed in the previous section, treatment programs designed to alter sexual dysfunction (LoPiccolo, J., & LoPiccolo, L., 1978), and the author's clinical experience.

Client Selection

Client selection is an extremely important factor to be taken into consideration (Lobitz, W., & Lobitz, G., 1978). Clients with similar types of sexual concerns are usually placed into homogenous groups. Although the demographic characteristics of the group participants do not have to be identical, clients with similar types of sexual problems are usually treated in the same group. For example, rapid ejaculators and men with erectile failure are placed *into different treatment groups*. Likewise, preorgasmic and secondary inorgasmic women are treated *in separate group therapy programs*. Preorgasmic women have never experienced orgasm and initially will have concerns about their ability to reach orgasm. The secondary inorgasmic women have already learned to reach orgasm. Instead, they are dissatisfied with the frequency with which they reach orgasm or the method by which they become orgasmic

(McGovern, Stewart, & LoPiccolo, J., 1975). Since the preorgasmic and secondary inorgasmic women have different concerns and goals, a separate therapy program needs to be developed for each group. Although similar procedures are often used for both preorgasmic and secondary inorgasmic women, group members will have a better chance to reach their goals by participating in a group where the members are working toward similar goals.

In order to select eligible clients for a group therapy program, the co-therapists usually interview each prospective client for approximately 60 to 90 minutes. During this interview, the therapists can: (1) obtain a sexual history, (2) determine whether a client has a legitimate sexual problem, and (3) assess the motivational level of each client.

Since some eligible clients have other significant emotional concerns, a more extensive psychological assessment may be undertaken after the initial interview. Besides carefully evaluating these psychological factors, the clinician determines whether there are any germane medical factors that might be contributing to the sexual dysfunction. For example, certain medications can cause erectile failure. In other instances, cervical tears and abrasions can lead to painful intercourse.

Recently, a number of self-report questionnaires (Lobitz, W., & Lobitz, G., 1978) have been designed to provide therapists with valuable information about prospective clients. Besides outlining specific sexual problems, concerns, attitudes, and dysfunctional behaviors, some of these questionnaires give an index to a couple's marital compatibility. The combination of a screening interview and the administration of several self-report questionnaires can provide the clinician with a wealth of pertinent information about prospective clients.

The motivational level of each member is another extremely important variable to assess. In order to develop a cohesive and productive group therapy program, the therapists need to include motivated clients who will take an active part in their therapy program. Resistance, spotty attendance, or an inability to complete specific homework assignments are variables that will significantly alter the group's efforts. Since most behavioral group therapy programs are structured and incorporate reasonable homework assignments, the group members are expected to complete assignments, attend meetings, and cooperate with a group during the scheduled meetings. Individuals who are unable to attend meetings lose their incentive and motivation. Spotty attendance or passive resistance can hamper the group's progress and discourage other group members. In order to evaluate each client's level of motivation, some therapists ask clients to attend pregroup sessions prior to a group therapy program (Yalom, 1970). In addition, clients can be asked to read books, complete a set of self-report questionnaires, and/or keep a record of their daily sexual behaviors prior to the beginning of a group therapy program. With these specific assignments, a person's motivational level can be assessed.

A client's level of motivation may also be enhanced by specific contingencies, including a waiting list, a limited number of therapeutic sessions, and/or a penalty fee deposit. For illustrative purposes, some therapists have utilized a penalty fee deposit to insure maximum cooperation (Lobitz, W., & LoPiccolo, J., 1972). During the assessment phase, clients are expected to deposit a set amount of money with the co-therapists. The amount of the deposit will depend upon the socioeconomic status of the client. If the client misses an appointment without reasonable notice or cannot complete a homework assignment, he or she will lose a portion of the deposit for the first violation, and a portion of the deposit for the second violation. If a third violation occurs, the client loses the remaining portion of the deposit and is terminated from the program.

A penalty fee deposit is extremely effective, especially if a client has been placed on a waiting list for 3 to 6 months. Another positive aspect of the penalty fee deposit is that the therapist can always refund a portion of the penalty fee deposit during the therapy program. For example, a couple may have lost $50 (one-third of the deposit) because of their inability to complete a homework assignment between sessions 4 and 5. Several weeks later, the therapists may observe that the penalized couple have completed all of their weekly assignments plus the assignment they weren't able to complete between sessions 4 and 5. At this point, the therapist may decide to reinforce these positive behavioral changes by returning the $50 that the couple had forfeited. In summary, these contingencies can enhance a client's level of motivation.

Co-Therapists

Behavioral group treatment programs are usually coordinated by trained co-therapists. These co-therapists have already learned through structured professional activities and supervised clinical experiences how to coordinate behavioral group treatment programs. In addition, these clinicians have completed a sufficient number of graduate courses (in the area of human sexuality) designed to teach basic clinical assessment and treatment procedures. These trained therapists realize that there is a major difference between coordinating a sexual counseling program for one couple and monitoring a group therapy program for four couples. Besides understanding group dynamics, the co-therapists are expected to: (1) design and implement the group therapy program, (2) monitor each individual's weekly progress, (3) coordinate group activities, and (4) provide the group with reasonable models for role-playing activities.

As the co-therapists are designing a therapy program, they need to establish the number of sessions, length of sessions, goals for each session, and the assignments that will be given to their clients at the end of each meeting. By establishing a specific number of sessions, they help participants in the group understand that they are expected to reach their goals within a limited period of time.

Each program's format is usually based upon the specific treatment needs of the participants, established treatment procedures, and the therapists' own clinical experiences. For illustrative purposes, the co-therapists may decide to coordinate two separate treatment groups for preorgasmic women. In the first group, the eight women participants have strong religious convictions and are reluctant to engage in any self-stimulation procedures. In contrast, the eight women participants in the second group have fewer religious concerns and are more willing to openly discuss self-stimulation procedures. In group one, the co-therapists may decide to spend the first three sessions reviewing physical anatomy, sexual myths, fears, expectations, and the clients' sexual histories. Self-stimulation may not be introduced to these group participants until the seventh or eighth session. The co-therapists may also decide to run this group for 20 sessions.

In the second group, the therapists may spend only one to two sessions discussing sexual myths, fears, expectations, and physical anatomy. At the end of the first session, they may decide to encourage the participants to practice step one of a nine-step self-stimulation procedure (LoPiccolo, J., & Lobitz, W., 1972) at home before their next session. Since there are no absolute guidelines for each program's format, the co-therapists need to rely upon their professional training, established clinical procedures, and their own clinical experiences.

During the course of group psychotherapy, the group members will be required to complete a series of homework assignments between each therapy session. Group participants are asked to write out their reactions to these homework assignments on a specific form (Lobitz, W., & LoPiccolo, J., 1972). Prior to each therapy session, the co-therapists review these reaction forms. They use this information to plan for the next therapy session.

Co-therapists can also coordinate behavioral rehearsal sequences for their clients. For example, some couples with sexual dysfunction often have a difficult time expressing their particular likes and dislikes to their partners. The co-therapists can demonstrate various forms of verbal communication through behavioral rehearsal procedures. After the co-therapists have provided the group with communication models, each group member can then practice these verbal behaviors with another group member. As these new behaviors are acquired, the co-therapists can provide the participants with constructive feedback.

With co-therapists, the larger group can be divided into smaller, specific subgroups (McGovern, Kirkpatrick, & LoPiccolo, J., 1976). For example, couples A and B may have a difficult time communicating with their partners, whereas couples C and D may not understand how to adequately apply the stop-start technique for rapid ejaculation. The co-therapists may decide to work on these problems separately. One of the therapists might assist couples A and B with their communication problems, while the other therapist provides couples C and D with a more thorough explanation of ways to modify rapid ejaculation.

In some situations, the woman co-therapist may decide to meet with the women clients separately while the male co-therapist meets with the male clients. During these subgroup discussions, the men and women have an opportunity to carefully discuss some particular concern or a new therapeutic procedure. For example, the preorgasmic women may want to discuss specific aspects of self-stimulation more thoroughly, while the men decide to debrief their reactions to the stop-start technique for rapid ejaculation. With co-therapists, the group can be subdivided to resolve specific problems that evolve during the course of therapy.

Successes and Failures

The successes and failures experienced by group members need to be carefully monitored. Quite often a couple or an individual might exaggerate a therapeutic success. For example, some clients seem to feel the need to report that they had the best erotic fantasy or sexual interaction between each therapeutic session. During the course of the week, they report having had multiple orgasms, while other group members are still trying to experience their first orgasm through 40 minutes of self-stimulation. Clients who are overenthusiastic or who overrate their progress can discourage other group members. Since these "rapid cure" statements can significantly affect other group participants, the co-therapists need to carefully observe the group's reaction to their weekly assignments. Instead of prematurely reinforcing "rapid cure" statements, the group leaders should carefully determine whether these claims are exaggerations or actual therapeutic changes.

Sometimes a group member may become discouraged by another participant's success. In order to avoid these disappointments, the co-therapists could share with the group members that some of them are going to reach their goals more quickly than others. In addition to these individual differences, a variety of environmental factors may affect an individual's progress. For example, a cumbersome work schedule, an illness, or a problem at home may legitimately affect an individual's ability to complete a set of homework assignments. These legitimate problems should be discussed during the course of therapy.

Clients who cannot contribute to the group and who do not complete their weekly homework assignments can have an adverse effffect upon the other participants. The therapists may be tempted to spend an inordinate amount of therapeutic time with these clients. Or, other group members may unintentionally reinforce these resistive behaviors. Since these types of setbacks can affect the group's morale, continuous observations and timely confrontation by the co-therapists can decrease the frequency of resistive behaviors. Some therapists utilize a penalty deposit to discourage resistive couples or clients.

Fears and Expectations

Clients usually have fears and expectations regarding their sexuality. For example, some preorgasmic women may fear that they will not be able to reach orgasm through any mode of stimulation. Another dysfunctional client may fear that his unique sexual history will alienate other group members. Others may expect to resolve their sexual problems in two sessions. These concerns need to be carefully assessed during the screening interview and periodically throughout the group therapy program.

Sexually dysfunctional clients may not have had previous experience with individual and/or group psychotherapy. They may not know what to expect from the co-therapists or from the group participants. Some clients may have already read a number of uncomplimentary articles about unusual group therapy practices. Others may have been warned about encounter groups. In addition to these concerns, clients with sexual dysfunction are often afraid to discuss their own sexual concerns around other people. Others may feel they will have to stand in the nude or engage in coital group activities. These concerns can be quickly resolved by a skilled group leader. Some therapists elect to use a series of warm-up exercises to resolve these uncomfortable feelings, fears, and misperceptions.

During a behavioral group treatment program for sexually dysfunctional couples, McGovern, Kirkpatrick, and J. LoPiccolo (1976) utilized several warm-up exercises. These activities were designed to enhance group cohesiveness and to allow each group participant to feel at ease with each other. These warm-up procedures were employed during the first two group meetings. During the first warm-up exercise, a group milling experience, the group participants were instructed to walk around the room and verbally or nonverbally greet each other. After several minutes of walking among the group members, participants were then asked to exchange one written piece of information about themselves to another group member other than their spouse. This basic exercise allowed the group members to become acquainted.

At another point in the same session, the hope and fear exercise was introduced. Each participant was instructed to write out his or her hopes or fears pertaining to his or her sexuality or to the group experience on index cards. These cards were then collected, shuffled, and redistributed among the group members. Each one of the group members then read aloud the hopes from his or her index card. After these hopes were adequately discussed, the fears were read aloud by each group member. Through this process, group members had a better understanding of what the expectations and fears were for each group member. The discussion following the distribution of these cards was a valuable learning experience for the participants and co-therapists.

Behavioral Contracts

Co-therapists are advised to establish a written behavioral contract with each prospective group member. The basic elements of this document can be reviewed by each group participant after the intake interview. At the second assessment meeting, a variety of topics can be discussed including attendance, confidentiality, group participation, client responsibility, homework assignments, fee schedules, and record keeping. After each participant has had an opportunity to carefully read the contract and discuss these topics, the co-therapists and the participants can sign the contract. At this point, the co-therapists may also provide the clients with a brief outline of what will occur during the scheduled therapeutic sessions. During the first therapy session, the co-therapists can again review the behavioral contracts with each group participant. With a therapeutic contract, each client will have an adequate understanding of what he or she will be expected to accomplish during the course of the group therapy program.

Alleviating Myths

Many sexually dysfunctional clients have learned erroneous information regarding human sexual behavior. For example, some individuals believe that they will never be able to have an orgasm, whereas others are concerned that they must have an erect penis in order to adequately satisfy the needs of their sexual partner. A number of clients assume that women can only be satisfied through direct coital activity. Others are concerned that certain sexual problems are signs of latent homosexuality. During the course of therapy, the group participants are encouraged to identify, discuss, and resolve these and other sexual myths.

Homework Assignments

At the end of each group therapy session, clients are given a set of reasonable homework assignments to complete before the next scheduled session. For example, in a preorgasmic women's group, clients may be asked to examine their genitals in a mirror and to start practicing self-stimulation exercises. Men with erectile failure may be encouraged to stimulate themselves to a high level of arousal and then allow themselves to lose their erection. After they have relaxed for a period of five minutes, they will be expected to stimulate themselves to a high level of arousal a second time.

After each homework assignment has been completed, the group members are instructed to write out their reactions to these assignments on a reaction form. These completed forms are brought to the co-therapists 24 hours before the next scheduled meeting. By reviewing these forms each week, the co-therapists will understand: (1) what assignments have been completed, (2) what problems have occurred, and (3) what therapeutic gains have been experienced. After the co-therapists have had an opportunity to carefully examine this information, they will be better prepared to plan the next therapy session.

Audiovisual Materials

Since sexually dysfunctional clients are often lacking adequate information about human sexual behavior, behavioral group therapy programs are usually complemented by a reasonable array of audiovisual materials and books. As the group members begin to discuss their own sexual concerns, feelings, and discomforts, they should have access to sensible articles, manuals, films, and/or slides. As the group participants read these materials and discuss their perceptions and attitudes within the group structure, they usually feel more comfortable about their sexuality. Many clients need a reference point from which they can examine their attitudes and perceptions. Although other group members and the co-therapists can act as a set of reference points, clients are often reassured about their sexuality when they have an opportunity to read about their concerns in legitimate books and/or articles. A specific chapter or article may alleviate more anxiety than a group discussion or a germane statement made by a co-therapist.

As the group provides a supportive atmosphere for openness and reasonable discussion, the members will be able to learn more adaptive sexual attitudes and behaviors. The group members will also learn that other individuals have similar thoughts, fears, and emotions. As the similarities become more apparent, the group members will begin to identify with each other and develop a strong sense of cohesiveness. As defined by Yalom (1970), "cohesiveness is both a determinant and effect of intermember acceptance: members of a highly cohesive therapy group will respond to each other in this manner more frequently than will the members of a noncohesive group; groups with members who show high mutual understanding and acceptance are, by definition, cohesive" (p. 38). With a cohesive atmosphere, clients can develop more reasonable attitudes and perceptions about themselves.

Maintenance Programs

During the last several sessions, each client is encouraged to develop an appropriate maintenance program. These maintenance programs are designed to insure that each group participant will continue to experience attitudinal and behavioral changes after the group therapy program has been terminated. The group participants are expected to write out a useful behavioral schedule that can be followed after the program has ended.

For illustrative purposes, one couple attending a group treatment program for sexual dysfunction adopted the following maintenance program. First, the couple decided to spend a minimum of 4 hours a week engaging in some form of sexual intimacy. They also agreed to have their sexual interactions occur before 10:00 P.M. Before therapy, the couple had a difficult time initiating any form of sexual activity prior to 10:00 P.M. Most of their sexual activities would occur after the children were asleep. During the course of therapy, they discovered they would find their sexual interactions more pleasant if they occurred at an earlier hour.

This couple also agreed to spend at least another 2 hours a week engaging in sensate focus exercises (Masters & Johnson, 1970). These nongenital and genital pleasuring sessions became an important part of their sexual repertoire. During the group therapy program, this couple learned how to receive and give each other high levels of sexual pleasure through a variety of noncoital sexual activities.

In addition, prior to therapy, the husband never initiated any sexual activities. While constructing their maintenance program, the couple agreed that the husband would initiate approximately 70% of their sexual contacts. Finally, the couple decided to keep a daily diary of their sexual interactions. These materials were reviewed each Saturday morning. While following this basic maintenance program, this couple was able to maintain the behavioral and attitudinal changes learned during the course of therapy. By adhering to maintenance schedules, sexually dysfunctional clients can enjoy a more satisfying sexual relationship once the formal therapeutic program has terminated.

In addition to the maintenance programs, group participants are encouraged to attend several follow-up therapy meetings. At these sessions, the co-therapists will review with each participant what specific goals have been accomplished and what particular problems still need to be resolved. The clients' maintenance programs are also discussed. By attending these follow-up sessions and adhering to the maintenance programs, the group participants will obtain the maximum benefit from their group therapy program.

Training

Behavioral therapists who are offering clinical services to sexually dysfunctional clients should be adequately trained. In my opinion, a recognized graduate degree in the health care sciences would be a basic requirement. As part of this training, qualified sex therapists would complete, in 1 year, a series of professional seminars designed to review basic theoretical, sociological, anatomical, physiological, cultural, psychological, and ethical issues. During these seminars, the trainees would discuss their own personal experiences, attitudes, emotional reactions, and biases regarding human sexuality.

These basic seminars would be complemented by a series of clinical training courses whereby trainees could observe and discuss ongoing therapeutic cases. When each trainee had demonstrated adequate clinical judgment, he or she could then advise clients with a supervising co-therapist. As a co-therapist, the trainees would also be expected to observe other ongoing cases or therapy groups and attend weekly supervision and planning seminars. After the supervised co-therapist became proficient in the assessment and treatment of sexual dysfunction, a clinical supervisor would continue to monitor the trainee's clinical skills for an additional year at a ratio of 1 hour of clinical supervision to 8 hours of clinical practice. Since the training of sex therapists is a highly controversial area, the reader is encouraged to review other pertinent articles (LoPiccolo, J., 1978; Waggoner, Mudd, & Shearer, 1978).

LIMITATIONS

Although the preliminary results of the behavioral group treatment programs appear promising, many of these studies were hampered by methodological issues, including small sample size, limited statistical analysis, inadequate control groups and other confounding variables (Edwards, 1964). Besides these important empirical considerations, there are a number of practical concerns that should be discussed. One major limitation is that the co-therapists may have a difficult time finding a sufficient number of eligible clients. Since many prospective clients feel uncomfortable discussing their sexual concerns in a group setting, they may decide not to participate in a group therapy program. In addition, group therapy programs may also be adversely affected by a higher attrition rate. Since some clients feel intimidated or insecure in a group therapy program, they may decide to leave the program after the first several sessions.

Another limitation is that most behavioral group therapy programs are designed to meet a specific set of therapeutic goals for all group members. Since these programs are structured and time limited, there are few opportunities to modify the basic therapeutic procedures to meet individual problems that occur during the course of therapy. In many cases, these individual problems are set aside for another meeting or referred to another program or therapist. For example, in a rapid ejaculation treatment program, one or two men may begin to discuss their social fears and inadequacies during the course of therapy. As they elaborate upon these concerns, the co-therapists may decide that these individuals need to learn a variety of social skills. However, since the major goal of the group therapy program is to teach all group members how to control their ejaculatory response, the co-therapists may not have an opportunity to provide these men with additional social skills training.

Some clients cannot adequately express themselves in a group setting. They are concerned that other group members will not understand their problems. Other clients are overly aggressive or assertive during group therapy meetings and can cause continuous discomfort among other group members. In addition, some clients will frequently challenge the co-therapists' understanding of human sexuality. Romantic entanglements among group members represent another problem that can arise during the course of group therapy. These and other related issues have been discussed elsewhere (McGovern, Kirkpatrick, & LoPiccolo, J., 1976; Yalom, 1970).

A group therapy program may also be too powerful. In other words, both the group members and group structure can be important reinforcers. In this setting, group members are reinforced for learning adaptive behaviors. In some instances, group members complete their behavioral assignments in order to obtain reinforcement from the co-therapists and the other group members. Once the program has terminated, each individual loses an important source of reinforcement. Sexually dysfunctional clients attending group programs report that they look forward to their group therapy sessions. They find these meetings highly informative and worthwhile. After the group has ended, they no longer have an opportunity to discuss their sexual concerns or to be reinforced for learning a set of adaptive behaviors. Once this source of encouragement is no longer available, some clients lose their incentive and spend less time following their maintenance programs. Further research studies may demonstrate that there is a higher regression effect among group members than among individuals or couples obtaining consultation from a therapist or a co-therapy team.

ADVANTAGES

There also seem to be a number of realistic advantages. Since most sexually dysfunctional clients are lacking adequate knowledge about human sexual behavior, a significant percentage of the co-therapists' time is spent providing basic information about human sexual behavior. Co-therapists are often required to: (1) teach their clients basic or fundamental information about anatomy, (2) resolve a number of sexual myths, and (3) provide a supportive atmosphere where individuals can discuss relevant information regarding human sexuality. From a practical point of view, information about human sexual behavior can be more reasonably provided in a group setting. Since many individuals need to learn accurate information about human sexual behavior, a group therapy program provides a forum where this information can be shared with a greater number of people.

Clients attending these groups will also learn that their past and present sexual thoughts and behaviors are not unique. Unfortunately, many clients with sexual concerns feel they are abnormal or unusual. They are concerned that other individuals with similar backgrounds are not bothered by similar fears, anxieties, or inadequacies. Although therapists treating sexually dysfunctional couples or individuals normally take a sexual history, these clients do not have an opportunity to contrast their past with the history of other clients. In a group therapy program, participants can compare their sexual histories and their present sexual thoughts and behaviors with others in the group. Through self-disclosure, both clients and therapists realize that many people have experienced similar sexual thoughts and behaviors. Clients are relieved to learn that other "normal" people have similar types of sexual histories and concerns regarding their sexual behavior.

Another advantage is that the group serves as an important source of continuous support. As the members begin to identify and change their dysfunctional attitudes, perceptions, and/or behaviors, they receive encouragement from the group members. Since many of the group members are working on similar goals, each of the participants can provide valuable insights, thoughts, and suggestions that enhance the therapeutic process. In many cases, group members provide major contributions which allow personal growth to occur among other group members.

SUMMARY

Sexually dysfunctional clients who attend group therapy programs can learn adaptive sexual attitudes and behaviors. In the group, clients observe that their own sexual concerns are not unique and that other individuals experience uncomfortable thoughts, feelings, or behaviors. While attending each session, the group members are encouraged to discuss their sexual concerns and to develop a set of behavioral assignments that are completed between each session. As the members begin to learn more reasonable attitudes and/or behaviors, they receive a great deal of encouragement from the co-therapists and the other group members. During the last few therapeutic sessions, the clients are taught how to maintain these behavioral gains in the future. Through these procedures, sexually dysfunctional clients can learn how to resolve their sexual concerns.

Hopefully, in the future, clinical researchers examining the effectiveness of behavioral group therapy programs will utilize more rigorous research designs. A number of the behavioral group treatment studies discussed in the previous sections could be empirically challenged on the basis of: (1) small sample size, (2) inadequate research design, (3) marginal statistical design, (4) the exclusion of contrast control groups, and (5) the nonrandomization of therapists and clients. As better designed studies are being developed, clinicians are encouraged to carefully evaluate the advantages and limitations of these behavioral group treatment programs. When these additional research projects are completed, clinicians will know what types of sexually dysfunctional clients are best assisted by behavioral group treatment programs. Finally, these projects will also demonstrate which specific therapeutic variables are vital components of behavioral group therapy programs designed to modify sexual discomfort.

REFERENCE NOTES

1. Price, S., & Heinrich, A. *Group treatment of secondary orgasmic dysfunction*. Paper presented at the American Psychological Association Convention, San Francisco, August 1977.
2. Golden, J., Price, S., Heinrich, A., & Lobitz, W. C. *Group versus couple treatment of sexual dysfunctions*. Paper presented at the American Psychological Association Convention, San Francisco, August 1977.
3. Heinrich, R., & Price, S. *Group treatment of men and women without partners*. Paper presented at the American Psychological Association Convention, San Francisco, August 1977.

REFERENCES

Annon, J. *The behavioral treatment of sexual problems* (Vol. 1: Brief therapy). Honolulu: Enabling Systems, Inc., 1974.

Barbach, L. G. Group treatment of preorgasmic women. *Journal of Sex and Marital Therapy*, 1974, *1*, 139–145.

Barbach, L. G. *For yourself: The fulfillment of female sexuality*. Garden City, N.Y.: Anchor Press/Doubleday, 1976.

Edwards, A. L. *Experimental design in psychological research*. New York: Holt, Rinehart, & Winston, 1964.

Gambrill, E. *Behavioral modification: Handbook of assessment, intervention, and evaluation*. San Francisco: Jossey-Bass, 1977.

Heiman, J., LoPiccolo, L., & LoPiccolo, J. *Becoming orgasmic: A sexual growth program for women*. Englewood Cliffs, N.J.: Prentice-Hall, 1976.

Heimberg, R. G., Montgomery, D., Madsen, C. H., & Heimberg, J. S.

Assertion training: A review of the literature. *Behavior Therapy*, 1977, *8*, 953–971.

Kaplan, H. S. *The new sex therapy*. New York: Brunner/Mazel, 1974.

Kaplan, H., Kohl, R., Pomeroy, W., Offit, A., & Hogan, B. Group treatment of premature ejaculation. *Archives of Sexual Behavior*, 1974, *3*, 443–452.

Lobitz, W. C., & Baker, E. Group treatment of single males with erectile dysfunction. *Archives of Sexual Behavior*, in press.

Lobitz, W. C., & Lobitz, G. K. Clinical assessment of sexual dysfunction. In J. LoPiccolo & L. LoPiccolo (Eds.), *Handbook of sex therapy*. New York: Plenum, 1978.

Lobitz, W. C., & LoPiccolo, J. New methods in the behavioral treatment of sexual dysfunction. *Journal of Behavior Therapy and Experimental Psychiatry*, 1972, *3*, 265–271.

LoPiccolo, J. The professionalization of sex therapy: Issues and problems. In J. LoPiccolo & L. LoPiccolo (Eds.), *Handbook of sex therapy*. New York: Plenum, 1978.

LoPiccolo, J., & Lobitz, W. C. The role of masturbation in the treatment of orgasmic dysfunction. *Archives of Sexual Behavior*, 1972, *2*, 163–171.

LoPiccolo, J., & LoPiccolo, L. (Eds.), *Handbook of sex therapy*. New York: Plenum, 1978.

LoPiccolo, J., & Miller, V. H. A program for enhancing the sexual relationship of normal couples. *Counseling Psychologist*, 1975, *5*, 41–45.

LoPiccolo, J., & Steger, J. The sexual interaction inventory: A new instrument for assessment of sexual dysfunction. *Archives of Sexual Behavior*, 1974, *3*, 585–595.

Masters, W. H., & Johnson, V. E. *Human sexual inadequacy*. Boston: Little, Brown & Co., 1970.

McGovern, K., Arkowitz, H., & Gilmore, S. The evaluation of social skills training programs for college dating inhibitions. *Journal of Counseling Psychology*, 1975, *22*, 505–512.

McGovern, K., & Burkhard, J. Initiating social contact with the opposite sex. In J. D. Krumboltz & C. E. Thoresen (Eds.), *Counseling methods*. New York: Holt, Rinehart & Winston, 1976.

McGovern, K., Kirkpatrick, C., & LoPiccolo, J. A behavioral group treatment program for sexually dysfunctional couples. *Journal of Marriage and Family Counseling*, 1976, *2*, 397–404.

McGovern, K., Stewart, R., & LoPiccolo, J. Secondary orgasmic dysfunction: 1. Analysis and strategies for treatment. *Archives of Sexual Behavior*, 1975, *4*, 265–276.

Schneidman, B., & McGuire, L. Group therapy for nonorgasmic women: Two age levels. *Archives of Sexual Behavior*, 1976, *5*, 239–247.

Semans, J. Premature ejaculation: A new approach. *Southern Medical Journal*, 1956, *49*, 453–458.

Waggoner, R. W., Mudd, E. H., & Shearer, M. L. Training dual sex teams for rapid treatment of sexual dysfunction: A pilot program. In J. LoPiccolo & L. LoPiccolo (Eds.), *Handbook of sex therapy*. New York: Plenum, 1978.

Wallace, D. H., & Barbach, L. G. Preorgasmic group treatment. *Journal of Sex and Marital Therapy*, 1974, *2*, 146–154.

Yalom, I. D. *The theory and practice of group psychotherapy*. New York: Basic Books, 1970.

Zilbergeld, B. Group treatment of sexual dysfunction in men without partners. *Journal of Sex and Marital Therapy*, 1975, *1*, 204–214.

Chapter 5

Group Treatment of Sexual Dysfunction: Coping Skill Training for Single Males

W. Charles Lobitz
Elgan L. Baker, Jr.

Abstract

Nine men with chronic erectile dysfunction (three primary, six secondary) who had no regular sexual partner were treated in two 12-session all-male psycho-educational therapy groups. Treatment interventions addressed specific factors which inhibited adequate sexual function with a focus on coping skills to overcome those factors. Pretreatment, posttreatment, and follow-up behavioral self-report data and responses on a goal attainment scale questionnaire indicated that the treatment groups were successful for five men with secondary and one man with primary erectile dysfunction. Subjective report and pretreatment and posttreatment fantasy productions to Thematic Apperception Test (TAT) cards for the first group indicated that all men significantly improved their attitudes about sexuality and their sexual self-concept. The results suggest that this is a viable, cost-effective treatment for secondary erectile dysfunction, but not for primary erectile dysfunction unless supplementary individual therapy is provided.*

*Portions of this chapter will appear in the *Archives of Sexual Behavior* and were presented at the American Psychological Association Convention, San Francisco, September 1977.

INTRODUCTION

Since the success of direct treatment approaches for couples with sexual dysfunctions (Kaplan, 1974; Lobitz, W., & LoPiccolo, 1972; Masters & Johnson, 1970), clinicians have turned their attention to dysfunctional individuals who do not have regular partners. Using a directed masturbation program as a central focus (LoPiccolo, & Lobitz, W., 1972), treatment groups for preorgasmic women have proven to be highly successful (Barbach, 1974; Heinrich, Note 1). However, erectile dysfunction in patients without regular partners would appear to be less amenable to treatment because of the importance of the female partner's role in both maintaining and relieving the dysfunction (Kaplan, 1974; Lobitz, W., LoPiccolo, Lobitz, G., & Brockway, 1976; Masters & Johnson, 1970). Despite this potential problem, some positive efforts have been made in this direction. Zilbergeld (1975) has reported the outcome of brief treatment for single men. In therapy groups consisting of men with either premature ejaculation or erectile dysfunction, he reported a "complete success" for two-thirds of the groups' members. Although not specific about the criteria for success and the variables contributing to it, nor the outcome for erectile dysfunction, this report has been the most promising to date for the group treatment of single men.

At the University of Colorado Medical Center Human Sexuality Clinic, we have been conducting similar treatment groups for men with chronic primary or secondary erectile dysfunctions who do not have regular partners. The general treatment goals for the men in these groups are: (1) enhancement of their sense of adequacy and comfort with heterosexual relations, and (2) development of self-control skills to facilitate the acquisition and maintenance of an erection sufficient to complete heterosexual intercourse. The first goal involves changes in the men's attitudes and expectations about themselves, women, and sexual performance. Interventions directed at this goal include education, cognitive restructuring, and fantasy training.

The second goal involves a specific set of cognitive/behavioral skills for coping with sexual and interpersonal anxieties. These interventions include relaxation and sensory awareness training, role playing, and a self-directed *in vivo* desensitization process. The emphasis on coping skills derives from hypotheses about the nature of erectile dysfunction, as well as the particular vulnerabilities of men who do not have regular partners. In addition to the general vulnerability of the erectile response to anxiety, Kaplan

(1974) has hypothesized that men with erectile problems may have an "especially reactive vasocongestive genital system" (p. 265), rendering their sexual responses more vulnerable to stress than other men's responses. In the man without a regular partner, this vulnerability is compounded by the uncertainty and concomitant anxiety in his interpersonal relationships with women. Given both a constitutional and interpersonal vulnerability, erectile failure is highly probable for these men on any sexual encounter. Consequently, specific skills for coping with any given sexual situation are necessary for the resolution of their erectile dysfunction and the maintenance of their improvement.

The present report describes the treatment procedures and results of two six-man therapy groups for men without regular partners. The first group was composed homogeneously of men with chronic primary ($n = 1$) or secondary ($n = 5$) erectile dysfunction. The second group was heterogeneous, consisting of two men with primary erectile dysfunction, one with secondary erectile dysfunction, two with chronic premature ejaculation, and one with retarded ejaculation. Table 1 describes the demographic characteristics of the six men in the first treatment group (A through F) and the three men with erectile dysfunction in the second group (G through I). All of these patients had chronic erectile dysfunctions of many years' duration except for A and B whose onset was within a year of treatment. Three (E, H, and I) had primary erectile dysfunction, i.e., in the presence of a woman they never had achieved an erection sufficient for intercourse. All of the men with secondary erectile dysfunction also reported a less severe problem of premature ejaculation. Since the focus of this report is the treatment of erectile dysfunction, the remaining three men in the second group are not included. Their outcome is footnoted in the results.

All group members were initially seen for a brief screening interview to assess their general level of social skills and to rule out any severe psychopathology. In addition, they were examined by a physician to rule out organic factors in their dysfunctions. To be appropriate for these groups, the men needed to have a level of social skill sufficient for successfully initiating a date and a sexual encounter. Men who had never dated or never had a sexual encounter with a woman were excluded.

Many of the group members had additional psychological or medical problems and had received previous medical or psychosocial treatment. For example, A had been successfully treated for a severe reactive depression. C had been treated in psychoanalysis for 5 years for an obsessive-compulsive neurosis. E was currently being followed by a therapist in the military for a borderline personality

Table 1
Demography and Diagnosis

Patient	Age	Marital Status	Religion	Education	Occupation	Erectile Dysfunction	Additional Psychiatric/ Medical Diagnoses
Group 1							
A	30	Divorced	Protestant	M.A.	Teacher	Secondary	Depressive Neurosis
B	29	Divorced	Protestant	M.A.	Teacher	Secondary	Depressive Neurosis
C	32	Single	Jewish	M.A.	Social Worker	Secondary	Obsessive-Compulsive Neurosis
D	27	Divorced	Catholic	B.A.	Store Manager	Secondary	Hodgkin's Disease
E	23	Single	Catholic	H.S.+1	Military-Enlisted	Primary	Borderline Personality Disorder
F	55	Widowed	Protestant	B.A.	Business Executive	Secondary	None
Group 2							
G	25	Divorced	Catholic	H.S.+1	College Student	Secondary	None
H	25	Single	Catholic	B.A.	Economic Analyst	Primary	Anxiety Neurosis
I	30	Single	—	B.A.	Government Clerical Worker	Primary	Depression, Passive-Dependent Personality Disorder

disorder. Although not initially in treatment, H was experiencing severe heterosocial anxiety such that he had episodes of nausea when dating. He was seen for individual treatment of his social anxiety concurrent with his participation in the second group. D had Hodgkin's Disease which had been arrested through chemotherapy; however, this treatment apparently had precipitated his erectile dysfunction. Part of his dysfunction appeared organic in that he was never able to obtain a complete erection either during masturbation or while sleeping. However, his erections under those conditions were sufficient to permit sexual intercourse, whereas he was unable to obtain even minimal erections with a woman. Despite their histories of medical problems or psychopathology, all of the men, with the exception of H, were without symptoms other than their erectile dysfunction at the beginning of the groups. Although not confident in their sexual abilities, all of the men in each group were unambivalently heterosexual in orientation.

TREATMENT

The groups consisted of six male patients and two male co-therapists, viz., the authors in Group 1 and the first author and a psychiatric resident in Group 2. The groups met for 12 sessions of 90 minutes each. Group 1 met twice weekly for the first six sessions and once a week thereafter. Group 2 met once a week throughout. In both groups the process was similar to that described by Zilbergeld (1975). Most communications were directed toward the co-therapists. Some sessions were primarily didactic, whereas others involved an exploration of members' attitudes, feelings, and behaviors. Each session ended with a "homework" assignment which was debriefed at the beginning of the subsequent group.

In keeping with a multimodal assessment and treatment model for sexual dysfunctions (Lobitz, W., & Lobitz, G., 1978) and psychosocial problems in general (Lazarus, 1973), specific interventions were directed at the following identified problem areas.

Sexual Performance Anxiety

In these men, as in most cases of erectile failure (Masters & Johnson, 1970), anxiety appeared to be the central factor in their dysfunction. Although they were able to obtain erections through masturbation, the performance pressure which they felt in the presence of a female partner prevented their erectile response from occurring. The men were taught progressive relaxation exercises

(Bernstein & Borkovec, 1973) which they practiced at home. In addition, they were instructed in a self-directed step-wise *in vivo* desensitization program which had two principal components. One was the desensitization to fears over losing their erections. Similar to the procedure described by Zilbergeld (1975), as part of their "homework" they were instructed to masturbate to a full erection, let it subside, relax, and restimulate another erection. This process was repeated daily until the men could gain, lose and regain erections without subjective anxiety. The second desensitization component consisted of instructions for a graduated series of steps to be followed with a partner when and if they were involved in a sexual encounter. These were adapted from Masters and Johnson's (1970) step-wise approach, beginning with nongenital sensate focus and progressing through nondemand genital contact, to penile insertion without thrusting and, ultimately, to full intercourse. The pace of these steps was self-determined, with anxiety being a sign not to proceed to the next step until anxiety had abated. In addition, most of the men had anxieties about ejaculating prematurely. They were instructed in the use of the start-stop (Semans, 1956) and squeeze techniques (Masters & Johnson, 1970) and were shown films of the procedures.

Inhibited Communication with Women

The success of the step-wise program required the participation of a female partner. This depended on the openness of their communications with women and on the women's responses. The men believed that women would not accept their problem. Consequently, they would never discuss their problem with a woman and would try to disguise their dysfunction by making excuses, becoming intoxicated, or avoiding any sexual contact altogether.

To overcome this problem, group members were encouraged to broach the topic of sex in a graduated manner, first by discussing it generally with a woman, then by sharing some of their anxieties about sexual performance, followed by self-disclosure of their specific problem, and finally by suggesting the step-wise model to their partners as something which would work. Female co-therapists from the Clinic joined each group for one session to share their personal reactions to the men's self-disclosures and to allow each man to role play these communications, followed by feedback from the women. These communications included self-assertive responses by the men about what they would and would not like to do sexually (e.g., "I wouldn't feel comfortable having intercourse tonight, but I would love to make out for awhile and bring you to orgasm if you'd like.").

Destructive Attitudes about Women's Expectations

The men in the groups generally viewed women as demanding ogres. In part this was based on previous experience, but largely it was due to misinformation from books, other men, or their own cognitive distortions. The following are some of the more common distortions: (1) men should always be ready for sex, especially intercourse, (2) the man is responsible for his partner's arousal and pleasure, (3) women need an erect penis to be satisfied, and (4) if a man can't get an erection, he is probably a "latent homosexual." Each of these distorted cognitions was addressed throughout the group by the male co-therapists and, in particular, by the female therapists' self-disclosures about the importance of affection and caring rather than male performance. The leaders also acknowledged that indeed some women expected "magnificent performances" by their partners, but that there were many who did not.

Ignorance about Human Sexual Response

One of the factors which contributed to the men's destructive attitudes was their sexual ignorance. For example, some of the men believed that their "impotence" was a function of muscular weakness, requiring more "effort" if they lost their erections (several men in the groups were compulsive weight lifters). Other men believed that women were most easily orgasmic through penile intercourse without any concurrent manual clitoral stimulation. This resulted in the "Look Ma, no hands" syndrome (Lobitz, W., & Lobitz, G., 1978), in which the only kind of stimulation attempted in intercourse was through penile-vaginal contact. The male co-therapists presented didactic material and films on the anatomy and physiology of sexual response, including information on the enervation of the clitoris as compared to the vagina and the effect of "efforting" on a man's erectile response.

Insensitivity to Physical Sensations

Many of the men were so preoccupied with their "performance" that they were insensitive to the sensations in their bodies during lovemaking. This was addressed through sensory awareness exercises similar to those used with couples for sexual enrichment (LoPiccolo & Miller, 1975). The men were instructed to practice sensory awareness regularly at home and to incorporate it into their masturbation sessions, as well as practicing sensate focus with a female partner if, and when, they had one.

Impoverished Sexual Imagery

For some men, "sensing" without engaging in some mental process was difficult to achieve in spite of their sensory awareness training. To help the men utilize their thought processes in constructive ways, the co-therapists provided sexual fantasy training, including a guided group fantasy. Group members were instructed to rehearse erotic fantasies during masturbation and to switch their attention from a thinking-performance channel to an erotic fantasy channel whenever they were having thoughts which interfered with their arousal with a partner. Sexual fantasy training was employed not only as a coping skill, but also as one means of enhancing a sense of sexual adequacy through covert rehearsal. Literature on the relationship between psychopathology and impoverished fantasy formation suggests that an impairment of symbolic activities via daydreaming is associated with an impaired ability to function adaptively in a variety of ways, including decreased impulse control, decreased self-concept, increased anxiety level, inability to anticipate the results of one's behavior, and decreased awareness of alternative behavioral responses in a particular situation (Arlow & Brenner, 1964; Singer & Fowe, 1962; Baker, Note 2; Frazier, Note 3). The ability to engage in sexual fantasy has also been positively correlated with sexual response (Hariton, 1973).

RESULTS

Formal and informal assessments were made pretreatment, posttreatment, and at 4-month and 9-month follow-up meetings with Groups 1 and 2 respectively. (Follow-up data on Subject C were limited to 3 months due to his moving to another country at that time.) Data pertaining to the specific incidence of erectile dysfunction are based on the men's self-reports and are shown in Table 2. Prior to treatment, eight men reported difficulties obtaining or maintaining an erection on 50% to 100% of their coital opportunities. The one exception was B, who reported erectile dysfunction for 10% of his attempts, although the figure for his encounters with new partners was 75%. Immediately after treatment, two-thirds of the men in each group reported decreases in the incidence of their erectile dysfunction. This incidence was reduced even further on follow-up assessments, to a range of 0–50%. The one-third of each group who did not report a change had not attempted sexual intercourse at either the posttreatment or follow-

Table 2
Percentage of Reported Erectile Dysfunction

Patient	Pretreatment	Posttreatment	Follow-up*
Group 1			
A	75%	50%	25%
B	10%	10%	0%
C	100%	—	—
D	100%	75%	50%
E	100%	—	—
F	50%	25%	0%
Group 2			
G	50%	25%	10%
H	100%	75%	30%
I	100%	—	—

*Group 1 was tested 9 months after termination (except 3 months for C) and Group 2 was tested 4 months after termination.

up periods.[1] Including the data on the three men who had not had any sexual contact during or after treatment, these changes were statistically significant using t-tests for dependent data. (Pre vs. post: $t(8) = 3.16, p < .02$; pre vs. follow-up: $t(8) = 3.28, p < .02$, two-tailed.)

Although it was expected that the group members would show some improvement in their absolute ability to obtain or maintain an erection sufficient for intercourse as seen above, the principal goals for treatment were: (1) to improve their comfort with their sexuality, and (2) to develop their self-control skills to enable them to function sexually with a female partner even if they lost their erections. These goals were assessed by breaking them down into a 14-item "Goals for Sex Therapy" questionnaire in which the men rated their satisfaction with various feelings and abilities on a 7-point scale where 1 = much less than satisfied, 4 = satisfied, and 7 = much more than satisfied. The 14 items were as follows:

(1) Being able to anticipate (think about) having intercourse without fear of anxiety
(2) Being able to get an erection by stimulating myself when I am alone

1. The two men in Group 2 with premature ejaculation had also not attempted intercourse. Although they reported subjective increases in their comfort with sexuality and latency to orgasm in masturbation, neither of them were dating at the time of follow-up. The man with retarded ejaculation was transferred to another state after the sixth group session and did not complete treatment.

(3) Being able to get an erection during foreplay with a woman while both of us are clothed
(4) Being able to get an erection during foreplay while both of us are nude
(5) Being able to regain an erection if I lose it during foreplay
(6) Being able to get an erection sufficient to begin intercourse
(7) Being able to keep an erection during intercourse until I ejaculate
(8) Being able to regain an erection if I lose it during intercourse
(9) Being able to engage in intercourse for as long as I like without ejaculating
(10) Being able to stimulate my partner to orgasm
(11) Feeling like I am sexually desirable to my partner
(12) Feeling comfortable about my own sexuality
(13) Being able to enjoy a sexual encounter without having intercourse
(14) Being able to anticipate a sexual encounter without feeling I should have intercourse

Table 3 describes the mean satisfaction scores at pretreatment, posttreatment, and at follow-up. Prior to treatment, all of the men rated themselves as less than satisfied with their sexual coping skills and attitudes. Immediately posttreatment, three men reported being more than satisfied (mean score > 4.0) and three other men were nearly satisfied (3.8–3.9). All nine men showed an increase in their satisfaction level. At follow-up, four of the nine men exceeded their criteria for satisfaction and two others were nearly

Table 3
Goals for Sex Therapy (GST)
Individual Mean Satisfaction Scores

Patient	Pretreatment	Posttreatment	Follow-up
Group 1			
A	2.4	3.9	5.3
B	3.4	6.3	6.4
C	2.1	3.8	3.9
D	2.5	3.8	4.2
E	1.8	2.1	1.9
F	3.6	4.1	4.4
Group 2			
G	3.2	4.8	5.1
H	1.8	3.3	3.6
I	2.3	2.7	2.7

satisfied (3.6–3.9). These overall changes in goal attainment satisfaction ratings were statistically significant. (Pre vs. post: t (8) = 3.60, $p < .01$; pre vs. follow-up: t (8) = 3.76, $p < .01$, two-tailed.) Examination of the individual items revealed that, although positive changes occurred across all items, the greatest changes occurred in items pertaining to being able to get an erection (Nos. 4 and 6), regain an erection in either foreplay or intercourse (Nos. 5 and 9), engage in intercourse as long as desired (No. 9), and stimulate the female partner to orgasm (No. 10). Thus, the greatest changes occurred in areas pertaining to specific skills for coping with erectile failure and premature ejaculation.

Changes in the men's general and sexual self-concept were also assessed through their fantasy productions to 10 cards of the Thematic Apperception Test (TAT) which had a demonstrated stimulus value in eliciting specific fantasy content (Stein, 1948). The cards selected were Cards 8 GF and 7 BM (View of females), Cards 9 BM, 17 BM, and 7 BM (View of males/Self-concept for males), Cards 13 MF and 10 (Sexual concerns and attitudes), and Cards 12 M, 1, and 14 (Passive vs. active approach to conflict resolution). These cards were administered in a standard order in a group session, with each patient requested to write a fantasy story for each card. This assessment was administered during the first group session and again during the last regular session at the end of treatment for Group 1 only. The stories from each patient were disguised for both patient identity and treatment condition (pre- or post-) and were then rated independently on each of the seven dimensions by two advanced graduate students in clinical psychology. Each dimension was rated on a 3- or 5-point scale where 1 represents a negative, conflicted view (or no mention) of the dimension and the upper end of the scale represents a positive, unconflicted attitude.[2] An interrater reliability coefficient of .86 was obtained.

Table 4 presents the pretreatment and posttreatment ratings for each subject on each of the seven fantasy dimensions rated: (1) View of females, (2) View of male-female interactions, (3) View of males/Self-concept, (4) View of sexuality, (5) Creativity of fantasy, (6) Activity (vs. passivity) of main characters, and (7) Conflict resolution. Repeated-measures analysis of variance of these data indicated a significantly higher rating of fantasy after treatment (F (1,83) = 65.1; $p < .001$), suggesting a globally more mature and more adaptive quality to fantasy on the dimensions evaluated. Item

2. Copies of the "Sexual Fantasy Rating Scale" and specific descriptors for each point on the scales for each dimension are available from E. L. Baker on request.

Table 4
TAT Fantasy Rating Score*

Dimension	1		2		3		4		5		6		7	
Patient	Pre-	Post-	Pre-	Post-	Pre-	Post-	Pre-	Post-	Pre-	Post-	Pre-	Post-	Pre-	Post-
A	2.0	2.5	1.0	2.5	3.0	3.0	1.0	4.0	2.0	2.0	1.5	3.5	3.0	3.5
B	1.5	2.5	1.5	2.0	1.0	2.5	1.0	3.0	1.5	2.0	2.0	3.0	2.5	4.0
C	1.5	2.5	2.5	3.0	1.0	3.0	2.0	4.5	1.5	2.0	1.0	3.0	2.0	3.5
D	2.0	2.0	1.0	3.0	2.5	3.0	2.0	1.0	1.0	1.5	1.0	1.5	1.5	3.5
E	1.0	1.5	1.0	2.0	1.5	2.0	1.5	2.0	1.0	1.0	2.0	2.0	1.0	3.0
F	2.5	3.0	3.0	3.0	2.0	2.5	1.0	5.0	1.5	2.0	2.5	3.0	3.5	3.5

*Administered to Group 1 only.

analysis indicated that the greatest improvement occurred on Dimension 4 (View of sexuality), Dimension 7 (Conflict resolution), and Dimension 6 (Range of activity).

The three men who were not sexually active at the end of treatment reported that they were not able to meet women with whom they felt comfortable becoming sexually involved. Two of them dated infrequently (less than five dates each) during the follow-up period, and one did not date at all. Of the two who dated, one did not engage in any sexual contact, whereas the other was involved in heavy petting with one woman but did not attempt intercourse.

The six men who were sexually active by the end of treatment reported that they were engaging in intercourse on the average of one to two times per week during the follow-up period. They were all actively dating, and G was engaged to be married to a woman he had dated during treatment. All six men reported that they regularly employed some of the procedures covered in the group treatment. Each discussed his problem with prospective sexual partners and reported that this relieved some of his anticipatory anxiety and usually resulted in the partner's cooperation. They used the self-directed, step-wise desensitization process with new partners. Most of them practiced relaxation, sensory awareness, and fantasy exercises both while alone and with their partners. Despite the fact that some of them continued to experience episodic losses of erection (see Table 2), they reported being able to cope with that by relaxing and employing the above procedures to enhance the sensuality of the experience. Typically, they would regain their erections. When they did not, they refrained from resensitizing themselves to failure by not "efforting" at intercourse and instead engaged in noncoital sexual behaviors.

DISCUSSION

These results indicate that the groups were a qualified success in treating men with erectile dysfunction, despite the fact that female partners were not involved in treatment. Two-thirds of the men in each group showed significant improvements in their ability to obtain and regain erections sufficient for intercourse by the use of a series of coping strategies learned in the groups and practiced at home. These improvements were corroborated by informal reports of their increased sexual self-confidence and pleasure in their level of function. Although formal control group data were not available, the men served as their own controls in that several of the men in both groups were on the waiting list for up to six months with no significant change in their reported level of sexual function during that period. In general, the chronic nature of the men's dysfunctions, despite previous nonspecific therapy in some cases, suggests that the groups were probably responsible for the treatment effects.

Although it is not possible to determine which factors in the group treatment accounted for which changes, the use of coping strategies applied *in vivo* appeared to be particularly important. This probably accounts for the continued improvement from post-treatment to follow-up for those men who used them. In conjunction with this, as Zilbergeld (1975) has identified, the use of female therapists is an important dimension. When asked what the most important factors were in the groups, the men stated that the attendance of the female therapists was primary. Their feedback was confirmed by the dramatic increase in the degree to which the men approached women outside of the group after the session with the female co-therapists. However, the men also stated that they would not have felt comfortable with women in the group during the initial sessions.

Positive changes in the men's social-sexual behaviors coincided with positive changes in their fantasy productions in response to the TAT cards. Fantasy characterizations of both women and men became more positive with a view of females as more nurturing, supportive, and less threatening and males as more competent and adaptive. Both of these changes probably reflect positive experiences within the group with female co-therapists, as well as with other male group members. In fact, many of the patients' stories describe an increasing sense of camaraderie and mutual support with other men. Perceptions of male-female interactions moved from threatening and conflicted to a greater degree of mutuality and a sense of the potential for positive relationships. The patients' fantasies also indicated an increasing sense of activity and personal adequacy in problem solving rather than a more passive, reactive stance which characterized the fantasies before treatment. The most dramatic change in their fantasy productions reflects an increase in direct, positive references in the stories to sexuality, sexual involvement, and intimacy. Pretreatment productions portrayed sexuality as a conflicted and anxiety-producing topic or the subject was avoided and denied altogether, even when the sexual content on the stimulus cards was quite obvious. After treatment, sexuality had become an open topic, no longer taboo, which could be contemplated with less fear and dread.

Although the overall results suggest that this form of group treatment is effective for cases of secondary erectile dysfunction, it does not appear to be a sufficient treatment for primary erectile dysfunction. At follow-up, one of the three men with primary erectile dysfunction was able to complete intercourse on 70% of his attempts. However, these gains were achieved with concomitant individual therapy for his severe social anxiety. Since the other two men did not even attempt sexual intercourse during either the treatment or follow-up periods, this suggests that additional individual therapy for social anxiety or other psychosocial problems may be necessary to supplement the group treatment.

The major qualification to the success of these groups was the failure of three of the men to make any significant gains in their sexual behavior, despite some improvements in their attitudes toward sex. Although the exact reasons for these failures are unclear, several possibilities emerge. The three men were initially more dysfunctional sexually than the six who improved. Two of them were experiencing primary erectile dysfunction and the third was experiencing complete erectile failure at the beginning of treatment, even though he had previously had successful intercourse on a few occasions. Similarly, as compared to the successful group members, these three men had more severe and long-standing psychopathology which interfered with their heterosocial behavior. None of these men sought out social contacts with women during the course of treatment. Thus, not only did they seem to manifest a heterosocial shyness, but also they did not avail themselves of the group support and reinforcement for approaching women. As suggested above, the best indicator of likely success in this form of group treatment for erectile dysfunction seems to be the presence of heterosocial comfort and skill. Future group treatments should either build in a stronger social skill training component or should employ a pretreatment condition where those individuals who are deficient in this area receive special training before the treatment of their sexual dysfunction begins.

REFERENCE NOTES

1. Heinrich, A. G. *The effect of group and self-directed behavioral-educational treatment of primary orgasmic dysfunction in females treated without their partners.* Unpublished doctoral dissertation, University of Colorado, 1976.
2. Baker, E. L. *A comparative investigation of fantasy in normal and behaviorally deviant latency-aged boys.* Unpublished doctoral dissertation, University of Tennessee, 1976.
3. Frazier, J. *An investigation of daydreaming in obsessive-compulsive and hysterical personalities.* Unpublished doctoral dissertation, University of Tennessee, 1974.

REFERENCES

Arlow, J., & Brenner, C. *Psychoanalytic concepts and the structural theory.* New York: International Universities Press, 1964.

Barbach, L. G. Group treatment of preorgasmic women. *Journal of Sex and Marital Therapy,* 1974, *1,* 139–145.

Bernstein, D. A., & Borkovec, T. D. *Progressive relaxation training.* Champaign, Ill.: Research Press, 1973.

Hariton, E. The sexual fantasies of women. *Psychology Today,* 1973, *6,* 39–44.

Kaplan, H. S. *The new sex therapy.* New York: Brunner/Mazel, 1974.

Lazarus, A. A. Multi-modal behavior therapy: Treating the "basic id." *Journal of Nervous and Mental Disease,* 1973, *156,* 404–411.

Lobitz, W. C., & Lobitz, G. K. Clinical assessment of sexual dysfunction. In J. LoPiccolo & L. LoPiccolo (Eds.), *Handbook of sex therapy.* New York: Plenum, 1978.

Lobitz, W. C., & LoPiccolo, J. New methods in the behavioral treatment of sexual dysfunction. *Journal of Behavior Therapy and Experimental Psychiatry,* 1972, *3,* 265–271.

Lobitz, W. C., LoPiccolo, J., Lobitz, G. K., & Brockway, J. A closer look at "simplistic" behavior therapy for sexual dysfunction. In H. J. Eysenck (Ed.), *Case studies in behavior therapy.* London: Routledge and Kegan Paul, 1976.

LoPiccolo, J., & Lobitz, W. C. The role of masturbation in the treatment of orgasmic dysfunction. *Archives of Sexual Behavior,* 1972, *2,* 163–171.

LoPiccolo, J., & Miller, V. H. A program for enhancing the sexual relationship of normal couples. *The Counseling Psychologist,* 1975, *5,* 41–45.

Masters, W. H., & Johnson, V. E. *Human sexual inadequacy.* Boston: Little, Brown & Co., 1970.

Semans, J. Premature ejaculation: A new approach. *Southern Medical Journal,* 1956, *49,* 453–458.

Singer, J., & Fowe, R. An experimental study of some relationships between daydreaming and anxiety. *Journal of Consulting Psychology,* 1962, *26,* 446–454.

Stein, M. *The Thematic Apperception Test.* Cambridge: Addison-Wesley, 1948.

Zilbergeld, B. Group treatment of sexual dysfunction in men without partners. *Journal of Sex and Marital Therapy,* 1975, *1,* 204–214.

Chapter 6

A Broad-Spectrum Behavioral Group Approach to Smoking Reduction

Steven P. Schinke
Betty J. Blythe
Howard J. Doueck

Abstract

This chapter describes the clinical application and evaluation of a broad-spectrum behavioral group approach to smoking reduction. Over the course of eight weekly, 90-minute meetings, group members employed multiple interventive techniques to reduce their cigarette smoking and cigarette urges. To evaluate the efficacy of this approach, training condition participants and control condition participants monitored cigarette urges and cigarettes smoked at baseline, throughout the interventive period, and at three intervals during a 6-month follow-up. Urge and smoking levels both showed between-condition differences beginning with the second group meeting and across the three follow-up periods, 13, 21, and 34 weeks after intervention: training condition mean scores showed decreases in urge and smoking levels; control condition mean scores remained at baseline levels. Advantages and disadvantages of the broad-spectrum group approach are discussed, with special attention to the effects of group process on specific behavioral techniques. Guidelines for future work suggest continued efforts to apply and refine this interventive approach.*

*This research was partially supported by Maternal and Child Health Project No. 913 from the Bureau of Community Health Services (United States Public Health Service, Dept. of Health, Education, and Welfare), and by Grant No. HD 02274 from the National Institute of Child Health and

Human Development (United States Public Health Service, Dept. of Health, Education, and Welfare). Portions of this chapter were presented at the meeting of the Association for Advancement of Behavior Therapy, Atlanta, December 1977. The authors are indebted to Dr. Katharine Briar for her support and assistance throughout the study.

INTRODUCTION

Demands for effective methods of reducing cigarette smoking have increased in recent years. Behavioral researchers have responded by examining myriad interventive strategies including aversion techniques involving: shock (Conway, 1977), noxious hot air (Schmahl, Lichtenstein, & Harris, 1972), fear arousal (Rogers & Deckner, 1975), rapid smoking (Relinger, Bornstein, Bugge, Carmody, & Zohn, 1977), and satiation (Dericco, Brigham, & Garlington, 1977), as well as self-control techniques involving positive reinforcement (Brockway, Kleinmann, Edleson, & Gruenewald, 1977), contingency contracting (Winett, 1973), stimulus control (Levinson, Shapiro, Schwartz, & Tursky, 1971), covert sensitization and thought stopping (Wisocki & Rooney, 1974), systematic desensitization (Wagner & Bragg, 1970), cognitive conditioning (Berecz, 1976), hypnosis (Pederson, Scrimgeour, & Lefcoe, 1975), and relaxation (Sutherland, Amit, Golden, & Roseberger, 1975).

Despite isolated successes, most of these individual techniques have not resulted in long-term behavior change (cf. Bernstein & McAlister, 1976; Hunt & Matarazzo, 1973; Lichtenstein & Danaher, 1976). A more promising approach to the reduction of smoking and maintaining that reduction, as suggested by Bernstein (Note 1) and Conway (1977), is combining individual techniques into broad-spectrum treatment packages. With the exception of a laboratory study by Lando (1977), however, such an approach has not been empirically tested.

The present chapter describes the clinical application and evaluation of a broad-spectrum behavioral group approach to smoking reduction. Since small groups provide many opportunities for reinforcement, feedback, modeling, and vicarious learning (Feldman & Wodarski, 1975; Rose, 1972, 1977; Schinke & Rose, 1976, 1977), group-mediated intervention was viewed as an integral component of the study. Behavioral techniques composing the present broad-spectrum group approach included rapid smoking, covert sensitization, contracting, relaxation, assertion training, thought stopping, and *in vivo* practice. To evaluate this broad-spectrum group approach, smoking behaviors of participants assigned to an interventive condition were compared with those of participants assigned to a waiting list control condition.

METHOD

Setting and Participants

The smoking reduction program was requested by a local community college seeking noncredit courses relevant to the nonstudent community. Responding to an announcement of course offerings, 17 persons interested in reducing or eliminating their cigarette smoking attended an organizational meeting. Since the number of persons requesting intervention exceeded available resources, nine participants were assigned randomly to an interventive condition; eight were assigned to a waiting list condition. Constituting a control group, waiting list participants were told that resource limitations would delay their training by 6 to 8 months. Geographic moves, lack of interest, and time conflicts reduced the two conditions to six and two participants. These seven women and one man were aged 16 to 51 years, with a mean (M) of 34.16 years and standard deviation (SD) of 9.88 years; participants had been smoking for 1 to 29 years ($M = 18.29$ years, $SD = 10.30$ years).

Data Collection

At the organizational meeting, all participants began monitoring daily cigarette "urges," defined as a strong desire to smoke, and daily cigarettes smoked. Urges were recorded on wrist counters; smoking was recorded on sheets attached to cigarette packs. Treatment condition participants returned their data at each group meeting, and control condition participants mailed their data. All participants mailed their data for three weekly follow-up periods, 13, 21, and 34 weeks after intervention. Any participant not mailing in data was contacted by telephone and reminded that the data were due.

Intervention

Treatment condition participants were involved in eight 90-minute, weekly group meetings. Led by two social work graduate students, all meetings were held in a community college seminar room. A description of each interventive technique follows.

Group sharing of progress. After the first group meeting, all meetings began with individual participants constructing a graph of the previous week's daily mean number of cigarette urges and cigarettes smoked. Group members then described experiences in various smoking situations, explaining these within a social learning framework whenever possible. Those who had changed stimulus conditions of smoking behavior received special recognition from group leaders and other participants. A group norm formalized this recognition by requiring at least three group members to socially reinforce the presenter (e.g., to praise, applaud, give a pat on the back) when positive data were shared. Such procedures helped participants take responsibility for group process and helped build group cohesion.

Rapid smoking. A rapid smoking method similar to that reported by Schmahl et al. (1972) was employed in the third and fourth group meetings. After reading precautions associated with the procedure and signing informed-consent statements, two persons decided to participate in rapid smoking. These group members smoked three cigarettes each, inhaled every 6 seconds, and described the aversive consequences they were experiencing.

Cigarette litter handling with covert sensitization. The remaining group members, advised not to rapid smoke for health reasons (cf. Dawley & Dillenkoffer, 1975; Hauser, 1974; Lichtenstein & Glasgow, 1977), participated in cigarette litter handling with covert sensitization. Following Dawley and Dillenkoffer's (1975) procedure, these participants handled the litter of approximately 20 spent cigarettes while smoking and inhaling at their regular rates. Covert sensitization procedures, similar to methods described by Wisocki and Rooney (1974), involved having participants imagine disagreeable consequences of cigarette smoking (e.g., bad breath, damage to heart and lungs, monetary expense, noxious fumes for others) while handling cigarette litter.

Contracting. At the end of the third meeting and at each subsequent meeting, group members signed weekly contracts agreeing to smoke all future cigarettes using rapid smoking or covert sensitization procedures. Although participants contracted only with themselves, each contract was read aloud in the group, adding an element of public commitment. Figure 1 depicts a weekly contract completed at the fifth group meeting.

Relaxation training. Training in deep-muscle relaxation (Jacobson, 1974) was given all group members in Meetings 3 through 8. After leaders modeled using relaxation as a behavioral response to cigarette urges, participants rehearsed the new response, receiving coaching and feedback from other participants and leaders.

Buddy system. Beginning with the third meeting, participant pairs exchanged telephone numbers and scheduled weekly calls to share smoking-reduction progress reports. The buddy system helped decrease dependence on the group and leaders, and gave a source of support for not smoking outside the group. It is noteworthy that one participant temporarily resumed smoking when her buddy moved to another state.

Incompatible responses. Introduced in the fifth meeting, this technique presented a list of responses to compete with smoking (substituting a walk for an after dinner cigarette, munching on low-calorie foods, becoming more active physically, fondling paper clips rather than a cigarette, and so forth). Group members selected a number of responses and agreed to use one or more when encountering situations in which they previously had smoked.

Figure 1. Weekly Contract

I, ___*Dick R.*___ , hereby agree that

beginning on ___5/11/76___ I will smoke all future
        (date)

cigarettes using either rapid smoking or (covert sensitization)

(circle one).

I will call my buddy, ___*Helen T.*___ , on

___*May 14*___ at ___*9:30 a.m.*___
        (date)   (time)

to tell her/him of my smoking-reduction progress.

This contract is in effect until ___*May 18*___ .

___*Dick R.*___
(Signature)

Assertive training. Using a format described by Schinke and Rose (1976), group members learned and practiced assertive responses during Meetings 6 and 7. Primarily, members practiced refusing cigarette offers and asking others not to smoke in various social contexts (e.g., food stores, buses, crowded waiting rooms).

Health information. Two films on smoking cessation, *The Time to Stop is Now* (American Cancer Society, 1965) and *Let's Call It Quits* (American Cancer Society, 1975), were shown and supplementary printed material was distributed during the seventh meeting. Group discussion of these materials related specific facts to participants' lives.

Thought stopping. Using a procedure outlined by Wolpe (1973), group members were taught thought stopping in the eighth meeting. First, leaders modeled use of the technique. Next, participants practiced stopping cigarette-related thoughts, with leaders and other participants giving coaching, feedback, and reinforcement. Group members then described how they would use thought stopping to combat cigarette urges.

In vivo practice. To practice interventive techniques in a high-demand smoking situation, the final group met at a restaurant. Several group members experienced a strong desire to smoke, especially after the meal. Participants selected appropriate treatment techniques to overcome this desire. For example, a participant craving a cigarette with his coffee practiced thought stopping and substituted a toothpick for the cigarette. Another group member changed stimulus conditions by drinking tea instead of coffee. This final meeting helped generalize behavior change from the group therapy setting to the natural environment, which is often unsupportive of smoking cessation.

Group process. Although not a specific interventive technique, the group context appeared to enhance the overall treatment package. For example, participants probably benefited vicariously from each other's experiences in sharing weekly progress reports, rapid smoking, handling cigarette litter with covert sensitization, contracting, and choosing responses incompatible with smoking. As well as providing additional sources of reinforcement and feedback, the group offered a number of models and coaches for relaxation and thought stopping exercises. Similarly, assertive training and *in vivo* practice occurred with a variety of protagonists and antagonists. As indigenous group leaders, participants may have gained self-help skills when assisting others in problem-solving efforts and facilitating the group's on-task behavior. Last, the buddy system and group discussion of health information are difficult to arrange outside a group context.

Figure 2. Daily Mean of Cigarette Urges and Cigarettes Smoked

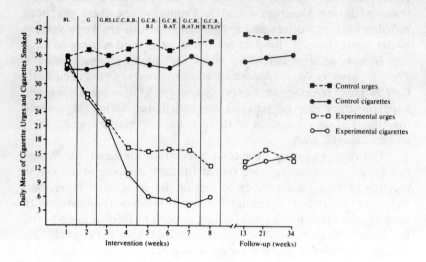

*Abbreviations represent the following treatment phases: BL, baseline; G, group sharing of progress; RS, rapid smoking; LC, cigarette litter handling with covert sensitization; C, contracting; R, relaxation training; B, buddy system; I, incompatible responses; AT, assertive training; H, health information; TS, thought stopping; IV, *in vivo* practice.

RESULTS

Participants in the interventive condition and those in the control condition provided records of cigarette urges and cigarettes smoked for the 8 weeks during which the interventive group met, and for three weekly periods over a 6-month posttreatment follow-up. Daily means for these data are presented in Figure 2.

Beginning with the second week of intervention, graphed means showed between-condition differences: treatment condition participants reported fewer urges and fewer cigarettes smoked during all phases of group training; control condition participants maintained and slightly increased their urge and smoking levels over this same period. Follow-up data at 13, 21, and 34 weeks after intervention showed that participants involved in group training still experienced fewer urges and smoked fewer cigarettes than did participants in the control condition.

DISCUSSION

Comparison data for the treatment condition and for an equivalent control condition show that this broad-spectrum behavioral group approach to smoking reduction is viable and effective. Participants in the interventive group decreased their cigarette urges and cigarettes smoked during 8 weeks of group training and at three follow-up periods; control condition participants showed no such decreases. For the interventive condition, low follow-up levels of smoking are impressive considering the posttreatment failure rates of many smoking-reduction programs (cf. Bernstein & McAlister, 1976; Hunt & Matarazzo, 1973; Lichtenstein & Danaher, 1976; West, Graham, Swanson, & Wilkinson, 1977; Yates, 1975).

The present findings indicate a number of advantages to a broad-spectrum group approach to smoking reduction. Confirming recent suggestions (Conway, 1977; Bernstein, Note 1), correlational research (Perri, Richards, & Schultheis, 1977), and nonclinical results (Lando, 1977), these findings document the clinical efficacy of a multitechnique package in reducing and maintaining reduced cigarette smoking. More important, this chapter has identified several benefits to the group delivery of such a package. As previously noted, the group context appeared to enhance each treatment technique. Further, the group itself served as an interventive resource and practice forum difficult to duplicate in individual counseling. Multiple agents for reinforcement, feedback, coaching, vicarious learning, and role playing are a unique strength of groups. Opportunities to provide leadership, by helping others in group and by serving as a buddy out of group, are additional benefits to behavioral group intervention. Finally, groups offer economy of time and expense; one group meeting reaches several people simultaneously, supplanting many individual sessions.

Certainly, there exist potential disadvantages to broad-spectrum group approaches such as the one described here. The inability to document the degree to which each specific interventive technique was responsible for change is one obvious limitation. In addition, the group may exert sufficient pressure on participants to result in lying or data fudging to meet group expectations. Although not an apparent problem in the present experience, group sharing of smoking-reduction progress has potential for such pressure. Group members also may become dependent on group support, reinforcement, and feedback, and thus diffuse responsibility for their own behavior change. Anticipating this problem in the present group, leaders worked toward transferring change by asking members to develop self-mediated contracts for the performance of all agreed-upon behaviors.

Additional smoking-reduction research could build upon results yielded by this study. One area of future work might isolate the relative efficacy of individual interventive components. In the present group, for example, interventive techniques introduced in Weeks 2–3 appeared to have reduced cigarette urges and cigarettes smoked more than did techniques introduced later. Different technique sequencing could test whether such reductions occurred because of less powerful techniques or because of "ceiling" limitations on the data. Future research could also focus intensely on lowering cigarette urges. Combining the present findings with the work of others (Danaher, 1976) indicates that cigarette urges do not subside until long after actual smoking decreases. Despite the need for future investigation, this study suggests that future smoking-reduction programs can profit from a broad-spectrum behavioral group approach.

Reference Notes

1. Bernstein, D. A. *The modification of smoking behavior: Some suggestions for programmed symptom substitution*. Paper presented at the meeting of the Association for Advancement of Behavior Therapy, Chicago, November 1974.

References

American Cancer Society. *The time to stop is now*. New York: Author, 1965. (Film)

American Cancer Society. *Let's call it quits*. New York: Author, 1975. (Film)

Berecz, J. Treatment of smoking with cognitive conditioning therapy: A self-administered aversion technique. *Behavior Therapy*, 1976, *7*, 641–648.

Bernstein, D. A., & McAlister, A. The modification of smoking behavior: Progress and problems. *Addictive Behaviors*, 1976, *1*, 89–102.

Brockway, B. S., Kleinmann, G., Edleson, J., & Gruenewald, K. Non-aversive procedures and their effect on cigarette smoking: A clinical group study. *Addictive Behaviors*, 1977, *2*, 121–128.

Conway, J. B. Behavioral self-control of smoking through aversive conditioning and self-management. *Journal of Consulting and Clinical Psychology*, 1977, *45*, 348–357.

Danaher, B. G. Coverant control of cigarette smoking. In J. D. Krumboltz and C. E. Thoresen (Eds.), *Counseling methods*. New York: Holt, Rinehart & Winston, 1976.

Dawley, H. H., & Dillenkoffer, R. L. Minimizing the risks in rapid smoking treatment. *Journal of Behavior Therapy and Experimental Psychiatry*, 1975, *6*, 174.

Dericco, D. A., Brigham, T. A., & Garlington, W. K. Development and evaluation of treatment paradigms for the suppression of smoking behavior. *Journal of Applied Behavior Analysis*, 1977, *10*, 173–181.

Feldman, R. A., & Wodarski, J. S. *Contemporary approaches to group treatment*. San Francisco: Jossey-Bass, 1975.

Hauser, R. Rapid smoking as a technique of behavior modification: Caution in selection of subjects. *Journal of Consulting and Clinical Psychology*, 1974, *42*, 625–626.

Hunt, W. A., & Matarazzo, J. D. Three years later: Recent developments in the experimental modification of smoking behavior. *Journal of Abnormal Psychology*, 1973, *81*, 107–114.

Jacobson, E. *Progressive relaxation* (3rd rev. ed.). Chicago: University of Chicago Press, 1974.

Lando, H. A. Successful treatment of smokers with a broad-spectrum behavioral approach. *Journal of Consulting and Clinical Psychology*, 1977, *45*, 361–366.

Levinson, B. L., Shapiro, D., Schwartz, G. E., & Tursky, B. Smoking elimination by gradual reduction. *Behavior Therapy*, 1971, *2*, 477–482.

Lichtenstein, E., & Danaher, B. G. Modification of smoking behavior: A critical analysis of theory, research, and practice. In M. Hersen, R. M. Eisler, & P. M. Miller (Eds.), *Progress in behavior modification* (Vol. 3). New York: Academic Press, 1976.

Lichtenstein, E., & Glasgow, R. E. Rapid smoking: Side effects and safeguards. *Journal of Consulting and Clinical Psychology*, 1977, *45*, 815–821.

Pederson, L. L., Scrimgeour, G., & Lefcoe, M. Comparison of hypnosis plus counseling, counseling alone, and hypnosis alone in a community service smoking withdrawal program. *Journal of Consulting and Clinical Psychology*, 1975, *43*, 920.

Perri, M. G., Richards, C. S., & Schultheis, K. R. Behavioral self-control and smoking reduction: A study of self-initiated attempts to reduce smoking. *Behavior Therapy*, 1977, *8*, 360–365.

Relinger, H., Bornstein, P. H., Bugge, I. D., Carmody, T. P., & Zohn, C. J. Utilization of adverse rapid smoking in groups: Efficacy of treatment and maintenance procedures. *Journal of Consulting and Clinical Psychology*, 1977, *45*, 245–249.

Rogers, R. W., & Deckner, C. W. Effects of fear appeals and physiological arousal upon emotion, attitudes, and cigarette smoking. *Journal of Personality and Social Psychology*, 1975, *32*, 222–230.

Rose, S. D. *Treating children in groups*. San Francisco: Jossey-Bass, 1972.

Rose, S. D. *Group therapy: A behavioral approach*. Englewood Cliffs, N.J.: Prentice-Hall, 1977.

Schinke, S. P., & Rose, S. D. Interpersonal skill training in groups. *Journal of Counseling Psychology*, 1976, *23*, 442–448.

Schinke, S. P., & Rose, S. D. Assertive training in groups. In S. D. Rose (Ed.), *Group therapy: A behavioral approach*. Englewood Cliffs, N.J.: Prentice-Hall, 1977.

Schmahl, D. P., Lichtenstein, E., & Harris, D. E. Successful treatment of habitual smokers with warm, smoky air and rapid smoking. *Journal of Consulting and Clinical Psychology*, 1972, *38*, 105–111.

Sutherland, A., Amit, Z., Golden, M., & Roseberger, Z. Comparison of three behavioral techniques in the modification of smoking behavior. *Journal of Consulting and Clinical Psychology,* 1975, *43,* 443–447.

Wagner, M. K., & Bragg, R. A. Comparing behavior modification approaches to habit decrement—smoking. *Journal of Consulting and Clinical Psychology,* 1970, *34,* 258–263.

West, D. W., Graham, S., Swanson, M., & Wilkinson, G. Five year follow-up of a smoking withdrawal clinic population. *American Journal of Public Health,* 1977, *67,* 536–544.

Winett, R. A. Parameters of deposit contracts in the modification of smoking. *The Psychological Record,* 1973, *23,* 49–60.

Wisocki, P. A., & Rooney, E. J. A comparison of thought stopping and covert sensitization techniques in the treatment of smoking: A brief report. *The Psychological Record,* 1974, *24,* 191–192.

Wolpe, J. *The practice of behavior therapy* (2nd ed.). New York: Pergamon Press, 1973.

Yates, A. J. When behavior therapy fails: 1. Smoking. In A. J. Yates (Ed.), *Theory and practice in behavior therapy.* New York: Wiley, 1975.

Chapter 7

Cognitive-Behavioral Group Therapy and Assertion Training

Arthur J. Lange

Abstract

Cognitive-behavioral approaches to group counseling and therapy offer unique emphases in the following areas: (1) the conceptualization of client problems, (2) the types of client changes sought, (3) the actions the therapist and client undertake to effect those changes, and (4) the process goals that enhance the client's potential for self-help in the future. This chapter describes one cognitive-behavioral approach, cites the uniqueness of the four dimensions noted above, and provides a number of case examples. Specific cognitive restructuring and behavioral principles and techniques for groups are described and the application of cognitive-behavioral principles to assertion training is briefly presented. References to the theory and techniques employed in this cognitive-behavioral approach are provided, along with recommended readings on related approaches.

INTRODUCTION

Cognitive-behavioral therapy is a synthesis of semantic/insight therapies (Beck, 1976; Ellis, 1971; Kelley, 1955; Mahoney, 1974; Meichenbaum, 1977; Phillips, 1956) and behavioral treatment modes (Lazarus, 1976; Malott, 1972; Rimm & Masters, 1974; Salter, 1949). A sophisticated approach to cognitive-behavioral therapy goes beyond simply employing the former and then the latter in succession. The model presented here will demonstrate an integrated approach where changing cognitions and behaviors both take place, but where behavioral principles and techniques are employed toward changing cognitions (Meichenbaum, 1977) and cognitive restructuring techniques are incorporated into behavior rehearsal, relaxation, and contingency contracting stages. Considerable support exists for the use of treatment modes which attempt to influence cognitions, feelings, and behaviors with appropriate emphases on all three components (Kanfer & Goldstein, 1975; Lazarus, 1976; Raimy, 1975). Cognitive techniques in therapy are rapidly emerging as extremely popular interventions among both lay persons and practitioners (Mahoney, 1977). The cognitive-behavioral model presented here (which is only one of many) is an effort to conceptualize the relationship between thoughts, feelings, and behaviors and to provide treatment modes to help clients modify any or all of these components of human functioning.

The cognitive-behavioral model is especially appropriate in a group context. First, in addition to helping clients accomplish specific individual changes, primary therapy goals are to teach group members: (1) the conceptual model, particularly emphasizing the influence of cognitions on feelings and behaviors; (2) a process of self-assessment; (3) specific cognitive restructuring procedures; and (4) behavioral change techniques. Thus, as one group member is working on a specific change, others learn the procedures which can be implemented by them not only in the group but, even more importantly, in their daily lives as well. Moreover, as group members become more knowledgeable and proficient in applying the principles and procedures, they are increasingly active in helping each other work through specific changes, particularly when under the primary direction of the therapist.

COGNITIVE RESTRUCTURING

The cognitive-behavioral model presented here places heavy emphasis on understanding the importance of one's belief system, i.e., the judgments, meanings, and other ideas one has about oneself and others in specific situations. What can we do with this belief system when it becomes faulty? A faulty belief system is self-destructive rather than self-enhancing. We might also ask *why* one's system becomes faulty. A simple answer is that, particularly at a young, impressionable age, we come to believe and act upon: (1) that which we think we see; (2) that which is told to us by significant, believable others; (3) that which keeps others happy and us safe; and (4) that for which we get attention.

However the original question —"What can we do when our belief system is faulty?"—is considered more important. The first basic assumption of the cognitive-behavioral approach is that individuals have the capacity to change their thinking, both their generalized beliefs and their specific thoughts in specific situations. Thus, although it would be interesting and sometimes valuable to understand why and how one developed certain beliefs, such knowledge is not a necessary condition for their modification.

Meichenbaum (1977) notes that the therapy process itself is an experience about which the client is making judgments. He suggests that one factor which may be critical for therapeutic success is that the client has a conceptual model of the process and believes in that process, at least believing that the steps toward change make sense.

Consequently, before people enter a cognitive-behavioral therapy group, they generally receive three or four individual sessions designed to help them understand how to think about their concerns in a cognitive-behavioral context. In an assertion group, which is typically time limited with everyone beginning at the same time, the first several sessions are devoted to this learning process. Didactic, modeling, and practice segments are designed to present the cognitive-behavioral principles they will need to know to work on specific changes later in the group (see Lange & Jakubowski, 1976). Thus, the cognitive-behavioral approach not only works toward effecting specific changes, but it is primarily concerned with teaching clients how to assess themselves and how to carry out their own changes. It is very much a self-help training program directed at learning to control one's own thinking, feelings, and behavior.

One important conceptualization to which all clients are introduced is a combination of Meichenbaum's (1977) and Ellis's (1971) work. Clients recognize that they are doing three things at all times: thinking, feeling, and behaving. Moreover, they understand that some aspect of these three states is what's "wrong." What we offer them is a conceptual model for understanding the *relationship* between their thoughts, feelings, and behaviors, which they can use any time to assess themselves and to change any of those dimensions. Learning Ellis's (1974) ABC's is the start. "A" represents any person or situation which might lead the client to feel excessively angry, anxious, depressed, or guilty (these are the four basic dysfunctional emotional reactions we have available to us). "B" represents the thinking one does in response to the awareness of "A," and "C" represents one's feelings and behaviors that result. Most people believe that "A" causes "C" (e.g., "He makes me so mad I could kill him," or Flip Wilson's "The devil made me do it!"). This model demonstrates the primary importance of one's own thinking in the process, places a great deal of responsibility on the client for the resultant feelings and actions and, most importantly, points the way to change.

This model can be presented as an exercise in the group. The leader asks for situations that lead to excessive emotional reactions, cites them as Step A on a blackboard, then gets the group to give examples of likely resulting feelings and specific behaviors at Step C. Then, he goes back to Step B and gets the group members to identify what kinds of thoughts would have to be present before such feelings and behaviors could exist. This is where Meichenbaum's concept of "internal dialogues" is so valuable (Meichenbaum, 1977). Group members are encouraged to recall the thoughts they had in a specific situation. We all think to ourselves all the time, and we do not pay enough attention to it. Sometimes these thoughts are inaccurate, exaggerated, and self-defeating. Group members learn that their thinking can be categorized as rational, irrational, or rationalized. They learn a set of criteria for each category to be used in and outside the group when doing cognitive restructuring (see below). For example, irrational thinking tends to be exaggerated, catastrophic ("what if . . ."), and absolutistic ("I *must* . . .") with a final, often unstated phrase like "That would be awful!" Rationalizations tend to exaggerate or distort reality in the opposite direction by overly minimizing the significance of events (e.g., "Who cares if I get this job? Besides, I feel lucky!" or "I can do anything" or "Every day, in every way, I'm getting better and better" or "I'm fine; it's everybody else!"). Rational thinking is an accurate representation of reality; it is logical and self-enhancing (the other two tend to be self-defeating).

The first stage in this cognitive-behavioral model, then, is to offer a conceptual framework by which the group members can think about the relationship between their thoughts, feelings, and behaviors in specific situations and recognize the contribution of each. In this model, all three are emphasized, but one's thoughts are considered to be the initiator of the sequence. Group members are taught to imagine themselves in a specific real situation and are asked to identify the thoughts they are thinking to themselves about themselves, about others in the situation, or about the situation in general. Most people have difficulty in doing this at first, and it takes a while for them to begin to recognize all the different issues, worries, criticisms, and opinions that emerge in relatively brief situations. Yet, once a bit of attention is applied, the dialogue becomes very rich. The dialogue or conversation with oneself is not usually entirely self-defeating, but is something like the following dialogue. A person sitting in a reception area waiting to go in for an important job interview might be thinking: "Oh god, I just shouldn't have arranged this interview so soon. I'm not ready! Look, relax, you'll do fine, don't worry. You can do it. But what if he starts asking things I can't answer? I'd die! I'd feel so stupid. Look, you're getting yourself all upset over nothing. Come on, you'll blow it before you even get in there. Ah no, is that him? He looks like a real hard-nose. He'll see right through me. Look at my hands shake. I can't do it!"

This type of dialogue, interspersed with riffling through an old magazine from the rack, is fairly representative in that there is a lot of worrying, some support, some self-criticism, and much ambivalence. Many people are only minimally or partially aware of such cognitions during their occurrence, but can recall them in retrospect.

The next stage is to teach the group members how to go through the four basic steps of cognitive restructuring. Again, "cognitive restructuring" is a widely used term and only one method is presented here. First, group members are given a brief explanation of what constitutes an internal dialogue. They are given examples of some dialogues in specific situations like the one cited above. Then, they explore the internal dialogues they recently had in real situations. Individuals share their dialogue with another group member who is primarily a listener and recorder, although they can ask a few questions like "What were you thinking about yourself . . . about the others . . . about the situation?" The listener can also help the explorer to keep thinking so that he does not stop before most of the thoughts emerge.

The second step of cognitive restructuring is to identify the general underlying irrational assumptions or beliefs which are supporting this situationally specific dialogue. Ellis (1974; Ellis & Grieger, 1978; Ellis & Harper, 1975) offers about 10 (the number varies with each new publication) general irrational beliefs which are self-defeating and which manifest themselves in infinite ways in specific situations. The identification of these underlying beliefs is a very important step for several reasons:

(1) The client is able to see recurring themes in a variety of settings which all have a common irrational belief at their base.

(2) Others in the group can see how a particular basic belief can manifest itself in many ways.

(3) The general irrational beliefs are very clear and clearly illogical and self-defeating, whereas the situationally specific dialogue often gets cluttered and confusing. When it is reduced to the basic irrationality it is much clearer and therefore easier to change.

Ellis and Harper's *A New Guide to Rational Living* (1975) is the best elaboration of these basic irrational ideas and is usually required reading for the group (see also Lange & Jakubowski, 1976; Jakubowski & Lange, 1978). The 10 irrational ideas* are always available in the group for reference, at least during the first few sessions. The first four are the most frequently found while the others are often additionally present in one's belief system.

(1) You must—yes, must—have sincere love and approval almost all the time from all of the people you find significant.

(2) You must prove yourself thoroughly competent, adequate, and achieving, or you must at least have real competence or talent at something important.

(3) You have to view life as awful, terrible, horrible, or catastrophic when things do not go the way you would like them to go.

(4) People who harm you or commit misdeeds rate as generally bad, wicked, or villianous individuals, and you should severely blame, damn, and punish them for their sins.

(5) If something seems dangerous or fearsome, you must become terribly occupied with and upset about it.

(6) People and things should turn out better than they do, and you have to view it as awful and horrible if you do not quickly find good solutions to life's hassles.

(7) Emotional misery comes from external pressures, and you have little ability to control your feelings or rid yourself of depression and hostility.

(8) You will find it easier to avoid facing many of life's difficulties and self-responsibilities than to undertake more rewarding forms of self-discipline.

*From the book, *A New Guide to Rational Living* by Ellis and Harper. Copyright 1975 by Institute for Rational Living. Published by Prentice-Hall, Inc., Englewood Cliffs, NJ.

(9) Your past remains all-important, and because something once strongly influenced your life it has to keep determining your feelings and behavior today.

(10) You can achieve happiness by inertia and inaction or by passively and uncommittedly "enjoying yourself."

The third step in cognitive restructuring involves challenging the thinking identified in the first and second steps. First the question is asked, "What is true in your thinking?"; then, "What is not true?" Although the questions seem simplistic, the process is quite revealing when pursued in terms of the characteristics of irrational (catastrophic and absolutistic), rational, and rationalized thinking. The case examples cited below may help to demonstrate what this step entails.

The fourth step consists of substituting more accurate, self-enhancing, reasonable, alternative thoughts for those which were inaccurate, irrational, and self-defeating. Very often persons doing cognitive restructuring therapy tend to stop prematurely with either having only identified the internal dialogue and irrational bases or having only challenged their appropriateness. It is important also to help the client develop several clear, brief cognitions which are believed and which counter the self-defeating cognitions. The client can then think these thoughts when an incident arises in which the previous, self-defeating cognitions might have emerged.

It is important to note here that this process of learning how to restructure one's cognitions is only the beginning of the therapeutic process. This is not the "cure"; changes take time and systematic effort. At this point group members have merely learned some new self-help skills. The process of applying them will determine the degree of change.

CASE STUDIES INVOLVING COGNITIVE RESTRUCTURING

Before going on to tie together the cognitive and the behavioral components of this model, some case studies of the cognitive restructuring process will be presented. After the group learns the basic conceptual model (either together or in individual sessions before entering the group), the therapist will work with each individual who wishes some time in that session. The process is similar to the traditional group psychotherapy model in that most interaction takes place between one group member and the therapist (that is, during the cognitive restructuring phase). As group members become more skillful, they start interacting among themselves, and they are often able to help each other work through the four stages. However, it is not at all like an encounter group.

Case Study

Robert White is an accountant for a chemical company and came to the group with concerns about being passive, depressed, and generally unhappy in his work and family relations. He is 52 years old and lives with his wife, Sarah, and two children, Robert Jr. and Amy, who are in their middle teens. (The names used in all the case studies are entirely fictional.)

Arthur Lange *(therapist):*	What is it you want to work on today, Bob?
R.W.:	Well, I've been feeling down in the dumps since I came back from vacation in San Francisco. My father-in-law has been on my back ever since.
Participant 1:	What for?
R.W.:	He thinks I should have taken better care of Sarah and Robert Jr. You see when we were ready to drive back from San Francisco, they decided they wanted to fly. Robert wasn't feeling well, so I drove them to the airport but it was fogged in. The airline said they'd bus them to Oakland airport nearby and they could fly out from there, so I left them and drove home with Amy. Well it turns out that Oakland got fogged in, too, and they had to stay overnight. Well, Mr. Graves was *very* unhappy with me. He got Amy over there and upset her terribly with his criticism of me, and he's brought it up several times at family dinners these past 2 weeks. He's been telling me I'm not a fit husband and that I don't really have what it takes to protect my family.
A.L.:	What's your response when he does this at dinner?
R.W.:	Well, I've been quiet, although I did say it wasn't my fault. I don't like to have hassles, and I do feel bad about their inconvenience.
A.L.:	What would you like to say to your father-in-law?
R.W.:	I'd like to tell him to shut up! Only I don't want to be rude.
A.L.:	So you'd like to tell him to stop, but not in a rude manner. OK. When he's berating you for being irresponsible, how are you feeling?

R.W.:   I get anxious and upset. . . . I'm probably angry too, but I'm mostly feeling cornered and put down.

Participant 2:   Almost like you've been a bad boy.

R.W.:   Yes, that's exactly it. And I'm a grown man with a family. I get really down on myself later because I let him get to me so easily.

Step 1: Identifying the Internal Dialogue

A.L.:   Let's take this one stage at a time. What do you think to yourself when you are feeling anxious and cornered?

R.W.:   I'm thinking, "Oh gosh, here he goes again. Why do I have to get this criticism? I know I goofed and I could have been better. He doesn't let me get a word in edgewise." Then when he persists in criticizing me no matter what I say to explain, I give up and I think, "Maybe he's right, I am irresponsible and thoughtless. I probably was wrong."

A.L.:   It also sounds like you decide that the only way to stop the hassle is to give in and you talk yourself into feeling guilty and wrong. Is that true?

R.W.:   Yes, that's very true. I do give up so that he'll let up!

A.L.:   That's what you are thinking to yourself about the immediate situation of arguing with your father-in-law. When you argue with him, what are you thinking to yourself about him and about you?

R.W.:   I think of myself as being very weak and vulnerable and of him as being strong and unbending.

Step 2: Identifying the Underlying Irrational Ideas

A.L.:   OK. That's an excellent analysis of your internal dialogue in this situation. Now, what do you think are the underlying irrational ideas supporting your thinking?

R.W: I think there are several. First, I get upset because he does not respect me and that really bothers me. Then, I worry that I was not adequate as a husband and father. Then, I believe I should feel guilty and that I deserve his wrath. I also believe that it's easier to avoid the conflict than to face it.

Participant 3:   It also sounds like at first you get pretty upset that he is treating you so unfairly and later you decide to avoid facing this hassle. Is that right?

R.W.:   Right, both are true.

Step 3: Challenging the Thinking of Steps 1 and 2

A.L.:   OK. Now, what *is* true about your father-in-law in this situation?

R.W.:   Well, it's true that he is angry with me and that in this case he doesn't respect me. He probably does not like many things I do. It's also true that he is very critical and demeaning when he doesn't like what I do. He is stubborn and does not change his opinions. I also think he competes with me over the attentions of my family.

A.L.:   Fine. Let's presume all you say is true. What is *not* true?

R.W.:   Although I'd like his respect, I don't *need* it, and I am not a bad person just because he doesn't respect me . . . . It's not awful when he criticizes me; it's annoying and unpleasant, but I don't have to get terribly upset. I don't *have* to change his opinion of me, I'd simply like to. He does not *make* me upset, I do.

Step 4: Substituting Alternative Rational Ideas

A.L.:   Good. Now what would you need to *think* to yourself about your father-in-law that would help you to stay more relaxed when he begins berating you?

R.W.:   "I'd like you to respect me. When you don't, I can live with it." Yes, that would really do it. I've been so worried about his approval that I've overreacted. I could also think, "I don't like it when you harass me, but I *can* handle it."

A.L.:   Great, Bob. What else can you think to yourself about the situation, particularly your feelings of vulnerability and seeing your father-in-law as being strong and overpowering?

R.W.:   I will think to myself, "He is overbearing and I don't like that, but I can stay in control of myself and keep my cool. I do not have to give up; I can stay assertive."

A.L.:   OK. Now, as you begin to practice how you

would like to respond to your father-in-law, will
you think these thoughts over and over to
yourself?

R.W.:   Sure. I can feel myself relaxing now.

Analysis. Several points warrant attention at this time. First,
all of the internal dialogue is challenged and restructured all the
time. When the dialogue is as extensive and multifaceted as in this
case, the therapist typically prioritizes the issues expressed (with
the agreement of the client) and works on one at a time. Second,
group members are often initially hesitant to help each other in the
cognitive restructuring process. This is partly due to a lack of
knowledge and skill in doing restructuring. Moreover, new group
members often do not see that part of their role in the group involves being helpful to other group members. Since the primary
goal is to help clients learn the process of cognitive restructuring,
active participation by group members with each other is highly
desirable when it stays relevant to the process. In fact, most group
members can learn the steps of restructuring and, with some practice and coaching, can participate actively in the restructuring process. The therapist is typically the primary helper, with group
members asking pertinent questions or making suggestions. Third,
at this point the therapist might go on to some behavioral practice,
since quite a bit of restructuring occurred. Not all clients are as
clear and efficient in their analyses of their thinking. This example
was intentionally "textbookish" to show the four steps of cognitive
restructuring clearly. It is also true, however, that the didactic
presentations of the conceptual model at the beginning of a group
will greatly increase the client's ability to assess himself or herself.
Fourth, this brief cognitive restructuring leads smoothly to the next
step of behavioral change. If Bob did not get upset and withdraw
guiltily after being briefly defensive, what *would* he like to do instead? That is the first step in the behavioral change process.

Clearly, a therapist could go in many other directions when a
client reports an incident like the one above. She could conceptualize and interpret Bob's behavior in terms of his low self-image, she
could analyze the interaction as a game in transactional analysis,
she could explore early developmental experiences which helped
shape Bob's image of himself as a "bad boy," or she could help
Bob to get more fully in touch with his feelings and to express
them. We could all make brilliant interpretations of the dynamics
and of the roles each person seems to be playing. The cognitive-
behavioral model does none of these things as a central part of the
process. Most experienced therapists do utilize more than one

therapeutic approach, but usually as an adjunct to the basic orientation. For example, one might explore past events that were similar, particularly childhood events, but for the purpose of identifying the belief system that manifested itself in this present situation. Or exploration of one's feelings would not be an end in itself but rather a means to identify other parts of the internal dialogue (one might explore feelings of anger and discover the client was angry because he believed he was inadequate in the situation). Or analyzing the ego states one moved through in a transactional analysis game could be helpful toward recognizing the changes in cognitions at various moments during an interaction.

The therapist's goals in the segment presented above were: (1) to identify the internal dialogue, (2) to identify the underlying irrational assumptions, (3) to challenge the accuracy of that dialogue, and (4) to generate a few simple counterthoughts to be substituted while practicing new behaviors and in future real situations. Such cognitive restructuring can be accomplished in a relatively short period of time. The art of this process lies in being able to recognize what the basic irrational issues are and being able to stay focused on them without being rigid, dogmatic, humorless, or mechanical. When two people are right on target identifying and restructuring one person's cognitions, it is an exciting process and a very human one.

Many critics of the cognitive and semantic therapies have only seen them done in a very directive manner and reject the principles because they are not comfortable with the style. The fact is that being directive and cognitively oriented are not synonymous with being insensitive or unfeeling. This cognitive-behavioral approach maintains a high regard for the client and requires considerable attention and sensitivity to the client's feelings.

Many casual investigators of cognitive therapy perceive it to be unconcerned with feelings. Some even suggest that the cognitive approach attempts to eliminate feelings. In fact, cognitive restructuring focuses very heavily on emotions. Most importantly, however, cognitive therapists presume that not all feelings are self-enhancing. Some are in fact self-destructive. Consequently, the task is to discriminate between those feelings that are disruptive, exaggerated, and excessive and those that are healthy and appropriate. Cognitive restructuring then becomes an effort to cope with, reduce, and even eliminate self-destructive feelings in order to enable us to experience those feelings which *are* desired. The issue is not one of deciding to have or not have feelings, but rather one of choosing what feelings we want to have.

Finally, since the client gets to do most of the work, the successful changes can be more fully valued and celebrated. Clearly, the implementation of the restructuring process between sessions is of primary importance. The work in the sessions merely provides the means and the direction for *in vivo* changes.

Case Study

Another case example might help to demonstrate the cognitive restructuring process. In this instance, the client did not give up her irrational thinking as readily as Robert did in the previous case. Barbara Bailey is a woman in her mid-thirties who felt a great deal of bitterness over her divorce 2 years earlier. During the past 2 years, she had had no intimate relationships and had managed to make herself quite miserable about that fact. After being in therapy for about 3 months, she made significant changes in her beliefs about herself and how she used her anger in self-destructive ways. She was now developing a new relationship with a man she considered to be wonderful. However, she was finding herself becoming increasingly tense and withdrawn and behaving in some dysfunctional ways which were quite upsetting. She was beginning to feel less in control and feared she was falling back to her old position of seeing herself as inadequate and others as rejecting. She reported an incident where she became so tense that she almost caused a serious accident on a ski lift, although she is an experienced skier.

B.B.:	(Stressed voice) I don't know what's going on. I've found someone who is so loving and caring I can't believe it, and here I am getting all tense and nervous and doing things that are just mortifying. (Note: Barbara is saying a great deal in this first statement. Not all of it can receive attention at this time. Moreover, some interpretations would warrant further verification. Nevertheless, she seems to be saying: (1) I'm stuck, I'm confused, I need someone to figure this out for me; (2) I'm angry with myself for doing what I'm doing; (3) help me; (4) I don't deserve him; (5) I'm losing him. It would be easy for a therapist to begin rescuing Barbara by doing her thinking for her. My goal was to get her to think clearly about what is happening and to reduce her agitation.)

A.L.:	What is it you want to work on?
B.B.:	Well . . . I want to figure out why I'm doing what I'm doing, and I want to stop it.
A.L.:	Great. That's very clear, and you *can* do both. You said you are getting tense and acting inappropriately. When do you find yourself getting tense?
B.B.:	Lately, it seems like all the time. I can't seem to relax. I'm distracted and jumpy.
Participant 1:	And what is it you are tense about?
B.B.:	Well, I guess it's because I'm worried about my relationship with Henry.
Participant 1:	You sound like you're not sure that is what's causing your tension.
B.B.:	Well, I hate to think I'm doing that to myself. It's so stupid.
A.L.:	After you find yourself getting tense or doing something "wrong," what do you think to yourself about yourself?
B.B.:	Ah, I get really angry and I tell myself what a dummy I am. I'm my own worst critic.
A.L.:	And when you hate to admit to yourself that you are doing something that's self-destructive, what assumptions are you making about yourself?
B.B.:	Ah! That I should be perfect and adequate and have no faults . . . and that it's easier to ignore my faults than face them.
A.L.:	Very good thinking. What do you need to think to yourself to challenge those beliefs so that you can work on these concerns without getting down on yourself?
B.B.:	It's clear now. I don't have to be perfectly together all the time and, even though I don't like what I'm doing, I can face it, and I don't have to get down on myself because I'm doing it.
A.L.:	Great. You may want to keep that in mind while we work on these things you are doing. OK?
B.B.:	OK.
Participant 2:	What are you getting yourself tense about lately?
B.B.:	Well, Henry is very interested in literature.

	He's an officer in the Literary Guild and we went to a reading and reception 2 weeks ago. I just don't know that much about writers and books. I felt like a log in that group. And Henry was just the center of attention, everybody came up to him and asked him questions. I felt so stupid I couldn't say a thing.
A.L.:	When you were at this meeting, what were you thinking to yourself about Henry?
B.B.:	At first, I was really impressed, but I began to feel jealous because he was getting all the attention and I wasn't getting any. Then I began to worry that he might realize how little I had to say.
A.L.:	So you thought that it wasn't fair that he was getting all the attention, and you wanted some. What is the underlying irrational assumption here?
B.B.:	Well, that I must be liked and respected by people significant to me all the time.
A.L.:	Good, and then you began to worry about Henry's possibly judging you to be inadequate.
B.B.:	Yes, I got really scared and withdrew even more.
A.L.:	And what's the irrational belief here?
B.B.:	I must be competent and adequate at everything I undertake all the time.
Participant 3:	And if you're not?
B.B.:	Oh! Then people like Henry will not like me, and he'll leave me.
Participant 4:	And that would be awful!
B.B.:	It would! I'd die. He's so wonderful. You don't know what it's been like these past 2 years and in my marriage.
A.L.:	So you think that if Henry left you, you would be alone and that would be terrible or you'd wind up with some louse who would be nasty to you.
B.B.:	Well, I don't know, but Henry is so nice. I don't know what I'd do without him now.
A.L.:	Let's consider the worst possible outcome, that Henry will find you boring and leave. What would you do?
B.B.:	I couldn't stand it. I'd probably fall apart.

A.L.:	Only if you convinced yourself that it was awful and terrible and horrible. But what *is* true about being alone without Henry?
B.B.:	Well, I wouldn't have his love and caring. I'd be alone without companionship or love.
Participant 4:	And how awful is that?
B.B.:	It feels terrible. I don't think I could stand it.
A.L.:	Only because you believe that you must be loved by someone significant all the time, otherwise you are not an OK person, which is baloney because there is no evidence to prove you are not OK. Even more important, it feels lousy to believe such a distortion of reality, and that's not good for you.
B.B.:	I know it's not doing me any good, but it only makes sense when I think about it here.
A.L.:	Exactly! The solution then is to learn how to continue to think accurately in other situations where you have been catastrophizing and making yourself miserable.
B.B.:	OK. So when I find myself getting anxious I can force myself to think clearly instead of upsetting myself. But sometimes it does feel awful.
A.L.:	Sure. First of all, you will not be able to control your irrational thinking completely (remember, you don't have to be perfect at this either), but you can get more and more control over the thoughts and worries which lead you to feel so anxious. What can you think to yourself that you know is true and will counter your catastrophizing about Henry?
B.B.:	Well, it's unlikely that Henry is displeased with me, but if he is and if he leaves me, I would be very unhappy, but I could live with it. It would not be awful. As I say that, I can feel that catastrophizing trying to creep in, but it's clear to me how different these thoughts are, and they *are* true. I just need to stick to them and not let the old worrying get in the way.
A.L.:	Exactly! To feel very sad to lose Henry makes sense, but you could live with that and it would not be the end of your world.

This case represents a complex combination of irrational beliefs which probably have a long history beginning in childhood. Barbara actually had several issues to work on: (1) her beliefs about herself as inadequate, (2) her resulting expectation that she would be judged inadequate and undesirable and would end up alone or in an unsatisfactory relationship, (3) her denial of herself as a source of support and caring, (4) her competitiveness for the attentions that are given out and her belief that she *needed* to be verified as OK regularly (the paradox here is that she often set it up to get negative attention, thus verifying her inadequacy), (5) her belief that she *should* be a better person and deserves to be miserable since she is not as good as she should be, and (6) her initial tendency to avoid facing her concerns because that would require admitting her inadequacies. The basic conflict is: I must be perfect and I am not; therefore, I will be rejected and deserve to be miserable, but I don't want to be miserable because it hurts.

In this transcript, we only worked on a portion of Barbara's issues, emphasizing her catastrophizing about being rejected for being inadequate. Another irrational assumption warranting restructuring is her belief that she must be charming, intelligent, and composed all the time or people will leave her. In fact, Barbara is a bright, personable, attractive woman, but, alas, she is not perfect.

Another conceptual approach that could facilitate valuable exploration of Barbara's belief system is a good script analysis from transactional analysis theory (Steiner, 1974). This process enables clients to identify ulterior messages communicated by significant persons to the client, particularly at an early, impressionable and vulnerable age, and emphasizes that the individual receiving the messages (e.g., "don't feel, go away, you are bad, don't exist, women/men are all bastards") actually makes a decision to believe those messages in order to survive and be safe. Although it can be a lengthy, speculative, and highly interpretive process, a well-directed therapist can utilize script analysis to identify important links between present irrational thinking (internal dialogues) and early decisions made about oneself, others, and situations. These connections can help clarify the areas of irrationality and make the restructuring easier.

Case Study

The following case example demonstrated a deeply embedded set of irrational beliefs which, being more pervasive, are more difficult to give up.

Jim Lowery is an architect who has been married for 5 years

to Susan, a botanist. They had been seeing a therapist for marriage counseling for about 3 months. Their presenting concerns were that Jim and Susan worked very hard, and each weekend it seemed they had to recreate their relationship since they were so out of touch during the week. This process had become more and more pronounced over the years. Both recognized the cycle, and they talked about it often, but no improvements resulted. Moreover, Jim seemed to be quite critical of Susan for being overly adaptive and for keeping a safe, low profile when he seemed annoyed about anything. Susan tended to fear his criticism and tried to act happy, avoid his criticism, and talk about something positive. Jim often expressed the belief that Susan would say loving, caring things to him only to keep things positive.

An exclusively behavioral approach might focus on increasing more direct communication between Jim and Susan and restructuring their time so that the weekends are not their only time together.

It would also be easy to presume that if they changed their styles (critical and adaptive) they would be happier together. This is a legitimate goal; however, the process of changing one's style varies with each theoretical model. This case example demonstrates how cognitive restructuring can be used in conjunction with a more developmental, psychodynamic approach to therapy. The focus of this segment of the session is on Jim.

A.L.:	Jim, you've agreed that you often become critical of Susan's behavior toward you. Tell Susan what it is that bothers you.
J.L.:	Well, you seem so afraid of my criticism that you act like you'll do or say anything just to avoid it. I feel manipulated.
S.L.:	I do worry about making you even madder. I know you say that bothers you, too, but it feels safer than speaking up.
A.L.:	Jim, when you get angry at Susan for being adaptive or trying to be so positive, what do you think to yourself?
J.L.:	I get really mad because she seems phony. I feel like I'm too powerful with her and that I can't trust what she's saying.
A.L.:	And what is it that's so very annoying about not being able to trust Susan?
J.L.:	Well, that's obvious, isn't it? We should be able to trust each other.
A.L.:	It would be better if you could. My concern is

that you understand what it is you want to be able to trust from Susan. What is it you would like to trust that her adaptiveness makes difficult to believe?

J.L.: (Pausing . . . responding with considerable feeling) I keep thinking of all the times when I believed that people didn't really like me. In high school, I was pretty popular, but I never had a really close friend or a girlfriend.

A.L.: When Susan acts adaptive, tell her what it is you don't trust.

J.L.: (Somewhat upset) I want to know that you really love me. That you really like me. Not because you're afraid of me, but because you just love me.

A.L.: And when you get angry with Susan, what's the anger about?

J.L.: (To Susan) I'm afraid you don't really care for me.

A.L.: So when Susan gets adaptive you are angry at her because she isn't showing you she really loves you, and you are afraid that she might not really care.

J.L.: Yes. I never really realized why I get so upset with her.

A.L.: Jim, it may also be true that you actually help the prophecy that you are not likeable to come true by being overly critical and not spending as much time together. It's also possible that when you do get honest caring you can find some way to distrust it or not value it. What do you think?

J.L.: It's really true. I can see that I do both. I just never fully realized what was behind it all, my wanting to know I'm really loved and worrying that I won't be.

A.L.: What *is* true about your likeableness?

J.L.: I haven't always been liked by people I wanted to like me, especially when I was younger. I expect people to probably not like me. I worry a lot about whether they do. And I tend to avoid situations where I might have to face a personal rejection.

A.L.:   What's *not* true?

J.L.:   I don't have to be rejected. I can handle it if it happens and things don't have to be the way they were. I can face it and not avoid it, or start getting critical of Susan to defend against what I think is a rejection. It's not awful if I do get rejected; it's worth the risk to go ahead and I don't have to protect myself by being critical.

A.L.:   OK, what could you think to yourself in one of these situations where you are wanting some indication that Susan really loves you?

J.L.:   (To Susan) I want to know you love me and, if you do, great. There is some chance that you don't, at least not all the time, and I can handle that. I can stay relaxed, and I don't have to be critical to defend myself.

A.L.:   Great. That's excellent thinking, Jim. Will you think those thoughts in specific situations with Susan this week?

J.L.:   Sure. It feels a lot better than what I've been doing.

A.L.:   Now, how would you like to act differently as you think these new thoughts?

This case example represents more complex dynamics. Those inclined toward hypothesizing motives and generating interpretations could generate elaborate conceptualizations to explain Jim's actions. In this cognitive-behavioral model, the primary issue was one of identifying the basic underlying beliefs prompting the dysfunctional behaviors. It would have been simple to presume Jim was too intolerant and that he irrationally always wanted things and people to be the way he wanted them to be, that he was full of "shoulds" about how people are to be. The therapist would then work toward Jim's giving up his perfectionist and critical thoughts and behaviors.

The art of cognitive restructuring is the ability to recognize what irrational beliefs are the basis of one's behavior and to challenge and change them. In this case, Jim's fear and expectation of not being liked prompted much of his behavior. It is exciting when the really critical issues are identified and challenged. Clients often become more alive and are able to understand their behaviors and the beliefs that support them so much more clearly. Such clarity greatly facilitates changing the undesired behaviors.

ALTERNATIVE COGNITIVE MODELS

There are a number of other cognitive or semantic therapies which have actually developed specific therapeutic approaches as well as conceptual models. Although this chapter does not permit elaboration of these therapies, they warrant investigation by the reader interested in this general approach. Of particular interest might be the work of Meichenbaum and his colleagues on stress inoculation (Meichenbaum & Cameron, 1972; Meichenbaum & Turk, 1976; Meichenbaum & Cameron, Note 1), Novaco (1975) on anger control, Maultsby & Ellis (1974) on rational-emotive imagery and disputing irrational beliefs, and Lazarus's multimodal therapy (1976). Of related interest are the areas of attribution theory and dissonance theory (Aronson, 1972; Festinger, 1957; Kopel & Arkowitz, 1975; Ross, Rodin, & Zimbardo, 1969; Valins & Nisbett, 1976).

BEHAVIORAL INTERVENTIONS

The cognitive restructuring stage of the total process should lead naturally into the development of behavioral responses. With the emphases on specific situations and clarifying and changing one's thinking, the most likely next step is to work toward behaving in some more desired manner in that situation. It is also worth noting that the cognitive stage is not purely cognitive. Meichenbaum (1977) points out that many behavioral principles (reinforcement, successive approximations, working in small segments, modeling, and rehearsal) are used to change one's cognitions in the restructuring process. Moreover, the new cognitions are continually being utilized by the client as the behavioral steps are carried out. The cognitive and behavioral aspects are intertwined in this process.

In order for group members to be efficient and effective when working on their own assertions and to participate in helping others in the group, the therapist might conduct several group exercises (Lange & Jakubowski, 1976) which not only focus on some aspect of assertiveness (e.g., making and refusing requests, expressing compliments), but also provide practice at some process skills (e.g., giving specific behavioral feedback, making suggestions for improvement, observing nonverbal behaviors). These exercises enable the therapists to coach group members to become more facilitative as they attempt to help each other. The examples of group member assistance in the case examples presented above are quite functional, but not at all unusual after some coaching.

As the group members begin to work on specific changes in

specific situations, the emphasis is on ultimately behaving more effectively. Behavioral techniques which can be applied at this point have been more elaborately described elsewhere (Bandura, 1969; Cotler & Guerra, 1976; Malott, 1972; Rimm & Masters, 1974; Watson & Tharp, 1972). The behavioral techniques most often utilized in this model are behavior rehearsal and contingency contracting. In the behavior rehearsal process, the client specifies behavioral goals not in terms of outcomes or others' behaviors, but in terms of client behaviors. For example, Bob in the first case example might want his father-in-law to treat him with respect or he might want a peaceful dinner, but he would have to specify his own desired behaviors in order to begin the behavioral process. These goals are changeable (and usually do change as the process goes on), but the focus is on the client's behaviors. For example, Bob first said he wanted to be able to explain his behavior without being overly defensive and shortly later decided that what he really wanted to do was to assertively state that he did not want to discuss the matter at all and to ask his father-in-law to stop raising the subject. This stage of goal clarification is extremely important. Particularly in matters involving assertiveness, a client might be assertively practicing asking a question ("What do you want to do tonight, John?"), when he would rather be expressing a preference and a request ("I'd like to go to the movies; would you like to go with me?"). The only way to find out what the client does want is to ask and to check periodically that *what* he is doing feels right, as well as *how* he's doing it. It is OK for the therapist to make suggestions for a particular mode of response, but the client makes the decisions.

After clarifying one's goals and desired behaviors, stimulus persons are then sought from among the group members to play the roles of others in the situation, and they are coached by the client in how to act. The client then sets up the situation and practices a brief interaction with the stimulus people, who are told to be cooperative the first time around (sometimes it's hard enough just to get the words out without having to handle a difficult reaction). The interaction is kept brief: (1) to prevent it from getting to a point where the client cannot handle it and it becomes a negative experience, and (2) to allow for accurate and manageable assessment. The first question goes to the client: What did you like about what you did and how you did it? Question 1 is very important since most people focus heavily on the negative to the exclusion of what they could continue to do and feel good about. The therapist should get a full answer to the first question and keep asking until the client cannot identify any more things he liked. Then the group members are asked to state what they liked *in behaviorally specific terms* (statements like "I knew you were sincere" are complimentary but warrant description, e.g., "Your voice was serious yet firm and your face looked relaxed"). No negative statements are to be entertained.

The therapist then asks the client for suggestions for improvement (not things he didn't like). This takes into account the undesired behaviors but puts them in the context of substituting alternatives for improvement (e.g., "I'd like to make more direct eye contact, and I'd like to state my preference more clearly and briefly"). Clients are urged not to work on more than three changes at a time; if more than three changes are desired, the group is asked for suggestions about which three should take priority. Again, the client makes the final decisions (although the therapist should not support behaviors which in her judgment are clearly self-destructive or self-defeating). The client then practices the situation, and the assessment process is repeated. The client can have the stimulus people escalate the situation by being obstreperous or dysfunctional in various ways, and the length of the interaction can be extended. The rehearsal should end when the client feels ready to do it and wishes to stop.

The processing of a rehearsal can be aided in several ways through the use of videotape playback. First, the asserter can analyze her own behavior more clearly when actually seeing those behaviors in retrospect. Habitual, almost unconscious, behaviors are more strikingly revealed when seen on videotape than when described by others. Moreover, the opportunity for self-analysis is increased. Second, the therapist might employ a modification of Kagan's Interpersonal Process Recall (1975), whereby the asserter can stop the tape and explore how she was feeling at that point, what thoughts she was having about herself or the others in the situation, or what judgments she was making about her efforts to be effective. Third, replaying an initial rehearsal and then immediately replaying the final rehearsal is often a striking example to group members of how much they can change toward greater interpersonal effectiveness. The therapist might also ask the client to try out the new behaviors and to report back at the next session.

Case Study

Claire Larson, a secretary for an academic dean at a large, midwestern university, wanted to be more confident and not to let others "push her around." In fact, she seldom expressed her opinions, feelings, or preferences and had gotten in the protective habit of not thinking about much of anything. She seemed bored and dissatisfied with herself and her present world. She successfully avoided many situations which she defined as threatening and scary.

In this case example, the behavioral procedure will be demonstrated. It is presumed that Claire has just completed some cognitive restructuring to reduce her anxiety and her tendency to withdraw. She chose to work toward being able to tell her boss, the dean, some things she did not want to do for him, but which he had come to expect her to do. She substituted such cognitions as: it is all right for me to say what I would like; it is not easier to avoid; I can handle this situation without getting overly upset; I can live with his displeasure should that happen; it's OK for me to have preferences.

Specifically, Claire wanted to stop getting the dean's lunch for him on her own lunch hour since it was often an inconvenience and it cut into her own time. There were several other instances in which the dean expected Claire to do tasks she believed were not appropriate to her job. She decided that rather than do them and later to get angry with him and with herself, she wanted to express her preference to not do them. She chose the lunch issue as a specific undesired task (particularly since she sometimes bent over backward and even refused to accept reimbursement for the dean's food). Rather than wait until the next time he asked, Claire decided she would raise the issue herself at a neutral time.

A.L.:	What is it you would like to see happen with your boss?
C.L.:	I'd like him to stop asking me to get him his lunch during my own lunch time.
A.L.:	OK, and what do you want to do to see that happen?
C.L.:	Well, I want to stop avoiding the situation and tell him what I think. (At this point Claire chose another group member to play the role of the dean, set up a physical arrangement which approximated the way they would really be, and began a brief practice of initiating the conversation.)
A.L.:	Without a whole lot of preparation, go ahead and initiate this conversation. Bob (playing the role of the dean), be cooperative this first time.
C.L.:	(To her "boss") "Uh, Dr. Haynes, uh, I'm sorry to bother you, but is it OK if I ask you something for a minute?"
Boss:	"Yes, come in. What is it?"

C.L.:   "Well, I don't think I should have to be your maid. I mean I think you treat me like I'm a servant, and I don't have to take it."

Boss: "Well, I didn't know you felt that way."

A.L.:   OK. Stop. Claire, what did you like about what you did and said?

C.L.:   Well, I liked that I did it at all. I got right to the issue when he asked me what I wanted. I didn't fall apart.

Participant 1:   Claire, your voice was clear and loud enough. You sat down and looked physically comfortable.

Participant 2:   You smiled pleasantly when you went in and then looked serious when you began to tell him what bothered you.

A.L.:   Claire, what would you like to do differently?

C.L.:   I thought I got to it, but I want to be more specific about what the problem is. I also thought I was sarcastic and defensive. I'd like to be more factual and not try to put him down indirectly. That's all I can think of.

A.L.:   Does anyone have a suggestion for Claire as to how she might respond more effectively?

Participant 3:   Claire, what if you started the discussion by telling him you would like to talk with him and asking to do it now, instead of being apologetic and giving him so much power?

C.L.:   Yes, I like that. I did feel like I was being overly hesitant the first time.

A.L.:   OK. Let's try it one more time, but first what are the three things you are going to work on?

C.L.:   I'm going to be more specific, less sarcastic and defensive, and I'm going to ask to talk with him more directly.

A.L.:   Great. Try it once more.

C.L.:   "Dean Haynes, I'd like to talk with you about something, can we do that now?"

Boss: "Sure, come on in. What is it?"

C.L.:   "When you ask me to get lunch for you on my own lunch time, it's often a real inconvenience and I'd prefer not to do that."

Boss: "Well, it's certainly a help to me since I'm often unable to do it myself."

C.L.:   "I can appreciate that but, when I do that for

	you, it takes away from my own lunch time. I would be willing to help you, but I'd rather do it on work time and take my full lunch."
A.L.:	Stop. That was excellent! What did you like particularly about the three changes.
C.L.:	Well, it felt really good. I started more directly, and I wasn't defensive even when he said it was such a big convenience to him. I got right to the issue.
A.L.:	You sure did. You changed quite a lot. What else did others like?
Participant 2:	Your voice was serious, yet pleasant. Not at all defensive.
Participant 3:	You looked more relaxed facially, yet you sounded like you meant what you said.
A.L.:	What would you like to do differently?
C.L.:	(Pause) I feel pretty good about it now. I would like to do it with the dean being more uncooperative and have him act like I should do these things.
A.L.:	Fine. Does anyone else have any suggestions?
Group:	No.
A.L.:	OK. Let's try escalating the situation with the boss being more defensive.

This case represents the steps in the behavior rehearsal process:

(1) Specify the situation.
(2) Specify the outcome goals and the goals for oneself.
(3) Set up the situation.
(4) Practice a small segment.
(5) Identify what the rehearser liked, then what others liked.
(6) Generate suggestions for change from the rehearser, then from others (never more than a total of three).
(7) Practice again and assess again with possible escalations by the role player ("the boss") and gradually lengthen the interaction.

It is important to note that this situation may not be a major event in one's life; however, for Claire to behave more affirmatively in this situation is a measurable move toward being more powerful and more confident.

When setting specific behavioral goals, the consequences of those actions are important considerations. When considering a particular behavior, the likely consequences may lead one to decide that, although that behavior is legitimate, the consequences might be more than one is willing to endure. Thus, one might choose not to carry out a particular behavior. For example, if Claire's boss is a particularly punitive and defensive person, she may choose not to express her concern because she might be fired from a position she needs. Most importantly, however, her decision would be based on a reasonable assessment of the likely consequences of her behavior, not a fear of asserting herself. On the other hand, many people rationalize their avoidances by convincing themselves that their assertions would do no good or fall on deaf ears. Accurate consideration of likely consequences is an important component in setting behavior changes.

The behavioral process is quite structured and is designed to enable the rehearser to improve gradually and to have the process of change be a positive and successful experience. Since some behavior changes involve larger increases in one's behavioral repertoire, a long-range plan including contingency reinforcers can be employed. This process has been articulated elsewhere (Jakubowski & Lange, 1978; Malott, 1972; Watson & Tharp, 1972) and fits nicely into the cognitive-behavioral approach. Clients can develop contingency contracts for changing cognitions as well as behaviors. For example, one client wanted to be able to approach and initiate a conversation with women he found attractive. His conversational skills were, in fact, quite good although he did practice a few new ones. The primary cause of his avoidance was catastrophic thinking in which he imagined what he would do when such an opportunity presented itself. Consequently, he set up a contingency plan which included a hierarchy of behaviors and situations which successively approximated the desired target behavior. He also planned a series of rewards each time he successfully completed a step in the behavioral plan. He began by simply saying hello to much older men and women. More uniquely, however, he also set up a series of coping thoughts he would think to himself in each situation and rewarded himself every time he managed to think those thoughts consistently in that situation. In fact, he reported that the systematic attention to changing his cognitions seemed more valuable toward reducing his anxiety and freeing him up to utilize the conversational skills he already had.

Basically, contingency contracting involves: (1) careful specification of desired behavior changes, (2) often the use of successive approximations and hierarchies toward approaching that behavior, (3) the use of reinforcers for successful accomplishment of each step toward the goal, and (4) a systematic monitoring of progress with appropriate adjustments of the plan.

COGNITIVE-BEHAVIORAL ASSERTION TRAINING

Differences and similarities exist between cognitive-behavioral therapy and cognitive-behavioral assertion training in terms of process and content. Differences in process are:

(1) Assertion groups typically include more information giving, particularly regarding issues like personal rights; discrimination between unassertive, assertive, and aggressive responses; the impact of nonverbal behaviors; and learning specific types of responses, like "I-messages" (specifying the undesired behavior someone else is doing, citing the consequences to you, and expressing how you feel about it in an appropriate, nonhostile manner) or "empathic" assertions (expressing understanding of another's position and being assertive as well, e.g., "I know that you're in a hurry, but I don't want to make this decision quickly").

(2) Assertion groups tend to be more structured in that they include more exercises for all participants, at least in the initial stages.

(3) There tends to be more interaction among group members in a therapy group, although in both groups the primary interactions are between the leader and the person working (excluding the behavior rehearsals).

(4) In assertion groups, members tend to begin and end together and the group is of relatively short duration (6 to 8 weeks); in the therapy group, people leave when they are done working and new people are added.

Differences in the content are:

(1) In assertion groups, the focus is exclusively on improving interpersonal behavior (recognizing that there are cognitive, affective, and behavioral elements to be dealt with toward this end). In a therapy group, other, more intrapsychic issues are also appropriate, such as: decision making; how one treats oneself; developing control of feelings of stress, anxiety, anger, frustration, guilt, and depression that are not completely interpersonally based; avoidance and phobic reactions; and self-destructive behaviors.

(2) In a therapy group, more attention is given to in-group behavior, although the primary emphasis is still on specific, out-of-group situations.

(3) Clients are often referred to therapy groups when they have heavier investments in holding on to their self-defeating thoughts, feelings, and behaviors. Often the pervasiveness,

      intensity, and tenacity of one's concerns are the criteria for determining the most appropriate intervention. Moreover, assertion training is often employed as an adjunct to longer-term group therapy.

(4) Other therapeutic interventions are more easily integrated into therapy groups because they are somewhat less structured, are not time limited, and are somewhat less educational in nature.

(5) In therapy groups, the whole cognitive-behavioral process is not always employed; that is, if a concern is fairly complex, the therapist might only do cognitive restructuring with the client and not feel obliged to get to behavior rehearsals with every client in every session. In an assertion group with a heavier emphasis on handling specific interpersonal situations more assertively, behavioral practice is an important component.

    Both therapy groups and assertion groups can utilize cognitive and behavioral principles, conceptualizations, and procedures. A primary emphasis is on specifying the manifestations of the client's problems and citing contexts. For example, if a person reports having a poor self-image, the first step is to identify how that poor self-image manifests itself (e.g., by avoiding talking with people, sleeping 12 hours a day, excessive drinking, self-defeating thoughts), in what contexts (at parties, with spouse, sexually, at work), and in what specific incidents (last night at the dinner table, today at work). Both interventions focus primarily on direct change of thoughts, feelings, and behaviors in the real and present world. The case examples presented to this point actually could have occurred in either a therapy group or an assertion group.

    The cognitive-behavioral assertion training model is a four-stage process involving: (1) identification of personal rights, (2) discrimination between unassertive, assertive, and aggressive behaviors, (3) cognitive restructuring, and (4) behavior rehearsal (Lange & Jakubowski, 1976; Lange, Rimm, & Loxley, 1975). The group typically last 6 to 8 weeks and includes four basic formats: brief didactic presentations, modeling and demonstrations, practice, and assessment. A variety of exercises are employed during the initial sessions of the group to enable participants to begin with common experiences which focus on some aspect of assertiveness and also to prepare the group members to do the cognitive restructuring and behavior rehearsals of specific real situations in later sessions. Typically, when working with a group member on a specific assertion situation, it takes about 20 to 30 minutes to go through the entire process. Many situations take even less time. The optimal group arrangement is to have 10 to 12 group members with 2 leaders. When the group works on specific situations, it can be split into 2 groups of 5 or 6 so that most people can work in every session. If the leaders have the time, they might also train the group members to coach each other in triads (Flowers & Guerra, 1974).

The concept of *responsible* assertive behavior is a major emphasis within this four-stage model. Much of the literature on assertiveness stresses being able to get what one wants. Such a goal is clearly legitimate and is usually a part of assertion situations. However, in many situations, particularly those that are ongoing or more intimate, a second goal is of equal importance: being able to express oneself in a manner which maintains a high regard for one's own personal rights *and* the rights of others, particularly for respect.

During the course of an assertion group, participants may only work on three or four personal situations. The primary emphasis is on teaching the group members the cognitive and behavioral self-help skills they can apply themselves in their daily lives. Participants thus may make several specific changes by the end of the group, but they will also have learned how to assess themselves, how to determine what they would like to be doing, how to identify and change those things which get in the way of the desired responses, and how to try out and evaluate efforts to accomplish the desired changes. Although many participants report significant increases in assertiveness before the completion of the group, the continued application of the knowledge gained is essential. Completing an assertion group is actually the beginning of the change process.

SUMMARY

Cognitive-behavioral therapy places great importance on learning coping skills which clients can employ in specific situations. Thus, the therapeutic intervention consists of more than insights on increasing one's behavioral repertoire. The very procedures experienced in therapy can be carried out by clients for themselves.

Further improvements in this therapeutic approach might focus on: (1) what specific interventions work best to modify what types of irrational or self-defeating thinking and why, (2) how do individuals come to develop specific belief systems and internal dialogues, (3) how does one's internal dialogue influence one's behaviors and feelings, (4) what new conceptualizations for thinking styles can be developed and how can they be integrated with behavioral changes.

The cognitive-behavioral approach is receiving increasing attention clinically and experimentally, and the marriage of cognitive and behavioral therapies may yield an exciting intervention utilizing the best aspects of both approaches.

REFERENCE NOTES

1. Meichenbaum, D. H., & Cameron, R. *Stress inoculation: A skills-training approach to anxiety management.* Unpublished manuscript, University of Waterloo.

REFERENCES

Aronson, E. *The social animal.* San Francisco: W. H. Freeman & Co., 1972.

Bandura, A. *Principles of behavior modification.* New York: Holt, Rinehart, & Winston, 1969.

Beck, A. *Cognitive therapy and emotional disorders.* New York: International Universities Press, 1976.

Cotler, S. B., & Guerra, J. J. *Assertion training.* Champaign, Ill.: Research Press, 1976.

Ellis, A. *Growth through reason.* Palo Alto, Cal.: Science and Behavior Books, 1971.

Ellis, A. *Humanistic psychotherapy: The rational-emotive approach.* New York: McGraw-Hill Paperbacks, 1974.

Ellis, A., & Grieger, R. *The handbook of rational-emotive therapy.* New York: Springer, 1978.

Ellis, A., & Harper, R. *A new guide to rational living.* Englewood Cliffs, N.J.: Prentice-Hall, 1975.

Festinger, L. *A theory of cognitive dissonance.* Stanford, Cal.: Stanford University Press, 1957.

Flowers, J., & Guerra, J. The use of client-coaching in assertion training with large groups. *Journal of Community Mental Health,* 1974, *10,* 414–417.

Jakubowski, P., & Lange, A. *The assertive option.* Champaign, Ill.: Research Press, 1978.

Kagan, N. *Interpersonal Process Recall: A method of influencing human interaction.* East Lansing, Mich.: Michigan State University, 1975.

Kanfer, F., & Goldstein, A. (Eds.). *Helping people change.* New York: Pergamon Press, 1975.

Kelley, G. A. *The psychology of personal constructs.* New York: Norton, 1955.

Kopel, S. A., & Arkowitz, H. The role of attribution and self-perception in behavior change: Implications for behavior therapy. *General Psychology Monographs,* 1975, *92,* 175–212.

Lange, A. J. Cognitive-behavioral assertion training. In A. Ellis & R. Grieger (Eds.), *Handbook of rational emotive therapy.* New York: Springer, 1977.

Lange, A. J., & Jakubowski, P. *Responsible assertive behavior: Cognitive-behavioral procedures for trainers.* Champaign, Ill.: Research Press, 1976.

Lange, A. J., & Jakubowski, P. *Responsible assertion: A model for personal growth.* Champaign, Ill.: Research Press, 1978. (A demonstration film directed by Norman Baxley).

Lange, A. J., Rimm, D. C., & Loxley, J. C. Cognitive and behavioral procedures for group assertion training. *The Counseling Psychologist,* 1975, *5,* 37–41.

Lazarus, A. *Multi-modal behavior therapy.* New York: Springer, 1976.

Mahoney, M. *Cognition and behavior modification.* Cambridge, Mass.: Ballinger, 1974.

Mahoney, M. Reflections on the cognitive-learning trend in psychotherapy. *American Psychologist,* 1977, *32,* 5–13.

Malott, R. *Contingency management.* Kalamazoo, Mich.: Behaviordelia, Inc., 1972.

Maultsby, M. C., Jr., & Ellis, A. *Technique for using rational-emotive imagery (R.E.I.).* New York: Institute for Rational Living, 1974.

Meichenbaum, D. H. *Cognitive-behavior modification: An integrative approach.* New York: Plenum, 1977.

Meichenbaum, D. H., & Turk, D. The cognitive-behavioral management of anxiety, anger, and pain. In P. O. Davidson (Ed.), *The behavioral management of anxiety, depression, and pain.* New York: Bruner/Mazel, 1976.

Novaco, R. W. *Anger control: The development and evaluation of an experimental treatment.* Lexington, Mass.: Heath & Co., 1975.

Phillips, E. L. *Psychotherapy: A modern theory and practice.* Englewood Cliffs, N.J.: Prentice-Hall, 1956.

Raimy, V. *Misunderstandings of the self.* San Francisco: Jossey-Bass, 1975.

Rimm, D. C., & Masters, J. C., *Behavior therapy: Techniques and empirical findings.* New York: Academic Press, 1974.

Ross, L., Rodin, J., & Zimbardo, P. Toward an attribution therapy: The reduction of fear through induced cognitive-emotional misattribution. *Journal of Personality and Social Psychology,* 1969, *12,* 279–288.

Salter, A. *Conditioned reflex therapy.* New York: Farrar, Straus, & Giroux, 1949.

Steiner, C. *Scripts people live.* New York: Bantam, 1974.

Valins, S., & Nisbett, R. Attribution processes in the development and treatment of emotional disorders. In J. Spence, R. Carson, & J. Thibaut (Eds.), *Behavioral approaches to therapy.* Morristown, N.J.: General Learning Press, 1976.

Watson, D., & Tharp, R. *Self-directed behavior.* Monterey, Cal.: Brooks/Cole Publishing Co., 1972.

Chapter 8

Behavioral Group Therapy with Adolescents: A Review and Pilot Program

Carl Schrader

Abstract

The literature on adolescent behavioral group therapy is reviewed, focusing on target problems selected for modification, behavioral techniques employed, significant problems encountered in treatment, and the effectiveness of this treatment modality. In general, while the literature indicates that behavioral group strategies hold promise for dealing with problems of juvenile delinquency, psychiatric maladjustment, drug abuse, and vocational indecisiveness, little systematic, methodologically sound evaluation research has been performed. Techniques such as modeling, role playing, behavior rehearsal, and peer feedback are used extensively. However, research is scanty on the relative effectiveness of these procedures. In an attempt to answer some of the unresolved questions in adolescent behavioral group therapy, a pilot program was designed and components of the program discussed. Specifically, session-by-session outlines of an assertiveness training, problem solving, and prevocational group are presented along with preliminary evaluation data.*

*The funding for the paper and for the Project Entry Program comes from a grant from the National Institute of Drug Abuse #81 DA01817-02. The author wishes to thank Athan Karras, Jeffrey Long, Carol Panzer, Richard Kornblath, Donna Gillet, Dennis Wagner, and Sandra Brandon for their assistance in the design of the Project Entry program and the preparation of this manuscript.

INTRODUCTION

This chapter reviews the literature on the use of behavioral techniques in a group setting with adolescent populations. A number of general areas will be explored including: the range of adolescent behaviors which have been selected for modification, the group techniques employed and their effectiveness, the problems inherent in working with adolescent in groups, and the future of adolescent group therapy. In addition, preliminary data from a behaviorally oriented adolescent day treatment program designed by the author and colleagues and featuring a number of groups of workshops will be presented.

Behavior modification techniques have been applied extensively to the problems of the individual adolescent. Excellent reviews are available detailing the treatment techniques employed with: juvenile delinquents (Braukmann & Fixsen, 1975; Burchard, Harrig, Miller, & Armour, 1976), drug abusers (Callner, 1975), disruptive students and underachievers (Drabman, 1976; O'Leary, 1977), and severe conduct disordered adolescents (Patterson, 1974; Tharp & Wetzel, 1969). The adolescent's interaction with his parents has also been a fertile research area, with numerous studies exploring the effectiveness of contingency contracting approaches (Blechman, Olsen, & Turner, 1976; Stuart, 1971; Stuart & Lott, 1972; Weathers & Liberman, 1975a, 1975b) and negotiation skills training (Kifer, Lewis, Green, & Phillips, 1974; Schrader, Panzer, Long, Gillet, & Kornblath, Note 1).

Despite the proliferation of studies on the effectiveness of behavioral techniques with individual adolescents, relatively few studies attempt to investigate the potential effectiveness of group approaches in the modification of selected target behaviors. This is, indeed, a curious oversight since the empirical basis for behavioral group therapy appears derivable both from fundamental behavioral principles and the literature on the effectiveness of groups in general. The most obvious advantages of such an approach include: the presence of a situation in which behavior can be observed and monitored; the possibility of greater generalization of behaviors learned in the group; the availability of peer prompting and reinforcement of the performance of target behaviors; the opportunity to employ modeling and behavior rehearsal techniques to teach specific skills in settings similar to those the client will experience in real life; and the opportunity for the client to receive feedback on his performance from someone other than a therapist whose opinion may be discounted.

THE GROUP PROCESS

The behavioral group studies which do exist can be broadly classified into two categories—studies which investigate ways to improve the group process itself and studies which investigate the actual content of the group sessions and the effect of the material discussed on the performance of specific target behaviors. More simply put, studies which fall into the first category are concerned with the question of how the group functions, while those in the second category address the question of what the group attempts to teach.

The studies which deal with group process have primarily focused on the verbal performance of group members. Operant techniques of reinforcement, both verbal and material, have been employed to: increase the frequency of group verbalizations (Carpenter & Caron, 1968; Hauserman, Zweback, & Plotkin, 1972), increase the frequency of self-disclosing statements (Abudabbah, Prandoni, & Jensen, 1972), and to reduce irrelevant or off-task verbalizations (Williams & Blanton, 1968). Typically these studies employ tokens and praise to reinforce appropriate responses.

Both individual and group contingencies have also been employed to manipulate the group process. In the case of individual contingencies, each group member is reinforced for reaching an agreed upon standard of performance, e.g., a certain number of self-disclosing statements or the absence of disruptive behavior within the group. Reinforcement usually comes in the form of tokens or points which are exchangeable for material goods or privileges. The success of individual contingencies depends upon an accurate assessment of each client's level of performance and the setting of performance standards which are within the client's reach. In this way, the technique of shaping may be employed to gradually increase desired performance without undue frustration or loss of reinforcement for the group member.

In contrast to individual contingencies which treat all group members as individuals, group contingencies refer to contingencies in which the criterion for reinforcement is based upon the performance of the group as a whole. The behaviors of all individuals are considered as a unit, and the group receives reinforcement only if the unit reaches an agreed-upon standard. In a variation of this procedure, the performance of select individuals serves as the criterion for reinforcement for the entire group. While group contingencies have been used with children in a classroom setting (Drabman, Spitalnik, R., & Spitalnik, K., 1974; Hamblin, Hathaway, & Wodarski, 1974; Litow & Pumroy, 1975) and psychiatric patients (Greenberg, Scott, Pisa, & Friesen, 1975), no examples of group contingencies were found in reviewing the adolescent group therapy literature.

In addition to individual and group contingencies, some researchers have investigated the utility of behavioral contracts in facilitating the group process. Behavioral contracting refers to a procedure in which both the client and counselor enter into an agreement for the reciprocal exchange of specified behaviors. In the group setting, clients can contract to: increase attendance and participation (Bardill, 1972), complete homework assignments (Schinke & Rose, 1976), reduce disruptive behavior (Jesness & DeRisi, 1973), and increase positive self-statements (Brown & Kingsley, 1975). The contract spells out the reinforcement that can be expected for engaging in the specified behaviors and, therefore, is a clear statement to the adolescent of the contingencies which are in effect. Given the "mixed messages" that many adolescents receive in other situations, most notably the home, the contract has obvious therapeutic advantages.

GROUP CONTENT

As indicated above, early studies of behavioral techniques in group therapy focus on the group process. It was felt that, by using operant techniques to increase group participation, conventional group therapy techniques and discussions could be enhanced (Bardill, 1972). Recently, however, behavior modifiers have been focusing on the content of the group itself, i.e., just what gets talked about in the group, what information is disseminated among group members, and what goals the group is trying to reach. Specific problem areas have been identified and groups have been designed to teach clients the skills they need to function effectively. With an adolescent population, skill training groups which have been reported include: social skills training (Sarason & Ganzer, 1973), self-control training (Cheek, 1972); decision-making and problem-solving training (Jones, 1976; Platt, Spivack, Altman, N., Altman, D., & Peizer, 1974); prevocational skills training (Barbee & Keil, 1973); career decision making (Bergland, Quatrano, & Lundquist, 1975; Birk, 1976); and training in appropriate assertiveness (Merritt & Walley, 1977). These groups tend to be highly structured, short-term, and problem-oriented. A fuller discussion of the content of some of these groups will follow when we examine group work with specific problem behaviors.

GROUP TECHNIQUES

Behavioral group techniques with adolescents are quite similar to those used with adults as enumerated by Frankel and Glasser (1974) and by Rose (1977). With adolescents, as one might expect, there appears to be more of an emphasis on contracting and individual contingencies than is the case with adult groups. However, a variety of techniques have been used with or could easily be applied to adolescent groups. A number of these techniques are discussed below.

Modeling

Although modeling has been shown to be a powerful and efficient approach for changing behavior in the laboratory (Bandura, 1969), few experimental analyses of the modeling phenomenon exist in the adolescent literature. Sarason & Ganzer (1973) investigated the effectiveness of modeling procedures compared to traditional group discussion approaches with juvenile delinquents. Youths acted out scripts which demonstrated appropriate behavior in problem situations, while other group members observed and summarized the main points of the scripts. This approach was found to be highly effective when compared to the group discussion method. The clinical use of modeling in adolescent groups is, no doubt, quite widespread although the experimental evidence of its effectiveness is scanty. Modeling appears to be the fundamental basis for some of the more complex procedures described below and, as such, deserves more empirical investigation with this population.

Behavior Rehearsal

The set of behaviors classified under the label "behavior rehearsal" appear to be varied and, as yet, nonstandardized. Behavior rehearsal can be seen as systematic role playing (Frankel & Glasser, 1974). The goal of behavior rehearsal is to enable clients to learn and to practice new behaviors in a therapeutic situation. The sequence of training is usually: (1) instructions (from therapist or other group members), (2) modeling of appropriate behavior, (3) client rehearsal of new behavior, and (4) feedback from other group members on the client's performance. Reports on the successful use of behavior rehearsal with adolescents include those of: Hedquist and Weinhold (1970), who worked with unassertive college freshmen; Cheek (1972), who employed behavior rehearsal with adolescent drug addicts; Anderson, Fodor, and Alpert (1976), who used it with disruptive adolescents as a method of teaching self-control; and Birk (1976), who worked with high school women to promote career exploration. Although used extensively, few comparative studies exist demonstrating the superiority of behavior rehearsal over various "discussion" techniques. Anderson et al. (1976) found a behavior rehearsal group to be superior to a traditional therapy group with disruptive adolescent boys. Likewise, Friedman (1972) provided empirical support for the effectiveness of a modeling, role-playing approach when compared to a group discussion control. Part of the difficulty in undertaking research with behavior rehearsal is the complexity of the procedure. Little standardization in techniques presently exists, and difficulties in evaluation will continue as long as the technique remains poorly defined.

Structured Exercises

Many investigators have employed a structured exercise format, at least in part, to teach specific skills. Lange & Jakubowski (1976) detail a number of exercises that can be employed in assertiveness training groups, and Merritt & Walley (1977) describe some of these techniques (e.g., giving and receiving compliments, introducing oneself, the trust circle) as they are used with adolescents. Platt, Spivack, & Swift (Note 2) in their problem-solving manual for use in group therapy present a number of exercises useful for teaching adolescents to solve problems. Birk (1976) discusses structured group exercises useful for helping adolescents explore career goals. Structured exercises with this population appear to be valuable in that they gain attention and can, indeed, be fun for participants, a fact which might increase both attendance and participation. Research into the comparative effectiveness of the structured exercise technique is lacking at the present time, but it certainly appears to be a worthwhile area for further study.

The Buddy System

Often it is difficult to assure generalization of treatment effects from the group setting to outside situations. One method employed to enhance generalization has been to pair each group member with another member or "buddy" who can monitor, teach, and reinforce newly learned behaviors. Rose (1969, 1977) has employed the buddy techniques with adult groups, while Fo and O'Donnell (1974) used a buddy approach with adolescent delinquents. Both investigators report success using this approach, but a great deal more research is needed. Employing a buddy system in groups to facilitate communication and learning in group sessions, as well as generalization of learned behavior to extragroup settings, appears to be a feasible treatment technique deserving of further attention.

Peer Counseling

Using peers as counselors is another poorly researched area in the adolescent therapy literature. Few evaluative studies exist comparing this form of counseling with more traditional, professionally led groups. Varenhorst (1976) describes a peer counseling program with high school students designed to help clients overcome problems with families, school relationships, and peer interactions. Although no systematic data have been collected, self-reports and behavioral observation of clients appear to demonstrate some effectiveness of this technique. Using fellow group members as co-leaders in groups seems to be a potentially effective variation of the peer counseling technique which, likewise, could be investigated under controlled conditions.

GROUP APPROACHES WITH SPECIFIC PROBLEM BEHAVIORS

Juvenile Delinquency

Delinquent behavior has received a great deal of attention in the adolescent behavioral literature. Reviews by Davidson and Seidman (1974) and Stumphauzer (1973, 1976) report the successful application of behavioral techniques to the problems of delinquent youth. The widespread use of contingency contracting and token reinforcement procedures in schools, institutions, and group homes attests to the popularity of the behavioral approach with this population.

Despite the extensive use of behavioral techniques with individual delinquents, group approaches are less well represented in the literature. Those studies which do exist rely primarily on modeling, role playing, and peer reinforcement in groups to effect therapeutic change. For example, Stumphauzer (1974) developed a "behavioral psychodrama" format in which a 10-step procedure is followed to teach appropriate behavior. Instructions, modeling, rehearsal, peer feedback and reinforcement, and encouragement to practice learned behaviors outside the group appear to be the active components in the treatment process. Sarason and Ganzer (Note 3) constructed a series of role-playing scripts which deal with problems faced by an institutionalized delinquent population (e.g., coping with authority figures, resisting negative peer pressure, handling anger). Clients enact the scenes which show both appropriate and inappropriate methods of dealing with the problem situations.

A comparison between the treated delinquents and nontreated counterparts indicated the superiority of the role-playing techniques, as measured by recidivism rates and scores on various paper-and-pencil tests of self-concept. In a variation of the role-playing technique, Kaufman and Wagner (1972) developed the "barb" technique to be used with adolescents on a group or individual basis. In this procedure, adolescents are given verbal and physical cues that would normally elicit aggression and were trained to make alternative responses. Reports from staff members on the unit indicated a decreased incidence of aggressive outbursts.

By far the most ambitious attempt to modify delinquent behavior on a large scale is represented in the work of E. L. Phillips (1968) and E. L. Phillips, E. Phillips, Fixsen, and Wolf (1974) at Achievement Place. Using ABA and multiple-baseline designs, these investigators have demonstrated convincing success in improving social behavior, self-governing skills, self-help skills, academic performance, and prosocial behavior. While much of the training is done individually, the youths live in a community and therefore are subject to group influence and control. The use of the family conference as a problem-solving forum and as a vehicle through which to teach appropriate interaction skills makes this group an important component of the Achievement Place program. The existence of a self-governing body of clients and the development of the peer program also involve skill development and feedback.

In other studies with delinquents in groups, Shoemaker (Note 4) employed group assertive training techniques with delinquents with an emphasis on standing up for legitimate rights assertively rather than aggressively. Fodor (1972) employed negative verbal feedback from staff in a group setting to decrease the frequency of runaway behavior in eight adolescent girls.

Drug Abuse

Studies of behavioral group interventions with drug-abusing adolescents are scanty. Most studies which are reported deal with hard-core drug abusers and involve residential treatment programs employing aversive conditioning and skill-training to teach alternative behaviors (Coghlan, Gold, Dohrenwend, & Zimmerman, 1973; Copeman, Note 5). The most comprehensive behavioral treatment program for hard-core adolescent and young adult drug abusers has been developed by Cheek (1972). Cheek, working with heroin, methadone, and barbiturate addicts, developed a self-control treatment program for use in a group setting. The program teaches clients anxiety management via relaxation and systematic desensitization, assertiveness skills, problem-solving skills, and positive self-imagery. Data obtained from this population indicate that this treatment is more effective than traditional group approaches to the problem (Cheek, Tomarchio, Standen, & Albahary, 1973).

Studies with adolescents who abuse nonaddicting drugs (e.g., marijuana, phencyclidine) are extremely rare. Warner and Swisher (1976) developed a program for "soft" drug abusers which focused on affective, behavioral, and cognitive attitudes toward drugs. The program, which consisted of six 1-hour group counseling sessions, stressed alternatives to drug abuse, consequences of drug usage, and reinforcement of behaviors incompatible with drug taking. While no objective long-term follow-up studies of any of the participants in the groups have as yet been carried out, preliminary data on attitudes toward drugs and self-reported drug use indicate changes in a positive direction (Swisher, Warner, & Herr, 1972).

Many of the studies cited earlier with delinquents usually add a drug abuse component to the treatment program. Sarason and Ganzer (Note 3) include a script on refusing peer pressure to "turn on." Stumphauzer's (1974) behavioral psychodrama likewise contains role-playing situations designed to address the problem of drug abuse.

Adolescents' drug abuse, particularly abuse of "soft" drugs, remains a significant problem which has not received nearly as much attention as it merits. Program development in the area is sorely needed, perhaps combining the techniques of modeling, role playing, contingency contracting, and problem solving, which have proven successful with other behaviors.

Psychiatric Problems

The influence of behavioral techniques in the area of adolescent psychiatric treatment is negligible. Some studies (e.g., Bardill, 1972; Hauserman et al., 1972; Zweback, 1976) report the successful use of reinforcement techniques to facilitate verbal initiations in conventional group therapy sessions. The pioneering study in this area was performed by Carpenter & Caron (1968), who used Green Stamps to facilitate communication with nonverbal adolescents. These studies attempt to manipulate only the quantity of responses, not the quality. The experimenters were not concerned about what kind of verbalizations to reinforce, but with increasing verbalizations of any kind.

The behaviors of "acting out" adolescents were addressed in a report by Elitzur (1976), who taught subjects relaxation in a group setting. While objective data on effectiveness are not presented, self-report of improvement in mood and staff reports of improved functioning are attributed to the relaxation program. Anderson et al. (1976) conducted a comparative study of three methods of teaching self-control to adolescent boys: token fading, behavioral rehearsal, and a traditional therapy group. Both the token fading group and the behavioral rehearsal group stressed self-evaluation, self-reinforcement, and discrimination training in identifying internal states of anger, depression, and frustration. Both behavioral groups proved to be superior to the traditional group therapy approach in establishing self-control in classroom situations.

Studies dealing with such problems as adolescent depression, social isolation, and deficits in assertiveness and self-control are lacking. Techniques applied to adults manifesting these problems have not, at this point, been applied to adolescents, although they would appear to be useful with some modifications. Possible psychiatric groups that might be adapted to an adolescent population include:

(1) A group for adolescents manifesting depressive behavior or social isolation. The goals of this group might be: (a) to increase general activity level and, specifically, the frequency of participation in positively reinforcing events; (b) to teach communication and conversation skills for improved interaction with same and opposite sex peers; (c) to teach the principles of modifying negative self-statements which maintain depressive and other maladaptive behavior problems; and (d) to teach the principles of self-reinforcement in order to maintain adaptive behaviors.

(2) A group for adolescents manifesting problems in self-control. This group, emphasizing the usefulness of relaxation, cognitive restructuring, and covert self-statements, could conceivably be helpful in dealing with drug and alcohol abuse, explosive anger, and impulsive behaviors of varying types.

(3) A group for adolescents manifesting excessive fears or phobias. The usefulness of group desensitization procedures with adults is well documented; however, little work has been done with adolescents. The relaxation and cognitive restructuring procedures appear applicable to the motivated adolescent and, if successful, could conceivably prevent more serious problems or extensive phobias later in life.

(4) A group designed to teach assertiveness with nonassertive or aggressive adolescents. While assertiveness training is

now commonplace in behavioral work with adults and in the popular literature, few studies attempt to teach adolescents who manifest psychiatric or other problems to be more appropriately assertive. The outline of a sample assertiveness group will be presented later in the paper.

The techniques employed in these groups might be similar to those used with adults. It has been the author's experience that many adolescents benefit from more "action" and less "talk" and that techniques such as behavior rehearsal, modeling, and videotaped feedback are quite useful. Behavioral contracting, specifying what is required of the group member and emphasizing the need to practice behaviors learned in the group in extragroup settings, also appears to be appropriate with this population. Capitalizing on the adolescent's susceptibility to peer feedback and pressure can enhance the group's effectiveness if one can enlist the cooperation of these peers in the therapeutic process. This is by no means an easy feat since the adolescent norms are often quite different from those of the therapist and can, in fact, work against group effectiveness. A more detailed discussion of problems faced in adolescent group therapy and possible solutions will be presented in a subsequent section of this paper.

Alienation

Warner and Hansen (1970) report the successful application of group behavioral counseling to the problem of alienated students. Verbal reinforcement and model reinforcement groups were conducted, focusing on feelings of powerlessness, social isolation, and normlessness. Verbalizations which reflected a positive attitude toward the student's position in the social structure or positive steps that could be taken to reduce feelings of helplessness or social isolation were reinforced by counselors. Results of the study indicated that both behavioral counseling groups were successful in reducing students' feelings of alienation when compared to a control group on a scale of alienation. A follow-up study (Warner, 1971) 6 months after counseling had terminated indicated that the behaviorally counseled students demonstrated both changed covert feelings and overt behavior reflecting less alienation. Raubolt (1975) reports the effectiveness of peer networks in modifying alienation. Although these studies indicate that behavioral group counseling may be effective in helping individuals overcome feelings of alienation, a great deal of controlled research is needed before this can be shown conclusively.

Vocational Deficits

Group work with adolescents manifesting vocational deficits falls into two categories: programs designed to ameliorate prevocational skill deficits (e.g., job interview skills, job search skills) and programs aimed at teaching vocational decision making and career exploration.

Barbee and Keil (1973) taught underprivileged adolescents job interview skills using a workshop format to review important aspects of the job interview. Pretesting and posttesting on a mock job interview indicated that the workshops were effective in teaching the requisite skills for successful job interviewing. Walker (1969) describes a program called "Pounce," which was designed to teach clients to recognize and take responsibility for solving their employment problems. The group process relies on confrontation in dealing with problems such as low motivation, poor job search skills, poor work histories, and poor job performance.

The second category of studies involves attempts to prepare clients to make career decisions and to reduce vocational indecisiveness. Numerous studies are reported which contain programs for vocational awareness. A problem-solving approach is usually adopted (e.g., Bergland et al., 1975; Birk, 1976; Stewart, 1969), with clients being given instruction in generating career alternatives, seeking information, discovering skills, evaluating the alternatives, and finally narrowing down the career options and making tentative choices. Krumboltz and Schroeder (1965) and Krumboltz and Thoresen (1964) used reinforcement techniques in a group setting to promote vocational information seeking and decision making. Yabroff (1969) employed a group decision-training program to counsel junior and senior high school students in their career choices. Magoon (1969) has developed the most comprehensive career decision-making model, called Effective Problem Solving. This counseling model takes the students through the various stages of career decision making in the form of a self-directed learning program. Clients learn to evaluate their interests and skills, obtain information about job opportunities, and correlate their interests and abilities with those of individuals working at selected jobs. While many of these programs hold great promise, long-term data concerning their ultimate effectiveness in helping individuals with career decisions are still lacking.

METHODOLOGICAL CRITIQUE OF BEHAVIORAL GROUP THERAPY STUDIES

The studies reporting on the use of behavioral group therapy with adolescents generally support the effectiveness of this approach. However, methodological difficulties in many of the studies make it impossible to state that the behavioral intervention was responsible for the improvement in the target behavior.

An important methodological concern is whether the observed changes in behavior are due to the experimental manipulation or to maturational or other factors. This appears to be a crucial question with an adolescent population since maturational factors which may influence results cannot be ruled out. One approach to dealing with this problem is to use a no-treatment control group against which results can be compared. Unfortunately, most of the studies reported do not make provisions for such an analysis. Of the studies reviewed, only 15% employed a no-treatment control condition as a comparison group. Most of the other studies report either anecdotal data, program designs, or comparisons between behavioral groups and traditional discussion groups. While many of these studies report interesting findings, the absence of a no-treatment control group opens the possibility that change may have occurred even in the absence of the experimental manipulation.

A second methodological concern is the absence of studies which systematically vary the treatment in an attempt to separate the effective components in the treatment package. The majority of the studies reported present an entire treatment program (e.g., modeling, role playing, group feedback, individual contracting), with no attempt made to tease out the necessary from the superfluous components. At this point, strategies of group intervention are extremely varied and ill-defined. Studies which systematically vary treatment components might enable us to develop a standardized group approach which could conceivably be applicable to a wide variety of populations and target behaviors.

A third consideration is the need for more overt measures of behavior change. The use of multiple dependent variables as outcome measures is highly desirable when evaluating the results of treatment. Self-report measures, reports from significant others, and measures of observed behavior, when taken as a battery, provide a good picture of treatment effectiveness. Unfortunately, reports and/or records from significant others (e.g., school and court records, employer ratings) and, to a lesser extent, measures of observable behaviors indicative of generalization effects are difficult to obtain. The reliance on self-report measures as the sole indicators of success in many of the studies reviewed represents a methodological shortcoming which reduces our confidence in the results obtained.

Finally, the absence of long-term follow-up data in the majority of studies does not permit statements about the long-term effectiveness of treatment. While short-term gains are desirable, treatment effectiveness becomes questionable if behavior is not maintained after treatment terminates. Particularly with an adolescent population, results from a 6-month and 1-year follow-up are crucially important in determining ultimate treatment outcome.

Given the previous methodological shortcomings and the large gaps in knowledge with this population, the program described below was designed to answer some of the research and clinical questions raised by those working with adolescents. Specifically, questions which relate to the range of techniques useful with this population, the comparative effectiveness of these techniques when compared to more traditional approaches, and the long-term effectiveness of a behavioral treatment strategy are addressed. The program, Project Entry, has as its goal the collection of empirical data which will document the relative success of a behavioral approach with adolescents.

THE PROJECT ENTRY PROGRAM

Project Entry is a behaviorally oriented vocational/educational program for drug-abusing adolescents. Funded by the National Institute on Drug Abuse, the program is designed to test the effectiveness of behavior modification techniques with this population and to compare the results with a control program serving the same population but using more traditional vocational and therapeutic techniques. The program serves a "soft" drug-abusing population (primarily marijuana, alcohol, and pills) whose drug use is functionally related to difficulties experienced in school, at home, and/or on the job. Many of the clients are truant from school, engage in delinquent behaviors, and experience problems at home and with peers.

The program loosely follows the Oxnard model developed by Liberman, King, and DeRisi (1976). Each client attends three groups or workshops, which are held each week for a period of 8 weeks. Clients earn points for attending and participating in groups, with the points being exchangeable for money, goods, and trips. The groups focus on teaching assertiveness, problem-solving, and prevocational skills as they apply to the specific problems of this population.

Assertion Training Group

The assertion training group attempts to teach adolescents the basic components of assertiveness. The group focuses on the common assertiveness problems of this population (e.g., dealing with authority figures, resisting peer temptation, asking for dates) and relies upon didactic instruction, modeling, behavior rehearsal, and peer feedback as clinical techniques. A session-by-session outline of the group follows.

SESSION 1
A. In Session:
   1. Lecture on content of group, requirements of participants, expectations of what group can provide; brief description of what assertive behavior entails.
   2. Each member introduces him/herself to the group member on his/her right; feedback provided on effectiveness of introduction (e.g., eye contact, voice quality, facial qualities).
   3. Members break up into dyads and are given assignments of learning more about each other; after 10 minutes, group reassembles and each member describes what he/she learned about the other member.
   4. Each member gives and receives compliments from the group member opposite; group members give positive feedback about what they liked about the way compliment was given or accepted; group discusses methods of accepting and negating compliments.
B. Session Goals:
   1. Establish positive feelings among group members and maximize each member's involvement in the group.
   2. Accustom members to giving feedback.
   3. Give members practice in self-disclosing.
   4. Demonstrate that positive interactions also involve assertiveness.
   5. Help members learn to give and receive compliments.
C. Homework:
   1. Have members introduce themselves to two other people during the week and notice the other person's nonverbal behavior.
   2. Have members give three compliments to others during the week and notice how others accept the compliment and how it makes the member feel.

SESSION 2
A. In Session:
   1. Review homework assignments; each group member discusses the results of his/her assertive behaviors.
   2. Begin in-depth discussion of assertive, aggressive, and nonassertive behavior.

    (A) Assertive Behavior:
      (1) Definition
      (2) Reasons for acting assertively rather than nonassertively
      (3) Reasons for acting assertively rather than aggressively
      (4) Nonverbal components of assertiveness
        (a) eye contact
        (b) body posture
        (c) gestures
        (d) facial expression
        (e) voice tone and volume
    (B) Nonassertive Behavior:
      (1) Reasons why people act nonassertively
      (2) Consequences of acting nonassertively
      (3) Examples of nonassertive behavior
    (C) Aggressive Behavior:
      (1) Reasons why people act aggressively
      (2) Consequences of acting aggressively
      (3) Need to maintain assertion in the face of someone's aggression
  3. Administer discrimination test on assertive, aggressive, and nonassertive behavior (see Lange & Jakubowski, 1976 for an example of a discrimination test); present audiotape of dialogue in situations calling for assertion and have group members determine if characters' verbalizations are aggressive, assertive, or nonassertive.
B. Session Goals:
  1. Present the concepts of assertiveness, aggressiveness, and nonassertiveness and teach the group discriminative ability between these behaviors.
  2. Present rationale and consequences for acting assertively and possible reasons for and consequences of nonassertive and aggressive behavior.
  3. Discussion of the myths that surround acting assertively.
C. Homework:
  1. Have members begin a log or diary in which they record situations in which they acted assertively and situations in which they were aggressive or nonassertive.

SESSION 3
A. In Session:
  1. Review homework assignment.
  2. Review definitions of assertion, aggression, and nonassertion.

3. Discussion of situations calling for assertion (e.g., dealing with teachers, parents, police, resisting temptation, meeting new people, refusing requests, giving negative feedback).
4. Dealing with anxiety around being assertive; teaching relaxation.
5. Introduction of role-playing techniques; members learn to role play specific scenes developed from problems brought to the group; all members encouraged to give positive feedback to other group members during role-played interaction on scale of 1–3.

B. Session Goals:
1. Introduce concept of relaxation and its usefulness in dealing with anxiety around assertion.
2. Present the variety of situations calling for assertive behavior.
3. Introduce role-playing methodology and demonstrate its effectiveness in dealing with problems in assertiveness.

C. Homework:
1. Continue making entries in assertion diary detailing situation, your behavior, and, if not assertive, what an assertive response would have been.
2. Practice relaxation at least once a day.

SESSION 4
A. In Session:
1. Review homework assignment; discuss and role play situations; discuss problems in relaxation.
2. Discuss cognitive aspects of assertiveness:
   (A) Cognition as the way we talk to ourselves.
   (B) Discussion of how our cognitions influence our behavior.
   (C) Discussion of how "self-statements" determine whether we act assertively, aggressively, or nonassertively.
3. Discuss 6 C's of assertive behavior (Cheek, 1972):
   (A) Keeping *cool*.
   (B) *Considering* the other person's side of the matter.
   (C) *Communicating* clearly what your feelings are.
   (D) *Clarifying* what you expect from the other person.
   (E) Explaining the *consequences,* both negative and positive, if behavior is not changed.
   (F) *Correct* timing.
4. Discuss the concept of self-reinforcement.

B. Session Goals:
1. Introduce the concept of cognitions as self-statements.
2. Demonstrate how our self-dialogues affect the way we act.

   3. Discuss common self-statements which make assertion more difficult.
   4. Discuss the 6 C's of assertiveness.
   5. Present the concept of self-reinforcement.
C. Homework:
   1. Continue practicing relaxation, particularly in situations calling for assertive behavior.
   2. Continue recording in assertion diary, adding a column for self-statements made during each listed situation.

Sessions 4 Through 8

Following the initial 4 or 5 sessions, the group can go in 2 different directions. First, members of the group can present problems they are experiencing with assertiveness in various areas and have group members role play alternative solutions. Conversely, the group can be presented with a theme for the session and all members discuss problems with the presented theme. Role playing of alternative solutions then follows. Regardless of which method is used or if a combination is employed, certain topics should be covered. These include: (1) handling criticism, (2) dealing with peer pressure (refusing requests), (3) handling anger assertively and expressing negative feelings, (4) dealing assertively with teachers and parents, and (5) initiating social interactions.

The role playing performed in the group usually follows a model which stresses:

   1. Instructions—member is given instruction in the components (both verbal and nonverbal) of an appropriate assertive response in a given situation.
   2. Modeling—the appropriate behavior is modeled by the trainer or other group members.
   3. Behavior rehearsal—member practices the appropriate behavior until it feels comfortable.
   4. Feedback—trainer and other group members provide feedback (sometimes in the form of a rating) on the quality of the response.

The interested reader can obtain additional information on running assertiveness training groups by consulting Lange and Jakubowski (1976), Cotler and Guerra (1976), and Alberti and Emmons (1974).

Problem-Solving Group

This group stresses the acquisition of problem-solving skills through instruction in the systematic approach to solving problems described by D'Zurilla and Goldfried (1971). Training in problem-solving follows the model developed by these authors and by Platt et al. as outlined in their manual (Note 2). The objective of the group is to teach the participants the sequential steps involved in problem solving: defining the problem, generating alternative solutions, evaluating the alternatives, and making a decision. During the training process, modeling, coaching, behavior rehearsal, and reinforcements are employed as the change procedures. A session-by-session outline for the group follows.

SESSION 1
A. In Session:
   1. What is a problem? Recognizing when you have a problem.
   2. Discussion of how group members usually attack a problem.
   3. Discussion of common problems that people face.
   4. Discussion of what it means to solve a problem.
   5. Advantages of a problem-solving approach:
      (A) Teaches you a step-wise plan of action
      (B) Prevents impulsive behavior
      (C) Helps you expand your options
      (D) Helps you discover more effective solutions to problems
B. Session Goals:
   1. General discussion of what it means to have a problem and what people do to solve their problems.
   2. Introduce concept of systematic problem solving and its possible advantages.

SESSION 2
A. In Session:
   1. Committing oneself to work on a problem:
      (A) Perceiving a problem when one exists—what are the feelings and behaviors involved.
      (B) Inhibiting the tendency to respond impulsively or by avoiding the problem.
   2. Defining a problem:
      (A) Presenting hypothetical situations and asking members to define what the problem is in each situation.
      (B) Stating the conditions that would exist if the problem were resolved.
   3. Obtaining information about a problem:
      (A) Learning to discriminate who has the problem.
      (B) Learning to separate fact from opinion (Platt et al., Note 2):
         (1) Clients play out skits and view pictures which teach them discrimination.

(2) Discussion of how one learns if opinions are also facts.

(C) Learning that others have different points of view and that there are differences in the way that people perceive events.

B. Session Goals:

1. Discussion of the need to commit oneself to recognizing and working on problems.
2. Learning to define a problem.
3. Learning to obtain information about a problem.

SESSION 3

A. In Session:

1. Learning to recognize how others feel:
    (A) Role reversal employed with a specific problem and group members attempt to see everyone's point of view.
2. Learning the prerequisites of problem solving:
    (A) Don't jump to conclusions, get the other person's point of view.
    (B) Think before acting.
3. Discussion of thought as a process of talking to oneself:
    (A) Monitoring what we say to ourselves in problem situations.
    (B) Discovering how our self-statements affect our problem-solving behavior.
4. Presentation of videotape of individual talking to himself during the problem-solving process.

B. Session Goals:

(1) Learning to recognize others' feelings and point of view.
(2) Discovering covert thoughts which influence problem-solving behavior.

SESSION 4

A. In Session:

1. Learning to generate and consider multiple alternative solutions to problems:
    (A) Discussion of the concept of brainstorming.
    (B) Practice in generating alternatives through brainstorming a hypothetical problem.
2. Learning to evaluate the alternatives:
    (A) Considering each alternative in light of information gathered about the problem and the possible solution.
    (B) Anticipating long-term and short-term benefits of each alternative.

3. Selecting the most desirable alternatives and implementing these alternatives:
    (A) Knowing the rationale for the choice of these alternatives.
    (B) Rank-ordering the alternatives in order of preference.
    (C) Detailing a plan to carry out the preferred alternatives.
4. Implementing specific plans related to alternatives:
    (A) Knowing and exhibiting the behaviors necessary to implement the plan for the chosen alternative.
    (B) Judging whether the alternative should be modified or a second alternative selected.

B. Session Goals:
    1. Introduce the step-by-step problem-solving sequence.
    2. Present a model to evaluate the effectiveness of the problem-solving procedure.

Sessions 4 Through 8

A. Review problem solving sequence.
B. Have group discuss and solve problems which they are experiencing while encouraging members to implement possible solutions and report back to group.
C. An alternative to the above would consist of the group leader presenting problems for the group to solve, e.g., "Should I stay in school?" "How do I deal with police, parents, girl/boyfriend?" "I feel helpless/hopeless."

Prevocational Group

The prevocational group is designed to teach a range of pre-employment skills with particular emphasis on job hunting, resume writing, obtaining and coming across well on a job interview, and dealing with job problems. Extensive use is made of videotape techniques in addition to trainer and peer modeling, behavior rehearsal, and feedback. Participants are given mock job interviews before and after training as one measure of their improved skills. A session-by-session outline follows.

SESSION 1
1. Discussion of clients' work experience and expectations:
    (A) Likes and dislikes
    (B) Job responsibilities
    (C) How work affects life style
2. Discussion of the papers needed before one can work.
3. Discussion of the importance of a resume.

SESSION 2
1. Learning to fill out a resume.
2. Learning to get references.
3. Discussion of the resources available to the job hunter.

SESSION 3
1. Learning to fill out a sample application form:
   (A) Answering problem questions.
   (B) How detailed answers should be.
   (C) What an employer can ask on an application.

SESSION 4
1. Preparing for the job interview:
   (A) Calling for an interview, role-play simple dialogues.
   (B) What to find out on the phone.
   (C) Appropriate attire.
   (D) Preparing for interviewer questions.

SESSION 5
1. The job interview:
   (A) Review possible questions employer might ask and questions to ask the employer.
   (B) Show videotape of good and poor job interview and discuss positives and negatives.
   (C) Have clients role-play an interview alternating in the roles of interviewer and applicant; have group give feedback on performance.
   (D) Discussion of call-back techniques.

SESSION 6
1. Discussion of employer expectations, clients generate list of job responsibilities.
2. Discussion of possible problems that can come up on the job and possible solutions.

SESSIONS 7 & 8
1. Being assertive in the work situation:
   (A) Handling criticism.
   (B) Asking for more/less responsibilities.
   (C) Asking for a change in jobs.
   (D) Dealing with anger.
   (E) Handling peer pressure to get high or not work.
   (F) Keeping personal problems at home.
2. Have clients role-play problem situations in the group; discuss alternative ways of handling problems.

Preliminary Data

All clients in the study are randomly assigned to either the Project Entry or comparison program.

The comparison program takes a more traditional approach to the problems of an adolescent population. The program is a long-term (average length of participation is approximately 9 months) day treatment facility which emphasizes group and individual psychotherapy, vocational assessment and counseling, and activities therapy as the major vehicles for change. While problems in assertiveness, self-control, and problem solving are common to the clients in both programs, Project Entry attempts to ameliorate these problems through a structured skills training approach, while the comparison group relies upon more nonspecific, "milieu" therapy interventions. Participants in each program receive approximately 8 to 10 hours of therapeutic services per week.

At intake all clients are administered: an Assertion Inventory (Gambrill & Richey, 1975), a series of audiotaped situations calling for an assertive response, the Means-Ends Problem-Solving Inventory (Platt, Spivack, & Bloom, Note 6), Wahler's Self Description Inventory (Wahler, 1971), and Rotter's Internal-External Locus of Control Scale (Rotter, 1966). Tests are administered again 16 weeks after treatment has begun, during which time the Project Entry clients attend both a Problem-Solving and Assertiveness Training Group.

In the area of assertiveness, significant differences (all statistics reported here were obtained through the use of analysis of covariance) have emerged between the clients in the two programs in terms of self-reported assertion, with Project Entry clients (N = 15) reporting greater ability to behave assertively in specific situations and less discomfort in acting assertively in general ($p < .01$). Analysis of responses to the assertion tapes supports the claims of improved assertiveness skills. Ratings of independent judges (reliability ranging from 86% to 93%) indicate significantly more improvement in the Project Entry clients' ability to respond assertively as measured by response fluency, voice quality, and response content ($p < .01$). Overt measures of assertiveness within the program, at school, and at home are currently being collected and will be reported when available.

In the area of problem solving, the preliminary data indicate that the Program Entry clients are able to generate significantly more alternative responses to solve hypothetical problems on the Means-Ends Problem Solving Inventory than comparison group clients ($p < .05$). Whether or not this indicates a greater problem-solving ability in real life situations is problematical, and we are currently searching for a more overt measure of problem-solving ability.

In the area of self-report measures of general adjustment, clients in the Project Entry project indicate that significantly more positive statements on the Wahler Inventory ($p < .01$) and significantly fewer negative statements ($p < .05$) apply to them after training than before training. Significant differences also are emerging between the two programs in overall positive change scores, with the Project Entry client demonstrating greater self-reported change. On the Rotter Internal-External Locus of Control Scale, Project Entry clients report significantly higher internal beliefs than before treatment began ($p < .01$). Clients in the comparison group report no significant change in either external or internal beliefs as measured by the Rotter scale.

The above data, although still preliminary, seem to indicate a number of positive outcomes of the Project Entry training program. Research is presently continuing in order to increase the sample size, develop more overt measures of assertion and problem-solving ability, and perform follow-up work on treated clients. The data should provide some answers to the questions surrounding the effectiveness of behavioral group treatment with adolescents.

PROBLEMS ENCOUNTERED IN ADOLESCENT GROUP TREATMENT

Reports in the literature are scanty regarding problems encountered in group work with an adolescent population. It is the author's experience that numerous problems must be overcome in order for effective treatment to take place. A partial list of these problems includes:

Poor Motivation

Many adolescents are literally brought or coerced into treatment. Significant others (e.g., parents, teachers, counselors, the courts) make referrals to treatment programs, often without the adolescents' consent. Many clients do not feel they have any significant problems and, therefore, should not be in treatment. Added to this is the negative second-order effect of being in treatment (Graziano & Fink, 1973) and the stigma which is attached, particularly for this population. These factors contribute to poor attendance and participation, disruptiveness, and high drop-out rates.

To combat this problem, token economy programs have been

developed with the aim of increasing attendance, participation, and general involvement in the therapeutic process. Behavioral contracts have also been employed to increase client motivation for change (Bardill, 1972; Stuart, 1971). While some success has been reported utilizing these techniques, low client motivation continues to be a major problem.

Deviant Group Norms

Many groups rely upon peer group sanctions and reinforcement to effect therapeutic change. However, in many adolescent groups, the peer group reinforces deviant or inappropriate behavior and punishes appropriate behaviors or verbalizations. Little research has been done on modifying deviant group norms, although these can be a significant problem in many groups. We are currently experimenting with the use of an "ideal" group member who will support members' positive behaviors while functioning in the role of a co-leader. Other techniques might include: enlisting the cooperation (through the use of various incentives) of a high sociometrically rated group member to reinforce prosocial behaviors; setting up a buddy system (Schinke & Rose, 1976); and instituting group contingencies for the performance of appropriate behavior of group members.

Reluctance to Self-Disclose

Often a group situation is frightening to an adolescent. Hesitancy to discuss personal problems, share experiences, or role-play is quite common. Group pressure often makes the situation worse rather than better so other techniques are necessary. These can include shaping the reluctant member's self-disclosing contributions throughout the course of the group, providing individual counseling to supplement group work, and indicating specific participation requirements by means of behavioral contracting.

Scapegoating

Sometimes scapegoating, or consistently blaming other group members or other people for one's problems, occurs in the group. This externalization of responsibility interferes with change attempts and is detrimental to the group. To counter this behavior, it is sometimes helpful to bring it to the attention of the group and to ask if this behavior is helping the group or the member who is being scapegoated (Merritt & Walley, 1977). If this fails, scapegoating can be forbidden in the group and a point fine (if points are being used) can be levied for violations. Discussions centering around accepting responsibility for one's own behavior, using rational-emotive therapy techniques (Maultsby, 1975), might also be helpful.

Poor Group Interactions

Often faulty communication between group members can spell doom for a group. Behaviors such as harsh negative feedback, interrupting, not attending, disruptive, side conversations, and inappropriate or irrelevant statements detract from the work of the group. This behavior must be brought to the group's attention when it occurs, and, if possible, point fines should be imposed. Individual contracting with repeated offenders may also be employed.

Poor Generalization of Learned Behavior to Extratreatment Settings

Often behavior discussed and seemingly learned in the group does not generalize to situations where performance of the behavior would be appropriate. This is a problem inherent to therapy in general, not merely to group therapy. Increasing the likelihood of generalization may be achieved by: asking each member of the group to publicly state a behavior outside the group which he would like to change and reviewing each member's progress toward performing this behavior on a regular basis; instituting a buddy system to prompt and reinforce performance of the desired behavior; and drawing up a behavioral contract stipulating when and where behaviors learned in the group should be performed and providing various incentives for evidence of their performance.

SUMMARY

Behavioral group therapy with adolescents appears to be a potentially valuable therapeutic modality which at this time is still poorly researched. Behavioral groups provide a number of advantages for the change agent and group member including: the presence of a situation in which behavior can be observed and monitored; the availability of peer reinforcement and prompting to increase the likelihood of performance of the target behaviors; the opportunity to experiment with behaviors in an accepting, therapeutic group environment; and the availability of feedback to shape and modify behavior.

While advantages of this approach are clearly present, there are often problems inherent in group interventions including: clients' poor motivation for treatment, deviant group norms and reinforcement of inappropriate behavior, and reluctance of members to self-disclose and participate in group activities. Various ways of combating these problems were discussed and, in particular, the use of individual and group contingencies, establishing a buddy system, and group labeling and confrontations were recommended.

Research on the effectiveness of behavioral group therapy with adolescents is scanty. While behavioral interventions have been employed with delinquent, drug-abusing, psychiatric, and vocationally deficient youths to some extent, evaluative research has not been forthcoming. Evaluation studies with acceptable research designs are rare and conclusive statements as to the effectiveness of group intervention cannot at this time be made. It is recommended that future researchers concentrate their efforts on:

(1) Controlled research programs comparing the effectiveness of behavioral groups with traditional therapy groups and no-treatment control groups.

(2) Component analysis research designed to evaluate the effective components in the group process (e.g., role playing, contracting, information dissemination).

(3) Extending the range of populations to which the group process is applied (e.g., adolescent depressions, psychotic behavior, interpersonal fears, self-control difficulties).

(4) The development and analysis of innovative group approaches to problem behaviors (e.g., the use of peers as co-leaders, role playing vs. discussion groups, the use of videotape technology to represent overt and covert behaviors with, perhaps, the aid of dubbing).

The results of this type of research will go a long way toward resolving the unanswered questions in behavioral group work. Until this research is performed and evaluated, conclusions as to the effectiveness of group interventions for this population must be held in abeyance.

REFERENCE NOTES

1. Schrader, C., Panzer, C., Long, J., Gillet, D. J., & Kornblath, R. *Modifying maladaptive communication patterns in adolescent-parent triads.* Paper presented at the meeting of the Association for the Advancement of Behavior Therapy, Atlanta, Ga., December 1977.
2. Platt, J. J., Spivack, G., & Swift, M. S. *Interpersonal problem-solving group therapy* (No. 31). Philadelphia, Pa.: Hahnemann Medical College and Hospital, 1975.

3. Sarason, I. G., & Ganzer, V. J. *Modeling: An approach to the rehabilitation of juvenile offenders* (Final reports to the Social and Rehabilitation Service of the U.S. Dept. of Health, Education, & Welfare). Washington, D.C.: U.S. Dept. of Health, Education, & Welfare, 1971.
4. Shoemaker, M. E. *Group assertiveness training for institutionalized delinquents.* Unpublished doctoral dissertation, Fuller Graduate School of Psychology, Pasadena, Cal., 1974.
5. Copeman, C. D. *Aversive conditioning and social retraining: A learning theory approach to drug rehabilitation.* Unpublished doctoral dissertation, State University of New York at Stony Brook, Stony Brook, N.Y., 1973.
6. Platt, J. J., Spivack, G., & Bloom, M. *Means-ends problem solving (MEPS): Manual 7—Tentative norms.* Philadelphia, Pa.: Department of Mental Health Services, Hahnemann Medical College & Hospital, 1971.

REFERENCES

Abudabbah, N., Prandoni, J. R., & Jensen, D. E. Application of behavior principles to group therapy techniques with juvenile delinquents. *Psychological Reports,* 1972, *31,* 375–380.
Alberti, R. E., & Emmons, M. L. *Your perfect right: A guide to assertive behavior.* San Luis Obispo, Cal.: Impact, 1974.
Anderson, L., Fodor, I., & Alpert, M. A comparison of methods of training self-control. *Behavior Therapy,* 1976, *7,* 649–658.
Bandura, A. *Principles of behavior modification.* New York: Holt, Rinehart & Winston, 1969.
Barbee, J. R., & Keil, E. C. Behavior modification and training the disadvantaged job interviewee. *Vocational Guidance Quarterly,* 1973, *22,* 50–56.
Bardill, D. R. Behavior contracting and group therapy with preadolescent males in a residential treatment setting. *International Journal of Group Psychotherapy,* 1972, *22,* 333–342.
Bergland, B. W., Quatrano, L. A., & Lundquist, G. W. Group social models and structured interaction in teaching decision making. *The Vocational Guidance Quarterly,* 1975, *24,* 28–35.
Birk, J. M. Experienced-based career exploration. In J. D. Krumboltz & C. W. Thoresen (Eds.), *Counseling methods.* New York; Holt, Rinehart & Winston, 1976.
Blechman, E. A., Olsen, D. H. L., & Turner, A. J. The family contract game: Technique and case study. *Journal of Consulting and Clinical Psychology,* 1976, *44,* 449–455.
Braukmann, D. J., & Fixsen, D. L. Behavior modification with delinquents. In M. Hersen, R. M. Eisler, & P. M. Miller (Eds.), *Progress in behavior modification* (Vol. 1). New York: Academic Press, 1975.
Brown, W., & Kingsley, R. F. The effect of individual contracting and guided group interaction upon behavior disordered youth's self-concept. *The Journal of School Health,* 1975, *45,* 399–401.

Burchard, J. D., Harrig, P. T., Miller, R. B., & Armour, J. New strategies in community-based intervention. In E. L. Ribes-Inesta (Ed.), *The experimental analysis of delinquency and social aggression*. New York: Academic Press, 1976.

Callner, D. A. Behavioral treatment approaches to drug abuse: A critical review of the research. *Psychological Bulletin*, 1975, *82*, 143–164.

Carpenter, P., & Caron, R. Green stamp therapy: Modification of delinquent behavior through food training stamps. *Proceedings of the 76th Annual Convention of the American Psychological Association*, 1968, *3*, 531–532. (Summary)

Cheek, F. E. *Behavior modification training program*. Princeton, N.J.: New Jersey Neuro-Psychiatric Institute, 1972.

Cheek, F. E., Tomarchio, T., Standen, J., & Albahary, R. S. Methadone plus: A behavior modification training program in self-control for addicts on methadone maintenance. *International Journal of Addictions*, 1973, *8*, 969–996.

Coghlan, A. J., Gold, S. R., Dohrenwend, E. F., & Zimmerman, R. S. A psychobehavioral residential drug abuse program: A new adventure in adolescent psychiatry. *The International Journal of the Addictions*, 1973, *8*, 767–777.

Cotler, S. B., & Guerra, J. J. *Assertion training*. Champaign, Ill.: Research Press, 1976.

Davidson, W. S., II, & Seidman, E. Studies of behavior modification and juvenile delinquency: A review, methodological critique, and social perspective. *Psychological Bulletin*, 1974, *81*, 998–1011.

Drabman, R. S. Behavior modification in the classroom. In W. E. Craighead, A. E. Kazdin, & M. J. Mahoney (Eds.), *Behavior modification: Principles, issues, and applications*. Boston: Houghton-Mifflin, 1976.

Drabman, R., Spitalnik, R., & Spitalnik, K. Sociometric and disruptive behavior as a function of four types of token reinforcement programs. *Journal of Applied Behavior Analysis*, 1974, *7*, 93–101.

D'Zurilla, T. J., & Goldfried, M. R. Problem solving and behavior modification. *Journal of Abnormal Psychology*, 1971, *78*, 107–126.

Elitzur, B. Self-relaxation program for acting-out adolescents. *Adolescence*, 1976, *11*, 569–572.

Fo, W. S., & O'Donnell, C. R. The buddy system: Relationship and contingency conditions in a community intervention program for youth with non-professionals as behavior change agents. *Journal of Consulting and Clinical Psychology*, 1974, *42*, 163–169.

Fodor, I. The use of behavior modification techniques with female delinquents. *Child Welfare*, 1972, *51*, 93–101.

Frankel, A. J., & Glasser, P. H. Behavioral approaches to group work. *Social Work*, 1974, *19*, 163–174.

Friedman, P. H. The effects of modeling, role playing, and participation on behavior change. In B. A. Maher (Ed.), *Progress in experimental personality research*. New York: Academic Press, 1972.

Gambrill, E. D., & Richey, C. A. An assertion inventory for use in assessment and research. *Behavior Therapy*, 1975, *6*, 547–549.

Graziano, A. M., & Fink, R. A. Second order effects in mental health treatment. *Journal of Consulting and Clinical Psychology*, 1973, *40*, 356–364.

Greenberg, D. J., Scott, S. B., Pisa, A., & Friesen, D. D. Beyond the token economy: A comparison of two contingency programs. *Journal of Consulting and Clinical Psychology*, 1975, *43*, 489–503.

Hamblin, R. L., Hathaway, C., & Wodarski, J. Group contingencies, peer tutoring, and accelerating academic achievement. In R. Ulrich, T. Stachnik, & J. Mabry (Eds.), *Control of human behavior* (Vol. 3). Glenview, Ill.: Scott, Foresman, 1974.

Hauserman, N., Zweback, S., & Plotkin, A. Use of concrete reinforcement to facilitate verbal initiations in adolescent group therapy. *Journal of Consulting and Clinical Psychology*, 1972, *38*, 90–96.

Hedquist, F. J., & Weinhold, B. K. Behavioral group counseling with socially anxious and unassertive college students. *Journal of Counseling Psychology*, 1970, *17*, 237–242.

Jesness, C. F., & DeRisi, W. J. Some variations in techniques of contingency contracting in a school for delinquents. In J. S. Stumphauzer (Ed.), *Behavior therapy with delinquents*. Springfield, Ill.: Charles C. Thomas, 1973.

Jones, G. B. Evaluation of problem-solving competence. In J. D. Krumboltz & C. E. Thoresen (Eds.), *Counseling methods*. New York: Holt, Rinehart & Winston, 1976.

Kaufman, L. M., & Wagner, B. R. "Barb": A systematic treatment technology for temper control disorders. *Behavior Therapy*, 1972, *3*, 293–309.

Kifer, R. E., Lewis, M. A., Green, D. R., & Phillips, E. L. Training predelinquent youths and their parents to negotiate conflict situations. *Journal of Applied Behavior Analysis*, 1974, *7*, 357–364.

Krumboltz, J. D., & Schroeder, W. W. Promoting career explorations through reinforcement. *Personnel and Guidance Journal*, 1965, *44*, 19–26.

Krumboltz, J. D., & Thoresen, C. E. The effect of behavioral counseling in group and individual settings on information-seeking behavior. *Journal of Counseling Psychology*, 1964, *11*, 324–333.

Lange, A. J., & Jakubowski, P. *Responsible assertive behavior: Cognitive-behavioral procedures for trainers*. Champaign, Ill.: Research Press, 1976.

Liberman, R. P., King, L. W., & DeRisi, W. J. Behavior analysis and therapy in community mental health. In H. Leitenberg (Ed.), *Handbook of behavior modification and behavior therapy*. Englewood Cliffs, N.J.: Prentice-Hall, 1976.

Litow, L., & Pumroy, D. K. A brief review of classroom group-oriented contingencies. *Journal of Applied Behavior Analysis*, 1975, *8*, 341–347.

Magoon, T. M. Developing skills for educational and vocational problems. In J. D. Krumboltz & C. E. Thoresen (Eds.), *Behavioral counseling: Cases and techniques*. New York: Holt, Rinehart & Winston, 1969.

Maultsby, C. Rational behavior therapy for acting-out adolescents. *Social Casework*, 1975, *5*, 35–43.

Merritt, R. E., & Walley, D. D. *The group leader's handbook: Resources, techniques, and survival skills.* Champaign, Ill.: Research Press, 1977.

O'Leary, K. D. Token reinforcement programs in the classroom. In T. A. Brigham & A. C. Catania (Eds.), *The handbook of applied behavior research: Social and instructional processes.* New York: Irvington Press/Halstead Press, 1977.

Patterson, G. R. Intervention for boys with conduct problems: Multiple settings, treatments, and criteria. *Journal of Consulting and Clinical Psychology,* 1974, *42,* 471–481.

Phillips, E. L. Achievement Place: Token reinforcement procedures in a home style rehabilitation setting for predelinquent boys. *Journal of Applied Behavior Analysis,* 1968, *2,* 213–222.

Phillips, E. L., Phillips, E., Fixsen, D. L., & Wolf, M. M. *The teaching family handbook.* Champaign, Ill.: Research Press, 1974.

Platt, J. J., Spivack, G., Altman, N., Altman, D., & Peizer, S. D. Adolescent problem-solving thinking. *Journal of Consulting and Clinical Psychology,* 1974, *42,* 787–793.

Raubolt, R. R. Adolescent peer networks: An alternative to alienation. *Corrective and Social Psychiatry,* 1975, *21,* 1–3.

Rose, S. D. A behavioral approach to the group treatment of parents. *Social Work,* 1969, *14,* 21–29.

Rose, S. D. *Group therapy: A behavioral approach.* Englewood Cliffs, N.J.: Prentice-Hall, 1977.

Rotter, J. B. Generalized expectancies for internal versus external control of reinforcement. *Psychological Monographs,* 1966, *80* (1, Whole No. 609).

Sarason, I. G., & Ganzer, V. J. Modeling and group discussion in the rehabilitation of juvenile delinquents. *Journal of Counseling Psychology,* 1973, *20,* 442–449.

Schinke, S. P., & Rose, S. D. Interpersonal skill training in groups. *Journal of Counseling Psychology,* 1976, *23,* 442–448.

Stewart, N. R. Exploring and processing information about educational and vocational opportunities in groups. In J. D. Krumboltz & C. E. Thoresen (Eds.), *Behavioral counseling: Cases and techniques.* New York: Holt, Rinehart & Winston, 1969.

Stuart, R. B. Behavioral contracts within the families of delinquents. *Journal of Behavior Therapy and Experimental Psychiatry,* 1971, *2,* 1–11.

Stuart, R. B., & Lott, L. A. Behavioral contracting with delinquents: A cautionary note. *Journal of Behavior Therapy and Experimental Psychiatry,* 1972, *2,* 161–169.

Stumphauzer, J. S. *Behavior therapy with delinquents.* Springfield, Ill.: Charles C. Thomas, 1973.

Stumphauzer, J. S. *Six techniques of modifying delinquent behavior.* Leonia, N.J.: Behavioral Sciences Tape Library, 1974.

Stumphauzer, J. S. Modifying delinquent behavior: Beginnings and current practices. *Adolescence,* 1976, *41,* 13–28.

Swisher, J. D., Warner, R. W., Jr., & Herr, E. L. Experimental comparison of four approaches to drug abuse prevention among ninth and eleventh graders. *Journal of Counseling Psychology,* 1972, *19,* 328–332.

Tharp, R. G., & Wetzel, R. J. *Behavior modification in the natural environment.* New York: Academic Press, 1969.

Varenhorst, B. B. Peer counseling: A guidance program and a behavioral intervention. In J. D. Krumboltz & C. E. Thoresen (Eds.), *Counseling methods.* New York: Holt, Rinehart & Winston, 1976.

Wahler, H. J. *Wahler Self-Description Inventory.* Los Angeles: Western Psychological Services, 1971.

Walker, R. A. "Pounce": Learning responsibility for one's own employment problems. In J. D. Krumboltz & C. E. Thoresen (Eds.), *Behavioral counseling: Cases and techniques.* New York: Holt, Rinehart & Winston, 1969.

Warner, R. W., Jr. Alienated students: Six months after receiving behavioral group counseling. *Journal of Counseling Psychology,* 1971, *18,* 426–430.

Warner, R. W., Jr., & Hansen, J. C. Verbal-reinforcement and model reinforcement group counseling with alienated students. *Journal of Counseling Psychology,* 1970, *17,* 168–172.

Warner, R. W., Jr., & Swisher, J. D. Drug-abuse prevention: Reinforcement of alternatives. In J. D. Krumboltz & C. E. Thoresen (Eds.), *Counseling methods.* New York: Holt, Rinehart, & Winston, 1976.

Weathers, L., & Liberman, R. P. Contingency contracting with families of delinquent adolescents. *Behavior Therapy,* 1975, *6,* 356–366. (a)

Weathers, L., & Liberman, R. P. The family contracting exercise. *Journal of Behavior Therapy and Experimental Psychiatry,* 1975, *6,* 208–214. (b)

Williams, R. I., & Blanton, R. L. Verbal conditioning in a psychotherapeutic situation. *Behaviour Research and Therapy,* 1968, *1,* 97–103.

Yabroff, W. Learning decision-making. In J. D. Krumboltz & C. E. Thoresen (Eds.), *Behavioral counseling: Cases and techniques,* New York: Holt, Rinehart, & Winston, 1969.

Zweback, S. Use of concrete reinforcement to control content of verbal initiations in group therapy with adolescents. *Psychological Reports,* 1976, *38,* 1051–1057.

Part Three

Models for Behavioral Group Therapy Programs

Each of the five chapters included in this section represents an attempt to extend the scope and improve the technology of behavioral group therapy by building upon research and clinical findings from a number of diverse areas. Rather than reporting the results of extensive, well-controlled research projects, these papers instead present guidelines for developing new behavioral group therapy programs and extending their use to new clinical populations and settings. In this sense, they reflect an important recent trend in behavior therapy research—the shifting from a *basic research* to an *applied research* model. As Azrin (1977) has noted, while the basic research model emphasizes conceptual development, theoretical integration, the isolation of relevant variables, and homogeneous groupings of subjects, the applied research model emphasizes practicality, clinically significant outcomes, systems approaches (rather than single variables), and heterogeneous groupings of subjects. In the applied model, questions of experimental design, number of subjects, and control groups are redirected to the question of what it is necessary to do in order to demonstrate an effectiveness greater than that which has been experimentally demonstrated for alternate treatments.

In Chapter 9, Jeffrey Bedell and Lawrence Weathers present a model for the development and operation of a "psychoeducational" skills training program, one which combines social skills training and games technology in a group therapy format. Of special interest is their description of two applications of this model: a *therapist-facilitated* program, which is most suitable in situations in which a skilled behavior therapist can conduct the group, and a *game-facilitated* program, the structured nature of which permits its use by less skilled group therapists. The development of treatment packages of this type, particularly those which can be employed by lower-level professionals, paraprofessionals, and even the clients themselves, offers the potential for more efficient utilization of available manpower in providing treatment and greatly improved cost effectiveness.

Myles Genest and Dennis Turk, in Chapter 10, extensively review the literature on cognitive-behavioral approaches to pain management and formulate a group therapy model for treating patients with chronic pain. Here again, as with the programs and models presented in the other papers in this volume, a central role is given to the management of various aspects of the group process in order to enhance the effects of the behavior change strategies used, and the authors provide a series of practical guidelines for conducting therapy *through* the group.

In Chapter 11, Timothy O'Farrell and Henry Cutter bring together behavior therapy, couples group therapy, and alcoholism treatment approaches in formulating a model for a behavioral couples group for alcoholics and their wives. The goals of this type of group, pretreatment assessment procedures, the couples group treatment package, and methods to evaluate outcome are described in detail, and the advantages of incorporating such packages into on-going alcoholism treatment programs are discussed.

Chapter 12 by Kay Gustafson provides an interesting example of how behavioral group therapy can be conducted *through* a group interactive process as well as by therapist-to-client interactions *in* a group context. In the early stages of skill training, much of the communication is from therapist to individual group member. Later, group members themselves provide a good deal of shaping, modeling, and reinforcing of each other's behavior. Precisely defining the levels of skill required for advancement within the group is also innovative and shows promise for use with difficult populations such as hospitalized schizophrenics.

Judith Coché, Leonard Levitz, and Henry Jordan, in Chapter 13, review many antecedents for obesity in children and make a strong case for including an understanding of cultural and physiological factors as well as psychological factors in treating the problem. As with Gustafson's chapter, there is also a combination of *in* and *through* group methods, e.g., in the educative procedures and the group supportive procedures. Finally, the model proposed adds a systems orientation which distinguishes it from other approaches employing similar techniques.

REFERENCES

Azrin, N.H. A strategy for applied research: Learning based but outcome oriented. *American Psychologist*, 1977, *32*, 140–149.

Chapter 9

A Psycho-Educational Model for Skill Training: Therapist-Facilitated and Game-Facilitated Applications

Jeffrey R. Bedell
Lawrence R. Weathers

Abstract

The emphasis in psychology on social skill training and the formalized use of educational procedures has led to the advent of psycho-educational group therapy. Performance of this type of psychotherapy is not guided by a unifying model, however, and this results in the quality of programs being overly dependent on the skills of individual practitioners. The present chapter attempts to rectify this situation by presenting a model for psycho-educational treatment. Also, two applications of the model are reported. The first application, a therapist-facilitated program, is designed for use by the relatively well-skilled behavior therapist. The second application, a game-facilitated program, utilizes a technology shown to be effective in business and education for enhancing learning and involvement in skills training. The game program is well suited as an alternative to the therapist-facilitated program. The game format, because of its structure, objectivity, and processes, eliminates the need for a skilled behavioral therapist to operate these groups. Thus, the game-facilitated program is useful in a variety of natural settings for staff who may have little training in counseling and behavior therapy. The therapist- and game-facilitated programs appear to be radically different, but a comparison of their functions according to the overall model shows that they contain nearly identical processes. Finally, a brief description of the effectiveness of a residential treatment program based on this model of psycho-educational skill training is presented.

INTRODUCTION

An important development in contemporary psychotherapy is the emphasis now being placed on social skill training and formalizing the use of purely educational procedures (Alschuler, 1969; Drum & Knott, 1977; Goldstein, 1973; Ivey, 1977). These developments have led to psycho-educational treatment which combines psychological and educational methods to enhance social skills. Because the psycho-educational approach to psychotherapy has the potential to borrow the most effective procedures from psychology and education, it is a powerful behavior change tool.

The educational methods typically employed include the use of structured curricula and lesson plans, didactic teaching, and exercises to facilitate the application of knowledge. The psychological procedures have primarily been borrowed from the behavioral therapies and operant conditioning. Because of the structured and objective nature of these educational and psychological methods, an added benefit to the psycho-educational program is its usefulness to therapists with varying levels of skills, from psychologists to paraprofessionals.

The use of psychological techniques such as modeling, feedback, and reinforcement, which compromise some of the activities of a psycho-educational group, have been shown to facilitate the learning of social skills (e.g., Gutride, Goldstein, & Hunter, 1973; Pierce & Drasgow, 1969). However, the entire set of educational and psychological procedures that comprise this type of skill-training program has not been systematically delineated. Consequently, there is no unifying or guiding model to aid therapists in developing a psycho-educational program.

The lack of such a model requires that therapists rely on their own clinical and educational skills when attempting to develop and operate such a program. The quality of these programs is therefore directly dependent on the skills of individual practitioners. The absence of a model for a psycho-educational program makes it particularly difficult for the low and middle level counselor to conduct these procedures. The absence of a written unifying model may also limit the application of psycho-educational techniques to the few programs where they have been comprehensively developed. This situation makes them unavailable to many settings and therapists where they would be usefully employed. Given the potential power of such programs, and their suitability for wide application, the absence of a general unifying model is unfortunate.

The present study proposes to rectify this situation by presenting a model for the development and operation of a psycho-educational skill enhancement program. Also, two applications of this model are presented. Each of these applications has unique procedures suited for specific purposes. The first application is called the Therapist-Facilitated Program and would be best employed by a relatively skilled behavior therapist. The second application utilizes a therapeutic game-facilitated technology to supplement the talents of the group leader and is therefore suitable for use by therapists with less well developed group therapy skills. The therapeutic game-facilitated technology boosts the training capacity of the middle and lower level therapists so that they may conduct effective skill enhancement groups at a level that is comparable to a more highly skilled therapist.

Since the therapist-facilitated and game-facilitated applications of the model are important developments in their own right, they will be discussed and compared. Finally, a brief evaluation of the effectiveness of a psycho-educational program will be presented.

THE PSYCHO-EDUCATIONAL MODEL OF TREATMENT

There are three features that characterize the psycho-educational approach to therapy. First, the therapist role is modified in comparison to traditional treatments. He assumes the role of educator, trainer, and behavior change consultant. As an educator, he uses the treatment situation as an instructional setting to teach both the knowledge and the performance of social skills. The sheltered training situation is utilized as an analog of the natural environment to practice new social skills behaviors. By utilizing educational structures that support the educator-trainer role of the therapist, professionals and nonprofessionals at a wide variety of training levels can effectively conduct psycho-educational programs. This is important because other types of therapy programs that have not used educational orientations have largely been limited to use with specially trained, high-level staff (Repucci & Saunders, 1974).

Second, the role of the client is modified in the psycho-educational program. The client assumes the role of a student who is an active participant in an educational endeavor with a positive orientation, i.e., skills enhancement. He takes an active part in his own instruction and may also assist others in the learning of new behaviors. He is not the passive recipient of a "cure" but is responsible for his own development.

Third, an important component of the psycho-educational group stems from its educational style. In education, it is common practice to clearly define and delimit the realm of instruction for a given instructional or training program. Lesson plans describe and delimit the content of each meeting. The psycho-educational programs are consistent with this orientation, since the overall domain of content is clearly specified at the onset of training and each session has a planned agenda and content. This also facilitates its use by therapists with a wide range of skills.

Psycho-educational treatment is most effective when conducted in a group, particularly if participants have varying degrees of dysfunction in the same behavioral skill areas. Each member of the program benefits from the information and instruction provided by the teacher-therapist. Group members may learn skills from the other participants and may aid in the skill enhancement process by providing information and feedback, and by modeling appropriate behavior. In the group training situation, the ability to practice new skills is increased since participants may form dyads or small groups and may role-play by social interactions. The interactional features of the group format facilitate the shaping and reinforcement of appropriate social behaviors.

Figure 1 presents a model for psycho-educational treatment programs. As may be seen in this figure, the model characterizes the psycho-educational programs at two levels. First, the model depicts four broad stages that are oriented toward qualitatively different goals and that help separate educational and psychological components of the program. Secondly, the figure depicts discrete procedures within each of the four main categories. The model describes the activities of the therapist or group leader, and rarely depicts the activities of the client. The model is, therefore, a guide to the therapist and suggests the procedures associated with the operation of a psycho-educational program. Figure 1 is a dynamic model describing the changing activities of the therapist as the training program progresses. There are four major sequential stages to the operation of the program: (1) definition of the skill to be trained, (2) awareness training, (3) skill enhancement, and (4) generalization training. Each of these steps builds upon the former while preparing the group for the next stage of the skill training program.

Within each of these four major sections are the basic procedures for completing that phase of the program. These steps are sequential, and each must be completed before proceeding to the next step. Included in the procedure are evaluation points where clients' skills must be assessed. Inadequate performance at these assessment points branches the program back several small steps so that parts of the training may be repeated.

When reading Figure 1, note that all movement within the major sections of the model is indicated by a solid line and that the arrow indicates the direction of movement. Movement may be for-

Figure 1. A Model for Psycho-educational Treatment Programs

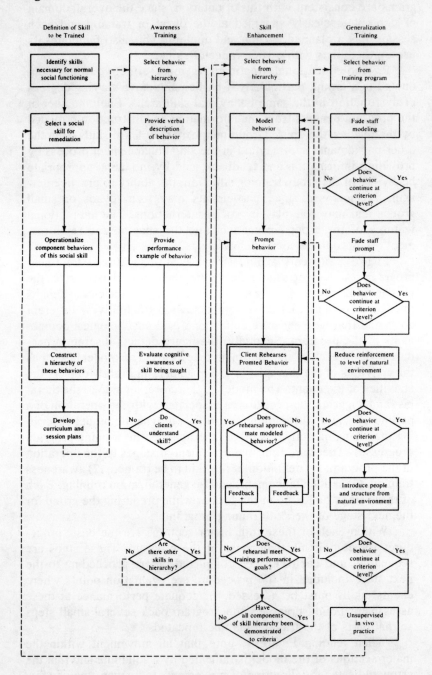

ward or backward within each step of the program. Interface between the four major sections of the program is indicated by a dotted line. All steps in the model refer to the actions of a staff member or group leader. The only exception is in the skill enhancement section, where there is a double outlined box indicating that the client rehearses a behavior. When the entire process of the program is completed, another social skill is selected for remediation as is depicted, and the entire procedure is repeated.

The operation of the program is complex and requires that the therapist be involved in a wide variety of educational and psychological tasks. For example, in the skill definition stage, the therapist is required to develop a curriculum and define the content of instruction for the program. This is an educationally oriented task. In comparison, in the skill enhancement section, the therapist must apply behavioral therapy and prompt the performance of successive approximations to the desired goal behavior. This is primarily a psychological task. This model simplifies the task of operating such a program by organizing the procedures and making them more objective and sequential.

Definition of Skill To Be Trained

The first step of the psycho-educational program is the definition of the skill to be trained. The constellation of adaptive social behaviors that are deemed to be important for good psychological functioning are delineated through a behavioral analysis of prosocial behavior. One of the many skills delineated in this process is selected for training and becomes the focus of the treatment. The skills that are not selected for a particular training group may become the focus of other psycho-educational groups, as indicated by the dotted line connecting the last step of the model back to the initial step. The behaviors associated with the identified skill are divided into components, specified, and operationalized. Finally, these behaviors are organized into a hierarchy ranging from the most simple and fundamental behaviors to the more sophisticated behaviors.

The skill definition section of the model is grounded in educational technology. This step is often omitted or only loosely applied in most contemporary psychological groups. The content of programs omitting this process is inclined to be less well organized and the parameters, goals, and procedures of the training session are therefore inconsistent.

Awareness Training

The second major section of the psycho-educational program acquaints the clients with the content and scope of the concepts and behaviors to be learned. The awareness training section explains to the clients much of the content that was concretized in the "Definition of Skills To Be Trained" section.

The major goal of the awareness training is to produce an understanding of the cognitive components of the skill being learned. An understanding is necessary to provide a cognitive model to organize the succeeding process of skill enhancement. Relying primarily on educational techniques, the clients are told about, and given examples of, the desired skill behaviors. This process increases the breadth and detail of their awareness and understanding of the behaviors they are to learn.

Skill Enhancement

The "Skill Enhancement" section of the program relies heavily on behavior modification techniques to train clients how to perform the actual social skill behaviors identified for training. The sequence of this training follows the commonly used procedures of behavioral psychology. First, a behavior is targeted for instruction from the standard hierarchy that was developed in the first stage of the program. Next, the behaviors are modeled by the therapist, and then the clients are prompted to perform the behavior at a level appropriate to their current skill level. Clients then perform (rehearse) the behavior and receive feedback on their performance. This chain of events is repeated as many times as necessary to teach the targeted behavior. This procedure provides the opportunity for repeated practice in the shaping of the clients' behavior until performance reaches criterion standards. After completing these procedures with one behavior from the hierarchy, another behavior is targeted from the hierarchy and the process is repeated.

Generalization Training

Generalization training is the last stage of psycho-educational treatment and primarily employs techniques from behavior therapy. This phase of treatment attempts to ensure that the skills learned in the sheltered therapy session are transferred to the natural environment. If treatment is to be considered successful, behaviors demonstrated with mental health staff and fellow clients must also be demonstrated with family, friends, and acquaintances in a variety of nontreatment settings. The ultimate goal of the skills enhancement program is for clients to use the new social skills in their behavioral repertoire in their unsupervised daily living.

During the generalization training phase of the treatment program, the artificial structuring aspects of the group that have expedited the development and maintenance of the client's new behaviors are systematically eliminated. First, staff modeling is reduced and eliminated, and then staff prompting of behavior is terminated. Next, the reinforcement associated with the performance of the new social behaviors is reduced to levels consistent with those occurring in the natural environment. Finally, natural reinforcers and settings are brought into the behavioral chain through the use of homework assignments.

If performance falters at any of these stages, the model depicts the appropriate level at which to reinstate the skill enhancement training procedures. Within this model, the client only repeats that portion of the training that is necessary to provide adequate practice of the subcriterion skill. Repeating more of the training than is necessary is wasteful of staff resources and unnecessarily repetitious for the clients. However, not re-introducing enough of the training sequence is likely to result in unnecessary failure for the clients.

APPLICATION OF THE PSYCHO-EDUCATIONAL MODEL

By employing the model for a psycho-educational treatment program, as depicted in Figure 1, it was possible to develop two comprehensive skill enhancement programs—a therapist-facilitated program and a game-facilitated program. The value of the model lies in the fact that its various steps needed only to be operationalized in order to develop a treatment program. It is important to keep in mind that there are a variety of ways to operationalize the model. In this chapter two examples of programs that have been derived from this model will be presented. Although the example programs were developed for use in a residential treatment setting that provided services for a general population of adult mental health clients, the programs were designed to have general application in a variety of treatment settings. Also, the procedures described here were developed for use by therapists with all levels of skill, from paraprofessional counselor to clinical psychologist. The programs that are described have been designed and used for the last 2 years at the Florida Mental Health Institute (F.M.H.I.).

The Therapist-Facilitated Psycho-Educational Program

As conceptualized in this model, a skill training program should address itself to a wide variety of social skill areas. The residential program developed under this model at F.M.H.I. has 14 different skill enhancement modules, such as communication skills, problem solving, assertion, relaxation, leisure skills, and family training.

Each of these skill areas is composed of a specific (although some-times overlapping) set of behaviors. The therapist-facilitated ap-proach can be used to teach each of these skills areas to mental health clients. The combination of all the individual treatment groups compromise the psycho-educational treatment program.

Since each of the many individual skill training groups are based on the same model, any one of them serves as a representa-tive example. The Interpersonal Communications group presented here will illustrate a therapist-facilitated application of the pro-posed psycho-educational model of treatment.

Definition of skill to be trained. The first step for the psycho-educational program was to identify the skills necessary for normal social functioning. From among these various skills, it was neces-sary to select one skill for remediation in each psycho-educational group. Based on experience with psychiatric populations, it was observed that these individuals often have significant deficits in their ability to communicate effectively, and communications skill training became the target for one group.

A review of research reports on behaviorally oriented com-munications training suggested that many of these programs were oriented toward merely increasing the frequency of verbalizations in clients who had low operant levels of verbal behavior. Rather than develop a program for increasing the frequency of verbaliza-tion, we were guided by the psycho-educational model to identify component behaviors of effective sophisticated communications, and to evolve a program to teach these qualitatively different behaviors. In doing so, the writings of Ivey (1974), Jourard (1971), Kagan (1975), Rogers (1961), and Truax and Carkhuff (1967) were used to determine the nature of the behavioral components of interpersonal communication. Based on the work of these writers, and the clinical expertise of the professional staff, the behavioral components of a comprehensive communications training program were delineated. The behaviors to be taught in the communica-tions program included: (1) nonverbal communication, (2) self-disclosure, (3) feedback, (4) paraphrasing, (5) open questions, and (6) feeling reflections.

Each of these components of communication was operational-ized in behavioral terms. For example, self-disclosure was defined as verbal behavior that communicates to another person the thoughts, feelings, or beliefs that an individual has about himself. Behaviorally, there are three parts to self-disclosure and each statement should contain the following components: (1) a situation-ally specific description of something that was seen, heard, or ex-perienced; (2) a statement of one's feelings about that experience;

and (3) a statement of what the individual would like to do with regard to his experience or feeling. An example of a first-rate self-disclosure statement which incorporates all the appropriate behavioral components would be, "When I hold my baby in my arms, I feel very affectionate toward her, and I hope that I will be able to continue this relationship with my daughter as she grows up." Regardless of the specific content of the statement, it is possible to determine if the three components of self-disclosure are present. An awareness of these content areas and the behavioral ability to perform them can be taught and shaped. They are clearly amenable to the psycho-educational approach to skill training.

All six of the component skills that make up the communications program were operationally defined the same way as illustrated above for self-disclosure behavior (see Table 1). They were arranged in a hierarchy according to their sequential level of difficulty as follows: (1) nonverbal communication, (2) self-disclosure, (3) feedback, (4) paraphrasing, (5) open questions, and (6) feeling reflections. Each time in the hierarchy then became a content area for the "Awareness Training" and "Skill Enhancement" sections of the program that followed. A discrete program was developed around each of these behavioral content areas.

For each of the six areas of the hierarchy, a curriculum and session plan was developed. These plans delineated the materials needed to conduct each treatment session, the approximate amount of time required for the training, and a thorough description of the procedures to be followed during the session. An example of a plan for an awareness training session and a skills enhancement session

Table 1
Definitions of Communication Skills

SKILL	DEFINITION
Self-Disclosure	A statement of what you feel or believe, along with a description of the situation which evoked it, and what you would like to happen.
Feedback	A form of self-disclosure relating to another person. It is comprised of a description of what you saw or heard, how that made you feel, and what you want to happen.
Paraphrasing	A rewording of what another person has said.
Open Question	A question that explores another person's statement without requiring an individual to respond "yes" or "no."
Feeling Reflection	An expression to a speaker of a feeling or emotion you have experienced in reference to his statement.

relating to self-disclosure are presented in Table 2 and Table 3 respectively. It was possible to develop these plans through the application of the model for psycho-educational treatment programs. The process and operations of each part of the training (e.g., awareness training, skill enhancement) were specified by the model. It was only necessary to develop plans in concordance with the model.

Table 2
An Example of a Plan for an Awareness Training Session on Self-Disclosure

Awareness Training: Self-disclosure

OBJECTIVES: 1. To develop a concrete understanding of the concepts of self-disclosure.
2. To establish a positive attitude toward self-disclosure by experiencing it in a supportive, nonthreatening atmosphere.

MATERIALS: Chart listing parts of self-disclosure statement (optional).

TIME: 30–45 minutes, depending on size of group.

   I. Conduct Didactic Lecture:
1. Explain the concept of feedback and include the following core material: (Self-disclosure skills are those which facilitate the expression of what you feel, believe, wish, intend, etc. There are three levels all utilizing the "I-message" format.)
Level I is a statement of what you feel or believe. (For example, "I feel angry.")
Level II is a statement of what you feel or believe, and additionally, a description of the situation which evoked this feeling or belief. (For example, "I feel angry when you make a mess in the kitchen.")
Level III is not only a statement of what you feel or believe, and a description of the situation which evoked it, but also a description of what you'd like to do. (For example, "I feel angry when you make a mess in the kitchen, and I'd like you to clean it up.")

  II. Conduct Exercise:
1. *Set up:* Arrange participants in a large circle.
2. *Instructions:* In this exercise each of you will have a chance to introduce yourself through the eyes of a friend. In order to do this, you are to pretend like you are a friend of yours, imitating his posture, voice, gestures, etc. While role playing your friend, you are to introduce yourself as you think your friend would. Introduce yourself through the eyes of your friend.
3. *Time:* Allow 2½ to 3 minutes speaking time for each member.
4. *Facilitator's role:* Encourge questions from other group members. Keep members within their roles and call time. Comment positively on appropriate participation by group members.

Table 3
An Example of a Plan for a Skill Enhancement Session on
Self-Disclosure

Skill enhancement: Self-disclosure

OBJECTIVES: 1. To learn self-disclosure behavior in a group setting.
    2. To perform self-disclosure in a variety of contexts.

MATERIALS: 1. Pencils for all group participants.
    2. Paper for all group participants.
    3. Blackboard.

  I. Briefly review didactic portion of awareness training on self-disclosure.
    TIME: 5 minutes

  II Conduct Exercise:
    TIME: 30 minutes
    Divide participants into small groups, of three or four.

INSTRUCTIONS: 1. Instruct the group to write 10 to 12 positive or negative descriptive adjectives such as: flashy, noisy, fast, etc.
    2. Write down on the blackboard a series of role types that all participants have or will have experienced such as: child, son/daughter, student, adult, grandparent, aging adult.
    3. Write on the blackboard a series of environmental events that all participants can relate to such as: in a group, using free time, having an ideal weekend, involved in a career.
    4. Instruct the group—"Each person should choose three of the descriptive adjectives out of the 10 or 12 he has written down. Read an adjective and describe why it applies to you, keeping in mind the self-disclosure model and skills."
    5. Go around the group having each participant take one adjective at a time until each has described three.
    6. Instruct the group—"Each participant should tell the group how he sees or imagines himself in each of the series of role types I have written on the board. Each group member should go through the whole series describing himself in each, again keeping in mind the self-disclosure model and skills."
    7. Instruct the group—"Each participant should tell the other group members how he sees or imagines himself in the different environmental situations I have written on the board. Each member should

take one situation at a time, going around the group until you all have described yourselves in relation to all four. Keep in mind the self-disclosure model and skills list.''

8. Instruct the group—''Each participant should tell the other members his beliefs about an issue that is important to him such as: politics, religion, sex.''

III. Conduct Exercise:
    TIME 5 minutes

1. When first time period is up (30 minutes), the facilitator calls time. If a player is in the midst of his turn, the turn should be completed and then play should be stopped. If players are between turns, a new turn should not be started.

2. Maintain playing subgroups. Instruct the group—''Each participant should take a turn at giving feedback in response to these statements:
'Tell one thing you have learned about yourself while doing this exercise.'
'Tell one thing you have learned about each of the other group members while playing this exercise.' ''

Break
    TIME: 10 minutes

IV. Conduct Exercise:
    TIME: 15 minutes

1. Tell the groups—''The purpose of this role play is to practice application of the self-disclosure skills you have just learned in the exercises.''

2. Facilitator should ask each player to tell the group something about himself.

V. Conduct Exercise:
    TIME: 30 minutes

1. Arrange participants into large group.
2. Setting up the exercises:
   a. Draw a continuum on the board to evalute participants' group involvement.

   _____
   involved   so-so   uninvolved

   b. Draw a continuum on the board to evaluate group member relationships.

   _____
   family   acquaintance   stranger

   c. Instructions:
      a. Ask each member of the group—''What are your strengths and why do you consider them strengths?''
      b. Ask each member of the large group—''What

are your weaknesses and why do you consider them weaknesses?''

c. Tell each member—''Please come to the board and mark where you see yourself in relation to other large group members in terms of involvement.'' Ask the group—''Why is this so?'' ''Keep in mind the feedback model and skills list.''

d. Tell each member to come to the board and mark where he sees the group in relation to himself. Ask the group, ''Why is this so?'' ''Keep in mind the feedback model and skills list.''

VI. Conduct Brief Discussion of What was Learned.

Awareness training. Awareness training emphasizes the presentation of didactic lectures and complimentary group exercises (see Table 2) to teach clients the concepts supporting each of the six component areas of effective communication. The rationale for learning these skills and an explanation of the goals of the training program are provided to clients.

The awareness training program requires 6 hours of client contact and is started by selecting the first skill from the hierarchy developed in the previous section. This skill is introduced by the therapist in an extensive didactic training session. During the didactic presentation, the therapist acts out behavioral examples of the communications skill. Immediately following this presentation, small group exercises are facilitated to help illustrate the content of the didactic lecture. These exercises allow the clients to role play social situations. Thus, clients are able to have a behavioral experience of the skill to which they have just been introduced. During the exercises, the group leader moves among the clients, helping them to perform the behavior correctly and ensuring that they understand the concept presented.

The goal of these exercises is to provide examples of behavior associated with the communication skill being taught. The examples help clients to gain an in-depth conceptual understanding of the skill being presented. Actual competence in the performance of the behavioral skill is not the goal of these sessions, but is the domain of the next section of training. Once the group leader is confident that the client has a good understanding of the content of the entire communication program, the skill enhancement phase is begun. The awareness training section of the communications group requires four sessions, each lasting 90 minutes in order to teach the six conceptual areas delineated for the program.

Skill enhancement. The goal of the skill enhancement phase of the psycho-educational program (see Table 3) is to establish behavioral competence in the performance of each of the communication behaviors (e.g., self-disclosure) identified in the first section of the program. Each new communication skill selected from the hierarchy is introduced with a brief summary of the didactic portion of the awareness training materials. Next, a small group exercise is facilitated, during which the group leader actively works to modify the client's communication behavior in the desired direction. The session is ended with a group discussion of what the client has learned during the exercises.

The small group activities outlined in Table 2 are the primary arena where clients learn the communication skills in the therapist-facilitated program. Each activity elicits the behavior that is intended to be trained in that session. Once elicited in some form, it is shaped and reinforced. The operation of the skills enhancement portion of the program follows the sequence detailed in Figure 1.

In accordance with these guidelines, the therapist first explains the procedures that clients are to follow in the small group exercise. Next, he models the proper communication behavior, such as self-disclosure, and indicates the three components of his self-disclosure statements. The group members then begin to carry out the structured exercise. As they become involved in these activities, the therapist circulates among them, providing prompts where necessary and reinforcing approximations of correct behavior. During this time, the most proficient clients are reinforced for providing feedback and support to other group members who are at a lower level of performance. As the session continues, the therapist shapes and reinforces behavior toward the desired goal, requiring closer approximations as time proceeds. As the session continues, the therapist provides fewer prompts and more intermittent reinforcement. Clients in the group are increasingly reinforced for being models of appropriate behavior and providing prompts for other group members.

Exercises used in the group sessions operate for at least one hour. At the end of the exercise, the facilitator leads the group members in a discussion of what they learned about communications during that session. After a rest break, the procedures described above are repeated with a different exercise for more sophisticated practice of the communication skills.

All skill enhancement sessions are operated according to this format, although the content of sessions differs for each of the six skills being taught. The skills enhancement section of the communications training program consists of 10 sessions, each lasting 90 minutes.

Generalization training. Insuring that skills performed in the psycho-educational training setting generalize to nontreatment environments is a critical phase of the psycho-educational program. There are generally wide individual differences in the extent to which clients will continue to perform the social skills they have learned once the facilitative influence of the therapeutic program is removed. Therefore, the procedures of this phase of the program are somewhat more individualized than other sections. As the model indicates, there is a considerable degree of decision-based interface between the skill enhancement section and the generalization training section of the model.

In applying the psycho-educational treatment model to the communications program, a number of training approaches were developed to facilitate generalization.

Fading. The modeling, prompting, and high levels of reinforcement employed during the skill enhancement phase of training are faded toward the end of the training sessions. Within each training session, the fading is begun during the second skill enhancement exercise. This procedure allows the therapist to determine whether the skill is firmly among the client's repertoire of behaviors, at least within the therapy situation. By the end of the second group exercise, it is most desirable to have as many of the clients as possible performing the task autonomously. Those clients who were most competent in the skill are urged to take the autonomous role of aiding the less competent. Thus, the direct role of the staff member is reduced. If, however, the client's performance of the desired skill falters, the group leader reinstates those portions of the skill enhancement procedures necessary to re-establish the behavior.

Generalization is also facilitated in a manner consistent with the treatment model through the use of exercises during skill enhancement that employ combinations of communication skills. After a number of the communication skills have been taught, exercises are employed that require previously learned skills to be practiced in combination with new skills. Using this technique, it is possible to chain component skills into larger socially functional units.

In the combination exercises, an example of which is shown in Table 4, the main focus of instruction is on the newly introduced behavior. There is planned modeling or prompting of the previously learned behaviors. If they are not performed when prompted, training is dropped back to the appropriate level, in accordance with the model. The combination of fading and combination exercises helps to determine whether the clients' behaviors could be performed within the sheltered therapy setting with a minimum of staff support.

Table 4
An Example of a Plan for a Combination Skills Enhancement Session

Skill enhancement: Listening and paraphrasing, asking open questions, and reflecting others' feelings.

OBJECTIVES: 1. To practice combining four elements of effective communication.
2. To integrate the use of the four elements of effective communication into a useful whole.

MATERIALS: 1. Blackboard.
2. Pencils and paper for participants.

I. Conduct Didactic Review:

TIME: 15 minutes

INSTRUCTIONS: 1. *Sample content for lecture on listening:* I have already covered the value of developing good listening skills, so now I will just review the definitions of the three basic listening skills, paraphrasing, asking open questions, and feeling reflection.
   a. *Paraphrasing:* Listening to what another person is saying and saying back to them what they have just said using different words.
   b. *Open questions:* A question that helps a person explore more rather than forcing a yes or no answer to a certain question.
   c. *Feeling reflection:* A response in which you say back to a person a feeling or emotion you think they are expressing.
2. Invite questions from group members on clarification of the listening skills.

II. Conduct Triad Exercise:

TIME: 30 minutes

INSTRUCTIONS: 1. Assign triads: Divide participants into subgroups of three or four.
2. Setting up the exercises.
   a. Assign roles to three members of triad: observer; listener; speaker. Give the observer a sheet of paper and a pencil. On that sheet of paper, the observer is to make three columns: one labeled paraphrase, one labeled feeling reflection, and one labeled open question.
3. Conducting the exercises.
   a. The speaker is asked by the facilitator to self-disclose to the listener. The listener then responds to the speaker using one of three basic listening responses. The observer keeps a frequency count on the number of responses that occur in each category. Continue role playing

for 10 minutes using this procedure, then have triad members change roles and play for another 10 minutes. This procedure should be repeated until all triad members have played each role (30 minutes of role playing). After each 10 minute segment, all triad members should discuss the frequency of the listeners' responses and what it implies.

III. Structured Processing of Exercise:

TIME: 5 minutes

INSTRUCTIONS: 1. After 30 minutes of exercises the facilitator should call time. If the group is in the midst of the exercise, the interaction should be continued until the exercise is completed.

2. Maintain triads. Have each participant take a turn at giving feedback in response to these statements.

   a. Tell one thing you have learned about yourself while doing this exercise.

   b. Tell one thing you have learned about each of the other triad members while doing this exercise.

Break

TIME: 10 minutes

IV. Conduct Role Play Exercise:

TIME: 15 minutes

INSTRUCTIONS: Knowledge of listening skills: Have participants return to triads. Assign roles to each triad member—listener, speaker, observer. Have the speaker make a self-disclosure statement. Have the listener respond to this self-disclosure using each of the three listening responses. The observer should give feedback after each response, and if the observer feels it is necessary, the listener should repeat the response. If there is time, have triad members change roles and repeat the process.

V. Conduct Group Exercises:

TIME: 30 minutes

INSTRUCTIONS: 1. Arrange participants into large group.

2. Setting up the exercises.

   a. Put a continuum on the board like the one shown below:

   passive listener   active listener

3. Conducting the exercises.

   a. The facilitator should act as a stimulus by making self-disclosure statements that either express a feeling (example: I feel tired today), describe a situation (example: My roommate uses my tools all the time, and I don't like it), or make a statement (example: I think I will go out tonight). The facilitator should direct statements to each large group member. The group member should then respond giving what he/she considers to be the best active listening response. The group's other group members should then give feedback to the listener evaluating their responses.

Sample statements:
(1) I feel angry that I failed my test.
(2) I am very tired of going to work every morning.
(3) I feel sick today.
(4) I am leaving town tomorrow.
(5) Tomorrow I am going to a party at my friend's house.
(6) The rent on my apartment is due tomorrow.
(7) My sister and I do not get along well.
(8) I don't like it when you bother me while I'm reading.
(9) I would like to punch Fred in the nose.

   b. Have each large group member come to the board and rate the other group members in terms of their active listening skills. After they rate each person they should tell why they placed them where they did on the continuum.
VI. Conduct Discussion of What Was Learned:
   A. Discussion Question:
      1. What is different about the four skills learned?
      2. How do you plan on using these skills?
      3. What was similar about the four skills learned?

Outside group assignments. In order to introduce people and structures from the natural environment into the chain of behaviors being trained, two types of outside assignments are encouraged. First of all, group member are assigned the task of performing some of their communication skills on the residential treatment unit where they are living. These interactions are performed with staff and clients who are not members of the communications therapy program. Group members report back their success or failure at performing these on-unit assignments. The performance of these assignments is observed by the treatment staff, and this additional feedback is available to determine the clients' level of skill and, according to the model, to provide the necessary repetition of previous training if required.

A second type of out-of-group assignment is "homework." Homework assignments are generally performed when the clients are given a pass to complete some activity in the community, or when they are home to visit friends or family on weekends. The homework assignments allow clients to practice new communication skills in settings outside of the residential treatment unit. If clients report success back to the group, they attempt other unsupervised practice of the communication skills. If they experience difficulty, the opportunity for additional training is available.

Having completed the 6-week psycho-educational skill enhancement program, the opportunity for continued training is still available. In the present program, clients enter a "transitional" phase of treatment to further prepare them for re-entry into the community. Many of the activities and behavioral assignments of the transitional program require clients to perform the social skills they have learned. If a client continues to experience difficulty in communication behaviors, he can re-enter the skill enhancement program for a refresher course. This process is followed by clients who either have severe communications deficits at the onset of the program or who have progressed very slowly in their acquisition of new behavioral skills.

A second alternative that is available to clients who have progressed to the transitional program is to act as a co-facilitator for a communications training group. In this situation, the client has an opportunity to teach others the communication behaviors he learned when he himself was a group member. Several writers have suggested the importance of allowing individuals to train others the skills they themselves are learning (Egan, 1975; Kalafat & Baroto, 1977). Training others in the performance of communication skills is considered to be an important step in solidifying the clients' new behaviors so they will continue in unsupervised, nontreatment environments.

As may be seen from this example, the psycho-educational model helps to clarify and structure this communications training program. The content of each treatment session is well defined, and the procedures are explicitly organized and arranged sequentially in a curriculum. However, some sections of the therapist-facilitated program require the talents of a skilled behavior therapist. The effective operation of this program depends on the ability of the therapist to generate interest and motivation in the clients. Also, the therapist must have talent in providing the critical functions of modeling, prompting, shaping, and reinforcing the behavior of the clients.

The therapist-facilitated model is therefore reserved for use by a skilled therapist. Such a treatment program provides an excellent therapy experience with many desirable features not associated with non-psycho-educational groups.

A Game-Facilitated Approach
to Psycho-educational Treatment

The parts of the therapist-facilitated communication program that require sophisticated leadership skills are mostly associated with the skill enhancement section of the model. The activities associated with this section of the program make it formidable for other than an experienced behavior therapist to undertake the operation of the group. Because of our desire to develop programs for use in state hospitals, prisons, and other mental health programs where staff often have little training in behavioral therapies, we also developed an alternative skill enhancement technology. The alternative program employs a game-facilitated technology in place of the sophisticated behavior techniques typically used to direct the skills enhancement section of the communication program.

The therapy games used in this alternative group are similar to those shown to be effective in education and business (Boocock, 1968; Uretsky, 1973) to facilitate feedback, discussion, and personal involvement in learning. Previous applications of games have shown this technology to be effective for training problem solving, counseling skills, and the therapeutic manipulation of emotions (Inbar & Stoll, 1972).

Although no reported study has used this type of game as an alternative to therapist-facilitated groups, several features of therapeutic games make them very useful for skill enhancement. Of prime importance, games are structured, objective, and they focus on overt behavior. Game procedures can be developed to prompt social skills behaviors and reinforce their performance. Also, the therapeutic game format can be addressed to a wide variety of skill enhancement areas to teach a multitude of individual and group behaviors.

The use of the model for psycho-educational programs presented in this paper is important in guiding the development of the communication game procedures. Primarily, the model was employed to identify the processes that should occur during the gaming group. The games were therefore designed and constructed so that they would facilitate the occurrence of these processes.

The actual operation of the therapist-facilitated and game-facilitated programs appear to be radically different during the skill enhancement section. On closer examination, however, it is apparent that although the technology is different, the processes are very similar. The major difference between the programs is that in the therapist-facilitated group, a staff member facilitates and controls the behavior procedures (modeling, prompting, reinforcement); in the game program, the format of the games themselves facilitates and controls the operation of these behavioral procedures. The game, because of the procedures and content built into it, in many ways takes the place of the skilled behavior therapist. As the game program is described, its similarity to the therapist-facilitated program will become apparent, despite their surface differences. After the description of the gaming application of the psycho-educational model, a more thorough comparison of the therapist-facilitated and game-facilitated technologies will be provided.

The procedures of the game program for communications training are identical to those of the contemporary therapist-facilitated program during three phases: (1) definition of skill to be trained, (2) awareness training, and (3) generalization training. These sections were left unchanged since they were a very effective "educational" orientation that could be operated by relatively unskilled staff with good social skills, the ability to follow directions, and the ability to conduct didactic lectures. Operation of the generalization training segment was aided by interfacing it with other programs (e.g., a transitional program). The primary focus on the game technology is in the difficult-to-operate skill enhancement section. The following description will explain the procedures of the skill enhancement game technology.

The game version of our communication skills program follows the model illustrated in Figure 1. First, the specific behavior to be trained in a particular therapy session is selected from the hierarchy developed in the skill definition stage of the program. This target behavior is modeled by a staff member in conjunction with the presentation of an abbreviated version of the awareness training associated with the target behavior. The procedures for eliciting (prompting), rehearsing, and reinforcing approximations of the targeted communication behavior are built into the game format. A description of a communication game will serve to illustrate how the game therapy model develops social skills.

Description of Communication Games

There are seven basic components to each communications game: (1) a playing board to focus and organize the sequence of the training (an example of a self-disclosure game board is present in Figure 2), (2) a set of playing rules to explain how the game oper-

Figure 2. Self-Disclosure Game Board

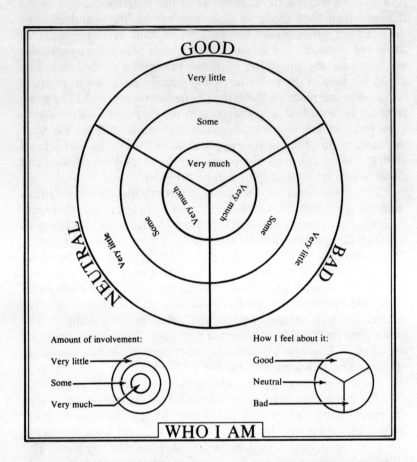

ates (the rules of procedure, etc.), (3) stimulus items such as cards with written instructions on them to prompt behavior, (4) a written set of criteria for evaluating and providing feedback on the performance of the prompted behaviors, (5) a scoring system for recording and providing feedback on performance, (6) play money for providing token reinforcement, and (7) markers to move around the playing board to record progress and the number of rehearsal trials.

Eight different games have been developed to teach communications skills. There are two self-disclosure games, two feedback games, and two games for instructing paraphrasing, open questions, and feeling reflections in a combined fashion. In addition, there are two games for teaching and reviewing all of the communications behaviors together. The section on nonverbal communication is taught by a lecture; no game is necessary for that skill.

Client and Staff Roles

In addition to participating in the game and learning the component behaviors of communications, players take on roles such as game manager, banker, vote caller, and vote recorder. Clients are totally responsible for organizing and managing the group experience after the operation and rationale of the game have been explained by a staff member.

This peer management model is consistent with the psycho-educational model of treatment, which assumes that it is therapeutic for clients to have responsibilities and for them to help each other to the fullest possible extent in the treatment program. When clients must depend on staff, their feelings of helplessness and inadequacy may be reinforced. The structure, concreteness, and simplicity of the games help clients to interact therapeutically with each other. Furthermore, peer pressure helps to ensure active participation of everyone, both in taking turns during the game and in evaluating each other's communication behavior. A patient whose attention is distracted by hallucinations, for example, receives continued reminders from other patients to participate since he will hold up the normal progress of the game.

The staff have a minimal role during skill enhancement when games are used. The staff member explains the rules of the game procedure and is available to help interpret these rules, resolve disagreements between players regarding the accuracy of reinforcement, and explain the meaning of a stimulus item, if necessary. The complicated and sophisticated tasks of prompting, rehearsing, and reinforcing the targeted communication behavior are taken care of by the game format.

An Example of a Game

Discussion of one of the communications games will serve to illustrate this technology. "Who I Am" is a self-disclosure game. The materials consist of one "Who I Am" board for each group of four players, a set of 50 "Who I Am" cards, $1000 in play money, and four sets of vote cards (each set has a 0, 1, and 2 card). The player selected as Game Manager sets up the game and reads an explanation of the game to the group.

Each "Who I Am" card has one word on it which probably has had an impact on the players' lives. The cards contain words such as "travel," "sister," "mother," "religion," and "job." The circular board (see Figure 2) is divided into three color-coded segments for players to rate how they feel about the word on the card as either "good," "neutral," or "bad." Each of these three segments cuts through three concentric circles for rating the amount of involvement one's life has with this word. These circles are labeled "little," "some," or "very much."

The first round of the game starts with the shortest player (or youngest, or oldest) drawing a card from the deck. He reads the word, rates how he feels about it, and identifies the appropriate color coded segment to represent it on the circle. Next, the client decides the amount of his life that is involved with the word ("very much" for example) and places the card on the appropriate section of color. He then explains to the group why the card was placed there, using an appropriate self-disclosure statement. The Vote Caller then calls for feedback on the self-disclosure statement from all persons other than the player. Each person selects a vote card (0 = poor response, 1 = acceptable response, 2 = excellent response) and places it face down in front of him. Votes are cast according to a clearly defined outline for rating self-disclosure (each player has a copy of the criteria outlined previously). When all decisions are made, the cards are turned over. The Vote Recorder sums and records the votes, and the player who made the self-disclosure statement receives from the Banker a payment in play money equal to the total number of votes received. The better the statement, the higher the number of votes and the more token reinforcement in play money he receives. The game continues with the player to the starter's right relocating the same card to reflect his own feelings and involvement. The feedback process is repeated. After all four players have responded to the card, a new one is drawn and play continues. The game ends when the allotted time period is up and the player with the most money wins.

The game is played for 45 minutes, then play stops and clients have a chance to discuss what they have learned and to take a rest break. Play is then resumed for another 45 minutes, followed by a structured processing of what has been learned about self-disclosure. Within a group format, clients are asked to respond to such questions as: What did you learn about self-disclosure? In what situations in your life could you make use of this skill? When do you have the most trouble self-disclosing?

COMPARISON OF THE CONTEMPORARY THERAPIST-FACILITATED
AND GAME-FACILITATED METHODS OF TREATMENT

Figure 3 illustrates the comparative operations of the therapist- and game-facilitated programs. As may be seen in this Figure,

Figure 3. Game Facilitated and Therapist Facilitated Skill Enhancement

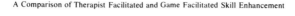

A Comparison of Therapist Facilitated and Game Facilitated Skill Enhancement

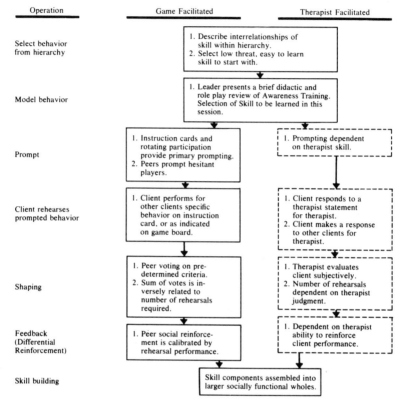

Operation	Game Facilitated	Therapist Facilitated
Select behavior from hierarchy	1. Describe interrelationships of skill within hierarchy. 2. Select low threat, easy to learn skill to start with.	
Model behavior	1. Leader presents a brief didactic and role play review of Awareness Training. Selection of Skill to be learned in this session.	
Prompt	1. Instruction cards and rotating participation provide primary prompting. 2. Peers prompt hesitant players.	1. Prompting dependent on therapist skill.
Client rehearses prompted behavior	1. Client performs for other clients specific behavior on instruction card, or as indicated on game board.	1. Client responds to a therapist statement for therapist. 2. Client makes a response to other clients for therapist.
Shaping	1. Peer voting on predetermined criteria. 2. Sum of votes is inversely related to number of rehearsals required.	1. Therapist evaluates client subjectively. 2. Number of rehearsals dependent on therapist judgment.
Feedback (Differential Reinforcement)	1. Peer social reinforcement is calibrated by rehearsal performance.	1. Dependent on therapist ability to reinforce client performance.
Skill building	Skill components assembled into larger socially functional wholes.	

several elements are indistinguishable between the game and the therapist models. The procedures for "selecting behavior from hierarchy," "modeling behavior," and the last two steps of the skill enhancement phase which are called "skill building" proceed in an identical manner for both training approaches. These three areas are, however, peripheral and supportive to the critical hub of skill development activities. Prompting, rehearsal, shaping and differential reinforcement are the critical working elements in the skill enhancement phase of the model. These procedures are based directly on experimental learning research in psychology.

The similarities and differences between the game- and therapist-facilitated models within this core of the learning steps can be organized in a number of ways. One important point of comparison has to do with the roles of the group leader and the clients. The systematic structure and content of a game technology vastly reduces the dependency on the leader's skill for the group to be successfully operated. Many of the functions that usually are associated with the leader's skill and knowledge of sophisticated techniques are built directly into the game's mechanics. This allows less skilled therapists to perform as well as more sophisticated professionals, since they are called on to do little more than set up, explain, and proctor the game. In many treatment settings, this feature increases the quality of therapy available to clients and certainly increases cost-effectiveness of the treatment process. The one difficulty with the high level of structure and independent operation of the game is that it does not provide opportunities for the highly skilled therapist to modify the learning experience to suit individual client needs unless he chooses to modify the game itself. This, of course, is only a difficulty to the extent that highly skilled therapists are available to make these sophisticated clinical discriminations.

The role of the client in sustaining the treatment process is substantially increased within the gaming model. The client is called upon to take an active responsibility for his own treatment and the treatment of others. The client conducts this function in much the same way that a therapist does in more traditional group therapy approaches. In many ways, a significant part of the role usually allocated to the therapist is structured and reallocated to the client. In the game format, there is also less variability in the help that each client is given, particularly in terms of prompting, rehearsal, shaping, and differential reinforcement, because each one of these elements is built into the rotating structure of the game process. This is in sharp contrast to the implicit or explicit voluntarism that largely controls client participation and activity within the therapist-facilitated program.

In gaming, roles are clearly defined. There is no question about what is expected of each person, what he is going to do, and what he will receive in return. It is identical for each participant. In actual practice, the game format seems to increase the participation of many clients, particularly of the lower-level clients. Games seem to have less impact upon those clients who are already well motivated and actively involved in their treatment process.

The actual procedures and processes of skill enhancement are another point of comparison between the therapist- and game-facilitated programs. In both of these approaches, the skill enhancement process begins identically, with the selection of a behavior to be trained. Behaviors are selected from a social skills hierarchy in a systematic way, since all behaviors of the hierarchy are interrelated on such dimensions as performance sequence, complexity, threat, and difficulty. The initial skills to be trained early in the performance sequence are simple, low threat, and relatively easy to learn. As communication skills are developed and a foundation is laid, more complex and potentially anxiety-provoking skills are trained.

At the beginning of each game- or therapist-facilitated session, there is a brief review of the didactic portion of the awareness training section, with specific emphasis on the skill to be trained during that session. The leader gives a short lecture reviewing the concept, then role plays the exact behaviors to be practiced during the training session. Clients are given an opportunity to ask questions during this time, but they do not have the opportunity to actually participate in active practice.

It is in the prompting process that the game- and therapist-facilitated approaches begin to sharply diverge. In the gaming approach, prompts are primarily provided by the game through the use of instruction cards, information written on the game board, and by rotating the players' turns to participate. These procedures give clear instructions as to what specific behavior is to be performed, to whom, and when. An illustration of what an instruction card might say is, "Tell the group about why some people dislike me." Such prompts provide low ambiguity and high consistency of training across clients.

When the prompted client does not perform the expected behavior within a limited amount of time after the game prompts him, the peer prompting comes into operation because his hesitancy holds up the other players' opportunity to play. Other players of the game begin to direct the client to rehearse the behavior requested by the stimulus card. In the gaming approach, the game and the peers take all the responsibility for prompting, and they reprompt the rehearsal by reiterating the instructions and by modeling the appropriate behavior. If a client delays his rehearsal, a peer immediately restarts the rehearsal.

For the gaming model, the decision processes that are the essence of shaping are performed on a peer basis through a structured voting mechanism. Each player has several cards in front of him which allow him to evaluate how adequate he considers the client's rehearsal. These judgments are based on specific behavioral criteria outlined in the game instructions. The games are designed so that, as the sum of the peer evaluations of a particular rehearsal decreases, the number of times that the behavior will have to be rehearsed increases. This ensures that the amount of practice is tailored to each client's specific skills deficit. The leader has essentially no role in this shaping and decision-making process.

In contrast, in the therapist-facilitated approach, the decision for repetitive behavior rehearsal is primarily the responsibility of the leader and highly dependent upon his clinical skills and judgment. Typically, the amount of rehearsal in the therapist-facilitated approach is more closely related to the client's willingness to volunteer and to initiate rehearsal than it is to the quality of his performance. Thus, poor performers may dominate the group if they are willing to volunteer. Typically, however, those who perform poorly tend to volunteer less frequently, unless the leader specifically intervenes to structure repetitions of the behavior. The less skill possessed by the therapist, the less likely these functions will be adequately performed.

Within the gaming approach, clearly structured reinforcement is an integral part of the scorekeeping and peer voting process. Token points are awarded and clients move their markers around the playing board as a clear indication of their performance. The provision of peer social reinforcement is also proportional to the individual's quality of performance. Such a system applies clear contingencies relating to the behavioral performance. Since these token and social reinforcers are integrated within the obvious character of the game structure, they provide a sense of equity to the differential reinforcement process, and the client seldom feels picked on or unfairly treated as a function of his evaluation.

In the therapist-facilitated model, differential reinforcement of rehearsed performance is somewhat catch-as-catch-can. It is solely a function of the leader-client interaction and depends upon the therapist's clinical skills, judgment, and reinforcing qualities. If the leader is called upon to operate more than one cluster of client exercises, his ability to provide the reinforcing element is greatly reduced. Catch-as-catch-can reinforcement of client behavior makes the contingencies for appropriate performance extremely vague and irregular. Under these conditions, clients have difficulty developing an appropriate expectancy for differential reinforcement of performance.

As each of the skills is learned, in either the therapist- or game-facilitated approach, they have to be assembled into larger, more functional, units in order for them to be useful in a natural social setting. In the flow chart of procedures relating to this process (Figure 1), the two decision diamonds are critical. The first diamond determines whether the skill has been shaped to meet a high level of competency and whether shaping can, therefore, be terminated. The second diamond initiates the shaping of a new skill from the hierarchy of behaviors to be trained. In the game-facilitated program, progression of this sort is more highly structured and automatic, whereas, in the therapist-facilitated program, these processes are decided by the therapist.

As may be seen, there are many similarities and differences between the therapist- and game-facilitated programs. They both can be expected to have similar training effects with clients. The prime variable that should be considered when selecting which procedure to use is the level of behavior therapy skill of the therapist. The less skilled the therapists available, the more helpful the game-facilitated program is in ensuring that clients receive a good program of skill enhancement.

Evaluation of the Psycho-Educational Program

There are many ways to evaluate the model and programs presented in this chapter. Overall evaluations will be discussed here, while more molecular assessments will, by necessity, be reserved for future reports. In evaluating the materials presented here, we will focus primarily on program issues.

First of all, it is necessary to make some judgment with regard to the usefulness and heuristic value of the model proposed in this paper. In our work, this model has made an extremely important contribution to our understanding of the psycho-educational processes of the programs we have developed and conducted. We now have a much clearer understanding of the necessary procedures for social skill training. This clarity is shared by individual therapists conducting groups within our residential program and results in increased consistency of services. The importance of consistency in behavioral (particularly research) programs has been well documented (Patterson, 1976).

The model also has proven to be helpful for training new staff and for staff development. The procedures to be performed in the group are clearly defined in the model and may easily be mastered by new staff. Training is especially easy when compared to that required for undefined and open-ended groups. The model permits and encourages the development of treatment handbooks that specify the nature of and procedures for each skill training module. These handbooks make our programs more readily available for use by our staff and by therapists in other agencies.

Another consideration is the extent to which psycho-educational group treatment can be used as the foundation of a rehabilitative program. In this regard, our experience clearly demonstrates that a major treatment program can be based on skills training guided by this model. At our institution, therapist- and game-facilitated programs are the basis of treatment for a 32-bed residential psychiatric facility, whose staffing pattern is similar to that of a state mental hospital. With this staff, an active and intense rehabilitation program has been established. All levels of treatment competency are represented on the residential unit; staff from all these levels conduct meaningful psycho-educational programs.

The clients have also responded well to these programs. They are actively involved in their treatment and function well in the groups. In the present program, the clients have a heavy schedule of groups to attend each day. These groups include training in communications, problem solving, relaxation, leisure, sex, nutrition, and assertion, among others. In fact, each client is involved in an average of over 10 hours of training per day. This amount of direct treatment is much greater than the amount that is typically provided by residential settings operating in accordance with other models of treatment. The primary reason for this large amount of direct treatment is because all the staff, not just the highly skilled psychologists, psychiatrists, and social workers, are capable of operating psycho-educational groups. In terms of facilitating structured staff-client contact, these programs are an overwhelming success.

An evaluation of the game technology presented in this chapter is also worthy of comment. The game technology was developed so that the psycho-educational training groups could be operated by professional staff with a limited capacity to conduct more conventional groups. We had observed that, in many mental health settings, a large number of staff have the desire to provide active treatment, but due to a lack of specific skills they are relegated to monitoring and supervising the clients' general ward activities. The treatment groups and active interventions in these settings are primarily conducted by psychologists, psychiatrists, and other highly trained mental health personnel. These highly trained staff, of course, always represent the great minority of the personnel available. This situation results in the underutilization of the largest segment of the available manpower. Technologies that would alleviate this situation would permit better utilization of staff resources.

We have found that the therapeutic games can, in fact, be effectively conducted by lower level staff, paraprofessionals, and even clients. These individuals need only brief training in how to present the awareness training and how the games work. After this training, they need minor supervision and support from higher-level staff.

In addition to their use on the present unit, these games are being used in a number of other clinical settings such as state hospitals and mental health centers. They are recognized as technological innovations that facilitate the utilization of a wide range of mental health staff to increase the amount of services delivered to clients.

Cost-effective mental health treatment has been a desirable side effect of the game technology. Not only do games allow for the full utilization of inexpensive staff (or paraprofessionals), they allow for each staff member to have contact with a greater number of clients. On our program, the contemporary therapist-facilitated programs required at least one (and often two) staff for each group of 10 to 12 clients. Using the gaming procedures, we have conducted comparable treatment groups employing one staff person for 20 clients. This is possible since each board game involves four clients, and the therapy activities merely involve the simultaneous operation of five replications of the same game. The amount of staff involvement that is required to conduct five replications of the game is only slightly greater than when a single game is being played. The awareness training portion of the gaming groups, because of its classroom orientation, is easily presented to 20 clients.

Does a client's behavior change as a function of these psychoeducational groups? Evaluations of specific treatment groups are in progress and long-term follow-up data on behavioral changes attributable to the overall program are also being collected. In lieu of these data, clinical assessments of the program will be presented.

As with all treatment programs, the psycho-educational method seems to work best with the most highly motivated client. Surprisingly, however, we have found that many of the low-level and unmotivated clients respond very favorably to the educational format of much of our training. The game technology has been particularly effective in capturing the interest of clients and teaching them new skills. In general, the vast majority of our clients show a substantial increase in social skills after experiencing the six-week training program we employ. In fact, the clients often become such good assertive communicators that the staff cannot "push them around" and often find themselves complying to a wide array of clients' desires. Of course, on occasion an assertive wife will return to us from a visit home sporting a black eye that was given to her by an "aggressive" husband unused to her new mode of interaction. These cases become a target for our family-training program.

It is important to note that the residential program that is built on this psycho-educational model has a fixed duration. Every client is discharged at the end of 9 weeks of treatment, which includes 6 weeks of skill training, and 3 weeks for transition back into the community. Nearly all of our clients would have been sent to a state psychiatric hospital had they not entered our program. With this information in mind, it is significant that after the 9 weeks of our program no client has ever been discharged to a state hospital. Of 96 randomly selected clients who have been discharged, only 5 have entered a supervised mental health setting (half-way house). Most of the clients were rehabilitated to the extent that they were discharged to family, friends, or to a boarding home (63, 11, and 2 respectively). In this sample, 15 of the clients were discharged to independent community living situations. These data certainly suggest that clients receiving our services have been diverted, at least temporarily, from the mental health system and have been returned to community living. The long-term community adjustment of these clients currently is being evaluated, and these data will be reported when available.

A final point of evaluation is of relevance to psychologists and nonmedical practitioners. The psycho-educational model described here appears to be an effective augmentation to the medically oriented treatment of residential psychiatric clients. The major therapeutic activities of this program are delivered at the hands of low-level counselors and "specialists" under the supervision of social workers, rehabilitation therapists, and psychologists. The need for medical support on the program is important, but it is minimized. The routine medical services are supplied by a staff psychiatrist and nurses; additional medical services are purchased from neighboring hospitals. This aspect of the psycho-educational model is certainly desirable and merits further attention and application to a variety of settings.

REFERENCES

Alschuler, A. The origins and nature of psychology education. *Educational Opportunity Forum,* 1969, *1,* 3–18.

Boocock, S. S. An experimental study of the learning effects of two games with simulated environments. In S. S. Boocock & E. D. Shild (Eds.), *Simulation games in learning.* Beverly Hills, Cal.: Sage, 1968.

Drum, D. J., & Knott, J. E. *Structured groups for facilitating development.* New York: Human Sciences Press, 1977.

Egan, G. *The skilled helper.* Monterey, Cal.: Brooks/Cole, 1975.

Goldstein, A. P. *Structured learning therapy: Toward a psychotherapy for the poor.* New York: Academic Press, 1973.

Gutride, M. E., Goldstein, A. P., & Hunter, G. F. The use of modeling and role playing to increase social interaction among psychiatric patients. *Journal of Consulting and Clinical Psychology,* 1973, *40,* 408–415.

Inbar, M., & Stoll, C. *Simulation and gaming in social science.* New York: Free Press, 1972.

Ivey, A. E. Microcounseling and media therapy: State of the art. *Counselor Education and Supervision,* 1974, *13,* 172–182.

Ivey, A. E. Cultural expertise: Toward systematic outcome criteria in counseling and psychological education. *Personnel and Guidance Journal,* 1977, *55,* 296–302.

Jourard, S. *The transparent self.* New York: Van Nostrand-Reinhold, 1971.

Kagan, N. Influencing human interaction: Eleven years with IPR. *Canadian Counsellor,* 1975, *9,* 75–97.

Kalafat, J., & Baroto, D. R. The paraprofesional movement as a paradigm community psychology endeavor. *Journal of Community Psychology,* 1977, *5,* 3–12.

Patterson, R. L. (Ed.), *Maintaining effective token economies.* Springfield, Ill.: Charles C. Thomas, 1976.

Pierce, R. M., & Drasgow, J. Teaching facilitative interpersonal functioning to psychiatric inpatients. *Journal of Counseling Psychology,* 1969, *16,* 295–298.

Reppucci, N. D., & Saunders, J. T. Social psychology of behavior modification: Problems of implementation in natural settings. *American Psychologist,* 1974, *29,* 649–660.

Rogers, C. *On becoming a person.* Boston: Houghton-Mifflin, 1961.

Truax, C. B., & Carkhuff, R. R. *Toward effective counseling and psychotherapy.* Chicago: Aldine, 1967.

Uretsky, M. The management game: An experiment in reality. *Simulation and Games,* 1973, *130,* 643–647.

Chapter 10

A Proposed Model for Behavioral Group Therapy with Pain Patients

Myles Genest
Dennis C. Turk

Abstract

A cognitive-behavioral framework for psychological interventions with pain patients is presented. The program begins with an individualized cognitive-behavioral assessment, using experimentally induced pain. This provides a source of information for the therapist, as well as a basis for patients reconceptualizing their pain problems. In this initial phase of therapy, patients are encouraged to conceptualize pain in a manner that incorporates the idea that they can do something *to alter the experience. To ensure maximally that this conception is adopted, all of the training encourages patients to take a very active role, collaborating in the development of the techniques that are then implemented. A range of potentially useful techniques is described: life style change, relaxation and biofeedback methods, attentional focusing strategies, and direct alterations of self-statements concerning pain and change. It is noted that attention to the way in which techniques are received by patients is as important as the specific interventions that are used.**

*The authors are indebted to Donald H. Meichenbaum for his helpful editorial comments. Please address correspondence to Myles Genest, Department of Psychology, University of Waterloo, Waterloo, Ontario, Canada, N2L 3G1.

Whether regarded as an occasion for compassion, punishment, or vengeance or for endurance, prayer, or therapy, the infliction and assuaging of hurt are two of the dominant influences in "civilized" human thought and action and apparently have always been so. (Fink, 1976, p. 278)

This chapter is a proposal for a model of group intervention to deal with the complex phenomenon of pain. Several lines of research are converging to implicate the role of cognitive factors in the experience of and amelioration of pain: (1) the literature on response to stress, both in the laboratory and *in vivo*, (2) laboratory studies of the psychology of pain, (3) clinical therapy programs for the treatment of severe pain problems, and (4) the growing area of cognitive-behavioral research. All of these sources seem to share some common elements, elements that we are inclined to view as "effective ingredients" in nonmedical pain therapy. After briefly examining these literatures and noting some specific therapy programs, we will proceed to outline a proposal for a broadly applicable model of group treatment of pain patients.

AN OVERVIEW OF PAIN LITERATURE AND RESEARCH

The Stress-Response Literature

One source of information concerning the psychological aspects of pain is research examining response to stress, including pain (e.g., Beecher, 1946; Bond & Pearson, 1969; Caston, Cooper, L., & Paley, 1970; Egbert, Battit, Welch, & Bartlett, 1964; Janis, 1958, 1971; Lazarus & Alfert, 1964; Pervin, 1963; Wolff & Langley, 1968; Zborowski, 1969). These investigations, carried out with such populations as surgical patients, have typically implicated other factors as determinant of a person's response to stress. Wolff and Langley (1968) and Zborowski (1969), for example, suggested that a person's socio-cultural background is important, partly in that it alters the personal meaning attributed to a painful event. Beecher (1946, 1951, 1959) similarly argued that the personal meaning of an event is an important determinant of its painfulness.

A message from such studies of reactions to stress, which is potentially useful in planning interventions with pain sufferers, seems to be that the physical stimulus or objective events (that is, those observed by others) are not the only, or perhaps even the major, determinants of the amount of pain one feels. How one *appraises* or interprets the pain plays an important role. Beecher noted:

The common belief that wounds are inevitably associated with pain, and that the more extensive the wound the worse the pain, was not supported by observations made as carefully as possible in the combat zone. . . . The data state in numerical terms what is known to all thoughtful clinical observers: there is no simple direct relationship between the wound per se and the pain experienced. The pain is in very large part determined by other factors, and of great importance here is the significance of the wound. (1959, p. 165)

Laboratory Studies of Pain

A currently burgeoning source of psychological information concerning pain is the laboratory research using experimentally induced pain. Melzack (1973), Turk (Note 1), and Weisenberg (1977) have reviewed this literature extensively. Once again, the evidence strongly suggests the importance of psychological variables in the experience of pain. Numerous influences have been implicated, such as anxiety (e.g., Hill, Kornetsky, Flanary, & Wilker, 1952; Nichols & Tursky, 1967; Schalling, Note 2), the use of coping skills (e.g., Barber & Cooper, B., 1972; Bobey & Davidson, 1970; Kanfer & Goldfoot, 1966), individual differences (e.g., Adler, R., & Lomazzi, 1973; Barnes, 1975; Davidson & McDougal, 1969; Petrie, 1967), motivation (e.g., Buss & Portnoy, 1967; Lambert, Libman, & Poser, 1960), and attentional focus (e.g., Blitz & Dinnerstein, 1971). Collectively, the laboratory studies of pain suggest that, although the mechanisms are not yet clear, pain is amenable to influence through psychological and, in particular, cognitive means. It is essentially on the basis of this research evidence that the current proposal for a therapeutic strategy is based.

Therapeutic Programs for Pain

Yet another perspective on pain is offered by treatment programs for pain problems. With the advent of pain clinics and the specialty of studying and treating pain (dolorology) (e.g., Cherry, 1977), more and more patients with a primary complaint of pain are being identified and treated as a separate group (Bonica, 1974; Gerbershagen, Frey, Magin, Scholl, & Müller-Suur, 1975; Sternbach, 1974a). This has made cross-disciplinary expertise available to patients with the complex medical problems that often accompany pain (Bonica, 1974; Melzack, 1973) and has resulted in specialized treatment-programs (e.g., Bonica, 1973; Fordyce, 1976; Gottlieb, Strite, Koller, Madorsky, Hockersmith, Kleeman, & Wagner, 1977; Greenhoot & Sternbach, 1974; Mitchell, K., & Mitchell, D., 1971; Sternbach, 1974a; Swanson, Swenson, Maruta, & McPhee, 1976). Both assessment and treatment in these programs involve attention to psychological contributions to the patients' problems, as well as the physiological components. We will later examine some of these interventions in more detail.

Cognitive-Behavioral Research

The recent literature from the cognitive-behavioral viewpoint (e.g., Goldfried, 1977; Mahoney, 1974; Meichenbaum, 1974, 1977) offers some integration to our view of the various psychological findings concerning pain. The cognitive-behavioral view holds that attention to an individual's processing of stimuli is as important as the stimuli themselves in understanding behavior. A person's appraisals, motives, expectancies, images, etc.—the "internal dialogues" concerning situations—along with the observable characteristics of situations themselves, are multideterminants of behavior.

This approach has been applied to a wide range of research and treatment areas, such as creativity (e.g., Meichenbaum, 1975a; Henshaw, Note 3), anxiety (e.g., Meichenbaum, Turk, & Burstein, 1976; Meichenbaum & Cameron, Note 4, Note 5), anger-control (e.g., Novaco, 1975), and depression (e.g., Rush, Beck, Kovacs, & Hollon, 1977).

Turk (in press) summarized the implications of this view for a consideration of pain problems:

> All stress episodes are comprised of a transaction between the individual and the threatening environment. The individual is not a passive recipient of information. To become a source of stress, an event must be judged or appraised as potentially harmful—the individual imposes meaning onto his predicament. The appraisal of the event, the individual's internal dialogue regarding the situation, various stimulus events and the attitudes and expectancies held concerning the capacity to master the situation contribute to and modulate cognitive and behavioral responses (Lazarus, 1974; Meichenbaum, 1977). As Meichenbaum (1977) notes, it is frequently not the situation and physiological arousal per se that is debilitating but rather what the individual says to himself about the arousal and situation and his ability to cope effectively or ineffectively that determine emotional reactions. It is this appraisal or internal dialogue that mediates the perception of the noxious event and subsequent responses.

Recently, several investigators have applied a cognitive-behavioral approach to the investigation of pain. These studies typically have found that a broad range of cognitive and behavioral strategies can be useful in learning to cope with or reduce pain. (See Holroyd, Andrasik, & Westbrook, 1977; Horan, Hackett, Buchanan, Stone, & Demchik-Stone, 1977; Johnson & Rice, 1974; Mitchell, K., &

White, 1976; Stone, Demchik-Stone, & Horan, 1977; Turk, Note 1, Note 6; Genest, Note 7; and Knox, Note 8. See also reviews by Turk, in press, and Turk & Genest, in press.) The usefulness of various techniques is not unqualified, however, for the research contains many apparently conflicting findings. This confusion may partly result from a failure to take into account individuals' evaluations of their ability to alter feelings of pain, in addition to the particular coping skills they employ. Genest, Meichenbaum, and Turk (Note 9) suggested the importance of this personal appraisal variable in one's evaluation of the painfulness of a stimulus. Once again, emphasis is placed on cognitive processing, that is, on the internal dialogue, in influencing the experience of pain.

Integrating the Literature

The view of pain as a multifaceted experience, involving cognitive and behavioral as well as physiological events, provides a framework within which we can work toward an integration of the literature and a formulation of a clinical treatment approach. As we mentioned above, investigations of response to stress have noted the importance of personal appraisal. In addition, the laboratory studies of pain have implicated numerous cognitive variables, such as anxiety, coping skills, and attentional focus, which can be seen as contributing to a person's evaluation of the situation. And, we will argue, the various treatment approaches to pain that have been developed can profitably be conceptualized as, in part, means of altering personal internal dialogues concerning the patients' problems, as ways of directly and indirectly influencing the manner in which they view and react to their situations, and, as a result, the amount of pain and suffering they demonstrate. We see a confluence of research evidence, leading to an integrative view of pain interventions, which may result in more effective and efficient group-based treatment.

AN OVERVIEW OF THREE THERAPIES FOR PAIN

Let us now briefly examine three therapeutic approaches, and then more explicitly consider the elements they share and the ways in which they affect the personal appraisals of patients. We will then turn to a proposal for making this appraisal process the cornerstone of a group treatment.

The Operant Approach.

Fordyce and his colleagues (Fordyce, 1974a, 1974b, 1976; Fordyce, Fowler, & DeLateur, 1968; Fordyce, Fowler, Lehmann,

DeLateur, Sand, & Trieschmann, 1973) have described the use of operant conditioning in the treatment of chronic pain. This behavioral approach involves manipulating the consequences that are hypothesized to exert control over the continuation of a patient's "pain behavior." In a well-controlled hospital setting, all of the possible direct influences on pain behaviors, such as attention from physicians, nurses, and family members in response to complaints of pain, are used to reduce, rather than increase, pain behavior. In addition, the possibilities for avoiding aversive activities, such as work and initially painful movement, are greatly reduced, thereby avoiding indirect reinforcement of pain-avoidant behaviors. Last, Fordyce provides contingent reinforcement of "well behaviors," such as uncomplaining activity. In such behavioral programs attention is explicitly not paid to patients' feelings, thoughts, and other cognitive events, since doing so is seen as potentially reinforcing "pain behavior."

The Transactional Analysis Approach

Sternbach and his colleagues (Greenhoot & Sternbach, 1974; Sternbach, 1974a, 1974b; Sternbach & Rusk, 1973) have used a multidimensional approach to the treatment of chronic pain, with an emphasis on interfering with the "pain games" of patients (Sternbach, 1974b; Sternbach, Murphy, Akeson, & Wolf, 1973).

Sternbach begins his contact with a patient whose pain is disproportionate to medical findings with an uncompromising confrontation. In contrast to assuming, as is usually the case in the medical treatment of pain, that a patient (1) really wants to be cured, and (2) given the right treatment, can be cured, this approach questions both of these assumptions.

Sternbach continues in this forthright manner to challenge the patient to give up "pain games" for more adaptive functioning. An assumption in this instance is that the patient usually can control his own "pain behavior" if he can be sufficiently motivated and rationally convinced to do so, and if he learns how.

Learning how, in this program, involves the patient's working with the therapist to develop a set of specific, realistic, behavioral goals and steps to achieve them. Sternbach has used both individual and group therapy sessions to promote patient progress, to modify behavioral programs when necessary, and to "*challenge . . . as resistance* (fear of risking current security) any failure in the patient's progress, and . . . [urge] him to be brave and do it, or quit and be doomed" (Sternbach & Rusk, 1973, p. 323, original emphasis).

A Comprehensive Rehabilitation Program
for Patients with Chronic Low-Back Pain

Gottlieb and his colleagues (Gottlieb et al., 1977) have reported a broad treatment program "aimed at teaching the patient to self-regulate key psychophysiological events contributing to pain" (p. 107). They employed this program with the traditionally refractory population of chronic, low-back-pain patients (Levine, 1971; Maruta, Swanson, & Swenson, 1976; Sternbach, Wolf, Murphy, & Akeson, 1973). Intervention was comprised of eight components: (1) biofeedback training to reduce both muscle tension and galvanic skin response (as an index of anxiety); (2) individual, group, and family psychotherapy aimed primarily at learning "constructive, self-control skills for the expression of emotional reactions to stressful, anxiety-producing situations" (Gottlieb et al., 1977, p. 104), with therapy for depression and sexual dysfunctions, when appropriate; (3) a self-administered medication-reduction program, in consultation with a physician; (4) patient-participant case conferences; (5) individualized physical reconditioning focused on physical progress rather than pain levels; (6) a vocational counseling program, which also offered assistance in placement; (7) educational lectures and discussions concerning the psychophysiology of back pain; and (8) a recovery-oriented therapeutic milieu.

Gottlieb et al. concluded that a cognitive, social-learning view of the low-back-pain patient's problems can lead to success in treating many patients with whom conventional medical and surgical interventions fail. Stressing self-regulation, their program used both behavioral and cognitive components along with more traditional medical interventions.

A COGNITIVE-BEHAVIORAL INTEGRATION OF PAIN THERAPY

Let us examine three aspects of the therapies that have been described (Fordyce, Sternbach, and Gottlieb et al.): (1) their implicit and explicit conceptualization of pain and of therapy, (2) the learning of methods of change, and (3) the patient's cognitions concerning change, as it is accomplished. (Meichenbaum, 1976b, 1977, has suggested the importance of these elements in psychotherapy in general.)

Conceptualizations of Pain and Therapy

Although the three programs that have been described differ in their approach to pain treatment, there are similarities in conceptualization. Clearly, each treatment assumes that the patient's pain can be altered by psychological means, that is, that some sort of nonphysiological intervention is worthwhile. This basic axiom has crucial implications for the patient's view of her problem. Because the treatments hold psychological intervention to be useful, and because through their interventions they convey that view (with varying explicitness) to the patient and patients in groups convey it to each other, in each instance the patient is encouraged to change her own conceptualization of the pain problem.

Sternbach and Rusk (1973) noted that pain patients view their problems in purely physical terms, rejecting psychological explanations of symptoms. Thus, patients are likely to approach therapy with a view of their problems that is quite different from the therapist's and that does not render them amenable to change. In fact, pain patients do not usually welcome contact with any mental health worker as, for example, people experiencing acute anxiety are likely to do (Sternbach, 1974a). A psychologist is likely to be viewed as a threat to a pain patient's self-esteem, to the veracity of her complaint, to the legitimacy and dignity of her patient status. So, also, is a group treatment modality likely to be seen as irrelevant. "I don't see what good talking to a bunch of people is going to do me. The problem is this *pain* in my head," argued one of the authors' (M.G.) patients recently.

The problem at the outset of therapy, then, is to alter the patient's conceptualization of the situation so that a treatment intervention is feasible. At the same time, the therapist needs to be sensitive to the patient's views and to appear not totally unwilling to change his beliefs or attitudes to accommodate evidence presented by the patient. Until some *shared conceptualization* of the therapeutic situation is reached, therapist and patient are likely to be working toward dissimilar goals and may undermine each other's efforts (Meichenbaum, 1977).

Let us take a closer look at the least professedly cognitive of the treatments we have outlined, and note the elements contributing to patients' conceptual shifts. Fordyce (1976) reaches a shared conceptualization primarily by imposing an operant view of pain behavior upon the patient. After a comprehensive medical evaluation, he "orients" selected patients (and spouses, if appropriate) by means of a didactic presentation of the procedures of, and the learning theory basis for, the treatment program. (See Fordyce, 1976, Chapter 8, for a sample patient/spouse orientation session.) Although Fordyce emphasizes the operant nature of his program, it is clear from his orientation sample that the contingency manipulations do not take place in a vacuum. Patients are "educated" to believe that the program will work, that is, that their pain can be altered through nonmedical intervention. They are strongly impressed with a new conceptualization of their problem, one that paves the way for the behavioral program, by making sense of it and making it seem like a plausible method of pain therapy. Consider, for example, such statements to the patient as these (Fordyce, 1976):

(1) The evaluation process is now complete. The results indicate that we are not going to be able to do much about the physical problem from which your pain originates. There is a real chance, however, that we can help to reduce how much it hurts. (p. 153)

(2) It is possible for you to train your system not to feel the pain so much. (p. 153)

(3) The very best evidence we have about your case indicates both that a specialized treatment approach such as I will describe looks promising as applied to your case *and* that we don't see another way to go that offers a better chance of being helped. (p. 151, original emphasis)

(4) To the extent that your pain is now controlled mainly by learning factors, we can probably help your system to unlearn it and thereby to get rid of the surplus pain. Even if your pain is not now primarily learned, these procedures can probably help you to get along with the problem and have a decrease in the amount of interference from it. (p. 153)

Such communications and others like them, whatever their intention, do not merely gain patients' cooperation in the program. If they are accepted—and they *are* persuasive communications—they are very likely to alter the way in which most patients view their problems: from a "pain equals physical disorder" view to a "pain equals physical disorder and/or learned behavior" view. Furthermore, patients come to believe that there is hope, that something may be able to be done about their long-standing problems, and that, in fact, they have key roles to play (e.g., Statement 2 above). In other words, the patients shift from a hopeless, passive appraisal to a hopeful, active one that encourages a sense of self-efficacy. In sum, the conceptualization of pain offered to Fordyce's patients conveys that patients may be active contributors to the experience of pain, *and,* conversely, that they can engage in behaviors that will reduce the pain.

This conceptualization aspect of therapy is common to the three approaches that have been outlined. Each of the therapies involves a "translation" process whereby the patients come to view their problems in different terms, in effect using a different sort of language. The translation is from the terms of physical medicine, with pain seen as a direct result of tissue damage, to the terms of the particular theoretical approach employed. Fordyce encourages viewing pain as learned, operant behavior; Sternbach, as a means of expression rooted in pain "games" (Berne, 1964; Sternbach, 1974b); and Gottlieb et al., as having a "cognitive-emotional-stress" component, susceptible to self-regulation (1977). Common to all three of these particular translations is the notion that pain is not solely a *physical event,* but is a complex, multifaceted and multidetermined process—a process that the patients influence, and *can change.*

This reconceptualization is begun at the outset of the therapy, when it is first introduced to patients (as we have seen with Fordyce's orientation session). It is not completed here, however; it continues throughout therapy. The types of questions the therapist asks, the homework assignments she offers, the responsibilities she assigns to patients, and other aspects of the continuing patient-therapist dialogue, all contribute to the patients' emerging reconceptualizations. The cognitive-behavioral model (as described below) underscores the importance of this translation process in the treatment of pain patients.

Acquisition and Rehearsal of Skills

Following an initial reconceptualization and planning effort, therapy usually proceeds to a skills-acquisition and rehearsal phase (Meichenbaum, 1976b, 1977). In this part of therapy, patients both undertake new cognitive and behavioral strategies, and strengthen their skills by rehearsal in using these and other appropriate strategies that may already be within their repertoires.

Let us take a brief look at this phase of Sternbach's pain therapy (Greenhoot & Sternbach, 1974; Sternbach, 1974a; Sternbach & Rusk, 1973). As has been noted, these phases are not clearly delimited, and, although the "treatment contract" that Sternbach uses may be viewed as part of the reconceptualization process, it can also be considered as partly a skills-acquisition method. Once a patient is committed to this therapy, he and the therapist work together to achieve: a set of specific, behavioral goals of treatment, and the steps that will be taken to achieve those goals. Both involve the acquisition and rehearsal of cognitive and behavioral skills.

Setting goals, in this program, involves not simply drawing up a list of ideal events or states. Instead, the patient is asked how she would live if her pain were removed, and then each goal that the patient presents is challenged by the therapist. The therapist may argue, for example, that returning to work sounds like a strange goal, for who really likes to work? A need for more money can be dealt with in other ways, such as by obtaining an increase in pension or disability benefits, but it hardly seems like a reason for having work as a primary goal in pain therapy.

> In a similar vein we question and challenge each goal, and encourage the patient to come up with a set of goals about which he can get enthusiastic, and which seem realistically attainable rather than goals which he obediently recites in response to assumed expectations of the therapist or "society". . . . Most patients come up with three to five specific behavioral goals they wish to achieve, such as (a) to accomplish a certain amount on a task (job, housework) each day, (b) to visit with friends each day, (c) to cultivate a best friend, or (d) to go fishing (or play golf, etc.) at least once a week. (Sternbach & Rusk, 1973, p. 323)

This process of contracting for goals clearly has an impact on the patient's view of his situation and of what constitutes realistic means of changing. Setting goals, then, amounts to achieving a new cognitive repertoire, a new set of thinking patterns that come into play when the patient attends to his pain. As we noted, the experience of pain is partly determined by ongoing cognitive processes. Through the transactional therapy sessions in which the patient's goals are elicited, challenged, and reformulated, he comes to engage in different cognitions concerning pain. The patient's thoughts, images, self-statements, and so on, concerning pain are gradually altered. From a tendency to engage in hopeless, anxiety-engendering, depressive, and in other ways counterproductive cognitions, he is likely to begin developing more realistic, hopeful, resourceful, and positive cognitions. In turn, he is being influenced to give up self-defeating pain-game behaviors and to begin to engage in self-efficacious behaviors that lead to improvement.

Specifying the steps to attain the goals amounts to obtaining a series of smaller, discrete goals that lead to the final ones. Again, Sternbach uses transactional techniques in establishing these steps and motivating the patient to carry them out. These "may be no more than writing a letter, or making a phone call, or finding out about the meeting of a singles club, or about a night class" (Sternbach & Rusk, 1973, p. 323).

Similar changes in cognitions and behavior are accomplished in these sessions. The patient's awareness of her pain behaviors becomes the stimulus for her to engage in different cognitions and behaviors, ones that the therapist believes are conducive to improvement.

Whereas Sternbach emphasizes the patient's adoption of new strategies, Fordyce (1976) notes that some desirable behaviors are already within the patient's repertoire, but are "not occurring often enough and need to be increased or strengthened" (p. 77). One might add that the same is likely to be true of the patient's cognitive coping strategies; that is, some coping cognitions (thoughts, feelings, images, etc.) are familiar to, and perhaps sometimes engaged in, by the patient, but they may not be employed at appropriate times, nor be dominant enough, nor be "believed in."

We have illustrated this central portion of therapy, the acquisition and/or rehearsal of skills with some examples from Sternbach's type of pain therapy. In fact, this part of a treatment is usually seen as its core, as the effective ingredient, what differentiates one approach from the next. The present authors are inclined to make much less of the particular techniques used, and to see no great advantage in exclusive concentration on one method. Rather, we view the skills-acquisition and rehearsal phase as following from the conceptualization employed in each instance, and depending in part on the patient population and the therapist's orientation. As Frank (1974) and, recently, Cameron (in press) have suggested, perhaps more important than the specific therapy undertaken is the patient's commitment, the belief that therapy will be effective and that change is possible, indeed, likely. Once a conceptualization of the problem and what might be done to help has been agreed upon by both therapist and patient (whether imposed upon the patient or mutually arrived at), the steps of intervention are more or less determined. If, for example, the pain is viewed as an operant, then the contingencies need to be changed, or if the problem is considered to be based in pain games and a painful lifestyle, then the games need to be undermined and different means of expression and satisfaction substituted. If the problem is viewed as both cognitively and behaviorally determined, then multiple interventions are called for.

It is not only the nature of the problem that determines the conceptualization. Both the therapist's and patient's beliefs and inclinations are also important. A behavioral program such as Fordyce's may stress operant techniques to change behaviors (along with reconceptualization and didactic presentations to change cognitions). A game-based program such as Sternbach's may focus on transactional techniques. A multifaceted, cognitively oriented program such as that of Gottlieb et al. may concentrate on a variety of behavioral and cognitive learning techniques. All share the assumption that a change in the amount of pain at least partly depends upon learning new skills and practicing them, or practicing existing ones, or both.

Treatment Generalization and Persistence

Finally, all therapies are concerned with the generalization and, particularly, the persistence of therapeutic change. Fordyce's (1976) procedure typifies gradually fading therapeutic intervention but maintaining contact as the patient gradually achieves independence and until she has a stable status in the community and home. Gottlieb et al. (1977) also deliberately encouraged self-sufficient cognitions by emphasizing the patient's self-regulation throughout the program. The use of time-limited therapeutic groups may encourage patient independence from the therapist, while enabling patients to provide long-term sources of support for each other.

As Davidson (Note 10) noted, patients will carry treatment effects with them as far as they are given the means to do so, and perhaps the most effective means involve altering their cognitions concerning a problem and how to deal with it.

A COGNITIVE-BEHAVIORAL GROUP MODEL

In reviewing some of the literature concerning pain and examining the cognitive-behavioral elements of pain therapies, we have attempted to establish a foundation for an integrative group model of nonmedical pain treatment. The model combines elements used in the Fordyce, Sternbach, and Gottlieb et al. treatments, as well as others, in a group therapy setting. We are not attempting to present a definitive treatment program here. In our view, such an attempt would be premature. Rather, we will sketch a framework and suggest alternative means of filling in the details, to encourage practitioners and researchers to develop and assess their own trial programs, which would gradually contribute to the evolution of this new treatment modality. We will be eclectic and, we hope, provocative.

Let us begin by noting some of the problems facing the therapist: (1) she requires information concerning the psychological contributions to the patient's complaint; (2) she must elicit this information from a patient who may be skeptical of any psychological interpretations of his condition, and therefore may be both unwilling and unable to contribute much of what may be relevant; (3) the patient is likely to have some investment in his status as a pain patient, and therefore may be resistant to both psychological assessment and treatment; (4) the assessment information, once gained, must be used therapeutically in a manner that is sensitive to the patient's expectations and encourages, rather than discourages, a therapeutic alliance. We will continue to be concerned with these problems as therapy proceeds, for they influence the therapist's response to the patient's problems.

Conceptualization

Turk (in press, Note 1) suggested that the uneven performance of many experimentally imposed cognitive strategies in dealing with pain results, in part, from the unwarranted assumption that a useful strategy is useful for everyone. Although some people may find one means of coping with pain useful, others may not, but may be inclined to use a different means. Furthermore, the presence of absence of specific strategies for dealing with pain may be less important than the attitudes of individuals toward using these strategies—specifically, their evaluations of the *usefulness* of coping mechanisms and their ability to employ such strategies. It is suggested, therefore, that one begin an intervention with a detailed assessment of each patient's cognitions preceding, during, and following a particularly painful episode. The intention is to ferret out "which cognitions (or the failure to produce which key cognitions), under what circumstances, are contributing to or interfering with adequate performance" (Meichenbaum, 1977, p. 236), which in this case consists of behavior more in line with the patient's physical condition.*

The methods of conducting this assessment are various (see, for example, guidelines in Cautela & Upper, 1976; Meichenbaum, 1976a). They include the use of interviews, behavioral tests, record keeping, questionnaires, and so forth. Whichever methods are used, the intention is for the therapist to come to appreciate the sequential psychological events and processes (Meichenbaum, 1977, p. 236) involved in the patient's problem. Additionally, this cognitive-functional analysis of the pain provides the basis for the patient's reconceptualization of her pain as therapy proceeds. Methods that offer fairly clear, easily understandable interpretations to the patient are the most valuable in facilitating the patient's translation of pain problem into new terms.

---

* We are not, here, examining the question of whether or not the patient's behavior *ought* to be changed. It is assumed that the many-layered screening process that typically precedes a patient's receiving the specialized help of a pain clinic or dolorologist will have established that some change is desirable. This assumption is not always justified, however, and we would do well to note Fink's (1976) cautionary note, that we ought not to rush headlong into modification of pain behaviors (or any behaviors) without first examining the social and psychological desirability of doing so.

A situational analysis. To facilitate a situational analysis of the patients' pain, they may be asked to keep records of the course of pain over time. This process may be initiated in the course of a group session, in which it is explained that such a record can help to determine what might cause each person's pain to get worse, and what might help it to abate. Notice that even with the introduction of this assessment procedure the patients' views of pain are beginning to be influenced. For example, it is being implied that pain varies in intensity over time (something that not all patients attend to), and that it may be influenced by external, diurnal events, such as the activities or sympathy of other people, patterns of activity and rest, etc. As a result of the assessment procedures and questions considered by the group, patients are given a more differentiated view of pain. Instead of seeing pain as an "all-or-none" experience, they become sensitized to changes in intensity, setting, and so on.

One method of keeping a record of pain level involves describing an arbitrary scale of pain intensity to the patients, for example, with 0 defined as no pain and 100 as sufficient pain to induce you to commit suicide if you had to endure it for longer than a few minutes (Sternbach, 1974a). Patients may be asked to record the intensity of their pain throughout the day, taking time to note it on record cards or sheets as they are experiencing it. (See Figure 1 for an example of a record card we have used, with a 5-point scale modeled after Budzynski, Stoyva, Adler, C., & Mullaney, 1973.) The intention here is twofold: the records may provide clues to events that exacerbate or relieve pain; they also demonstrate to patients that their pain is not always at the same level, that it has its ups and downs, so that they can break their *painful existences* into smaller, more manageable units. Thus, this assessment technique also contributes to the translation process, the reconceptualization of pain as controllable, alterable, and susceptible to the patient's influence.

The pain records that are kept by patients may be used as a basis for group discussion. The therapist can encourage the members to share with each other their respective pain records, and then to begin to speculate on reasons for the changes in pain levels. In this way, the group members themselves can begin to suggest some of the complex relationships between behavior, cognitions, environmental events, and pain that will form the basis for later interventions. They may note, for example, that for some patients pain is typically most severe during the evening when they are tired and have little in which to involve themselves. Patients can offer similar experiences and can consider whether this pattern is ever

Figure 1. Sample of Daily Pain-Rating Card *

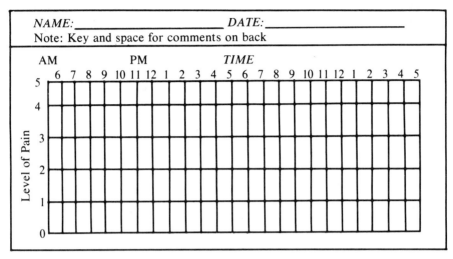

Side 1

	KEY
5	= incapacitating, intense, severe pain
4	= pain severe, but undemanding tasks possible, concentration difficult
3	= painful, but able to continue job
2	= pain can be ignored at times
1	= low level pain only when attended to
0	= no pain

COMMENTS:

Side 2

*Adapted from EMG biofeedback and tension headaches: A Controlled outcome study. *Seminars in Psychiatry*, 1973, *4*, 397–410.

broken. If so, what breaks it? Has there perhaps been an occasion in which a patient has been totally occupied by something during a typically "bad" time, and afterwards has noted that she "missed" the pain that day? In a similar vein, the therapist can guide the group to conduct detailed situational analyses of their pain, attempting to identify environmental events that influence intensity or "intrusiveness."

We should note at this point that by means of this collective effort, the therapist also encourages the group members to view the formulation of their problems and strategy planning as cooperative efforts, not as interpretations and techniques rigidly imposed on them by the therapist. It becomes apparent that the views and particular problem areas of individuals are of the essence in the therapeutic process. This may be important with many patients for, as Cameron (in press) recently noted, "The client is likely to be resistant to attempts to educate him if he believes that the therapist is mechanically imposing a prefabricated conceptualization upon his problem. . . . While it is undoubtedly advantageous for a therapist to be enthusiastic with clients, clients need to believe that they can honestly report lack of understanding, misgivings or lack of progress." The group setting can be used to facilitate such interchanges.

By relating environmental antecedent and consequent events to pain, the group, guided by the therapist, is conducting a *behavioral* situational analysis. As the patients begin to become comfortable with the assumption that their pain is related to outside events and to their own behavior—and patients may vary greatly in their resistance to this idea—then they may also be urged by the therapist to consider the relationship of *cognitions* to pain, if the patients themselves have not already introduced such material. The therapist may, for example, simply ask someone how he *feels* when the pain is worse, or what kinds of thoughts, emotions, or images seem to be concurrent with severe pain. By focusing on specific episodes, patients may gradually begin to describe such cognitive events in relation to their problems with pain (see Meichenbaum & Genest, 1977, for ways of using imagery procedures in this group assessment of patients' cognitions).

A behavioral trial. The analysis of cognitive contributions to the patients' pain may be facilitated by having them individually undergo some experimentally induced pain, report on their cognitions during this event, and then consider, as a group, the implications of this shared experience for their problems. Sternbach and his colleagues (Sternbach, 1974a; Sternbach, Murphy, Timmermans, Greenhoot, & Akeson, 1974) report that they routinely provide "a physical stimulus against which the patient may match his clinical pain" (Sternbach et al., 1974, p. 283). Craig (Note 11) also reported his use of such an exposure to induced pain in helping to sort out the psychological contributors to cases of chronic low-back pain. This behavioral trial may be employed in different ways (the reader is referred to Sternbach, 1974a, and Sternbach et al., 1971, for the technical details of those authors' procedure).

Among the available means of safely inducing experimental pain, perhaps the most useful here because of their close similarity to a chronic sort of pain, is muscle ischemia, with its slowly mounting deep pain (Smith, Egbert, Markowitz, Mosteller, & Beecher, 1966; Smith, Lowenstein, Hubbard, & Beecher, 1968; Sternbach, Deems, Timmermans, & Huey, 1977), and cold water, which produces a much more rapidly mounting pain (Kunkle, 1949).

A behavioral trial such as the muscle ischemic or "cold pressor" task provides the opportunity of making both therapist and patients aware of how their thinking styles may contribute to their distress and behavior. Following exposure to the stressor, patients can be encouraged to discuss pain in the context of the specific trial situation, which is by then a common experience among them. Meichenbaum (1977) summarized this introspective process, and its development in the group:

> The client can explore in some detail his thoughts and feelings during the assessment situation. The clinician may try to have him ascertain what were the particular aspects of the environment [or, in this case, the event] that triggered specific self-statements and images. At what point did the client begin to feel anxious? When was anxiety greatest? What were the self-statements and images that the client emitted at different points in the assessment? . . . [The group] can explore the common behaviors, thoughts, and feelings. A shared exploration of the common set of self-statements and images is invaluable in having the clients come to appreciate the role thoughts play in the behavioral repertoire. The recognition that other individuals have similar thoughts and feelings, similar internal dialogues, provides an additional impetus for self-examination and self-disclosure (1977, pp. 252, 258).

In effect, what is being accomplished is a *cognitive* (including affective) situational analysis of the pain, which will complement the primarily behavioral analysis described earlier.

An experimental illustration. An idea of the clinical usefulness of an assessment-related exposure to a painful stressor is provided by an investigation reported by Genest et al. (Note 9). In a study employing the cold-pressor task, female university students were asked to report on the train of cognitions that occurred before, during, and following the pain. Subjects were asked to endure the sensations of discomfort for as long as possible, and to give ratings of pain at irregular intervals, using an open-ended scale anchored at 0 and 10, with subjects encouraged to go beyond 10 if they were able (Hilgard, Cooper, L., Lenox, Morgan, & Voevodsky, 1967).

We can ascertain what happens physiologically while a person's hand is in the cold water, i.e., the blood-pressure, heart-rate, and other changes that occur (Lovallo, 1975). But we have only recently begun to develop the technology to attempt to capture the thoughts, feelings, and images that are likely to precede, accompany, and perhaps significantly affect such an experience. Some of the possible means of studying these congitions include asking the person to talk aloud during the task, interrupting him at various points and asking for reports, or administering some sort of questionnaire after the task is completed. Certainly, there are problems with such methods (e.g., see Bloom & Broder, 1950). It is difficult, if not impossible to distinguish post hoc rationalizations from actual ongoing thoughts. Further, the demand characteristics and social desirability components are formidable, and verbalizing thoughts in itself changes the thought process. We ought not to delude ourselves into the belief that we can ever "capture" a person's cognitive events. Such problems of reactivity and inference exist in all forms of assessment and therapy, however, and we cautiously proceed nonetheless. It is through converging evidence from several sources and the considered use of the data acquired that we come to reach a common ground with both experimental subjects and patients.

To "catch a glimpse" of cognitions, we used a procedure that we called videotape-reconstruction. After the subjects had removed their hands from the water, either of their own volition or upon instruction from the experimenter at the 5-minute limit (pain tends to level off beyond that point as numbness gradually sets in), they were immediately interviewed about the experience. Subjects were asked to describe everything they had been feeling and thinking during the immersion, "even if it was brief or random, and even if it seems trivial." To aid the recollection, each subject was shown a videotape of herself made during the cold-pressor task, and she was reminded of the pain ratings she gave at each request point. The subjects' descriptions were taped and transcribed verbatim.

This process yielded reconstructed chains of cognitions, with accompanying sequences of pain reports, which led to several interesting findings. First of all, the subjects naturally clustered into two groups, according to their tolerance times for the stimulus. Different cognitions were found to be characteristic of these two groups: high-tolerance and low-tolerance subjects. The high-tolerance group "seemed to feel that they could *use strategies to affect both the pain and their power to persevere* despite the pain, whereas the low-tolerance group used strategies with less conviction of their usefulness, and less sense of their own ability to influence their situation, other than by removing their hands from the water. In a sense, the high-tolerance group was displaying a conviction of self-efficacy, of their ability to remain in control" (Genest et al., Note 9).

A few, brief examples of reconstruction provided by subjects in this study convey the sort of information that can be gleaned from such reports and how the reports could be used in clinical situations.

One subject focused quite exclusively on the pain he was experiencing and the associated physiological changes:

> It's really bugging me now. . . . I guess I was just thinking that it was really sore and that I wasn't prepared. . . . I was looking at my hand an awful lot. It was swelling and getting white. I was really upset then. . . . I was just looking around, trying to keep my mind off my arm, but . . . I wasn't really thinking about anything else except . . . the pain.

Were a patient to provide a reconstruction such as this, the issue could be raised whether the patient's attention is similarly occupied when he is experiencing his chronic pain. If so, might a change of attention focus be helpful, and how could it be accomplished?

Another subject also focused on the pain, and the desire for it to end, but there was a complete absence in the protocol of any constructive attempts to handle the sensations in any way:

> It hurt. . . . I was thinking about taking my arm out of the water. It really started to hurt. It really got painful here. I was thinking about taking my arm out of the water and I told myself that I couldn't take it any more. The only thing I remember thinking was about taking my arm out of the water. . . . I was saying to myself, "I can't keep it in here any longer."

Again, with a similar clinical protocol, the patient could examine whether she had such a nonproductive orientation to her own pain. Is there any *action* that might be taken instead of simply dwelling on wishing the pain away?

As part of a clinical intervention, then, the type of reconstruction of cognitions that has been described can be used both to identify the range of cognitive events that characterize each patient's attempts to deal with a painful stressor, and to provide a sense of the patient's thinking style, the components of his appraisal of pain and his ways of coping with it.

When the patient's individual experiences are later shared with the group, both similar experiences and dissimilar responses are likely to be evident. The group can use these similarities and differences in reflecting on the range of behavioral and cognitive possibilities that is open to each of them: the shared problems and feelings, the various, individual difficulties, and the alternative means of handling the situation. In this process, they are continuing the translation of pain into controllable terms, relating it to cognitive events that they can change themselves.

Comparing clinical and experimental pain. The group can also attend to how the experimental pain situation was similar to, and how it differed from, each member's chronic pain. The therapist can, as a homework assignment, encourage them to carry out a similar cognitive reconstruction of a particular episode of severe pain. Patients can then note how different cognitions may be elicited by different situations, and how these may differently affect the pain. They may also note similarities and differences in their responses across time and situations. The discussion of any such material can contribute to the patients' emerging reconceptualizations of pain in a cognitive-behavioral framework, in contrast to the previous physiological, stimulus-response one.

The comparison of clinical and experimental pain may be facilitated by: (1) having the patients use the same scale for pain records and pain reports during the behavioral trial, and (2) asking patients to report, during the induced pain, the point at which the pain intensity is equivalent to the *average* level of chronic pain. Sternbach (1974a; Sternbach et al., 1974) has found that patients tend to estimate higher average levels in absence of the induced pain than they do when matching their pain against a concurrent stimulus. He interprets a marked difference of this sort as reflecting a patient's tendency to overestimate the level of his chronic discomfort. In this case, the reasons that the patient provides to explain the discrepancy may provide some directions for subsequent therapy.

The sharing of such assessment information among group members may further contribute to the reconceptualization. As Sternbach put it, "The patients quickly realize that they are not alone, that others have been struggling and suffering and manipulating as they have, and that there is understanding of what they have been through" (1974a, p. 103). Perhaps most importantly, patients are likely to be encouraged by the presence of similar patients to be honest in reporting both their thoughts and feelings and their recognition of the relationship of pain to cognitive and behavioral factors (e.g., Gottlieb et al., 1977; Sternbach, 1974a).

Additional assessment procedures. The methods of performing a cognitive and behavioral assessment of the patients' pain, and of using that assessment to contribute to the reconceptualization, are by no means limited to those we have described. For further examples the reader is referred to other sample sources: interview (Linehan, 1977; Morganstern, 1976; Peterson, 1968), self-report inventories and checklists (Bellack & Hersen, 1977; Cautela & Upper, 1976; Walls, Werner, Bacon, & Zane, 1977), self-monitoring procedures (Mahoney, 1977; Nelson, 1977), and other cognitive-behavioral methods (Meichenbaum, 1976a).

We should note a few particular possibilities, however. The cognitive reconstruction that we described in conjunction with the use of a painful stressor can also be employed using imagery instead of, or in addition to, an *in vivo* stressor. Patients, in a group, can be asked to close their eyes and to imagine themselves during a particularly severe episode of clinical pain. The same notice can be taken of thoughts, images, and behaviors related to the pain as the therapist guides them through "running a movie" in their heads of a stressful experience. This has the advantage of allowing the patients to represent their own clinical pain situations, rather than the artificial situation of laboratory-induced pain. But it may have the disadvantage of less immediacy. Future comparisons of the two procedures would be worthwhile to establish their differential efficacy.

In addition to the pain-report scales and methods we have described, other instruments and techniques for monitoring and reporting clinical pain are available. Probably the most comprehensive to date is the McGill-Melzack Pain Questionnaire (Melzack, 1975). This instrument provides quantitative measures of clinical pain which can be treated statistically, as well as separate indices of sensory, affective, and evaluative aspects of pain and an index of pain intensity (Melzack, 1975). Agnew and Merskey (1976), Bailey and Davidson (1976), and Bakal and Kaganor (1976), to name a few, have also reported on the qualitative evaluation of pain.

The Minnesota Multiphasic Inventory (MMPI) has been used in the evaluation of psychological contributors to pain (e.g., Carr, Brownsberger, & Rutherford, 1966; Sternbach, 1974a). Sternbach (1974a) described four MMPI profiles common among patients suffering from chronic disorders, including pain. He characterized these as reflecting symptoms of hypochondriasis, reactive depression, somatization reaction, and manipulative reaction, and he outlined the problems specific to each type of patient.

The translation. All the assessment methods that we have described provide possibilities for both defining the patients' problems more clearly and aiding them in reconceptualizing their problems as a first step toward change. The assessment methods suggest specific directions to the therapist, as well as providing the basis for the treatment group's dealing with their problems.

We have not clearly separated the assessment and therapy phases of intervention in this model. Certainly, at the outset assessment will be more emphasized than specific therapeutic methods. But as we have emphasized, from the very beginning of the patients' contacts with a therapeutic agent, the process of translation has begun. And this translation, we have argued, is the cornerstone of therapy. Assessment does not cease at some specific time; the emphasis merely gradually shifts to intervention techniques, but continual reassessment and revisions of goals and strategies are stressed. We therefore prefer to consider both "assessment" and "treatment" methods as part of the overall therapeutic process.

As we have noted, the translation process is fostered and intervention planning begun when the therapist and group examine the thoughts and feelings they had in their assessment experiences. Patients can explore the range of situations in which their thoughts are similar and consider how these cognitive events might influence their pain. The group itself may be particularly helpful in this process, since, as attributional research regarding "actors" and "observers" suggests (Jones & Nisbett, 1976), members may be readier to attribute situational influences to others than to themselves; thus, the group as a whole may gradually be encouraged to perceive pain as at least partly situationally modulated.

In addition, the group members can discuss their early experiences with pain, and how these may have affected their present reactions to pain. Particularly important is the notion that other aspects of their lives may influence their pain. For example, their activity level may be noteworthy: do they have anything to do besides think about pain or illness, are there other people in their lives who encourage or discourage pain behavior, and so on. At this point the individuals in the group may simply begin to discover that their own thoughts and behaviors, the situations in which they place themselves, and the reactions of others all contribute to their problems. They will find that other members of the group experience similar thoughts and behaviors, and that these patterns are alterable.

The importance of this reconceptualization aspect of therapy cannot be overstressed (see Cameron, in press). The aim is not to "convert" the patients to a "true" conception of their problem, but simply to encourage them to adopt a way of looking at it that inherently allows for change. Information concerning theories of pain may be helpful in this regard. Patients might, for example, be introduced to Beecher's (1959) model of pain, which assumes two elements: sensory input, and one's reactions to the sensory input. Or, they might be introduced to Melzack and Wall's (1965, 1970) more complex, gate-control model (with three interacting components: sensory-discriminative, motivational-affective, and cognitive-evaluative). Whichever of these or other pain theories are offered to the particular group, the theory's validity is not at issue. Meichenbaum succinctly stated the goals of such reconceptualizations in any therapeutic intervention:

> The scientific validity of a given conceptualization is less important than the aura of its plausibility. The aim of the therapist is not primarily to impart precise, scientific information, but rather to provide . . . a conceptualization that will facilitate therapy . . . [and make] its rationale comprehensible. . . .
>
> More specifically, the goal of the conceptualization phase is to have the client talk to himself differently about his presenting problem. An attempt is made to have the client change his perception, attributions, sense of control, and sense of helplessness about his presenting problem—in short, to alter the client's internal dialogue regarding his appraisal of his . . . behaviors. (Meichenbaum, 1976b, pp. 240–241)

To summarize the goals of the translation process in pain therapy, the idea that should evolve cooperatively from the group's experiences and discussions under the guidance of the therapist is that the level of pain that one experiences at any given moment is influenced by many factors, which may include a physiological disorder, and intentional or unintentional cognitions. Not only is there evidence to support this contention, as has been noted, but also, viewing pain solely as a physiological event is not conducive to psychotherapy. If the pain is regarded by the patients as completely beyond the control of any interventions, save intrusive medical ones, they will not be amenable to other kinds of assistance. The cognitive-behavioral model, therefore, encourages the therapist intentionally to focus on patients' cognitions concerning pain, and expectancies concerning the therapy process as they are revealed during the assessment tasks. These cognitions can then be incorporated into the intervention; that is, the therapist can plan to modify whichever cognitions need to be modified and to capitalize on useful ones. Therapy can thereby attempt to subsume patients' resistances and maladaptive behaviors so that the patients come to entertain the possibility that cognitive events, social stimuli, and learned patterns of responding are all important influences on the experience of pain, *in addition to* somatic factors.

Learning New Patterns

Once the patients have embarked on a process of reconceptualizing their pain in terms that are potentially amenable to therapy, they can begin to develop, with the direction of the therapist, ways of changing. Our intention here is not to detail the various therapeutic methods that are possible, but to illustrate the range of alternatives available, and to suggest some guidelines for incorporating techniques into the group therapeutic package.

To encourage the patients' commitment and belief in therapy, every effort should be made to involve the patients as *collaborators* in the planning of therapy. Following from the conceptualization phase and guided by the therapist, the group members can consider various methods of change and undertake together whichever ones are deemed appropriate. Naturally, not every type of therapy may be useful for all patient groups, and it is part of the therapist's role to introduce what is likely to be helpful for his particular population.

By the time patients begin to learn new patterns of behaving and thinking, *experience of pain has become a problem to be solved, not a reaction to a physiological process*. The group, when viewed as collaborators, can actively contribute to the problem-solving process by offering suggestions, i.e., behavioral and cognitive alternatives. The responsibility for learning new patterns is shared by both the therapist and group members. Group members are encouraged to search their repertoires to consider what skills and alternatives that already exist may be employed in the treatment of their pain behavior. Such discussions can be supplemented by the therapist's "teaching" a variety of other behaviors.

Thus, one aim of this phase of therapy is to provide the patients with whatever skills they may need and to help them to eliminate unwanted ways of behaving and thinking so that they can both reduce their pain and cope more effectively with whatever level of pain remains.

Turk (in press) outlined the possible routes that may be decided upon in light of the ongoing assessment process:

> Some individuals may require minimal cognitive and behavioral control information [e.g., Cohen & Lazarus, 1973; DeLong, 1971]; some, more extensive information; some, reinforcement of already established coping skills [e.g., Kendall, Williams, Pechacek, Graham, Shisslak, & Herzoff, Note 12]; and still others, additional coping skills training [e.g., Mitchell, K., & White, 1977]. The ability of all patients to benefit from such information should be assessed.

This assessment is partly through trial and error, since we really have very little information concerning the effects of different approaches with different populations. The assessment is also part of the therapeutic process itself, since the interventions should follow logically from the translation process while taking into account any clinical information available to the therapist. For example, in the course of self-monitoring the occurrence of headaches and environmental events, a group of headache patients may come to view their problems as at least partly caused by tension. It may be suggested to them that a biofeedback technique will aid them to reduce tension levels. The therapist, in introducing this technology, knows both: that the patients are likely to see it as appropriate given their current conceptualization of the problem, and that it has been found useful with headache patients in the past. Under these dual criteria, then, biofeedback therapy may very well be a worthwhile undertaking. In sum, the therapist needs constantly to be mindful of both the patients' cognitive events and the range of potentially useful intervention techniques, and he must try to achieve a match between the two.

Cognitive techniques. With pain, cognitive techniques have been used primarily to alter (1) the individual's appraisal of the painful situation, and (2) his attentional focus away from the pain. The methods of achieving these goals overlap, since each is often served by the same means. We will briefly note two primary means of intervention: (1) communications to patients concerning the nature of stressors (e.g., details concerning noxious medical procedures, such as changing burn dressings), the sensations associated with them, and behaviors appropriate to deal with them (e.g., muscular relaxation), and (2) training and rehearsal in cognitive coping skills, which emphasize attentional distraction.

(a) Communications about pain. Pain patients may benefit from informative communication, as Gottlieb et al. (1977) suggested. Consider, for example the group "educational lecture" described by those authors:

Utilizing a lecture-discussion format with audiovisual aids, patients were presented with information about the back, how it works and how psychophysiological stress plays a role in back pain. Lecture content ranged from the neurophysiological and anatomical components involved in back disorder, the role of nutritional and weight factors, the effects and proper use of pain medication, and the phenomena of pain, to attitudes regarding work, sexual activity, and the value of medication in management of stress, anxiety, tension and pain. (p. 105)

Although Gottlieb et al. did not report on the separate contribution of this component to their multifaceted therapy, such communications appear likely to be of some use in light of both the related research on preparatory communications (Turk, in press), and the way in which giving information may contribute to the patients' reappraisal of their pain and the therapy. The information contained in such communications can be consolidated and related to their own problem situations by the therapy group. Discussions can also aid in clarifying and modifying any information presented by someone other than the therapist (for example, by a film), to deal with resistance that might otherwise go unnoticed.

(b) Attentional focusing. Often despite any physical or other therapeutic measures that might be undertaken, pain persists. This is especially true of cases in which the person has suffered an injury or disease process that has resulted in a permanent or long-term bodily disorder. In these cases an important focus of therapy is cognitive coping processes, particularly attentional control.

Turk (in press, Note 1) reviewed the many different attentional techniques that have been used to ameliorate pain. He categorized them on the dimensions of inclusion of imagery, content of thought, and internal versus external locus. These different procedures can be incorporated into a therapeutic package in a paradigm that permits patients to expand their own range of techniques while emphasizing a guided, cafeteria-style offering. A particular strategy is not forced on people who do not feel comfortable using it.

Genest has used these attentional techniques experimentally in a bibliotherapy format (in press, Note 7). This mode of presentation (including both written and cassette-tape materials) is amenable to use by a group. One section of the bibliotherapy manual can be read at a time, either individually or (especially the taped sections) in the group. Members can then discuss and practice the exercises in group sessions, thereby consolidating the material with their own experiences and allowing the therapist the opportunity to deal with any problems in interpretation or resistance that arise.

A sense of the nature of attentional diversion strategies is conveyed by this excerpt from the bibliotherapy manual:

> *Focusing on a train of thoughts.* You can engage in mental activities other than images. Making a list of things to do before the weekend, or planning a day's activities, are things that some people have previously used to control attention. Remembering and/or singing the words to a song is another example. Mental arithmetic, such as counting backwards from 100 by sevens, is also attention-demanding.
> *Focusing on sensations in your body.* Analyzing the sensations in one part of your body and perhaps comparing them to another part;

or analyzing the intense stimulation as if you were preparing to write a biology report regarding the sensations experienced (heat or cold, pressure, tingling, etc.); comparing the sensations to feelings you have experienced before—all of these are means of directing your attention away from the unpleasant feelings themselves. You may allow yourself to experience discomfort, but you can control the context of that discomfort, so that it is no longer simply pain, but rather it is of some "scientific" interest—you are more "objective," not so much experiencing the sensations as observing them. You may choose to rate your pain on some scale and watch how the pain changes. Notice that pain does not always remain at the same level. On the other hand, you may focus on another part of your body exclusively, so that the painful portion is not in the forefront. (Genest, in press)

In addition to the two options described above (focusing on a train of thoughts and focusing on sensations in one's body), this manual outlines the following classes of attentional strategies: pleasant imagery; imagining similar sensations, but in a far different situation (imaginative transformation of context); attending to the environment; and thought-stopping.

Self-instructional training. The individuals' belief in their own abilities to master pain may be more important than the actual skills within their repertoires. One means of attending to these belief systems in the course of therapy is through the use of self-instructional methods (Genest, in press; Meichenbaum, 1975b; Meichenbaum & Turk, 1976; Turk, Note 1). The assumption underlying the use of self-instructional techniques is that "it is not only the manipulation of environmental consequences per se which is of primary importance in the therapy process, but what the client says to himself about those consequences" (Meichenbaum, 1975b, p. 358).

The cognitive-behavioral model being proposed emphasizes attention to the patients' ongoing cognitions during therapy. Through the group use of a variety of procedures (see Meichenbaum, 1975b), the patients' negative, maladaptive, or self-defeating "self-statements" and images are identified and changed to positive, adaptive, coping ones. Modeling of coping responses (Kazdin, 1974; Meichenbaum, 1971; Turk, Note 1), role playing (Turk, Note 1, Note 6), and thought stopping (Bain, 1928; Rimm & Masters, 1974) have all been suggested as useful in altering self-statements and images.

The therapist can encourage the group to develop a combined list of negative self-statements and images that the patients find themselves using, and a list of positive ones with which they can replace the others. Patients are thereby exposed to a variety of possibilities, but they can also be encouraged to pick out the ones they find personally most useful. The self-statements are not to be used as a "psychological litany," but rather as a set of cognitive strategies that will aid patients in bringing their pain experience under self-control. Following are some examples of coping self-instructions that were used in Genest's bibliotherapy study (in press):

(1)   STOP worrying. Worrying won't help anything. What are some of the helpful things I can do instead?

(2)   Alright, I'm feeling tense. That lets me know that I should take some slow, deep breaths as I relax more.

(3)   I won't get overwhelmed. I'll just take one step at a time. Let me just use my skills to handle a bit at a time.

(4)   STOP these negative thoughts. Let me just concentrate on one of the strategies to do something positive. What are the alternatives I can try?

(5)   I knew the sensations would rise. But I can keep them under control.

(6)   I won't think about any pain. I will focus my attention on remembering details of the movie I saw last night.

(7)   Things are going pretty badly. I can't take any more—no, wait—just pause. I shouldn't make things worse. I'll review my planned strategies to see what I can switch to.

These examples point out that patients should *plan* in advance how they will deal with critical or difficult episodes of pain. As they will have noted in filling out pain reports over the course of several days, pain levels fluctuate, and there are some times that are particularly difficult to deal with. By having strategies for these periods planned in advance (e.g., specific attention-diversion cognitions, involving activities, resources to call upon), they will be better able to cope than if unprepared. Patients need also to expect some variation in the effectiveness of their strategies. Otherwise a "failure" of pain relief on one occasion may result in the therapy's complete loss of credibility. Some instructions such as the following may be helpful: "One other point should be noted here. At various levels of pain, or different stages, you may find particular coping strategies more effective than others. For example, sometimes, at moderate pain levels, relaxation and imagery may be very useful. As the sensations mount, more active mental strategies, such as mental arithmetic, humming a tune, or thought stopping may be more useful. The rhythmical nature of some techniques helps you to hold your attention. Or just carefully focusing on your slow breathing may be best at this stage for you. Once again, there is no reason that you shouldn't try anything at any time. But you may find that not all strategies are uniformly effective during the whole stressful situation.''

Such examples underline the importance of teaching clients how and when to use such cognitive strategies in the pain experience. Particular cognitive strategies such as imagery diversion may work at low intensities, while at high intensities of pain the client may have to employ bodily and mental relaxation. The intent is to have the clients in the group view the various techniques as tools to be tried, experiments to be engaged in, and then to be brought back to the group and discussed.

In sum, a variety of cognitive intervention techniques is available from several literature sources. The therapist may find several of these useful in focusing on the contributions of patients' thinking style, images, feelings, and appraisals of their own coping abilities as well as therapy itself.

Life style changes. The goals of treatment should often include altering pain-engendering environments, in addition to teaching self-control techniques. The group discussions at the beginning of therapy may provide leads to life style intervention appropriate for the patients. In the course of group sessions, it may be noted, for example, that numerous patients evidence a life style devoid of stimulation that is unrelated to illness or pain (as Le Shan, 1964, noted is often the case with chronic pain patients).

Sternbach (1974a) noted the contribution of the group setting to uncovering such information. Within a transactional analysis framework, he describes the benefits of both group support and group pressures:

> Group support makes less difficult the ability of patients to become aware of how they use their pain to receive payoffs such as sympathy, narcotics, financial compensation, or admiration for bravery. Such payoffs are usually not consciously conceived by the patients, and when this is presented in didactic fashion, the group tends to rally and protest their good intentions. However, once an individual patient has his pain game described to him by other patients who have had similar games, he is more inclined to accept it and analyze his behavior. This is more effective than when feedback is provided by the staff. Patients may deceive themselves and the staff, but they cannot long deceive the other patients with whom they are living, and feedback from the others, given supportively, soon stops the game playing. (pp. 103–104)

The group may consider how such patterns of activities develop, and, with the therapist's assistance, may come to initiate a plan for change. Resistant patients may be goaded with the observation that if nothing seems to have much effect on the level of pain, then they might as well be active as inactive. Inactivity hasn't helped; perhaps in the long run increased activity will (Cairns, Thomas, Mooney, & Tace, 1976). Fordyce (1976), Gottlieb et al. (1977), Khatami and Rush (Note 12), K. Mitchell and D. Mitchell (1971), Sternbach (1974a), and Swanson et al. (1976) all provide examples of how life style changes may be used in therapy for chronic pain.

In such interventions, an attempt can be made to: (1) manipulate the social system in which the patients find themselves so that they are less rewarded by pain behaviors and more rewarded for a normal life style, and (2) to alter how patients view their life situation in relation to pain. Families may be involved, and, in the course of group and/or individual therapeutic sessions, patients can plan how to alter their environments gradually, setting significant but realistic goals. These goals are generally activity- and life-style oriented, rather than pain-centered (e.g., Greenhoot & Sternbach, 1974). A *reduction in level* of pain may result from such changes, which attempt to reduce the *importance* of pain for patients. But the elimination of pain is not usually considered to be a realistic goal for most chronic pain patients.

Multifaceted intervention. We have described some of the cognitive and behavioral techniques available to a pain-therapy group. Within the broad contexts of group therapy, other modes of interaction may be used. As we have noted, bibliotherapy materials may be useful adjuncts, as may audiotapes (e.g., Mitchell, K., & White, 1977). In addition, the therapist or team treating the patients may have group members engage in other, individualized treatment programs in addition to the group sessions, as is desirable in each case (e.g., Mitchell, K., & White, 1977; Greenhoot & Sternbach, 1974).

An example of such an individual treatment program that lends itself to pain therapy is training in the self-regulation of physiological processes. Relaxation exercises, as we have mentioned, may be used in group sessions to foster patients' sense of control over their own bodies and pain levels. Although the source of the efficacy of such treatments is as yet unclear, they have been found helpful for many patients, especially those suffering from headaches (e.g., Budzynski et al., 1973; Cox, Freundlich, & Meyer, 1975; Haynes, Moseley, & McGowan, 1975; Sargent, Green, & Walters, 1972; Tasto & Hinkle, 1973). Biofeedback may enhance the effectiveness of exercises in physiological self-regulation, perhaps because of the additional apparent potency of the sophisticated technology involved.

Relevant to a consideration of the use of such technologies as biofeedback is Cameron's (in press) comment that the patient needs to believe that the intervention proposed is proportional to the severity of his problem. A back-pain patient with a history of surgical interventions, for example, may readily accept the value of electromyographic biofeedback therapy to train him in muscular relaxation, whereas he might be very skeptical of simple, progressive relaxation exercises that had the same aim. Once again, we are reminded of the importance of awareness of the patients' internal dialogues during therapy.

Such techniques as relaxation, biofeedback, and others all contribute to a multifaceted, group-based therapeutic intervention. The goal is a broadly based therapeutic approach that includes patients as collaborators, taking into consideration individual differences, the range of patients' available coping repertoires, and the patients' appraisals, attributions, and self-statements—their internal dialogues about their problems and their ability to change and cope effectively. The therapist is the arranger and conductor, orchestrating the therapeutic movements with all the means available. The cognitive-behavioral vantage point affords him the use of a broad range of potential strategies, while providing a framework within which to employ them and to encourage the patients' self-sufficiency.

SUMMARY

We have presented a cognitive-behavioral framework for psychological interventions with pain patients. An individualized cognitive-behavioral assessment, using experimentally induced pain was suggested. This provides a source of information for the therapist, as well as a basis for patients reconceptualizing their pain problems. In this phase of therapy, patients are encouraged to conceptualize pain in a manner that incorporates the idea that they *can do something* to alter the experience. To maximally ensure that this conception is adopted, all of the training encourages patients in a very active role, collaborating in the development of the techniques that are then implemented. We described a range of potentially usefull techniques: lifestyle change, relaxation and biofeedback methods, attentional focusing strategies, and direct alterations of self-statements concerning pain and change. It was noted that attention to the way in which techniques are received by patients is as important as the specific interventions that are used.

REFERENCE NOTES

1. Turk, D. C. *Cognitive control of pain: A skills-training approach.* Unpublished masters' thesis, University of Waterloo, 1975.
2. Schalling, D. *Anxiety, pain and coping.* Paper presented at the Conference on Dimensions of Anxiety and Stress, Oslo, Norway, June 29 through July 3, 1975.
3. Henshaw, D. *Cognitive mediators in creative problem solving.* Unpublished doctoral dissertation, University of Waterloo, 1978.
4. Meichenbaum, D. H., & Cameron, R. *An examination of cognitive and contingency variables in anxiety relief procedures.* Unpublished manuscript, University of Waterloo, 1972.
5. Meichenbaum, D. H., & Cameron, R. *Stress inoculation: A skills-training approach to anxiety management.* Unpublished manuscript, University of Waterloo, 1972.
6. Turk, D. C. *A coping skills-training approach for the control of experimentally produced pain.* Unpublished doctoral dissertation, University of Waterloo, 1977.
7. Genest, M. *Controlling pain: A cognitive-behavioral bibliotherapy approach with experimentally produced pain.* Unpublished masters' thesis, University of Waterloo, 1978.
8. Knox, V. J. *Cognitive strategies for coping with pain: Ignoring vs. acknowledging.* Unpublished doctoral dissertation, University of Waterloo, 1972.
9. Genest, M., Meichenbaum, D. H., & Turk, D. C. *A cognitive-behavioral approach to the management of pain.* Paper presented at the annual meeting of the Association for the Advancement of Behavior Therapy, Atlanta, December 1977.
10. Davidson, P. C. *Therapeutic compliance.* Presidential address at the annual meeting of the Canadian Psychological Association, Toronto, Ontario, June 1976.
11. Craig, K. Personal communication, December 28, 1977.
12. Kendall, P., Williams, L., Pechacek, T. F., Graham, L. E., Shisslak, C., & Herzoff, N. *The Palo Alto medical psychology project: Cognitive-behavioral patient education interventions in catheterization procedures.* Unpublished manuscript, University of Minnesota, 1977.
13. Khatami, M., & Rush, A. J. *A pilot study of the treatment of outpatients with chronic pain: Symptom control, stimulus control, and social system intervention.* Paper presented at the annual meeting of the Association for the Advancement of Behavior Therapy, New York, December 1976.

REFERENCES

Adler, R., & Lomazzi, F. Perceptual style and pain tolerance: 1. The influence of certain psychological factors. *Journal of Psychosomatic Research,* 1973, *17,* 369–379.

Agnew, D. C., & Merskey, H. Words of chronic pain. *Pain,* 1976, *2,* 73–81.

Bailey, C. A., & Davidson, P. C. The language of pain intensity. *Pain,* 1976, *2,* 319–324.

Bain, J. A. *Thought control in everyday life.* New York: Funk & Wagnals, 1928.

Bakal, D. A., & Kaganor, J. A. A simple method for self-observation of headache frequency, intensity and location. *Headache,* 1976, *16,* 123–128.

Barber, T. X., & Cooper, B. J. Effects on pain of experimentally induced and spontaneous distraction. *Psychological Reports,* 1972, *31,* 647–651.

Barnes, G. E. Extraversion and pain. *The British Journal of Social and Clinical Psychology,* 1975, *14,* 303–308.

Beecher, H. K. Pain in men wounded in battle. *Annals of Surgery,* 1946, *123,* 96–105.

Beecher, H. K. Pain and some factors that modify it. *Journal of Anesthesiology,* 1951, *12,* 633–641.

Beecher, H. K. *Measurement of subjective responses.* New York: Oxford University Press, 1959.

Bellack, A. S., & Hersen, M. Self-report inventories in behavioral assessment. In J. D. Cone & R. P. Hawkins (Eds.), *Behavioral assessment: New directions in clinical psychology.* New York: Brunner/Mazel, 1977.

Berne, E. *Games people play.* New York: Grove Press, 1964.

Blitz, B., & Dinnerstein, A. J. Role of attentional focus in pain perception: Manipulation of response to noxious stimulation by instructions. *Journal of Abnormal Psychology,* 1971, *77,* 42–45.

Bloom, B. S., & Broder, L. J. *Problem-solving processes of college students: An exploratory investigation.* Chicago: University of Chicago Press, 1950.

Bobey, M. J., & Davidson, P. O. Psychological factors affecting pain tolerance. *Journal of Psychosomatic Research,* 1970, *14,* 371–376.

Bond, M. R., & Pearson, I. B. Psychological aspects of pain in women with advanced cancer of the cervix. *Journal of Psychosomatic Research,* 1969, *13,* 13–19.

Bonica, J. J. Fundamental considerations of chronic pain therapy. *Postgraduate Medicine,* 1973, *53,* 81–85.

Bonica, J. J. Organization and function of a pain clinic. In J. J. Bonica (Ed.), *Advances in neurology* (Vol. 4). New York: Raven Press, 1974.

Budzynski, T., Stoyva, J., Adler, C., & Mullaney, D. EMG biofeedback and tension headaches: A controlled outcome study. *Seminars in Psychiatry,* 1973, *4,* 397–410.

Buss, A., & Portnoy, N. Pain tolerance and group identification. *Journal of Personality and Social Psychology,* 1967, *6,* 106–108.

Cairns, D., Thomas, L., Mooney, V., & Tace, J. B. A comprehensive treatment approach to chronic low back pain. *Pain,* 1976, *2,* 301–308.

Cameron, R. The clinical implementation of behavior change techniques: A cognitively oriented conceptualization of therapeutic "compliance" and "resistance." In J. P. Foreyt & D. Rathjen (Eds.), *Cognitive behavior therapy: Research and applications.* New York: Plenum, in press.

Carr, J. E., Brownsberger, C. N., & Rutherford, R. C. Characteristics of symptom-matched psychogenic and "real" pain patients on the MMPI. *Proceedings of the 74th Annual Convention of the American Psychological Association*, 1966, *1*, 215–216. (Summary)

Caston, J., Cooper, L., & Paley, H. W. Psychological comparison of patients with cardiac neurotic chest pain and angina pectoris. *Psychosomatics*, 1970, *11*, 543–550.

Cautela, J. R., & Upper, D. The Behavioral Inventory Battery: The use of self-report measures in behavioral analysis and therapy. In M. Hersen and A. S. Bellack (Eds.), *Behavioral assessment: A practical handbook*. New York: Pergamon Press, 1976.

Cherry, L. Solving the mysteries of pain. *New York Times Magazine*, 30 Jan., 1977, *50*, 12–13.

Cohen, F., & Lazarus, R. S. Active coping processes, coping disposition, and recovery from surgery. *Psychosomatic Medicine*, 1973, *35*, 375–389.

Cox, D. J., Freundlich, A., & Meyer, R. G. Differential effectiveness of electromyograph feedback, verbal relaxation instructions, and medication placebo with tension headaches. *Journal of Consulting and Clinical Psychology*, 1975, *43*, 892–898.

Davidson, P. C., & McDougal, C. E. A. Personality and pain tolerance measures. *Perceptual and Motor Skills*, 1969, *28*, 787–790.

DeLong, R. D. Individual differences in patterns of anxiety arousal, stress-relevant information, and recovery from surgery. *Dissertation Abstracts International*, 1971, (University Microfilms No. 71, 554).

Egbert, L. D., Battit, G. E., Welch, C. E., & Bartlett, M. K. Reduction of postoperative pain by encouragement and instruction of patients. *New England Journal of Medicine*, 1964, *270*, 825–827.

Fink, B. R. Pain in perspective, 1975. *Perspectives in Biology and Medicine*, 1976, *19*, 278–284.

Fordyce, W. E. Pain viewed as learned behavior. In J. J. Bonica (Ed.), *Advances in neurology* (Vol. 4). New York: Raven Press, 1974. (a)

Fordyce, W. E. Treating chronic pain by contingency management. In J. J. Bonica (Ed.), *Advances in neurology* (Vol. 4). New York: Raven Press, 1974. (b)

Fordyce, W. E. *Behavioral methods for chronic pain and illness*. St. Louis: C. V. Mosby, 1976.

Fordyce, W. E., Fowler, R. S., & DeLateur, H. An application of behavior modification technique to a problem of chronic pain. *Behaviour Research & Therapy*, 1968, *6*, 105–107.

Fordyce, W. E., Fowler, R. S., Jr., Lehmann, J. F., DeLateur, B. J., Sand, P. L., & Trieschmann, R. B. Operant conditioning in the treatment of chronic pain. *Archives of Physiological Medicine*, 1973, *54*, 399–408.

Frank, J. *Persuasion and healing: A comparative study of psychotherapy* (Rev. ed.). New York: Schocken Books, 1974.

Genest, M. Learning to control pain. In N. E. Hankins (Ed.), *Behavioral self-control*. Chicago: Nelson-Hall, in press.

Gerbershagen, H. U., Frey, R., Magin, F., Scholl, W., & Müller-Suur, N. The pain clinic: An interdisciplinary team approach to the problem of pain. *British Journal of Anaesthesia*, 1975, *47*, 526–529.

Goldfried, M. R. The use of relaxation and cognitive relabeling as coping skills. In R. B. Stuart (Ed.), *Behavioral self-management: Strategies, techniques and outcomes.* New York: Brunner/Mazel, 1977.

Gottlieb, H., Strite, L. C., Koller, R., Madorsky, A., Hockersmith, V., Kleeman, M., & Wagner, J. Comprehensive rehabilitation of patients having chronic low back pain. *Archives of Physical Medicine and Rehabilitation,* 1977, *58,* 101–108.

Greenhoot, J. H., & Sternbach, R. A. Conjoint treatment of chronic pain. In J. J. Bonica (Ed.), *Advances in neurology* (Vol. 4). New York: Raven Press, 1974.

Haynes, S. N., Moseley, D., & McGowan, W. T. Relaxation training and biofeedback in the reduction of frontalis muscle tension. *Psychophysiology,* 1975, *12,* 547–552.

Hilgard, E., Cooper, L., Lenox, J., Morgan, A., & Voevodsky, J. The use of a pain-state report in the study of hypnotic analgesia to the pain of ice water. *Journal of Nervous and Mental Disease,* 1967, *114,* 501–513.

Hill, H., Kornetsky, C., Flanary, H., & Wilker, A. Studies on anxiety associated with anticipation of pain: 1. Effects of morphine. *Archives of Neurology and Psychiatry,* 1952, *67,* 612–619.

Holroyd, K. A., Andrasik, F., & Westbrook, T. Cognitive control of tension headache. *Cognitive Therapy and Research,* 1977, *1,* 121–133.

Horan, J. J., Hackett, G., Buchanan, J. D., Stone, O. I., Demchik-Stone, D. Coping with pain: A component analysis of stress-innoculation. *Cognitive Therapy & Research,* 1977, *1,* 211–221.

Janis, I. L. *Psychological stress.* New York: Wiley, 1958.

Janis, I. L. *Stress and frustration.* New York: Harcourt, Brace, Jovanovich, 1971.

Johnson, J., & Rice, V. H. Sensory and distress components of pain: Implications for the study of clinical pain. *Nursing Research,* 1974, *23,* 203–209

Jones, E. E., & Nisbett, R. E. The actor and the observer: Divergent perceptions of the causes of behavior. In J. W. Thibaut, J. I. Spence, & R. C. Carson (Eds.), *Contemporary topics in social psychology.* Morristown, N. J.: General Learning Press, 1976.

Kanfer, F. H., & Goldfoot, D. A. Self-control and tolerance of noxious stimulation. *Psychological Reports,* 1966, *18,* 79–85.

Kazdin, A. Covert modeling, model similarity, and reduction of avoidance behavior. *Behavior Therapy,* 1974, *5,* 325–340.

Kunkle, E. C. Phasic pains induced by cold. *Journal of Applied Physiology,* 1949, *1,* 811–824.

Lambert, W., Libman, E., & Poser, E. The effect of increased salience of a membership group on pain tolerance. *Journal of Personality,* 1960, *28,* 350.

Lazarus, R. S. Psychological stress and coping in adaptation and illness. *International Journal of Psychiatry in Medicine,* 1974, *5,* 321–333.

Lazarus, R. S., & Alfert, E. Short circuiting of threat by experimentally altering cognitive appraisal. *Journal of Abnormal and Social Psychology,* 1964, *69,* 195–205.

Le Shan, L. The world of the patient in severe pain of long duration. *Journal of Chronic Diseases*, 1964, *17*, 119–126.

Levine, M. E. Depression, back pain, and disc protrusion: Relationships and proposed psychophysiological mechanisms. *Diseases of the Nervous System*, 1971, *32*, 41–45.

Linehan, M. M. Issues in behavioral interviewing. In J. D. Cone & R. P. Hawkins (Eds.), *Behavioral assessment: New directions in clinical psychology*. New York: Brunner/Mazel, 1977.

Lovallo, W. The cold pressor test and autonomic function: A review and integration. *Psychophysiology,* 1975, *12*, 268–283.

Mahoney, M. *Cognition and behavior modification*. Cambridge, Mass.: Ballinger, 1974.

Mahoney, M. J. Some applied issues in self-monitoring. In J. D. Cone & R. P. Hawkins (Eds.), *Behavioral assessment: New directions in clinical psychology*. N. Y.: Brunner/Mazel, 1977.

Maruta, T., Swanson, D. W., & Swenson, W. M. Low back pain patients in a psychiatric population. *Mayo Clinic Proceedings*, 1976, *51*, 57–61.

Meichenbaum, D. H. Examination of model characteristics in reducing avoidance behavior. *Journal of Personality and Social Psychology*, 1971, *17*, 298–307.

Meichenbaum, D. H. *Cognitive behavior modification*. Morristown, N. J.: General Learning Press, 1974.

Meichenbaum, D. H. Enhancing creativity by modifying what subjects say to themselves. *American Educational Research Journal*, 1975, *12*, 129–145. (a)

Meichenbaum, D. H. Self-instructional methods. In F. H. Kanfer & A. P. Goldstein (Eds.), *Helping people change*. New York: Pergamon Press, 1975. (b)

Meichenbaum, D. H. A cognitive-behavior modification approach to assessment. In M. Hersen & A. S. Bellack (Eds.), *Behavioral assessment: A practical handbook*. New York: Pergamon Press, 1976. (a)

Meichenbaum, D. H. Toward a cognitive theory of self-control. In G. E. Schwartz and D. Shapiro (Eds.), *Consciousness and self-regulation: Advances in research* (Vol. 1). New York: Plenum, 1976. (b)

Meichenbaum, D. H. *Cognitive-behavior modification: An integrative approach*. New York: Plenum Press, 1977.

Meichenbaum, D. H., & Genest, M. Treatment of anxiety. In G. Harris (Ed.), The group treatment of human problems: A social learning approach. New York: Grune & Stratton, 1977.

Meichenbaum, D. H. & Turk, D. The cognitive-behavioral management of anxiety, anger, and pain. In P. O. Davidson (Ed.), *The behavioral management of anxiety, depression and pain*. New York: Brunner/Mazel, 1976.

Meichenbaum, D. H., Turk, D. C., & Burstein, S. The nature of coping with stress. In I. Sarason & C. Spielberger (Eds.), *Stress and anxiety* (Vol. 2). New York: Wiley, 1975.

Melzack, R. *The puzzle of pain*. Harmondsworth, Eng.: Penguin, 1973.

Melzack, R. The McGill Pain Questionnaire: Major properties and scoring methods. *Pain*, 1975, *1*, 277–299.

Melzack, R., & Wall, P. Pain mechanisms: A new theory. *Science,* 1965, *150,* 971–979.

Melzack, R., & Wall, P. Psychophysiology of pain. *The International Anesthesiology Clinic,* 1970, *8,* 3–34.

Mitchell, K. R., & Mitchell, D. M. Migraine: An exploratory treatment application of programmed behavior therapy techniques. *Journal of Psychosomatic Research,* 1971, *15,* 137–157.

Mitchell, K. R., & White, R. G. Control of migraine headache by behavioral self-management: A controlled case study. *Headache,* 1976, *16,* 178–184.

Mitchell, K. R., & White, R. G. Behavioral self-management: An application to the problem of migraine headaches. *Behavior Therapy,* 1977, *8,* 213–222.

Morganstern, K. P. Behavioral interviewing: The initial stages of assessment. In M. Hersen & A. S. Bellack (Eds.), *Behavioral assessment: A practical handbook.* New York: Pergamon Press, 1976.

Nelson, R. O. Methodological issues in assessment via self-monitoring. In J. D. Cone & R. P. Hawkins (Eds.), *Behavioral assessment: New directions in clinical psychology.* New York: Brunner/Mazel, 1977.

Nichols, D. C., & Tursky, B. Body image, anxiety, and tolerance for experimental pain. *Psychosomatic Medicine,* 1967, *29,* 103–110.

Novaco, R. W. *Anger control: The development and evaluation of an experimental treatment.* Lexington, Mass.: Heath & Co., 1975.

Pervin, L. The need to predict and control under conditions of threat. *Journal of Personality,* 1963, *31,* 570–585.

Peterson, D. *The clinical study of social behavior.* Englewood Cliffs, N. J.: Prentice-Hall, 1968.

Petrie, A. *Individuality in pain and suffering.* Chicago: University of Chicago Press, 1967.

Rimm, D. C., & Masters, J. C. *Behavior therapy: Techniques and empirical findings.* New York: Academic Press, 1974.

Rush, A. J., Beck, A. T., Kovacs, M., & Hollon, S. Comparative efficacy of cognitive therapy and pharmacotherapy in the treatment of depressed outpatients. *Cognitive Therapy and Research,* 1977, *1,* 17–38.

Sargent, J. D., Green, E. E., & Walters, E. D. The use of autogenic feedback training in a pilot study of migraine and tension headaches. *Headache,* 1972, *12,* 120–124.

Smith, G., Egbert, L., Markowitz, R., Mosteller, F., & Beecher, H. An experimental pain method sensitive to morphine in man: The submaximum effort tourniquet technique. *Journal of Pharmacology and Experimental Therapeutics,* 1966, *154,* 324–332.

Smith, G., Lowenstein, E., Hubbard, J., & Beecher, H. Experimental pain produced by the submaximum effort tourniquet technique: Further evidence of validity. *Journal of Pharmacology and Experimental Therapeutics,* 1968, *163,* 468–474.

Sternbach, R. A. *Pain patients: Traits and treatments.* N. Y.: Academic Press, 1974. (a)

Sternbach, R. A. Varieties of pain games. In J. J. Bonica (Ed.), *Advances in neurology* (Vol. 4). New York: Raven Press, 1974. (b)

Sternbach, R. A., Deems, L. M., Timmermans, G., & Huey, L. On the sensitivity of the tourniquet pain test. *Pain,* 1977, *3,* 105–110.

Sternbach, R. A., Murphy, R. W., Akeson, W. H., & Wolf, S. R. Chronic low-back pain: The "low-back loser." *Postgraduate Medicine,* 1973, *53,* 135–138.

Sternbach, R. A., Murphy, R. W., Timmermans, G., Greenhoot, J. H., & Akeson, W. H. Measuring the severity of clinical pain. In J. J. Bonica (Ed.), *Advances in neurology* (Vol. 4). New York: Raven Press, 1974.

Sternbach, R. A., & Rusk, T. N. Alternatives to the pain career. *Psychotherapy: Theory, Research and Practice,* 1973, *10,* 321–324.

Sternbach, R. A., Wolf, S. R., Murphy, R. W., & Akeson, W. H. Traits of pain patients: The low-back "loser." *Psychosomatics,* 1973, *14,* 226–229.

Stone, C. I., Demchik-Stone, D. A., & Horan, J. J. Coping with pain: A component analysis of Lamaze and cognitive-behavioral procedures. *Journal of Psychosomatic Research,* 1977, *21,* 417–457.

Swanson, D. W., Swenson, W. M., Maruta, T., & McPhee, M. C. Program for managing chronic pain: 1. Program description and characteristics of patients. *Mayo Clinic Proceedings,* 1976, *51,* 401–408.

Tasto, D., & Hinkle, J. E. Muscle relaxation treatment for tension headaches. *Behaviour Research and Therapy,* 1973, *11,* 347–349.

Turk, D. C. Coping with pain: A review of cognitive control technique. In M. Feuenstein, L. B. Sacks, & I. D. Turket (Eds.), *Psychological approaches to pain control,* in press.

Turk, D. C., & Genest, M. Regulation of pain: The application of cognitive and behavioral techniques for prevention and remediation. In P. C. Kendall & S. D. Hollon (Eds.), *Cognitive-behavioral interventions: Theory, research, and procedures.* New York: Academic Press, in press.

Walls, R. T., Werner, T. J., Bacon, A., & Zane, T. Behavior checklists. In J. D. Cone & R. P. Hawkins (Eds.), *Behavioral assessment: New directions in clinical psychology.* New York: Brunner/Mazel, 1977.

Weisenberg, M. Pain and pain control. *Psychological Bulletin,* 1977, *84,* 1008–1044.

Wolff, B. R., & Langley, S. Cultural factors and response to pain: A review. *American Anthropologist,* 1968, *70,* 494–501.

Zborowski, M. *People in pain.* San Francisco: Jossey-Bass, 1969.

Chapter 11

A Proposed Behavioral Couples Group for Male Alcoholics and their Wives

Timothy J. O'Farrell
Henry S. G. Cutter

Abstract

Although couples group therapy is popular in alcoholism treatment, has received empirical support, and is considered by some the treatment of choice for married alcoholics, behavioral approaches for such a group have not been developed. After briefly reviewing current developments in behavioral treatments for both alcoholism and marital conflict, we propose a behavioral couples group format for male alcoholics and their wives. The goals of this type of group, pretreatment assessment procedures, the couples group treatment package, and methods to evaluate outcome are described in detail.*

*Portions of this material were presented at the Eighth Annual Brockton Symposium on Behavior Therapy, VA Hospital, Brockton, Massachusetts, May 13, 1977.

BACKGROUND

Marital conflict and excessive drinking are widespread, and often related, problems in America today. Although some alcoholics never marry, a majority of them either are or have been married. It comes as no surprise, therefore, that Keller (1974) has called marital and family treatment the most notable current advance in the psychotherapy of alcoholism. Steinglass (1976), tracing the development of marital and family treatment approaches to alcoholism, indicated that the field started with the treatment of each spouse separately in either individual or group therapy and developed into the conjoint treatment of the spouses. More recently, the marital treatment of alcoholics has progressed to the most popular current method—multiple-couples group therapy.

Cadogan (1973) has found that couples group therapy produces results superior to having husbands alone receive treatment for their alcoholism. In the light of their clinical experience with 118 couples, Gallant, Rich, Bey, and Terranova (1970) concluded that couples group therapy is the treatment of choice for married alcoholics. Surprisingly, the alcoholism literature in this field fails to mention behavioral approaches to the increasingly popular couples group. In fact, recent reviews of the marital and family treatment literature for alcoholism make little or no mention of behavioral approaches of any kind (Janzen, 1977; Steinglass, 1976).

In this chapter, we propose a behavioral couples group format for male alcoholics and their wives based on current developments in behavioral marital therapy for nonalcoholics and on a broad spectrum behavioral approach to the treatment of alcoholism. We will begin with a brief review of the current status of behavioral treatments for both alcoholism and marital conflict, since developments in these areas provided the groundwork for our behavioral couples group.

Behavioral Treatment of Alcoholism

Behaviorists, historically, considered alcohol abuse a function of simple conditioning factors; consequently, the behavioral treatment of alcoholism almost exclusively employed aversion conditioning techniques. The Department of Health, Education, and Welfare (H.E.W.) report on alcohol and health (Keller, 1974) appropriately comments on the more recent "maturation" of behavioral treatment approaches to alcoholism. Current behavioral treatment has become more comprehensive in response to: (1) the increasing number of research findings questioning a simple classical conditioning model (see Franks & Wilson, 1975), and (2) recent reviews of controlled evaluation studies questioning the efficacy of aversion procedures (Nathan, 1976; Wilson, Note 1). A wide variety of nonaversive behavioral treatment strategies are now used to reduce excessive alcohol consumption and to enhance social, marital, emotional, and vocational functioning.

More recent behavioral approaches to alcoholism emphasize the initiation and maintenance of behavior patterns that are alternative to and incompatible with excessive alcohol consumption. Behavioral procedures are designed to modify the antecedent and consequent events associated with excessive drinking. Alcoholics are taught to avoid certain antecedents or to deal with them more effectively. This includes new ways of dealing with stressful social, marital, and vocational situations. Consequences can be rearranged either by the alcoholic himself through self-management procedures or through the cooperation of significant others in his environment. Within this operant framework, significant persons in the environment are taught ways of reinforcing new, sober behavior patterns and of punishing or ignoring excessive alcohol consumption.

A recent analysis (Miller, P., Note 2) of controlled follow-up studies indicates that comprehensive behavioral treatment programs are clearly superior to more traditional hospital treatment for alcoholism (Azrin, 1976; Hunt & Azrin, 1973; Sobell, M., & Sobell, L., 1973, 1976; Vogler, Compton, & Weissbach, 1975). For more comprehensive reviews of the literature in this area see: P. Miller, 1976, Note 2; Nathan, 1976; Nathan and Briddell, 1977; Nathan and Marlatt, in press.

Since behavioral group therapy is a relatively recent development in all areas of behavior therapy, it is not surprising that it is only in the last few years that reports of behavioral groups have started to appear in the alcoholism literature. Adinolfi, McCourt, and Geoghegan (1976) reported successful use of group assertiveness training with chronic alcoholics. In a related article, Foy, Miller, P., Eisler, and O'Toole (1976) used social skills training to teach alcoholics to refuse drinks effectively so they can resist social pressure to drink, a major factor in over 50 % of relapses (Marlatt, Note 3), When Azrin (1976) modified his already successful community-reinforcement program (Hunt & Azrin, 1973) so that all counseling was conducted in groups, the median counseling time per client was reduced by over 40 %. In another broad spectrum approach, Johnson (Note 4) reported on group behavior therapy with inpatient chronic alcoholics using many of Lazarus's (1971) techniques. Frederiksen and P. Miller (1976) studied the process of peer-determined and self-determined reinforcement in behavioral group therapy with alcoholics. Initially self-determination led to underrewarding and peer determination to overrewarding (compared with an objective standard), but these patterns were reversed in later sessions.

As in the wider behavioral group therapy literature, some of the studies using behavioral groups with alcoholics (e.g., Azrin, 1976; Johnson, Note 4) seem to do individual behavior therapy within a group primarily for the economy this provides. Adinolfi et al. (1976), however, go a step further in using the group setting to teach the interpersonal skill of assertiveness; they find that a group provides more varied and more realistic modeling and feedback than is available in individual therapy. Even more creative are the studies that consider the literature on the influence of social factors on alcoholic drinking (Griffiths, Bigelow, & Liebson, in press) and do therapy through the group. An individual therapist can never simulate realistic peer pressure to drink as well as fellow career drink-pushers; Foy et al. (1976) have capitalized on the ability of the group to provide a microcosm of social reality in their drink refusal training. Such a use of the group should promote transfer of therapeutic gains to real life situations. Another use of the group process itself is Frederiksen and P. Miller's (1976) attempt to study (in behavioral therapy groups) peer-determined and self-determined reinforcement, both of which are implicated in the maintenance of problem drinking. Future studies should exploit creatively the unique influence for change provided by a group setting and do therapy through the group, not just therapy in a group.

Our proposed behavioral couples group for alcoholics draws on developments in the behavioral treatment of marital conflict among both alcoholics and nonalcoholics. The discussion turns next to a synopsis of recent behavioral methods for intervening in troubled marriages where alcoholism is not a problem.

Behavioral Analysis and Treatment of Marital Conflict

In his behavioral conceptualization of marital conflict, Stuart (1969) suggests that marital discord is a function of the low rate of positive reinforcers exchanged by spouses. As an outcome of this low rate of positive reinforcement, spouses become less "attracted" to each other and mutually experience the relationship as less attractive. Partners are highly attracted to each other when they fall in love and must (from a behavioral viewpoint) be positively reinforcing each other at a high rate at that time. How, then, does marital discord develop? A behavioral explanation emphasizes what can go wrong when partners attempt to change each other to maximize their own reinforcement (a process assumed to happen in all marriages). Marital conflict occurs if one party fails to comply with explicit demands for immediate changes in behavior from the spouse.

Couples in marital discord generally engage in faulty behavior change operations. Rather than relying on positive control as the primary strategy for insuring rewards, cooperation, and compliance from the partner, spouses in distressed marriages make excessive use of aversive control techniques such as threats and nagging. As aversive stimulation escalates, the communication between the spouses becomes more and more ambiguous, vague, and inconsistent. Inadequate communication and reliance on aversive control by distressed couples makes them unable to solve problems in specific areas of conflict in the relationship. A backlog of unresolved problems and differences develops, and there is very little positive, reinforcing interaction. The evidence supporting these behavioral notions about marital conflict is summarized by Jacobson and Martin (1976).

Behavioral techniques for treating marital conflict can be roughly divided into two categories: (1) modification of couple interaction in the clinical setting, and (2) contingency contracting to change behaviors in the natural environment. In an effort to increase the rate of rewarding and decrease the rate of aversive interaction, behavioral marital therapists have focused on the couple's communication in the clinical or laboratory setting. Spouses are directed to alter their responses to each other on a variety of dimensions, two of which are: problem-solving interaction, i.e., the resolution of specific areas of conflict in the relationship (Weiss, Hops, & Patterson, 1973); and assertiveness, i.e., the verbalization of both positive and negative affect (Eisler, Miller, P., Hersen, & Alford, 1974; Fensterheim, 1972). The training in these varied communication skills consists of: (1) demonstrating to couples their self-defeating, destructive patterns of interaction by presenting them with feedback, (2) suggesting alternative methods by instruction and/or modeling, and (3) monitoring their attempts to practice techniques suggested or modeled by the therapist (behavioral rehearsal).

One of the most frequently used behavioral treatments for marital discord is contingency contracting. As applied to marriage therapy, contracting refers to the negotiation of written agreements between spouses; it is a "systematic procedure for setting forth behavior change agreements" (Weiss et al., 1973, p. 328). When used after adequate communication skills have been established, contracting provides a positive behavior change method that makes it possible for the couple to reverse the process of using aversive control for desired change.

In their recent review of the literature on the behavioral treatment of marital conflict, Jacobson and Martin (1976) conclude that: " . . . studies investigating behavioral marriage therapy, although not conclusive, strongly suggest the efficacy of a treatment approach combining contingency contracting with direct training of communication skills in the clinical setting. Furthermore, there is suggestive evidence that either of the two main components of this approach can be of some benefit when used alone" (pp. 553–4). In another review, Greer and D'Zurilla (1975) point out that, in addition to promising results, "the power of the behavioral method is found in its theoretical base, observational and treatment-relevant assessment, procedural specificity and quantification of outcome" (p. 299).

Although a behavioral couples group has been suggested (Gurman, 1975; Liberman, De Risi, & King, 1973; Weiss & Margolin, 1977), all of the studies reported in these two reviews of behavioral marital therapy have treated couples one at a time and not in a couples group. Liberman, Wheeler, and Sanders (1976) noted the economy of time a behavioral couples group provides and went on to list a number of other advantages:

> The group members provide a wide variety of models for each other in demonstrating alternative ways of relating, communicating and solving problems. It is sometimes easier for a spouse to identify with a fellow group member rather than with a more distant and dissimilar therapist. Feedback in the form of suggestions and positive reinforcement from peers in the group can be considerably more powerful than feedback from a therapist plus a possibly antagonistic spouse. . . . The opportunity to see fellow couples making progress and changes, even while one's progress is nil, decreases demoralization and helps to maintain favorable expectations. The cohesion in a group, mediated by mutual disclosure, problem-solving, informal pre- and post-group meetings, and refreshments has been shown to improve therapeutic outcome. (pp. 384–385)

Behavioral Analysis and Treatment of the Alcoholic Marriage

The behavioral treatment of married male alcoholics, like behavioral treatment of marital conflict in general, is based on a social-learning formulation of the alcoholic's marriage. According to this model, the marriages of male alcoholics and their wives are generally conflicted; the couple fight repeatedly about drinking and positively reinforce each other at a low rate. Marital interaction, under these conditions, is hardly a viable alternative to drinking.

In this behavioral view, certain antecedent and consequent events are assumed to maintain abusive drinking. An important antecedent to drinking by married alcoholics may be their lack of assertiveness in interaction with their wives. Wives who attend primarily to alcoholic behaviors, but virtually ignore positive non-drinking behaviors provide consequences likely to increase drinking. Wives, furthermore, often provide financial, emotional and sexual support when alcoholic husbands are actively drinking. A detailed consideration, however, of the evidence for and issues involved in a behavioral formulation of the alcoholic marriage is beyond the scope of this paper (see Paolino & McCrady, 1978 for more information).

There have been relatively few reports of behavioral marital therapy applied to alcoholic marriages. Cheek, Franks, Laucius, and Burtle (1971) attempted to teach 24 wives and relatives of treated alcoholics to apply behavioral principles and operant conditioning techniques to family interactions which were likely to threaten the alcoholics' sobriety. Unfortunately, none of the wives were able to apply this new learning consistently. The failure of this study may result from the fact that only the wives were treated in this program rather than both husbands and wives together and that more severe alcoholics were treated than in some of the case reports described below.

P. Miller (1972) successfully used contingency contracting with an excessive drinker and his wife to shape controlled drinking and an improved marital relationship. Soon after the contract was initiated the husband's drinking dropped to within acceptable limits and remained moderate at 6-month follow-up; the couple also reported improved marital relations in other areas.

Wilson and Rosen (1976) in a case study also employed a contract (specifying the amount and stimulus conditions for controlled drinking) as part of a multifaceted behavioral treatment program that also included blood alcohol concentration (B.A.C.) discrimination training, thought stopping, and assertive training. The wife observed treatment and provided feedback to the husband and to the therapists during therapy sessions. The couple, initially teetering on the brink of divorce, reunited with both reporting greater happiness. The husband was controlling his drinking at 6-month follow-up.

Eisler et al. (1974) reported a case in which they employed assertive training with an alcoholic to improve his marital relationship and drinking behavior. Results showed that the husband was more assertive in posttreatment videotaped interactions with his wife and that, apparently as a consequence, weekly B.A.C. (taken on a random basis for 6 weeks before and after therapy) decreased.

P. Miller and Hersen (Note 5) described a case of a 49-year-old male alcoholic whose wife had decided to divorce him if he did not stop drinking. This case report provides a good example of treatment-relevant assessment and the effective use of a more comprehensive marital treatment package. Assessment consisted of direct observation of the couple during interviews together, videotaped conversations in which the couple discussed various problem and nonproblem areas of their life, and audiotaped recordings of mealtime interaction at home on two occasions. In some of these assessment sessions the counselors were absent to allow for more "natural" interaction. On the basis of these assessments, specific behavioral goals were set and achieved by means of social skills training, assertive training, and contracting. Follow-up at 9 months indicated that the husband had taken Antabuse each day and was completely abstinent. Improvements also were noted in the interaction of the couple (videotaped in the clinic) and in their day-to-day behavior at home.

Hunt and Azrin (1973) and Azrin (1976) included a behavioral marital counseling procedure as part of their community-reinforcement treatment program for alcoholics. The marital counseling was based on an earlier study of a behavioral treatment package for nonalcoholic marriages (Azrin, Naster, & Jones, 1973). Homework assignments and various structured tasks taught couples to pinpoint specifically the behaviors that were pleasing to the other, those that were not, and the specific changes that would make the spouse's behavior more pleasing. Couples were instructed in the art of compromise and informal contracts were used to facilitate behavior change at home. In addition, a special social motivation program involving the wife cueing (when necessary) and reinforcing daily Antabuse-taking was part of the improved community-reinforcement program (Azrin, 1976). Rigorous evaluation of the treatment program, of which the marital counseling procedures were a part, showed it to be clearly superior to a less intensive, more traditional hospital program for alcoholics.

Hedberg and Campbell (1974), in an experimental clinical study involving outpatients compared the therapeutic efficacy of behavioral marital counseling, systematic desensitization, covert sensitization, and electric shock avoidance conditioning. At the 6-month follow-up, behavioral marital counseling was found to be the most effective treatment, with 74% of 15 alcoholic patients achieving their goal (either abstinence or controlled drinking) and an additional 13% showing "much improvement." For those who chose abstinence as their goal, behavioral marital counseling was, by far, superior to all other treatments. Communication training, instructions in the principles of learning, contracting, and assertive training were all part of the marital treatment. The sequencing, frequency, and total number of treatment sessions was the same for all patients irrespective of the type of therapy received.

This literature review shows that behavioral marital therapy in combination with social and vocational behavioral alcoholism treatment produces better results with state hospital alcoholics than a traditional alcoholism program (Azrin, 1976; Hunt & Azrin, 1973). Unfortunately, as Nathan (1976) points out, time in therapy was not equal for the two treatments in these studies. In addition, when intensity of treatment is held constant, behavioral marital therapy for outpatient alcoholics is not only superior to three alternative behavioral treatments, but clearly exceeds the outcome statistics in the nonbehavioral literature (Hedberg & Campbell, 1974). Finally, behavioral marital therapy (with the exception of the Cheek et al. (1973) study treating only the wife) has had positive results in 29 of 31 cases treated. Behavioral marital therapy for alcoholics and their wives, one must conclude, shows promise and deserves the further serious attention of behavior therapists. We have made detailed suggestions for much needed future research in this area elsewhere (O'Farrell & Cutter, Note 6).

Notably lacking in the literature, however, is any mention of a behavioral couples group for alcoholics and their spouses. Although couples group therapy is particularly popular in alcoholism treatment (Steinglass, 1976), has received empirical support (Cadogan, 1973), and is considered the treatment of choice for married alcoholics (Gallant et al., 1970), no behavioral format for a couples group for alcoholics has yet been proposed. A behavioral format for a couples group would facilitate incorporation of the very promising new behavioral marital methods in existing alcohol treatment programs, many of which now use nonbehavioral couples groups.

A PROPOSED BEHAVIORAL COUPLES GROUP FOR ALCOHOLICS

In a study related conceptually to the present proposal, Liberman, Levine, Wheeler, Sanders, and Wallace (1976) developed and evaluated a behavioral couples group treatment for nonalcoholics. The primary interventions in the behavioral couples group were: training in discriminating and monitoring pleasing behaviors given to and received from the spouse; behavioral rehearsal of communication skills using prompting, modeling, feedback, and homework assignments; and contingency contracting. Liberman, Levine, Wheeler, Sanders, and Wallace compared, among nonalcoholic couples with marital conflict, their behavioral couples group treatment with an interaction-insight couples group treatment. In the interaction-insight group, the leaders encouraged ventilation of feelings, problem-solving through discussion, and mutual support and feedback.

Liberman, Levine, Wheeler, Sanders and Wallace assessed treatment outcome on multiple levels before, during and immediately, 1 month, 2 months, and 6 months after treatment. Response measures included a variety of self-report measures of marital satisfaction and direct observation of clients through "live" time sampling during group sessions and through coding of videotaped problem-solving discussions before and after treatment. Both types of couples groups showed significant improvements on the self-report measures, with little or no differences between groups. However, the direct observational data indicated that couples in the behavioral group, as compared to the interaction-insight group, showed significantly more positive and mutually supportive verbal and nonverbal behaviors in their videotaped discussions after treatment.

Gurman (1977) is clearly correct in criticizing the serial rather than random assignment of couples to treatments, lack of an untreated control group, and possible therapist bias. He is on weaker ground when he states that the behavioral group received more intensive treatment. In spite of methodological deficiencies, it is important to note that Liberman provides a well-developed session-by-session group format, complete with a 95-page in-service training manual (Liberman, Note 7).

Liberman's "package," adapted for alcoholics using suggestions of P. Miller (1976), L'Abate (1975), and Marlatt (Note 3), is the basis of our behavioral couples group for alcoholics and their spouses. First we will describe the goals of the group, then the techniques to be used, and finally the methods for evaluating its effectiveness. Table 1 presents a tentative outline of goals and techniques.

Goals

Following P. Miller's (1976) suggestions, the first goal is to change alcohol-related interactional patterns presumed to maintain abusive drinking. Clinical experience suggests that one can get spouses to engage in behaviors more pleasing to each other, but if the alcohol-related interactional patterns are not changed, they soon return to arguing about past or "possible" future drinking. They then feel more discouraged about their relationship than before and are less likely to try pleasing each other again.

Table 1
Outline of Goals and Interventions for a Behavioral
Couples Group for Alcoholics and Wives

Goals

I. Alter alcohol-related interactional patterns.
II. Change general marital relationship so it becomes more of a positive reinforcer to the alcoholic than excessive drinking was previously.
   A. Identify and rehearse new behaviors in clinic.
   B. Transfer the new behaviors to "real life" with homework assignments, contingency contracting, and an explicit maintenance program.

Treatment Package

I. Pretreatment
   A. Conduct educational program on "alcoholism and marital and sexual problems."
   B. Complete pretreatment structured interview.
   C. Orient to group with instructions to promote therapeutic expectations.
   D. Phone daily to collect baseline data.
II. Treatment
   A. Negotiate agreement for husband to take Antabuse daily and wife to observe and reinforce Antabuse-taking and not to nag about past (or feared future) drinking.
   B. Display weekly records of pleasing and displeasing spouse behavior and give feedback in the group session.
   C. Increase "Pleases" and decrease "Displeases" by Love Days, shared recreational events, and sexual enhancement procedures.
   D. Train in communication skills using behavioral rehearsal, modeling, prompting, and feedback with emphasis on support-understanding, assertiveness, and problem-solving.
   E. Contingency contract to change targeted relationship behaviors using positive (not negative) control techniques.
III. Maintenance
   A. Drinking
      1. Identify steps that lead to drinking in the family.
      2. Suggest future actions to avoid drinking.
      3. Make a list of family rules to prevent future drinking.
      4. Rehearse methods to prevent future drinking.
   B. Marital interaction
      1. List behaviors that contributed to problems before therapy and how they have changed.
      2. List steps to deal with these problems if they recur.
      3. Repeat guidelines for communication, problem solving, and contracting to deal with new problems that will arise.
   C. Follow-up at gradually increasing intervals for maintenance of therapeutic gains and data collection.

The means by which a behavioral couples group improves the general marital relationship highlights the difference between traditional and behavioral couples groups. Behavioral groups emphasize communication skills training, using behavioral rehearsal in the group with specific homework assignments between sessions and contingency contracting; much less important are ventilation, sharing of feelings and insight into the marital relationship, emphasized in the traditional nonbehavioral group. Problem areas are pointed out and suggestions for change are offered in the nonbehavioral group, but no consistent concerted effort is made to teach new skills or to transfer new behavior to real life.

Assessment-Intervention Package

Pretreatment education consists of a discussion group after a live or videotaped presentation on the reciprocal relationship between alcoholism and marital and sexual problems. One of the goals of the education procedure is to overcome resistance to marital treatment by alcoholics and their wives (Hunt & Azrin, 1973, pp. 94–95). An attempt is made to introduce the notion of their mutual dependency on the husband's sobriety in preparation for the Antabuse procedure outlined below, and to describe briefly a social learning view of marriage.

Those expressing interest in couples group treatment after the educational meeting complete a questionnaire describing frequent past antecedents of abusive drinking and the precounseling questionnaires developed by the University of Oregon Marital Studies Program (Weiss et al., 1973; Weiss & Margolin, 1977). Following completion of the questionnaires, the co-therapists meet with each couple for a structured interview in order to make a preliminary list of marital problem areas, to further specify past antecedents of drinking using the Drinking Profile (Marlatt, 1975), and to videotape the couple trying to agree on solutions to problems identified by the questionnaires. Ideally, similar videotaped samples of problem-solving interaction would also be taken at home. During this interview, we also attempt to promote therapeutic expectations that active involvement in the group will produce a successful outcome. We describe to the couple the positive results obtained with couples groups for alcoholics (specifically with behavioral couples groups for nonalcoholics), and stress the group's emphasis on changing behavior before changing feelings, completing homework assignments, and actively participating in behavioral rehearsals.

At the end of the assessment-orientation interview, couples are instructed about the daily phone calls to collect data on pleasing and displeasing interactions at home for the 10-day "baseline" period prior to the start of the couples group. This assessment phase is done with each couple, one at a time, since behavioral group therapy uses the group to achieve specific aims that have been identified for each couple, at least partially, prior to the group. Finally, a deposit contract for group attendance and completion of homework assignments is negotiated at this time.

Behavioral couples group treatment starts with the leaders emphasizing the values of a group approach to marriage counseling. Groups provide more observers, more points of view, more interchange, and more stimulation. Groups provide multiple models for various styles of interrelating, and a wide range of behavioral options to emulate or to avoid. Exposure is offered to different interaction patterns, thus affording more learning opportunities. Group feedback carries more impact and is taken more seriously than feedback from a professional alone. As trust develops, groups offer a safe learning environment where couples can discover that exploring and experimenting with their own relationship is interesting and rewarding.

The ground rules for group sessions are the next topic of the first group meeting. Reports are limited to a present and future focus because bringing back the past is detrimental and interferes with making necessary changes to improve the marriage. Leaders interrupt such negative discussions. Group sessions are structured so that each couple has approximately 10 to 15 minutes to give reports on their progress, assignments, and problems. Couples who complete homework assignments have the full amount of time to report while those not completing an assignment have only 5 minutes. Of course, the noncompliers are encouraged to listen carefully to the others to learn by modeling. Throughout the group, the leaders refrain from giving a lot of negative attention to noncomplying couples, but rather use the 5-minute contingency and give a matter-of-fact request for better effort in the future. The greater successes of other couples hopefully will serve as a model for the more resistant couples through vicarious learning.

The next step consists of negotiating an agreement between spouses to insure daily Antabuse ingestion by the husband (Azrin, 1976). (In our setting, all patients are encouraged to take Antabuse prior to couples treatment.) Maintenance of the agreement is insured by rehearsing the new behaviors in the group and by monitoring compliance at the beginning of each session. This procedure is designed as a constructive way to deal with couples' desires to talk about drinking (rather than nondrinking issues) early in treatment. It is hoped that this avoids arguments about drinking until other treatment interventions build marital satisfaction to compete with future drinking. With the exception of regular tracking of urges to drink, drinking is downplayed as a topic in the group after the Antabuse procedure has been negotiated. Drinking becomes a major topic again when the maintenance of therapeutic gains is planned just prior to termination.

The rest of the interventions are described briefly since they have been presented in detail elsewhere (Weiss et al., 1973; Liberman, Note 7). Starting with the baseline period and continuing during the treatment period, couples track pleasing and displeasing behaviors at home and discuss these in the group. This is part of an effort to show the relationship between specific behaviors and daily marital satisfaction, to teach spouses to acknowledge pleasing behaviors, and to pinpoint behaviors that they wish to increase or decrease. A variety of techniques are used to increase pleasing behaviors: "Love Days," on which partners are asked to double the number of "Pleases" (i.e., pleasing behaviors) to each other; sexual enhancement procedures (LoPiccolo & Miller, V., 1975) starting with an educational film—"Tenderness" (Serber & Laws, 1974)—on improving communication between spouses about exchange of physical affection; and, finally, planning shared recreational events. This is particularly important since a recent retrospective alcoholism treatment outcome evaluation finds family participation in social and recreational activities to be one of the few family characteristics associated with positive treatment outcome (Moos, R., Bromet, Tsu, & Moos, B., Note 8).

Extensive training in communication skills focuses first on communicating support and understanding, second on assertiveness, and third on problem solving. Teaching partners in an alcoholic marriage to communicate support and understanding by using eye contact and rephrasing the partner's message before stating one's own position is a major accomplishment that must be carefully shaped. We start with nonproblem areas and provide repeated modeling and coaching by the therapist. Such learning may be impeded by a partner's failure to separate understanding his or her spouse from agreement with the spouse's position (Weiss & Birchler, Note 9). The second aspect of communication training involves teaching spouses to make pinpointed, assertive statements of their wants [e.g., "I would really like it if you would do (specific behavior)."]. In problem-solving training, spouses generate and evaluate possible solutions to relationship problems and then agree on a solution. In order to solve problems together, each partner must be able to state his own suggested solutions clearly and specifically and must show an understanding of the other's point of view; thus, each stage of communication training builds on skills that have been taught previously. Finally, remaining requests for change will be dealt with by using contingency contracting. The primacy of contingency contracting in early writing on behavioral marital therapy (e.g., Stuart, 1969) has given way to the current realization that, without a basis of adequate communication skills, a contract is not worth the paper on which it is written (Liberman, Levine, Wheeler, Sanders, & Wallace, 1976).

Explicitly programmed maintenance of therapeutic gains is important in all therapy, but it is especially important with addictions and other chronic problems. Hore's (1971a, 1971b) findings, which demonstrate a high frequency of drinking relapse following interpersonal conflicts with the spouse, underscores the importance of the procedures to prevent future drinking outlined in Table 1. L'Abate (1975) describes these procedures in detail. The couples should also be prepared to deal with future marital conflicts using the methods described in Table 1. In addition, recently suggested guidelines (Gottman, Notarius, Gonso, & Markman, 1976) for couples to use in getting through a crisis period in their relationship will also be used. After termination of the group, periodic follow-ups at gradually increasing intervals will serve both data-collection and maintenance functions (Sobell, L., in press).

We will, no doubt, encounter many problems in putting this proposal into practice. Pattison (1965) has described a subgroup of married alcoholics consisting of multiproblem families that require long-term supportive treatment to deal with their repeated family crises. Our group's time limit and focus on teaching couples problem-solving skills rather than providing a series of crisis interventions may not meet the needs of such families. Related problems we anticipate are calls about drinking episodes or intense conflict between group sessions. One solution is to prohibit such calls and to deal only in the group with any problems that occur. Another is to accept such calls and to provide suggestions for dealing with the crisis. A third possibility we are considering is to have the therapists available between group sessions for help in preventing or containing conflict or drinking. Couples will be instructed to try to call before a crisis occurs, with the understanding that such calls can be discussed in the group.

Methods to Evaluate Treatment Results

The methods behavior therapists have suggested for outcome assessment of marital and alcoholism treatment are proposed for use in evaluating the results of the behavioral couples group treatment.

Measures of marital adjustment based only on self-report have been criticized by behavior therapists and others for many reasons. The more global the self-report judgment and the larger the time interval being sampled, the more likely it will not be valid (Patterson, Weiss, & Hops, 1976). To counter these problems, behavioral researchers have suggested using a multicriteria approach to outcome assessment (Patterson et al., 1976; Weiss & Margolin, 1977). Measures should include at least one traditional global self-report measure such as the Locke-Wallace Marital Adjustment Scale (Locke & Wallace, 1959) to facilitate comparison of results with nonbehavioral studies. Self-report measures that are well-defined, of narrow bandwidth, sampled daily, and that measure reinforcing and punishing activities spouses engage in together should also be used. Examples are the Spouse Observation Checklist on which persons record daily pleasing and displeasing behaviors from their spouse, the number of shared recreational activities and the number of hours together each day, and the Areas of Change questionnaire on which desired partner changes are pinpointed (see Weiss et al., 1973, for details). Finally, the Marital Interaction Coding System (MICS) (Hops, Wills, Patterson, & Weiss, Note 10) should be used to code the videotaped samples of couples trying to solve their marital problems in the clinic and at home. The MICS describes what proportion of the couple's talk is devoted to reinforcing, punishing and problem-solving interactions.

Other indices of adjustment, according to recent suggestions by behavioral researchers (Miller, P., 1976; Sobell, L., in press), must be concise, communicable, and adequately defined. Global ratings and vague clinical judgments of "improved" versus "not improved" are not acceptable. Measures should be continuous and quantifiable, e.g., the actual number of days of missed work rather than "employed a majority of the time during a follow-up period." Multiple measures of treatment outcome should be used; in addition to drinking behavior, vocational and emotional adjustment should also be assessed. Finally, collateral reports from spouses and employers and in-field breath tests should be used to verify self-reports of drinking behavior.

If such a behavioral couples group proves superior to no marital treatment in an experimental study, then it should be compared with the interactional type couples group now most frequently used with alcoholics. This would help to determine whether the promising new behavioral treatment should be adopted widely by alcoholism treatment programs. Finally, before attempting to isolate the specific components of the treatment package responsible for the therapeutic gains (Azrin, 1977), the behavioral couples group should be compared with a behavioral intervention for one couple at a time to see which format better meets the needs of various types of couples and which is more cost-effective.

DISCUSSION

After briefly reviewing the current literature on behavioral treatment for alcoholism and for marital conflict among alcoholics and nonalcoholics, we have presented a behavioral couples group model for male alcoholics and their wives. We limited ourselves to male alcoholics because we see very few women alcoholics in our VA setting. However, behavioral and marital treatment for female alcoholics (Donaburg, Glick, & Fergenbaum, 1977) are neglected areas that could provide new frontiers for behavioral researchers and clinicians (McCrady & Hay, Note 11). Our use of Antabuse to achieve sobriety as a treatment goal is not a necessary component of the format we propose; the Antabuse contract procedure is only one way to reduce alcohol-related interaction patterns (such as arguments and nagging about past drinking) and to prevent unwanted future drinking. However, it is essential to deal with alcohol-related interaction patterns by means of a clear agreement between spouses about the goal of therapy and the role of each spouse in achieving and maintaining that goal. In addition, clinicians should use recently published guidelines (Miller, W., & Caddy, 1977) to choose carefully between controlled drinking and abstinence goals until empirical evidence for this decision is available.

We hope that our proposal may stimulate the inclusion of behavioral marital methods in more alcoholism treatment programs, as well as adding to the increasing number of reports in which behavioral group therapy is used with alcoholics.

REFERENCE NOTES

1. Wilson, G. T. *Aversive conditioning treatment programs for alcoholics: Issues, ethics and evidence.* Paper presented at Conference on Behavioral Approaches to Alcoholism and Drug Dependence, University of Washington, Seattle, August 1, 1975.
2. Miller, P. M. *Behavioral modification and biofeedback therapies in alcoholism treatment.* State-of-the-art review submitted to the National Institute on Alcohol Abuse and Alcoholism, January, 1977.
3. Marlatt, G. A. *Craving for alcohol, loss of control, and relapse: A cognitive behavioral analysis.* (Tech. Rep. 77–05). Seattle: University of Washington, Alcoholism and Drug Abuse Institute, 1977.
4. Johnson, J. W. *Group behavior therapy with inpatient chronic alcohol-*

ics. Paper presented at the Annual Meeting of the Association for the Advancement of Behavior Therapy, Chicago, December 1976.

5. Miller, P. M., & Hersen, M. *Modification of marital interaction patterns between an alcoholic and his wife.* Unpublished manuscript, 1975. (Available from Peter Miller, Weight Control Center, Hilton Head Hospital, Hilton Head Island, South Carolina.)

6. O'Farrell, T. J., & Cutter, H. S. G. *Behavioral marital therapy for alcoholics and wives: Review of literature and a proposed research program.* Paper presented at the NATO International Conference on Experimental and Behavioral Approaches to Alcoholism, Bergen, Norway, August 29, 1977.

7. Liberman, R. P. *Behavioral marital therapy: Group leaders guide.* Unpublished manuscript, 1975. (Available from BAM Project, 840 West 5th Street, Oxnard, Cal. 93030.)

8. Moos, R. H., Bromet, E., Tsu, V., & Moos, B. *Family characteristics and the outcome of treatment for alcoholism.* Paper presented at the Eastern Psychological Association meeting, New York, April 1977.

9. Weiss, R. L., & Birchler, G. R. *Adults with marital dysfunction.* Unpublished manuscript, University of Oregon, 1977.

10. Hops, H., Wills, T. A., Patterson, G. R., & Weiss, R. L. *Marital Interaction Coding System.* Unpublished manuscript, University of Oregon, December 1971.

11. McCrady, B. S., & Hay, W. M. Personal communication. November 22, 1977.

REFERENCES

Adinolfi, A. A., McCourt, W. F., & Geoghegan, S. Group assertiveness training for alcoholics. *Journal of Studies on Alcohol,* 1976, *37,* 311–320.

Azrin, N. H. Improvements in the community-reinforcement approach to alcoholism. *Behaviour Research and Therapy,* 1976, *14,* 339–348.

Azrin, N. H. A strategy for applied research: Learning based but outcome oriented. *American Psychologist,* 1977, *32,* 140–149.

Azrin, N. H., Naster, B. M., & Jones, R. Reciprocity counseling: A rapid learning-based procedure for marital counseling. *Behaviour Research and Therapy,* 1973, *11,* 365–382.

Cadogan, D. A. Marital group therapy in the treatment of alcoholism. *Quarterly Journal of Studies on Alcohol,* 1973, *34,* 1187–1194.

Cheek, F. E., Franks, C. M., Laucius, J., & Burtle, V. Behavior modification training for wives of alcoholics. *Quarterly Journal of Studies on Alcohol,* 1971, *32,* 456–461.

Donaburg, D., Glick, I. D., & Fergenbaum, E. Marital therapy of women alcoholics. *Journal of Studies on Alcohol,* 1977, *38,* 1247–1258.

Eisler, R. M., Miller, P. M., Hersen, M., & Alford, H. Effects of assertive training on marital interaction. *Archives of General Psychiatry,* 1974, *30,* 643–649.

Fensterheim, H. Assertive methods and marital problems. In R. D. Rubin,

H. Fensterheim, J. Henderson, & L. P. Ullmann (Eds.), *Advances in behavior therapy.* New York: Academic Press, 1972.

Foy, D. W., Miller, P. M., Eisler, R. M., & O'Toole, D. H. Social-skills training to teach alcoholics to refuse drinks effectively. *Journal of Studies on Alcohol,* 1976, *39,* 1340–1345.

Franks, C. M., & Wilson, G. T. Behavior therapy and alcoholism. In C. M. Franks & G. T. Wilson (Eds.), *Annual review of behavior therapy theory and practice.* New York: Brunner/Mazel, 1975.

Frederiksen, L. W., & Miller, P. M. Peer-determined and self-determined reinforcement in group therapy with alcoholics. *Behaviour Research and Therapy,* 1976, *14,* 385–388.

Gallant, D. M., Rich, A., Bey, E., & Terranova, L. Group psychotherapy with married couples: A successful technique in New Orleans Alcoholism Clinic patients. *Journal of the Louisiana Medical Society,* 1970, *122,* 41–44.

Gottman, J., Notarius, C., Gonso, J., & Markman, H. *A couples guide to communication.* Champaign, Ill.: Research Press, 1976.

Greer, S. M., & D'Zurilla, T. J. Behavioral approaches to marital discord and conflict. *Journal of Marriage and Family Counseling,* 1975, *1,* 299–315.

Griffiths, R. R., Bigelow, G. E., & Liebson, I. The relationship of social factors to ethanol self-administration in alcoholics. In P. E. Nathan & G. A. Marlatt (Eds.), *Behavioral approaches to alcoholism.* New York: Plenum, in press.

Gurman, A. S. Evaluating the outcomes of couples groups. In A. S. Gurman & D. G. Rice (Eds.), *Couples in conflict: New directions in marital therapy.* New York: Jason Aronson, Inc., 1975.

Gurman, A. S. Behavioral marriage therapy and the current empirical scene. *Association for Advancement of Behavior Therapy Newsletter,* 1977, *4,* 18.

Hedberg, A. G., & Campbell, L. A comparison of four behavioral treatments of alcoholism. *Journal of Behavior Therapy and Experimental Psychiatry,* 1974, *5,* 251–256.

Hore, B. D. Factors in alcoholic relapse. *British Journal of Addiction,* 1971, *66,* 89–96. (a)

Hore, B. D. Life events and alcoholic relapse. *British Journal of Addiction,* 1971, *66,* 83–88. (b)

Hunt, G. M. & Azrin, N. R. A community-reinforcement approach to alcoholism. *Behaviour Research and Therapy,* 1973, *11,* 91–104.

Jacobson, N. S., & Martin, B. Behavioral marriage therapy. *Psychological Bulletin,* 1976, *83,* 540–556.

Janzen, C. Families in the treatment of alcoholism. *Journal of Studies on Alcohol,* 1977, *38,* 114–130.

Keller, M. (Ed.), Trends in treatment of alcoholism. In *second special report to the U.S. Congress on Alcohol and Health.* Washington, D.C.: Department of Health, Education, & Welfare, 1974.

L'Abate, L. Behavioral program for families of alcoholics. In L. L'Abate

(Ed.), *Manual of family enrichment programs*. Atlanta, Ga.: Social Research Laboratories, 1975.

Lazarus, A. A. *Behavior therapy and beyond*. New York: McGraw-Hill, 1971.

Liberman, R. P. Reinforcement of cohesiveness in group therapy: Behavioral and personality changes. *Archives of General Psychiatry*, 1971, *25*, 168–177.

Liberman, R. P., DeRisi, W., & King, L. W. Behavioral interventions with families. In J. H. Masserman (Ed.), *Current psychiatric therapies* (Vol. 13). New York: Grune & Stratton, 1973.

Liberman, R. P., Levine, J., Wheeler, E., Sanders, N., & Wallace, C. Marital therapy in groups: A comparative evaluation of behavioral and interactional formats. *Acta Psychiatrica Scandanavica,*, 1976, Supplement 266, 1–33.

Liberman, R. P., Wheeler, E., & Sanders, N. Behavioral therapy for marital disharmony: An educational approach. *Journal of Marriage and Family Counseling*, 1976, *2*, 383–395.

Locke, H. J., & Wallace, K. M. Short marital-adjustment and prediction tests: Their reliability and validity. *Journal of Marriage and Family Living*, 1959, *21*, 251–255.

LoPiccolo, J., & Miller, V. H. A program for enhancing the sexual relationship of normal couples. *The Counseling Psychologist*, 1975, *5*, 41–55.

Marlatt, G. A. The drinking profile: A questionaire for the behavioral assessment of alcoholism. In E. J. Mash & L. G. Terdal (Eds.), *Behavior therapy assessment: Diagnosis and evaluation*. New York: Springer, 1975.

Miller, P. M. The use of behavioral contracting in the treatment of alcoholism: A case report. *Behavior Therapy*, 1972, *3*, 593–596.

Miller, P. M. *Behavioral treatment of alcoholism*. New York: Pergamon Press, 1976.

Miller, W. R., & Caddy, G. R. Abstinence and controlled drinking in the treatment of problem drinkers. *Journal of Studies on Alcohol*, 1977, *38*, 986–1003.

Nathan, P. E. Alcoholism. In H. Leitenberg (Ed.), *Handbook of behavior modification and behavior therapy*. Englewood Cliffs, N. J.: Prentice-Hall, 1976.

Nathan, P. E., & Briddell, D. W. Behavioral assessment and treatment of alcoholism. In B. Kissin & H. Begleiter (Eds.), *The biology of alcoholism* (Vol. 5). New York: Plenum, 1977.

Nathan, P. E., & Marlatt, G. A. (Eds.), *Behavioral assessment and treatment of alcoholism*. New Brunswick, N. J.: Rutgers Center for Alcohol Studies, in press.

Paolino, T. J., & McCrady, B. S. *The alcoholic marriage: Alternative perspectives*. New York: Grune & Stratton, 1978.

Patterson, G. R., Weiss, R. L., & Hops, H. Training of marital skills: Some problems and concepts. In H. Leitenberg (Ed.), *Handbook of behavior modification and behavior therapy*. Englewood Cliffs, N.J.: Prentice-Hall, 1976.

Pattison, E. M. Treatment of alcoholic families with nurse home visits. *Family Process,* 1965, *4,* 74–94.

Serber, M. & Laws, R. (Producers). *Tenderness.* San Luis Obispo, Cal.: Behavioral Alternatives, 1974. (Film available from Diane Serber-Corenman, Atascadero State Hospital, Atascadero, Cal.)

Sobell, L. C. A critique of alcoholism treatment evaluation. In P. E. Nathan & G. A. Marlatt (Eds.), *Behavioral assessment and treatment of alcoholism.* New Brunswick, N.J.: Rutgers Center for Alcohol Studies, in press.

Sobell, M. B., & Sobell, L. C. Individualized behavior therapy for alcoholics. *Behavior Therapy,* 1973, *4,* 49–72.

Sobell, M. B., & Sobell, L. C. Second year treatment outcome of alcoholics treated by individualized behavior therapy: Results. *Behaviour Research and Therapy,* 1976, *14,* 194–215.

Steinglass, P. Experimenting with family treatment approaches to alcoholism, 1950–1975: A review. *Family Process,* 1976, *15,* 97–123.

Stuart, R. B. Operant-interpersonal treatment for marital discord. *Journal of Consulting and Clinical Psychology,* 1969, *33,* 675–682.

Vogler, R. E., Compton, J. V., & Weissbach, T. A. Integrated behavior change techniques for alcoholics. *Journal of Consulting and Clinical Psychology,* 1975, *43,* 233–243.

Weiss, R. L., Hops, H., & Patterson, G. R. A framework for conceptualizing marital conflict, a technology for altering it, some data for evaluating it. In L. A. Hamerlynck, L. C. Handy, & E. J. Mash (Eds.), *Behavior change: Methodology, concepts, and practice.* Champaign, Ill.: Research Press, 1973.

Weiss, R. L., & Margolin, G. Marital conflict and accord. In A. R. Ciminero, K. S. Calhoun, & H. E. Adams (Eds.), *Handbook of behavioral assessment.* New York: Wiley, 1977.

Wilson, G. T., & Rosen, R. C. Training controlled drinking in an alcoholic through a multifaceted behavior treatment program: A case study. In J. D. Krumboltz & C. E. Thoresen (Eds.), *Counseling methods.* New York: Holt, Rinehart, & Winston, 1976.

Chapter 12

Step Group Therapy: A Behavioral Group Approach for Short-Term Psychiatric Inpatients

Kay Gustafson

Abstract

Step Group therapy-training is a three level, behavioral group therapy program for short-term psychiatric inpatients. The design combines relationship skills training with therapeutic group interaction. At each level, three basic relationship skills are defined and discussed and then specifically practiced during group discussion of member problem areas. The levels are progressively graded on skill complexity, personal risk and involvement required, and feeling emphasis. Modeling, instruction, reinforcement, feedback, and practice are prominent behavioral aspects. Preparation for therapy as well as group cohesion and homogeneity enhancing functions of the design are presented. Practical benefits, research support, and recent modifications and extensions are discussed.

INTRODUCTION

In recent years, behavioral methods have gained increasing recognition and acceptance. As in many fields, however, the translation of theory into practice is a major challenge facing direct service workers. In the case of the short-term inpatient psychiatric unit, the diversity of problems represented, plus the time and size constraints involved, combine to form a particularly challenging treatment context. In formulating a viable behavioral group therapy format for such a setting, one must consider the nature of the patients in interaction with the nature of the setting. Many of the patients would not be considered "good group therapy candidates" in that they are psychotic, unmotivated, or repeaters. In addition, the rapid turnover time plus the limited capacity of the unit combine to insure a constantly changing population representing a full range of levels of functioning. These forces plus changing staff availability put many practical constraints on the type of program applicable. Despite these challenging factors, however, this population deserves creative, specifically tailored treatment application of the best of our behavioral theories, if for no other reason than the large number of people involved.

The purpose of this chapter is to present a group-based behavioral program, Step Group Therapy, designed from both a theoretical and practical viewpoint to serve exactly this population. After considering the basic Step Group design and its evaluation, several modifications and extensions will be presented.

STEP GROUP THERAPY: BASIC DESIGN

Step Group Therapy was originally designed (Authier & Fix, 1977; Authier, Note 1) for the inpatient service of a university-based psychiatric institute, and it has been operating for over 4 years on the short-term psychiatric inpatient ward of a midwestern Veterans Administration hospital (Authier & Gustafson, Note 2). This unit is a 40-bed ward with an average stay of 3 weeks. The population of the unit by diagnosis includes a high porportion of schizophrenics in varying degrees of remission and chronicity, some depressed and manic patients, and smaller proportions of those with situational family crises and personality disorders. The entire ward population, with the exception of a few severely organically impaired patients, is included in the Step Group program. The program is coordinated by a clinical psychologist, with all levels of ward nursing staff also participating as group leaders.

The Step Group format follows a psycho-educational model as described by Authier, Gustafson, Guerney, and Kasdorf (1975) and seeks to combine behaviorally based training in basic relationship skills with a group therapy format. The practical as well as theoretical reasons for selecting such a combination include:

(1) The deficits of most psychiatric inpatients in basic relationship skills (Coleman, 1965; Libert & Lewinsohn, 1973; Stillman, 1971).

(2) The demonstrated capability of such a population to benefit from training in basic communication skills (Goldstein, 1973; Ivey, 1973; Orlando, 1974; Pierce & Drasgow, 1969; Vitalo, 1971).

(3) The economic necessity for a group, rather than an individual, therapy emphasis on most inpatient units.

(4) The inherent suitability of a small group as a practice ground for interpersonal skills.

(5) The converse suitability of most of the relationship skills in enhancing group member participation and thus group therapy process and outcome.

The name Step Group refers to the three levels of groups as pictured in Figure 1. Each step focuses on training in three specific relationship skills. As the arrows indicate, the skills from lower steps continue to be practiced as new skills are added in higher groups. All new patients, regardless of skill level or previous admissions, begin in Step I and move at individual rates to Steps II and III. Promotion to the next higher step is based entirely on that person's usage of the three skills of that step during group meetings. Step I meets once and Steps II and III meet twice weekly. The schedule is arranged so that a given member could move from step I on Monday to step III by Wednesday if he demonstrates the appropriate skills.

Although the skills taught may vary, the basic format of the group meeting remains the same across steps. Step I begins with an explanation of the basic format and purpose of the Step Groups, including the criteria for promotion. As in Steps II and III, the skills of that step are then presented to the members through either videotaped models or typed cards showing definitions and examples of the skills. Sometimes directed practice of some of the skills is also used at this point. After discussion of the skills, the members are instructed to practice the skills during the remainder of the meeting, which consists of group discussion of topics raised by the members. In addition to practicing the skills, the members are encouraged to use the meeting time to raise interesting and important topics for themselves.

Figure 1. Diagram of the Step Group Program

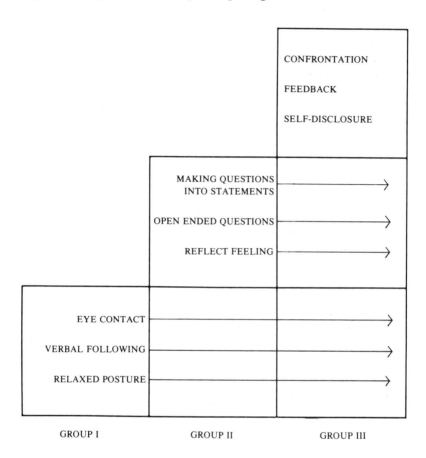

The Step Group leader's role is that of a combination teacher/ group facilitator. The leader introduces and explains the skills, provides examples and at times directs structured practice at the beginning of the meeting. During the discussion she models the skills, identifies and reinforces good skills usage by members, and makes suggestions regarding improvements or further appropriate opportunities for skills usage. At the end of each meeting the leader makes promotions and gives specific individual feedback to each member on his skills usage. A group list showing promotions and a weekly group note with further feedback are also prominently posted on the ward bulletin board. In addition to these primarily teaching interventions, however, the Step Group leader also functions as a group therapy facilitator. In this part of the dual role, interventions oriented toward group process or directed specifically toward an individual's role or interaction in the group are common. The emphasized elements of the leader's role tend to vary with the step level. The teacher role is most prominent in Step I, with the group facilitator elements becoming more prominent as one moves toward Step III.

Just as the leader's role changes, the nature of the skills and the expectations of the members become progressively more complex from Steps I to III. The skills taught were selected from the Enriching Intimacy program (Authier & Gustafson, Note 3), which is a relationship skills training program designed to teach the basic behavioral components of respect-warmth, empathy, and genuineness within a modified microcounseling format (Ivey, 1971). Although this program has been used primarily with students in the health professions, the skills are seen as basic relationship skills which should also be useful to patients or anyone in their day-to-day interactions.

The three skills of Step I—relaxed posture and appropriate gesturing, eye contact, and verbal following—are all basic attending behaviors. These are low-level, nonthreatening skills which are quickly mastered or demonstrated by many of the members. Many of the members spend only one meeting at this level. The leader's role at this stage is primarily that of a teacher and participation encourager. Any topic is acceptable for discussion as long as the skills are used and members are not pressed for in-depth discussion of intimate topics.

The skills of Step II are open-ended questions (questions that cannot be answered by yes or no), making questions into statements (presenting one's opinion or idea about a topic rather than "fishing" with a series of questions, e.g., "It sounds like you are most concerned about your oldest boy right now"), and reflection of feeling (stating how another person appears to be feeling, e.g., "You seem angry right now"). These skills are presented as those most useful in starting and carrying on a conversation and in getting to know someone new or a new aspect of a friend or relative. Most members spend about four meetings (2 weeks) in Step II. Reflection of feeling is usually the last skill mastered due to its feeling content and here-and-now emphasis. The nature of the Step II skills requires a more personal, feeling-oriented discussion topic if the skills are to be practiced. The leader's role is very much still that of a trainer, i.e., of refining and reinforcing skills. Beyond this, however, awareness of group process and individual reactions to the demands of the skills provide opportunities for valuable interventions that both facilitate group development and model and accent the usefulness of skills. For example, reflecting the feeling tone of the entire group in a boredom phase can help to move the group through that phase, as well as modeling the reflection-of-feeling skill. Similarly, reflecting a group member's hesitancy to try a reflection of another's feelings can shape and strengthen the skill while facilitating involvement in the group.

The Step III skills are confrontation (pointing out to someone in a concerned manner inconsistencies in his behavior, e.g., "You say you're angry, but you're smiling at me"), feedback (telling someone your specific feeling reaction to a specific part of his behavior, e.g., "I feel irritated and confused when you stop in the middle of the sentence"), and self-disclosure (telling someone of a specific personal reaction or experience and how it may relate to the other person's feelings or experience, e.g., "When my wife left me, I felt as depressed and anxious as you're feeling now"). These are taught as skills which are most useful in sustained, important relationships. A high degree of personal involvement and interpersonal risk taking is required if these skills are practiced consistently.

The leader here continues some trainer functions but also includes many traditional group therapy interventions. In fact, by simply using one of the Step III skills with a group member, the leader is performing both a trainer task of modeling the skill and a frequent therapist task of providing specific information to an individual member on his interpersonal impact or directing that member's attention toward an important personal area for consideration. Often the leader is in a participant/facilitator role, i.e., acting basically as a well-functioning member would for a short therapist-member interaction and then directing the focus back to further member-member interaction. Other group therapist interventions, as outlined by Authier and Gustafson (1976), include the identification of central themes of the discussion, the clarification of emerging group norms or stages of group development, and the continuation of basic group maintenance interventions such as beginning and ending on time or encouraging participation by all members.

It is quite apparent by now that movement from Step I to Step III represents a graded progression on several dimensions. Before looking at the practical benefits of such a program, let us examine the theoretical justification for such a design, first as a training program and, second, as a group therapy program.

STEP GROUP AS A SKILLS TRAINING PROGRAM

As a training program, Step Group relies heavily on the well-established behavioral principles of modeling, instruction, practice, specific feedback, and reinforcement. Sources of modeling include the videotape or typed examples, the leader's use of the skills, and other members' use of the skills. The leaders' identifications of their own skills usage, as well as their comments on member usage, serves the dual purpose of giving feedback and reinforcement to the user and providing a didactic component to the modeling which occurs throughout the meeting. This combination of instruction with modeling has repeatedly been shown to enhance learning and retention beyond demonstration alone because subtleties of skills usage can be identified and coded (Bandura, Grusec, & Menlove, 1966; Whalen, 1969). Modeling has also been found to be enhanced by similarity between the learner and the model (Bandura, Ross, D., & Ross, S., 1963; Bednar, Weet, Evensen, Lanier, & Melnick, 1974; Kanfer & Duerfeldt, 1967). The ready availability of modeling by other group members is insured by the inclusion of all new admissions in Step I regardless of the number of their past admissions or level of functioning. This policy, plus the individual rates of advancement through the system, provides for a nearly constant supply of appropriate member models within each step level. Reinforcement is highly visible within the group. The simple nature of the Step I skills requirements also tends to provide fairly immediate reinforcement through promotion for many of the members. This visible advancement tends to capture and maintain the members' involvement in the program.

The Step Group program thus incorporates basic learning principles within each step. The system appears to enchance learning by including individual rates of advancement, tangible and immediate reinforcement for skills usage, and abundant sources of modeling.

STEP GROUP AS GROUP THERAPY

Step Group as a group therapy program can be viewed as consisting of two phases: a preparation for therapy phase comprised of Steps I and II, and an active therapy phase comprised of Step III. The value of preparation for group therapy, in terms of clarifying norms, roles, and expectations, is one of the best documented and most consistent findings in the group therapy literature (Bednar et al., 1974; Truax, Shapiro, & Wargo, 1968; Yalom, Houts, Newell, & Rand, 1967).

The Step Groups are designed to provide a relatively nonthreatening introduction to group membership in Step I. This is particularly important in a primarily middle to lower class population for whom dealing on a psychological level, especially with a group of strangers, is likely to be a very novel and threatening experience. In addition, Step I members are primarily new admissions and those in the acute phase of their admissions problems, for whom even low-level demands can be very stressful. At the same time, however, the Step I skills do lay the groundwork for effective group membership by stressing basic listening skills and participation. Dies and Hess (1971) and Snortum and Myers (1971) have found that frequency of interaction itself is significantly related to group cohesion and outcome. In addition, many of the members are promoted quickly to Step II and move with several other member "winners" to Step II. This tends to ease the transition to a new group and to provide a core of cohesion on which to build.

Step II is designed to build on the participation norm and to move toward greater comfort in dealing with feelings and personal issues and increased risk taking in a here-and-now context. It is possible for a member who is uncomfortable in discussing his own personal problems to learn to use all of the Step II skills in an other-directed manner. That is, he can use the Step II skills to get to know the other members without revealing much of himself. It is also possible and even usual for new members of Step II to focus on the "open questions" and "questions-into-statements" skills before trying "reflections of feelings." This allows them the experience of participation and mastery in a somewhat more personally oriented context before moving into a potentially more threatening feeling-oriented context. Even if a member does choose to avoid disclosure of his own feelings entirely, he must take the risk of commenting on the here-and-now feelings of other members in order to move to Step III.

By the time the members reach Step III, they have developed a solid repertoire of basic communications skills, are well versed in the basic interactive group norms of participating directly with other members, have developed some familiarity and cohesion with at least several members of the group, and have tried out some interpersonal risk-taking on a here-and-now feeling level. They have been gradually prepared for the greater risk taking and personal involvement required on the Step III skills.

Once in Step III, the skills of interpersonal confrontation, feedback, and self-disclosure inherently demand the normative behavior of a well-functioning outpatient therapy group. Self-disclosure itself has been repeatedly cited (Bednar & Lawlis, 1971; Kahn & Rudestem, 1971) as an important element in group cohesion.

As defined here, self-disclosure includes not only revealing part of yourself but also relating your feeling or experience to that of another group member. This element of the definition is particularly instrumental in facilitating the universality (the knowledge that I and my problems are not that much different from other people and their problems) and instilling the hope which Yalom

(1975) cites as curative factors in group therapy. In addition, confrontation and feedback as defined here require a high degree of both awareness of others' behavior and the ability to comment on those specific behaviors. The availability of such specific information is important if one views increased awareness of one's interpersonal impact and experimentation with new behavior as major functions of group therapy. Indeed, Yalom (1975) reported this "interpersonal learning" as the curative factor ranked most important by group members. Finally, feedback also requires a clear statement of the member's own here here-and-now feeling. This increased awareness of one's own immediate feeling in reaction to someone else is again an important part of interpersonal learning.

The mastery of these skills is a large demand to make of this population and would be difficult to achieve without preparation. The Step Group design thus builds in this preparation in order to enhance the probability of benefit from the level of group therapy possible in Step III.

In applying one theoretical framework for group therapies, however, the combined emphasis of the Step Groups on training and therapy has made classification difficult. Glassman and Wright (Note 4) have proposed a conceptual framework for group psychotherapy composed of three categories: (1) therapy *in* the group—the central, directive therapist interacts successively with individual members while other members act as observers, (2) therapy *with* the group—the therapist acts as "expert participant" with emphasis on member-member interaction and here-and-now interpersonal relationships, and (3) therapy *of* the group—the therapist directs attention to the group as a whole, usually with a task focus and exploration of group processes. Step Groups represent a kind of hybrid in this system in that the leader's skill-training interventions primarily follow a leader-member or "therapy in the group" model, while most of the personally oriented discussion in the group is between members and this follows a "therapy with the group" model.

The need for elements from both of these models follows directly from the dual aims of the program. These are to teach interpersonal skills and to provide an interpersonally meaningful practice ground for those skills where individually relevant learning and behavior change can occur. The first aim requires considerable teacher-student interaction focused on the nature and performance of the skills (thus, the "therapy in the group" model). The second aim rests on practicing the skills with other members. Here the specific content of the skills is determined by the members and directed towards another member (thus, the "therapy with the group" model). The Step Group is unique in that the two models are interwoven temporally. Consider the following exerpt from a Step III meeting:

Bill:	John, you make me so angry.
Therapist:	Bill, you've told John your feeling. If you would tell him specifically what he has done that you're angry about, you would be using good feedback.
Bill:	Okay. John, every time I ask Bob a question, you answer for him before he has a chance to say anything, and then I get really irritated.
Therapist:	(To Bob) Good. (Looks at John)
John:	Well, I was just helping him out. You guys always pick on one person in here.
Therapist:	It sounds like you may have some feedback for the whole group, John.
John:	Yeah. It makes me really mad when you all pick on one guy!
Bill:	I wasn't picking on him. I just wanted to know why he's so quiet lately.
John:	Maybe he doesn't want to talk about it.
Bill:	There you go again—you just answered for him again!
Therapist:	John, I'd like to give you a little self-disclosure myself. I know that often, if I find myself protecting someone else, it's really partly to protect myself, like I'm wondering if I'm next. I wonder if this could be partly the case with you, too.
John:	Well . . . maybe. I don't like anybody prying into my business. I'm kind of shy and especially when I first got here, all they did was ask me question after question and I hated it.
Therapist:	John, you've almost got a good self-disclosure there yourself, if you would check that out with Bob and see if he feels the same way.
John:	Bob, I wonder if you feel shy and hate to be asked questions like I do.
Bob:	I don't like it sometimes but sometimes, if I make myself talk, it helps. I'm surprised you said you were shy, though. You laugh and joke and talk with everybody and don't seem shy at all.
Therapist:	Good confrontation, Bob. (Looks to John)

In this excerpt the active role of the therapist is apparent. Each of the seven therapist interventions involved a teaching component and was directed to an individual member. In only one case, however (the therapist's use of the self-disclosure skill), was the member's response directed back to the therapist. In the other six cases, the member went on to direct his response to another member. The form of that response was the primary focus of the therapist; however, the content was determined by that member's feelings and reactions. Thus the "therapy" (i.e., the interpersonal exchange of reactions, problems and thoughts), occurs primarily between patients, except occasionally where the therapist chooses to adopt a member role and to use the skills on a personal level (therapy with the group).* The "teaching" (i.e., the reinforcement and shaping of skills), occurs largely in one-direction statements from therapist to member (therapy in the group). The words "teaching" and "therapy" are put in quotations to highlight the relative nature of the distinction between them. Under the psycho-educational model, teaching is therapy. The blend of these two Glassman and Wright (Note 4) models in the Step Group design seems to depend on the therapist's maintaining the pre-eminence of a teaching role and interspersing content-oriented interventions primarily to model the skills and facilitate further member-member interaction. Through maintenance of this balance in the leader's role, both learning of skills "in" the group and therapeutic giving and receiving of input from others "with" the group is possible.

PRACTICAL ADVANTAGES OF THE STEP GROUP DESIGN

Perhaps the biggest practical difficulty facing the designer of either a training or group therapy program for the short-term inpatient unit is the constant patient turnover combined with the great heterogeneity of level of functioning. In addition, the absolute size of the population is usually small, thus limiting the total number of feasible groups. This generally means constantly changing group membership, with group process repeatedly returning to an introductory phase due to the disruptions of and adjustments to the lowest functioning, often psychotic, members of the group. The frustration engendered by such a situation does not foster good staff or patient morale. Often the choice is made to offer group therapy only to a small number of better functioning patients. Here, however, the limited time to work with a given person and the lack of attention to the larger proportion of those most in need are major drawbacks.

Rather than fight the disruptive realities of this type of unit, the Step Group program was designed to "go with the flow" and to

*In earlier chapters by Flowers and Sansbury this is referred to as "therapy *through* the group." [Eds.]

incorporate constantly changing group membership in a systematic way. Changing group membership is an expected part of the system, with the changes channeled in such a way as to enhance group homeogeneity. The assurance of more homogeneous groups, in turn, allows both greater appropriateness of level of skill teaching and more advanced phases of group process development. The program is therefore able to provide something for each member of the treatment population at a level individually appropriate for him. The disruptive impact of change in group membership on a given individual is further lessened by the interpretation of change as advancement within this system.

The visibility of each member's position and progress within the system is another major practical advantage of the system. It is often very difficulty for both the staff and the patient himself to gauge progress in a psychological area. The specific feedback and the objective evidence of improvement offered by the Step Group program seem to be welcomed by the patients and to be a major factor in insuring their involvement in the program. In view of the generally low self-esteem as well as high anxiety and pessimism levels of this population, this is a very important practical influence on their participation in their own treatment.

Our emphasis until now has been on dealing with constant patient turnover. Probably an equally important practical problem for most inpatient groups is the inconstancy of staff availability, especially where nursing personnel rotate irregularly to cover weekends and other shifts. Step Groups have the advantages of using a clear, easily teachable leader role and the expectation of the same leader for a maximum of 2 days, i.e., the two meetings in a week of Step II or Step III. It is thus possible for nearly all of the members of the nursing staff to be active therapists on a rotating basis in the program. This helps to insure cohesion and support for the program among the nursing staff while accomodating the reality of change in this sphere as well.

In general, the Step Group program has been a well-liked part of the treatment program by staff and patients alike. Involvement in the program has generally been easy to establish and maintain. A few exceptions to this will be discussed in the "Modifications" section following a brief consideration of the research evaluation of the program.

EVALUATION OF THE PROGRAM

To date only one formal evaluation of the Step Group program has been completed. The Petrick (Note 5) evaluation of the Step

Group program included direct behavioral counts of skills usage during videotaped Step Group meetings and during videotaped dyadic interventions with a patient from another unit, as well as a variety of indirect measures of the member's communication skills level in other meetings and on the ward. From the group meeting data, the question-into-statements skill was used significantly more frequently by Step II and III members ($p < .02$), and the open-ended questions skill was used significantly more frequently by the Step III members ($p < .01$). From the dyadic interaction data, Step I members demonstrated a significantly lower level of verbal following than Step II and Step III members ($p < .01$). The more frequent use of open-ended questions by the Step II and III members also was significant ($p < .03$). The direct measure of in-meeting and dyadic interaction skills usage thus provided only limited support for the efficacy of the Step Group program.

The more indirect measures, however, revealed a strong link between progress in the Step Group program and the quality of an individual's interpersonal communication in other ward settings. On weekly ratings by ward staff of the overall communication level of individual patients, highly significant differences were found between Step I, II, and III members ($p < .001$). There was little overlap between groups on this measure of general communication level on the ward. These differences remained highly significant with length of hospitalization covaried out ($p < .002$). The proportion of Step II and III members on each of the ward treatment teams was also found to be highly related to that team staff's rating of their satisfaction with the quality and quantity of the discussion in their daily team meetings. Pearson correlation coefficient indicating the relationship between the staff satisfaction with their meeting and the percentage of patients in each of the groups were $r = -.1413$ ($p < .08$) for Step I, $r = .2151$ ($p < .016$) for Step II, and $r = .2397$ ($p < .008$) for Step III.

These findings are suggestive of the generalization of improved communication ability to settings outside the Step Group meetings as the member progresses through the steps. Thus, they are very encouraging. Unfortunately, the relatively small number of subjects and methodological problems complicate interpretation of the less significant findings from the direct measures of skills usage during the meetings and the dyadic interactions. One such problem is the pooling of the skill counts for all members in a meeting rather than analyzing the skill counts for individual members. With pooled data, the frequency counts for a given meeting may be more reflective of the proportion of more disturbed or newer members who are just beginning to master the skills of that step than of the skill level of those members who are promoted. Perhaps looking at the skill usage of those members who are promoted to the next level would yield different results. Also, the coding of 40 utterances per meeting may not have been sufficient, and the sampling of the middle 30 minutes of the meeting may have tended to eliminate the more complex skills which are often not appropriate until the discussion has become more intimate as often occurs towards the end of the meeting. Similarly, the dyadic interactions were only 15 minutes long and thus were not really appropriate practice grounds for the Step III skills. Further study is needed, including investigation of several of the modifications in the basic format which have been developed to further facilitate the training of the less capable patients and the more complex skills.

MODIFICATIONS OF THE FORMAT

In general, a major test of a program's viability is the flexibility it allows for adaptations to changing demands. The Step Group program is currently operative in five different inpatient settings. The demands of each setting and the specific population treated have called for adaptations in the format. The first modification was the switch from the videotape model of the original university setting to the typed cards containing the definitions and examples of the skills in the VA setting. This change stemmed primarily from the practical lack of easily accessible video equipment in the VA hospital setting at that time. The workability of this less expensive alternative makes the Step Group a viable format for many other settings as well.

Most of the program modifications, however, have been made to tailor the program to the needs of the specific group member population. In the VA program, for example, it was found that a certain percentage of the population tended to get stalled in Step II. These were usually the more chronic, older patients, many of whom were waiting for placement in another institution. Although not eliminating the bottleneck entirely, a "structured practice" modification in the format of Step II has greatly decreased this problem. At the beginning of the first Step II meeting of the week, in addition to explanation and discussion of the skills, the open ended question and reflection of feeling skills are systematically practiced by each member. After the usual discussion of meaning and usefulness of the open ended questions skill, one member is urged to ask the member to his left anything he likes as long as it is an open ended question. After answering the question, the next person is asked to repeat the procedure until each person has had an opportunity to ask the person to his left an open ended question. This allows the leader to check the understanding of the skill of each member and to make additional teaching points as the questioning progresses around the circle. Again, after the reflection-of-feeling skill is discussed, one member is asked to reflect the feelings of the person directly across the circle from him. This process is repeated until each member has had an opportunity to practice the skill. Often the group interaction is also stimulated by interesting topics or questions arising during this practice. This additional repetition and practice has seemed to be the boost that some of the formerly stalled Step II members needed.

Similarly, a state hospital unit found that many of their patients were functioning at an even lower initial level than the patients in the VA or university settings. To suit the limits of their population, they retained the basic structure but modified the skills taught. Because much of their population was more withdrawn, they added an initiating conversations skill to Step I. Because reflection of feeling seemed a particular stumbling block to promotion to Step III for these patients, it was moved to Step III and replaced by paraphrasing in Step II. In addition, a tutoring component was added. That is, a staff member was designated to whom patients having particular difficulty with a given skill could be referred for individual help outside of the group. Another possibility in this regard would be to utilize higher-level group members as tutors for members of the groups below them. Although logistically complicated, this alternative would have the advantage of reinforcing the tutor's own learning through teaching similar to Ivey and Gluckstern's (1974) Do-Use-Teach model.

As outlined previously, the Step Group program was specifically designed to fit the demands of rapid turnover and short-term treatment. The program has, however, been successfully adapted to the quite different demands of a locked security unit of a state hospital which serves primarily state penitentiary inmates with psychiatric conditions. This setting has a much more constant population. A system of three levels of groups with three skills at each level was retained. Here, however, relatively stable small groups are formed which work on only one skill per meeting. Each of the three skills at a given step level is the major focus for either one or two entire meetings. At the end of that period, all the members of the group who have mastered the three skills move on to the next step level and those who have not mastered the skills begin the cycle over. The basic meeting format remains the same—definition, examples, and then practice of the skill during group interaction. This model suits the longer working time available in this setting, and the movement of most of the group as a unit to the next step level tends to build even greater cohesion in the groups. In addition to these structural changes, some changes were made in the skills taught. As in the state hospital program just discussed, an initiating conversations skill was added to Step I. In Step II instead of the making-questions-into-statements skill, an experiencing-and-expressing-personal-feelings skill is taught. As a further modification to help insure meaningful material for practice of this skill, a topic such as drugs, sex, or the penal system is set for the meeting, and attention is focused on discovering and expressing the feelings aroused during the discussion of that topic. Several meetings may be spent on different topics. In Step III, paraphrasing replaces feedback. Finally, Step IV, a further extension of the program, was added and will be discussed further in the next section.

EXTENSIONS OF THE STEP GROUP

The apparent deficits in other specialized skill areas among the inpatient group members, as well as their need for relevant contexts in which to further practice the basic Step Group skills, have provided the major impetus for the current extensions of the Step Group program.

In the case of the security unit program, just described, the longer length of stay has necessitated the development of a fourth step, entitled simply "Group Psychotherapy." This new level was developed to provide incentive for mastery of the Step III skills as well as continued involvement in the program. Those who have shown competency in each of the Step III skills are included in Step IV. Here the formal cards and teaching component are deleted, and a psychoanalytically based format similar to that developed by Bion (1959) is adopted. A personally disengaged leader who makes only group process interventions is the hallmark of Bion's approach. A here-and-now emphasis and issues of leadership are prominent. This is a theoretically interesting choice of group therapy models to follow in that the Bion-Tavistock model represents the third Glassman and Wright (Note 10) classification, "therapy of the group." By including this type of group as Step IV, elements of all three of Glassman and Wright's categories are included in this Step Group modification.

This model was chosen to follow the interest of the therapist involved and is a recent addition. Unfortunately, much of the evidence cited by Yalom (1975) suggests that the Bion model has not been very useful with a chronic patient population. Therefore, careful ongoing evaluation is necessary, and consideration must be given to the adoption of a more relationship-oriented model, where practice of the skills could continue to be modeled and encouraged by the leader. However, in a setting where length of stay allows a fourth step, the basic idea of a formal therapy group is promising. This would provide a personally relevant context in which to explore the usefulness of the skills as well as to learn more about oneself.

In the VA setting, a Step IIA has been instituted. This step includes selected members of Step II who have mastered some of the skills as well as most of the Step III members. The focus of Step IIA is training in some specialized skill area. Step IIA meets once a week for 1½ to 2 hours and constitutes a kind of mini-workshop. To date skill areas covered have included problem-solving training (Baker, Note 6), a life-planning workshop (Baker, Note 7), anger-coping skills (Novaco, 1977), and training in overcoming irrational ideas (Maultsby, Note 8). Many other areas, including relaxation training, assertiveness training, psychodrama, basic transactional analysis concepts, and job interview skills could be included. The constraint of a continually changing membership has necessitated modifications in the design of most of the training materials available in these areas to form essentially self-contained 1½ to 2 hour courses. These courses can then be repeated and extended as the continuity of membership allows.

Response to this new step has been excellent. Participation has to be an incentive and further reward for progression in the Step Group program. The content of the Step IIA training has also provided a further impetus for consideration of related topics in Steps II and III. The variety available here provides a kind of spice to the basic Step Group diet.

On a practical level, this approach has spoken to the varying treatment needs of the members as well as the limited number of patients on the ward at any given time who are capable of participating and likely to benefit from this more intensive training. Once a basic repertoire of training areas is established, topics can be easily changed to suit the needs of the current group. Also, various members of the nursing staff can become in-house experts in certain areas without competing for that limited resource—"the good candidate" patient-trainee.

Step IIA is too new for a firm evaluation. So far interest and involvement from staff and patients alike have been high. From a theoretical standpoint, Step IIA is a further commitment to the increasingly accepted psycho-educational model of treatment. The final evaluation of this as well as the basic Step Group design rests, however, on demonstrated improvement in member functioning in their daily lives as a result of the training. All of the pitfalls of any outcome study await attempts to assess such improvement. Until then, the Step Group therapy/training paradigm does seem to be a flexible, workable behavioral model for combining training in basic relationship skills with a group therapy context.

Many further modifications and extensions seem possible. It is hoped that this presentation of the Step Group design can serve as a model and, thus, a springboard for the development of further group treatment approaches for the short-term inpatient population.

REFERENCE NOTES

1. Authier, J. L. *A step group therapy program based on levels of interpersonal communication.* Unpublished manuscript, Nebraska Psychiatric Institute, 1973.
2. Authier, J. L., & Gustafson, K. M. *Step group therapy-training: A theoretical ideal.* Unpublished manuscript, Omaha Veterans Administration Hospital, 1976.
3. Authier, J. L., & Gustafson, K. M. *Enriching intimacy—A behavioral approach.* Unpublished manual, University of Nebraska College of Medicine, 1973.
4. Glassman, S. M., & Wright, T. L. *A conceptual framework for group psychotherapy.* Unpublished manuscript, Fort Logan Mental Health Center, Denver, 1969.
5. Petrick, S. *An evaluation of a combined group therapy and communication skills training program for psychiatric inpatients.* Unpublished doctoral dissertation, University of Nebraska, Lincoln, 1976.
6. Baker, R. R. *Problem-solving training program for patients.* Unpublished manuscript, Houston Veterans Administration Hospital, 1976.
7. Baker, R. R. *Life goals planning.* Unpublished manuscript, Houston Veterans Administration Hospital, 1976.
8. Maultsby, M. C. *The ABC's of solving your own emotional problems.* Unpublished manuscript, 1970.

REFERENCES

Authier, J. L., & Fix, A. J. A step group therapy program based on levels of interpersonal communication. *Small Group Behavior*, 1977, *8*, 101–108.

Authier, J. L., & Gustafson, K. M. Group intervention techniques: A practical guide for psychiatric team members. *Journal of Psychiatric Nursing and Mental Health Services*, 1976, *14*, 19–22.

Authier, J. L., Gustafson, K. M., Guerney, B., & Kasdorf, J. A. The psychological practitioner as a teacher: A theoretical, historical and practical review. *The Counseling Psychologist*, 1975, *5*, 31–50.

Bandura, A., Grusec, J. E., & Menlove, F. L. Observational learning as a function of symbolization and incentive set. *Child Development*, 1966, *37*, 497–506.

Bandura, A., Ross, D., & Ross, S. Imitation of film-mediated aggressive models. *Journal of Abnormal and Social Psychology, 1963, 66,* 3–11.

Bednar, R. L., & Lawlis, G. F. Empirical research in group psychotherapy. In A. E. Bergin & S. L. Garfield (Eds.), *Handbook of psychotherapy and behavior change: An Empirical Analysis.* New York: Wiley, 1971.

Bednar, R. L., Weet, C., Evensen, P., Lanier, D., & Melnick, J. Empirical guidelines for group therapy: Pretraining, cohesion, and modeling. *The Journal of Applied Behavioral Science, 1974, 10,* 149–165.

Bion, W. R. *Experiences in groups and other papers.* New York: Basic Books, 1959.

Coleman, J. *Abnormal psychology and modern life.* Glenview, Ill.: Scott, Foresman, 1965.

Dies, R., & Hess, A. An experimental investigation of cohesiveness in marathon and conventional group psychotherapy. *Journal of Abnormal and Social Psychology, 1971, 77,* 258–262.

Goldstein, A. P. *Structured learning therapy: Toward a psychotherapy for the poor.* New York: Academic Press, 1973.

Ivey, A. *Microcounseling: Innovations in interviewing training.* Springfield, Ill.: Charles C. Thomas, 1971.

Ivey, A. Media therapy: Educational change planning for psychiatric patients. *Journal of Counseling Psychology, 1973, 20,* 338–343.

Ivey, A., & Gluckstern, N. *Basic attending skills.* Amherst, Mass.: Microcounseling Associates, 1974.

Kahn, M. H., & Rudestem, K. E. The relationship between liking and perceived self-disclosure in small groups. *Journal of Psychology, 1971, 78,* 81–85.

Kanfer, F. H., & Duerfeldt, P. H. Learner competence, model competence and number of observation trials in vicarious learning. *Journal of Educational Psychology, 1967, 58,* 153–157.

Libert, J., & Lewinsohn, P. Concept of social skill with special reference to the behavior of depressed persons. *Journal of Consulting and Clinical Psychology, 1973, 40,* 304–312.

Novaco, R. W. Stress inoculation: A cognitive therapy for anger and its application to a case of depression. *Journal of Consulting and Clinical Psychology, 1977, 45,* 600–608.

Orlando, N. The mental patient as therapeutic agent: Self-change, power and caring. *Psychotherapy: Therapy, Research and Practice, 1974, 11,* 58–62.

Pierce, R. M., & Drasgow, J. Teaching facilitative interpersonal functioning to psychiatric inpatients. *Journal of Counseling Psychology, 1969, 16,* 295–298.

Snortum, J., & Myers, H. Intensity of t-group relationships as a function of interaction. *International Journal of Group Psychotherapy, 1971, 21,* 190–201.

Stillman, S. Mental illness and peer group popularity. *Journal of Clinical Psychology, 1971, 27,* 202–203.

Truax, C., Shapiro, J., & Wargo, D. Effects of alternate sessions and vicarious therapy pretraining on group psychotherapy. *International Journal of Group Psychotherapy*, 1968, *18*, 186–198.

Vitalo, R. Teaching improved interpersonal function as a preferred mode of treatment. *Journal of Consulting and Clinical Psychology*, 1971, *35*, 166–171.

Whalen, C. Effects of a model and instructions on group verbal behaviors. *Journal of Consulting and Clinical Psychology*, 1969, *33*, 152–155.

Yalom, I. D. *The theory and practice of group psychotherapy* (2nd ed.). New York: Basic Books, 1975.

Yalom, I. D., Houts, P., Newell, G., & Rand, K. Preparation of patients for group therapy: A controlled study. *Archives of General Psychiatry*, 1967, *17*, 416–427.

Chapter 13

Behavioral Group Psychotherapy for Overweight Children and Adolescents

Judith Coché
Leonard S. Levitz
Henry A. Jordan

Abstract

The purpose of this chapter is to discuss the psychological, cultural, and physical determinants of pediatric obesity, and existing treatment modalities. A proposed behavioral group psychotherapy approach for obesity in youngsters is discussed, and recommendations for the field of pediatric obesity are made.

INTRODUCTION

There is a clearly documented need for treatment of obesity in youngsters. Numerous articles by pediatricians, nutritionists, and psychologists have attested to the relationship between pediatric obesity and later psychological and physiological handicaps. For example, Friedman (1975) discusses the relationship between pediatric obesity and atherosclerosis, while Dwyer and Mayer (1973) discuss the physical and psychological difficulties faced by the obese adolescent girl. Furthermore, since the difficulty of weight loss among adults is well-known, it is thought that earlier treatment may be more successful, especially in terms of long-term maintenance.

Since a clear need exists for treatment, it is surprising that effective treatment programs are sparse and located only in a few areas throughout the United States and Canada. An earlier review (Coché, Jordan, & Levitz, Note 1) was able to point to work in the field done by Wheeler and Hess (1976), LeBow (1977),Rivinus, Drummond, and Combrinck-Graham (1976), and only a few others. The reasons for lack of appropriate treatment are complicated, but three will be touched on briefly.

First, the issue of overweight in youngsters is a very complex one, even more complex than overweight in adults, involving physiological factors such as the nature of adipose cell development, broad social and cultural factors, food intake habits, food likes and dislikes, and familial issues. Therefore, a professional equipped to deal with weight problems in children needs expertise in overlapping areas, including the medical, psychological, and nutritional fields. Over and above this, it is essential for the professional who wants to deal with children to have a working knowledge of normal child development.

Second, there is an inverse relationship between socioeconomic status and slimness in children: lower socioeconomic status children have a higher prevalence of obesity (Stunkard, d'Aquili, Fox, & Fillion, 1972). This puts the onus of responsibility onto public health care facilities, where excessive weight in children has been an unfortunately low priority item. Moreover, those families who can afford private practice fees are less likely to have children who are obese.

A third reason for the shortage of appropriate treatment facilities reflects a lack of recognition on the part of referral agents—first, that the problem exists, and second, that it is treatable. Pediatricians have been hesitant to refer clients, feeling that "the children will outgrow their baby fat.'' Mental health professionals, acutely aware of the psychological damage to an obese child, often wish that the child could lose weight, but are at a loss concerning recommendations for specific methods. Therefore, the problem often gets lost in the myriad of other problems which families bring to referring sources. Educators and school counselors are also acutely aware of the fat children in their schools, because these are often the children who are unhappy, late for school, and otherwise noticeable among the student population. However, educators who would recognize the problems of the obese child might not think of the weight as a treatable problem and would have a dearth of treatment possibilities should they want to refer a child. The *Diagnostic and Statistical Manual of Mental Disorders* (DSM-II), the diagnostic handbook for mental health professionals, does not include a diagnosis of pediatric obesity, which means that the problem is not really recognized as a mental health problem. In summary, the shortage in treatment opportunities exists because people do not recognize pediatric obesity as a problem, and because there is a shortage of programs in locations where the treatment is most needed.

SOME DETERMINANTS OF PEDIATRIC OBESITY

In order to effectively deal with the problem of the obese child it is necessary to have a firm understanding of the underlying determinants. There are numerous factors which may contribute to the over-ingestion of calories and/or decreased expenditure of energy. In order to achieve changes in a child's body weight, it is necessary to alter one or another (or both) of the essential determinants governing the equilibrium between caloric intake and caloric expenditure.

Certainly, biological processes contribute to a disorder of energy balance. While it is not feasible in this chapter to review the immense amount of work that has helped detail the effect of biological processes upon ingestion and body weight, it must be kept in mind that these factors are of primary importance in accounting for the behaviors involved in energy regulation. Two important biological determinants entering into and influencing regulation can be highlighted. First, during childhood there appear to be critical periods during which the number of fat cells in the body can dramatically increase (Hirsch & Knittle, 1970). Once these fat cells are formed they remain for life. This factor alone underscores the need for early detection, prevention, and treatment. Second, the biological foundations of taste play an important role in food selection and consumption. Studies have shown that in many cultures sweetened liquids are an integral part of early feeding experiences (Jerome, 1977). A study of Desor, Maller, and Turner (1973) with newborn infants showed that infants prefer sweet-tasting nutritive solutions in the first 24 hours of life. Their study clearly indicates that the preference for sweet substances is not merely a learned phenomenon but has a strong genetic basis.

Biological factors are indeed important, but they can be overcome or shaped by the nurturing process. For example, the breast-fed infant sucks until satisfied, and the mother does not know how much milk her child has ingested. Physiologically, the mother produces milk according to the demands of the child. This important biological feedback system is completely disrupted when the breast is replaced by a bottle. Fomon (1967) reported that in the United States since 1958 the frequency of breast feeding at 1 month of age has remained constant at only 20% of the infant population. By 4 months, breast feeding decreased to less than 10% of the infant population and, by age 6 months, to only about 5% of infants. Therefore, bottle feeding is the rule and breast feeding the exception. With bottle feeding, the mother has a visual cue and can see how much milk the child has ingested. She can use this cue to shape the child's eating behavior according to her own standards for how much the child should eat. It becomes possible for her to overfeed or underfeed her child. Beginning with this process, the parent assumes a much greater role in teaching and shaping feeding behavior.

As a child grows, the range and complexity of behaviors involved in eating and muscular activity increases enormously. It is this set of complex behavior patterns, in interaction with the person's biochemical make up, that governs the balance of energy and regulates the deposition of fat. As each child has different genetic and environmental influences, so he develops different behaviors that enter into the regulation of body energy and weight.

In most instances, these learned behaviors result in the regulation of normal body weight. However, Ullmann (1973) has outlined a number of ways by which a child may develop inappropriate eating habits that lead to disordered energy balance. For example, the child may learn to depend upon environmental cues for initiating eating. In the previous example of breast versus bottle feeding, the relationship between food delivery and the child's physiological needs is disrupted. If this occurs often, the child may learn to rely on cues provided by the parent rather than those provided by his own physiological needs. A common example of this process is the giving or withholding of parental approval in association with the amount of food remaining on the child's plate. Through repetition of this process, the cue for meal termination is no longer an internal satiety signal but becomes the act of cleaning the plate.

In addition, food itself is a strong reinforcer since it satisfies physiological needs. Therefore, food may come to satisfy multiple emotional needs by being strongly and repeatedly associated with parental attention, comfort, and affection. Through this association, food may become a general way of coping with various emotional states. For instance, food can be used to reduce anxiety, alleviate pain, lift depression, relieve boredom, distract from loneliness, counter fatigue, or even enhance happiness (Wooley, O. & Wooley, S., 1975).

Through eating in many situations and under a variety of conditions and experiences, ingestive behavior may come under the control of many influences other than those based on internal need. Not only may parents actively teach inappropriate behaviors and uses for food, but, because the child patterns his behavior after that of his parents, the eating behaviors of the parent become incorporated into the behavioral repertoire of the child. It is through such behavioral developments as these that a learning component enters into the regulation of energy balance.

Family eating practices have profound influences on the developing child, and there have been dramatic changes in American eating patterns in general. Currently, at least one-third of the food dollars in the United States are spent outside the home. By 1980 estimates indicate this figure will be 50%. Therefore, the impact of the family on learning food likes and dislikes is going to be less affected by what happens at home and more determined by what happens at fast food restaurants.

These broad social and cultural patterns influence the energy balance in many ways. For example, Stunkard et al. (1972) have shown that the prevalence of obesity is related to socioeconomic class, particularly among females. The remarkably early onset of class-linked differences in the prevalence of obesity underscores the need to prevent the disorder in childhood.

These broad psychological, cultural, and familial determinants are further modulated by factors which are present in the immediate environment and perception of the individuals. By varying greatly from one individual to another, these factors lead to important differences in the behaviors occurring immediately before, during, and after ingestion. Each person, because of repeated experience with these environmental factors, develops stable associations between the immediate factors and the behaviors involved in food intake. For example, infants do not eat three meals a day.

This temporal pattern of eating most often develops in our society through maturation of the biological system, through the socialization process in the family, and through cues in the immediate environment. This pattern, in fact, may become so overlearned that a person who could biologically afford to skip a meal will not do so. If the appropriate cues previously associated with eating are present in the immediate environment, he may eat without being in a state of energy deficit. On the other hand, if the cues are not present, he may not eat even if he is in a state of energy deficit.

Another important factor which shapes childhood eating habits is television. A recent report from the Council on Children, Media, and Merchandising (Choate & Engle, 1977), which summarized relevant testimony before the Federal Trade Commission in 1976–77, indicated that a typical television watching child is potentially exposed to between 8,500 and 13,000 food commercials each year. And approximately 40 million children under 12 are affected by television advertising of foods and beverages. In another report (McDonald, 1977), it was found that when a child sits down to watch Saturday morning cartoons he will see an average of 9.5 minutes of advertising per hour in the form of 20 to 30 second spots. Almost half of all commercial announcements were for cereal, candies, and other snacks. In after-school programs, 46% of the ads were for food, with nearly two-thirds of them being for sugared products.

In addition to advertising, there is an almost universal availability of food in our environment. Vending machines are placed in schools, stations, and stores. Supermarkets have thousands of items attractively arranged and easily available with candy and animal crackers always on children's eye-level shelves. There is little wonder that our children overeat; they are bombarded with food cues from the time they awake until the time they go to sleep.

EXISTING TREATMENT APPROACHES FOR OVERWEIGHT YOUNGSTERS

From the psychological literature, four approaches to the treatment of overweight youngsters have apparently been taken. Singly, or in combination with other approaches, these are psychodynamic, behavioral, family systems, and group therapy approaches. A complete review is not possible in this paper, but the interested reader is referred to writings by LeBow (1977).

Hilde Bruch is the best known psychodynamically oriented children's author on weight control. Her writings over the past 35 years are extensive. As she states (Bruch, 1973), her work concerns itself "with individuals who misuse the eating function in their efforts to solve or camouflage problems of living that to them appear otherwise insoluble" (p. 3). From her viewpoint:

> Obesity, although a faulty adaptation, may serve as a protection against more severe illness; it represents an effort to stay well or to be less sick. These individuals, overweight or otherwise, cannot function unless the underlying problems are clarified and resolved. For such people the actual weight loss must be considered a secondary question. Paradoxical as it may sound, for them reducing is not the cure of their problems. At best, as they are improving, dieting may become possible, a signal that the underlying problems are less disturbing and capable of a more rational solution. (p. 4)

Other treatment approaches are clearly behavioral in their reinforcement program, such as those described by LeBow (1977); Sash (1975); Dinoff, Rickard, and Colwick (1972); Aragona, Cassady, and Drabman (1975); and Foxx (1972). For example, Dinoff et al. (1972) describe a process of successive contracting for 10-pound weight reductions, resulting in a 30-pound weight loss in one youngster.

Many programs have favored a combination of behavioral, family-based, and group therapy techniques in working with pediatric obesity. For example, Rivinus et al. (1976) developed a 10-week program at the Children's Hospital in Philadelphia. Ten children aged 8- to 13-years-old were seen for 2 hours a week for 10 weeks. The mother of the child was seen simultaneously. Nine of the 10 children completed the program, and all lost weight during active treatment. The most remarkable aspect of this program was that at 120-week follow-up the group had continued to lose weight. The average percent overweight at the initiation of the program was 72%. At 120 weeks, the average percent overweight was 21%—a remarkable change. Authors attribute the success to not only the initial program content and structure but also to periodic follow-up contacts with these children and their parents.

The most successful programs are likely to be those involving work with the family, as evidenced by the programs described by Capell and Martin (Note 2), Kingsley and Shapiro (in press), Rivinus et al. (1976), Aragona et al. (1975), McReynolds (Note 3), and Wheeler and Hess (1976). Aragona et al. (1975) describe the creative use of reinforcement, and of parents as therapists. In their program, parents weighed their children and received information about exercise and nutrition. In addition, the parents' fees for the program could be reduced through clear cooperation and assistance in the child's weight loss program.

Group psychotherapy with homogeneous age groups has also been used (Stanley, Glaser, Levin, Adams, & Coley, 1970), and seems particularly suited to adolescents. The present authors, working with G. Emery (Emery, Coché, Levitz, & Jordan, Note 4), designed a 10-week group therapy program for overweight adolescents which was piloted in 1977. In a pretreatment information session, Emery discouraged those families in which the adolescent's weight was of more concern to the parents than to the adolescent from applying for treatment. He found it necessary to work on family dynamics involving eating and accomplished this by encouraging the adolescent to speak with her parents about maladaptive family eating patterns, and by directly speaking with the parents if necessary.

For example, Susan T., a 12-year-old weighing 312 pounds, had an obese mother who told Dr. Emery that Susan "hardly eats anything." On closer examination, Susan was found to have a low activity level, being fond of coming home from school and watching television rather than engaging in any physical activity. This, coupled with high-calorie trips to the Dairy Queen with her mother, resulted in severe overweight. Despite her mother's sabotaging, Susan lost 6 pounds in 10 weeks. For example, when Susan's mother got Dairy Queen ice cream for herself, Susan would say she didn't want any ice cream. Her mother nevertheless insisted on bringing her some. To counteract the sabotage, the therapist assisted Susan in speaking with her mother, and talked to the mother himself. In sum, a variety of individual, family, and group approaches have been tried with children and adolescents. Of these, the combination of a behavioral and family systems approach based on a group psychotherapy model would seem to have the highest likelihood of success.

A PROPOSED GROUP PSYCHOTHERAPY APPROACH TO PEDIATRIC OBESITY

Several factors involved in the regulation of body weight and previous experience in working with overweight adults and adolescents suggest the following model as a beginning in program development for overweight children and adolescents. The program would incorporate five basic principles.

The Program Would Be Behavioral

For example, records would be kept involving rate of eating, time of eating, amount, caloric density, and other factors important in gaining control of eating behaviors. In the case of younger children, the records would, of course, have to be adapted to the age of the child and might in fact be kept by one or both parents, or by the primary caretaker. Older children would be capable of keeping their own food records.

Although there are hundreds of individual techniques which can be used to alter eating behaviors, there are four major strategies under which all techniques fall: (1) increased awareness of eating, (2) altered exposure to problem eating situations, (3) changed susceptibility to the determinants, and (4) altered response in problematic situations.

The first line of defense is increased awareness. If one is going to change a habit, one must be aware of what the habit is and what influences its occurrence. In and of itself, an increased awareness of eating can produce adaptive changes in eating behavior. The food intake record itself is the most helpful method to increase awareness.

In addition, slowing down the rate of ingestion increases awareness of food. Rapid eating has been found to have two effects: first, it means the child is paying little attention to the taste and quality of the food, and second, it can override satiety signals generated by a particular quantity of food. If a child can slow down the rate at which he generally eats food, several effects important for weight control are often noted. By eating at a slower rate, physiological cues of satiety have a chance to operate. The youngster can find that he eats a smaller quantity of food, but, by eating it more slowly, he experiences as much or even greater satiety and satisfaction. But it is not enough to simply instruct patients to slow down their rate of ingestion. The therapist and child must devise very specific behavior changes which will result in a slower pace.

Beyond increased awareness, the second line of defense is to decrease exposure to situations in which maladaptive eating is likely to occur. One must first discover what areas are problematic, e.g., which place in the house, what social situation, what foods produce maladaptive eating. One must explore the child's daily routine and access to food supplies in order to see what changes can be made to decrease exposure to food.

At home, eating can be limited to one or two places. Food supplies can be rearranged. Cookies on the kitchen counter, cakes on the counter, or high calorie foods in the front of the refrigerator are important determinants of maladaptive eating. If these problematic foods are less visible and less available the probability of their being ingested is reduced. It does not mean "hiding" the food, nor does it mean that the child should not eat these foods.

Furthermore, the family and friends of the child have their

own habits concerning food, and one of them may be that they offer food to the patient as a reward or as a gift. The best way to deal with this is for the therapist to specifically ask the family to use other things for these purposes.

Meal times with the family may also present increased exposure to food. If a child is eating large amounts at meal times, it is especially important for the parents to limit the amount of food that the family has at the table. Keeping extra food away from the table can dramatically change the number of times the child takes second portions. Ideally, plates should be prepared in the kitchen and brought to the table while platters of food remain in the kitchen. In addition, the table should be cleared of extra food as soon after a person finishes eating as possible. These are but a few examples of the techniques which can be used to decrease exposure. The specific technique suggested must be carefully tailored to the child's unique situations.

However, a child cannot always control proximity to food. There will always be situations in which he is exposed to food. A third line of defense, then, is to change a child's susceptibility to the various environmental determinants. Understanding the relationship between eating and the forces influencing it can help to decrease susceptibility. Another way to decrease susceptibility is for the child and his family to preplan when and what they are going to eat, that is, to anticipate what situations they will be exposed to.

Preplanning one's daily food intake has a powerful effect on susceptibility. One can set up a time schedule and also plan what foods will be eaten. First, going too long a time without eating is not adaptive, since excessive feelings of hunger can significantly affect the amount and kind of food consumed. Once he is very hungry, a child is much more likely to take high-calorie foods requiring little preparation and to eat them very quickly. Second, the purpose of this technique is not to eliminate all snacks. Rather, snacks should be planned and scheduled. This is very useful for many children who have a pattern of eating very frequently during the day or evening. Parents can be very helpful in preplanning.

Preplanning causes a child and his parents to think and deliberate about his eating and choice of foods. This is of paramount importance in a society which pushes us toward rushed, automatic, mindless eating.

The fourth defense or strategy is to change the child's response to a problematic situation. If a youngster is in a situation which led to eating in the past, he may now make another response, such as engaging in a hobby, taking a walk, playing a game, anything instead of eating.

The disposition to eat can be lessened by having available other activities which are incompatible with the act of eating. The principle behind this method is that responding to these determinants with a new behavior is easier than trying not to respond at all. Not all activities can be used for this purpose; the best behavioral alternatives are those that: (1) are easily available so that the child can turn to them whenever he feels he is going to eat inappropriately, (2) are pleasant so that the activity can be enjoyable, and (3) are incompatible with eating. It should be difficult to eat and participate in the activity at the same time.

Although we have enumerated many strategies and techniques directed at decreasing the intake of calories, we regard increases in physical activity to be important in the control of body weight. For many children, it is their sedentary lifestyle which mainly contributes to a disordered energy balance. The same strategies of increasing awareness, changing exposure, changing susceptibility, and altering response apply in changing habits of physical activity. First, the child must become aware of how sedentary or active he is and what influences his inactivity. Second, exposure to activity must be increased. For example, the bicycle can be moved out of dead storage or the tennis racket can be made more available. Third, the knowledge that activity is an aid to weight control may increase the child's susceptibility to activity. Engaging in activities with friends and family increases the likelihood that the activity will occur more frequently. Last, a formerly sedentary response can be changed. Instead of sitting down after dinner, the child may walk the dog. Increasing physical activity must be done in small gradual steps, so that the child can gradually acquire physical and psychological conditioning.

The behavioral component of the treatment program, then, is composed of a wide variety of techniques, each providing a partial solution to the maladaptive habits of the obese child. Repetition of habit changes which are incorporated into the daily routine and lifestyle of the child, and which are seen by him to be directly related to weight loss, enhance long-term success. Through this process of daily record keeping, weekly analysis, and slow behavior change in both eating behavior and physical activity, the child assumes responsibility for his own behavior. This must remain the ultimate goal of the treatment program.

The Program Would Be Educational

The program would educate both parents and children about the basic factors involved in nutrition for children, with the educational emphasis placed on the food selection process. This might nicely be done as part of the initial phases of treatment in a group setting. Here the group would be an advantage, because they would be able to hear information from others which they would be hesitant to ask about for themselves.

In a program of this nature, as in any group therapy situation, the maintenance of high levels of participation and motivation is crucial to the success of the group experience. Motivation might be capitalized upon by gearing the group experience to the developmental level of the youngster. For example, it is important to run sessions for shorter time periods with younger children who are able to sustain interest for shorter time periods. For preschoolers and parents, sessions might last only 30 minutes, while 1 hour might be more appropriate for older youngsters. Moreover, one might gear the described rewards for weight loss to the developmental level of the child in the following manner: a 12-year-old boy might be told that he will have an easier time on the baseball field if he loses weight, while a younger child would respond to the knowledge that she might get less teasing on the school yard. Adolescents are interested in issues revolving around boy-girl issues and improving physical appearance.

During the group itself, it is important for the therapist to encourage increased member participation. Group interaction can be facilitated by encouraging members to talk with one another and by discouraging therapist-centered member participation. Comments like, "Why don't you ask Sharon about that?" or "Has anyone had a similar experience?" act to ease and encourage member participation. With younger children, age-appropriate games might be considered, such as "Uncle Wiggley's Weight Wagon," or other creative therapist attempts to engage the children's active interest.

Between-session motivation to keep records is also important to capitalize on. Records in bright colors with appealing mottos are helpful. The children's records at the Institute for Behavioral Education, for example, are bright blue and are titled "The Weekly Eater." Verbal reinforcement for homework well done is crucial (e.g., "Look everyone, Jane did a great job. She even put down how hungry she was at every meal").

The Program Would Be Supportive in Nature

Members in a group gain considerable support from one another, which enables them to change in desired directions more quickly than otherwise might be possible. This is particularly true because the authority dimension between client and therapist is lessened through the presence of other group members, who find it easier than the therapist at times to confront a client with his maladaptive eating patterns and behaviors. Moreover, there is value for one client in learning the experiences of another client as they are being discussed with the therapist and with other group members. Many clients gain personal insights simply by sitting passively and listening to others speak of their own problems, and it is not unusual for one to chime, "Yes, that has happened to me also." Finally, the group applies subtle pressure to the client to meet the norms of the group. This has been found to be quite true with adults and with adolescents, and it would most definitely be true of children who are developmentally past the age of parallel play, i.e., 6 or 7 years. Much as it does with adults, a children's group would function as a combination of support group, confrontation group, and educative experience for the children and the parents involved in it. Moreover, if the group were multigenerational, there would be the possibility for cross-generational sharings as well as sharings between members of the same generation.

The Program Would Be Systems-Oriented

The family, as a system, must be treated, rather than the individual child alone. Numerous authors have discussed the importance of working with the family in treating other disorders. Work by Liebman, Minuchin, and Baker (1974) at the Philadelphia Child Guidance Clinic with anorexia nervosa is especially worth mentioning, since they have achieved success with adolescent girls who have refused to eat. Working with the family is also essential when treating children who are overweight. Mayer (1965) states that a series of studies have shown that about 70% of the children of obese parents are also obese. Moreover, the parents' style of eating, discipline in the home concerning eating, and the value of food for the family are all important factors. Since all of these factors can be crucial in producing an obese child, a model program would involve a 1½-hour diagnostic session for the entire family, in order to learn the psychological factors surrounding eating for the child and other family members.

Treatment might be different for differing age levels, but would always involve three phases: (1) assessment of organic, psychological, and familial eating factors, (2) age-appropriate treatment, and (3) extended and adequate follow-up contacts. Age-appropriate treatment would always be with groups of family members (i.e., multifamily groups), but would differ in structure according to the developmental level of the overweight child. A preschool program would be most workable with three or four preschoolers and their parents, meeting bimonthly for 30 minutes. On the other weeks of the month, hour-long parent groups for 5 to 8 parent couples might encourage exploration of issues in parenting which could redirect the child's eating. Latency-aged children (ages 6 to 12), on the other hand, would best benefit from hour-long weekly meetings with one or both parents, and occasionally joined by siblings. Groups could consist of three or four families, and might concentrate directly on maladaptive family interaction as it contributes to maladaptive eating patterns.

For the adolescent, a slightly different emphasis is needed, since the adolescent is developmentally ready to assume a role of greater independence. An adolescent treatment program might involve a diagnostic workup with the parents and the brothers and sisters, so that the family eating patterns could be discussed openly. Primary treatment could focus on the adolescent, with secondary group meetings with the parents of the adolescent at a separate time. In this way, it would be possible for the therapist to work with the entire system without causing the adolescent to feel suffocated by continuing to come in with his family at all times.

The Program Would Involve Physical Activity

Minimally, there would be a strong therapist recommendation that physical activity appropriate to the age of the child be incorporated into the daily life of the child. The group would suggest appropriate activity resources, and it would follow through by making sure that the activities had, in fact, been initiated. This could be done by asking the youngsters at the beginning of each session their experience with homework assignments the week before. Furthermore, by using records one can ask youngsters to record each time they use a technique or initiate an activity. It is important to turn the promises of activity into the reality of behavior change, through continued follow-up on the activity in the group setting. Maximally, a program might directly introduce age-appropriate activities located at the treatment site. These activities could be incorporated into the group program itself. Other activities, such as dance or movement therapy, could be geared toward helping the obese child feel better about his or her body.

The program outlined above, with appropriate staff and facilities, is likely to to be effective because it would begin to address the complexity of issues involved in children's weight problems. The work by Rivinus et al. (1976), using many of these principles, attests to the possibility of an effective treatment program.

RECOMMENDATIONS FOR THE FIELD
OF PEDIATRIC WEIGHT CONTROL

Pediatric weight control is a field in its infancy, as has been documented earlier in this paper. As such, it is in need of considerable attention before programs like those outlined here can achieve widespread success. The first emphasis needs to be one of educating both the general public and the professional community to the necessity and feasibility of treating overweight children, and to the advisability of breaking down popular misconceptions of the relationship between food and health.

For example, there is a need to educate people about the dangers of "the fat and health baby" myth. Eden (1976) states, "Everyone loves those soft rolls of fat on a baby's tiny legs, thinks it's adorable that his neck is barely visible under his fat little chin. Not only that, but everyone thinks a fat baby is the healthiest baby. In truth, though nobody says, 'What a lovely *thin* baby!' the thin baby is actually the healthiest baby, the baby parents should strive for" (p. 71).

Perhaps the greatest impact on the lay population could come through articles in children's and parents' journals. A second source of education must be aimed at the professional community, the people who are in a position to first observe the problem and refer the youngster for help. Here, the educators, nutritionists, and pediatricians need to be made more aware of the dangers of allowing children to remain obese. It would be valuable, for example, to train students from a wide variety of disciplines to understand the factors involved in overweight children and to refer appropriate children for treatment. Until professionals are able to identify obesity as a treatable problem, too few children will be referred for help.

A final consideration is that the private practice model may not be the appropriate avenue for instituting pediatric obesity programs. The programs must be instituted at locations convenient to children of modest economic means: urban and rural hospitals, community mental health centers, and pediatric clinics. In the large cities, this location would probably center around the large urban hospitals near ghetto areas. In outlying rural districts, a local church might well provide the room for a team of professionals from a local community mental health center to provide treatment for the children of the area.

As the public and health providers become more aware of the inadequacy of current concepts, current facilities, and current treatment models, it is hoped that overweight children and adolescents will have more opportunities to gather in groups and receive the kind of assistance they require, via the type of program outlined above.

REFERENCE NOTES

1. Coché, J., Jordan, H., & Levitz, L. *The use of group psychotherapy in behavioral weight control for adults and children.* Paper presented at the 21st International Congress of Group Psychotherapy, Philadelphia, August 1977.
2. Capell, J., & Martin, J. *Obesity, multidisciplinary study, treatment, and prevention in the adult and pediatric rehabilitation program.* Paper presented at the poster session of the meeting of the Association for the Advancement of Behavior Therapy, San Francisco, December 1975.
3. McReynolds, W. *Family behavior therapy for obesity: Treatment and preventative implications.* Unpublished personal communication, 1977.
4. Emery, G., Coché, J., Levitz, L. S., & Jordan, H. A. Unpublished pilot study, 1977.

REFERENCES

American Psychiatric Association. *Diagnostic and statistical manual of mental disorders* (2nd ed.). Washington, D.C.: Author, 1968.

Aragona, J., Cassady, J., & Drabman, R. Treating overweight children through parental training and contingency contracting. *Journal of Applied Behavioral Analysis,* 1975, *8,* 269–278.

Bruch, H. *Eating disorders.* New York: Basic Books, Inc., 1973.

Choate, R. B., & Engle, P. C. *Edible TV: Your child and food commercials.* Washington, D.C.: Council on Children, Media, & Merchandising, 1977.

Desor, J., Maller, O., & Turner, R. Taste in acceptance of sugars by human infants. *Journal of Comparative and physiological Psychology,* 1973, *84,* 496–501.

Dinoff, M., Rickard, H. C., & Colwick, J. Weight reduction through successive contracts. *American Journal of Orthopsychiatry,* 1972, *42,* 110–113.

Dwyer, J., & Mayer, J. The dismal condition: Problems faced by obese adolescent girls in American society. In G. Bray (Ed.), *Obesity in perspective* (Vol 2). Washington, D.C.: U. S. Government Printing Office, 1973.

Eden, A. *Growing up thin.* New York: Berkeley Publishing, 1976.

Fomon, S. J. *Infant nutrition.* Philadelphia, Pa.: W. B. Saunders, 1967.

Foxx, R. M. Social reinforcement of weight reduction: A case report on an obese retarded adolescent. *Mental Retardation,* 1972, *10,* 21–23.

Friedman, G. Atherosclerosis and the pediatrician. In M. Winick (Ed.), *Childhood obesity* (Vol. 3). New York: Wiley, 1975.

Hirsch, J., & Knittle, J. L. Cellularity of obese and nonobese adipose tissue. *Federation Proceedings,* 1970, *29,* 1516–1521.

Jerome, N. W. Taste experience and the development of a dietary preference for sweet in humans: Ethnic and cultural variation in early taste experience. In J. M. Weiffenbach (Ed.), *Taste and development: The genesis of sweet preference.* Washington, D.C.: Department of Health, Education, & Welfare, 1977. (NIH 77–1068).

Kingsley, R. G., & Shapiro, J. A comparison of three behavioral programs for the control of obesity in children. *Behavior Therapy,* in press.

LeBow, M. The fat child and the behavioral scientist-practitioner: It's time to get together. *Canadian Psychological Review,* 1977, *18,* 322–331.

Liebman, R., Minuchin, S., & Baker, L. An integrated treatment approach for anorexia nervosa. *American Journal of Psychiatry,* 1974, *1314,* 432–436.

Mayer, J. Genetic factors in human obesity. *Annuals of the New York Academy of Sciences,* 1965, *131,* 412.

McDonald, M. Children and TV—How great an influence? *Psychiatric News,* March 19, 1977, p. 16.

Rivinus, T. M., Drummond, T., & Combrinck-Graham, L. A group-behavior treatment program for overweight children: Results of a pilot study. *Pediatrics and Adolescent Endocrinology,* 1976, *1,* 212–223.

Sash, S. E. Weight reduction in obese schoolboys. In A. Howard (Ed.), *Recent advances in obesity research* (Vol. 1). London: Newman, 1975.

Stanley, E. J., Glaser, H. H., Levin, D. G., Adams, P. A., & Coley, I. L. Overcoming obesity in adolescents: A description of a promising endeavor to improve management. *Clinical Pediatrics,* 1970, *9,* 29–36.

Stunkard, A. J., d'Aquili, E., Fox, S., & Fillion, R. D. L. Influence of social class on obesity and thinness in children. *Journal of the American Medical Association,* 1972, *221,* 579–584.

Ullmann, L. P., & Krasner, L. *Behavior influence and personality.* New York: Holt, Rinehart & Winston, 1973.

Wheeler, M. E., & Hess, K. W. Treatment of juvenile obesity by successive approximation control of eating. *Journal of Behavior Therapy and Experimental Psychiatry,* 1976, *7,* 235–241.

Wooley, O. W., & Wooley, S. C. The experimental psychology of obesity. In J. T. Silverstone (Ed.), *Obesity pathogenesis & management.* London: Medical & Technical Publishing Co., Ltd, 1975.

SUBJECT INDEX

AUTHOR INDEX